Casey Kochmer and Erica Frandsen

JSP™ and XML

Integrating XML and Web Services in Your JSP Application

Addison-Wesley

Boston • San Francisco • New York • Toronto • Montreal
London • Munich • Paris • Madrid
Capetown • Sydney • Tokyo • Singapore • Mexico City

The publisher offers discounts on this book when ordered in quantity for special sales.

For more information, please contact:

Pearson Education Corporate Sales Division
201 W. 103rd Street
Indianapolis, IN 46290
(800) 428-5331
corpsales@pearsoned.com

Visit AW on the Web: www.awl.com/cseng/

ISBN 0-672-32354-0

05 04 03 02 4 3 2 1

First Printing: March 2002

Executive Editor
Rochelle J. Kronzek

Acquisitions Editor
Michelle Newcomb

Development Editor
Mark Ray

Managing Editor
Matt Purcell

Project Editor
Christina Smith

Production Editors
Seth Kerney
Rhonda Tinch-Mize
Matt Wynalda

Indexer
Mandie Frank

Proofreader
Suzanne Thomas

Technical Editor
Craig Pfeifer

Team Coordinator
Pamalee Nelson

Interior Designer
Gary Adair

Cover Designer
Alan Clements

Page Layout
Rebecca Harmon
Michelle Mitchell

Contents at a Glance

Table of Contents

About the Authors

Casey Kochmer is a cofounder of the JSP Insider Web site. As president of AmberJack Software, Casey is a JavaServer Pages (JSP), HTML, XHTML, XML, DHTML, and Web service specialist. He was previously a senior programmer, trainer, and Internet expert for Starling Consulting, where he mentored users in JavaServer Pages, Active Server Pages (ASP), XML usage, and Internet practices. His job was to help customers integrate the latest technology at an appropriate time relative to the needs of a project. His mantra is that a project should implement usable and maintainable technology rather than using the latest technology for technology's sake. Casey codes and builds specialized applications using JSP, ASP, and various databases depending on customer needs. He has coauthored several books, including *Professional JSP, Second Edition* and *Beginning JSP Web Development.*

Erica Frandsen is an XML, ASP, and SQL Server expert. Experienced in TCP/IP networking, she is a founder of Sound Home Networks. While working as a network consultant, she installs, configures, and maintains networks for clients. Previously, Erica worked as a programmer and consultant for Starling Consulting, where she designed ASP and SQL systems using XML. Earlier in her career, she used these same technologies to create an online tax paying system for businesses in the state of Washington. She also was the Webmaster for several sites. In her free time, Erica brews beer, plays with computer hardware, and creates Web sites for worthy causes.

Dedications

Writing this book was a long process. As in all choices, this project had its rewards and its consequences. In the end, the most important lesson I learned was one of life, not JSP. I can share my thoughts in this poem. I dedicate the book to anyone who takes a moment to read my poetry.

Days of Wonder

Heaven and Hell are not after life
Heaven and Hell are part of life
It's in life we make our joy
It's in life we build our walls
To anyone who reads this
may you find your own heaven
may you find your own poems
Break free of your chains
Jump your walls
Live life as if in heaven
and don't make life hell

We have only one life
to relive over again in infinity
Don't regret as you move forward
Since the past is only for memories
The secret to life
is simply to be true to yourself and smile
then you will be able
to look upon each new day
with the wonder it deserves
It's all anyone can ever do

—Casey Kochmer

I dedicate this book to my family: Jim, Judy, Kristina, and my friends. You have made me what I am today, and for that I thank you.

Life is not measured by the number of breaths we take,
but by the moments that take our breath away.

—Erica Frandsen

Acknowledgments

I would like to thank Michelle, Mark, and Matt for their excellent work. Without their perseverance this book would never have happened. Thank you, guys!

Also, I pay tribute to Mari Nowitz and Nathan Hamilton. Without my most excellent neighbors, I might have died of starvation and lack of influence from the real world. Thanks for being there when I needed you!

I would also like to thank Steve and Brad at Kundalini for their excellent coffee.

—Erica Frandsen

Introduction

The purpose of this book is to teach you how to implement XML and Web services within a JSP Web application or site. The book will start very simply and then work its way up in complexity. This will make the book accessible to a wide range of readers.

The target audience includes new and intermediate JSP programmers. However, this book will be useful for any JSP programmer who wants to expand his or her XML or Web service implementation knowledge. The book is also geared towards helping a JSP programmer think in terms of the combination of JSP, XML, and Web services. The goal is to show how to usefully integrate these technologies into your projects and share the lessons we have learned in building Web applications.

On XML

We are programmers who spend quite a bit of time building Web applications. Over the past few years, we have been implementing XML in our projects. However, implementing XML is easier said than done at times. Even worse, many times XML is implemented in ways that can be harmful to a project. You should never use XML for XML's sake. This book is a reflection of our ordeals in learning the various tools and the methods of incorporating XML in a useful way into a Web site.

The problem for developers hasn't been about finding information on XML, but about using XML successfully within Web applications. While there are plenty of solid XML titles, no title really focuses on how to integrate XML into your JSP project. This book is written with the JSP developer in mind. We want to help teach XML, XSL, XPath, and the entire alphabet soup that goes along with XML. By showing how to use XML within a JSP framework, we intend to help make implementing XML both easy and advantageous for the JSP developer.

On Web Services

Web services are the latest fad. They are so new that many of the accompanying tools are still in beta or are only now being released into the marketplace. It's still very early to learn Web services. Web services are too new for anyone to truly be an expert in the field. This makes learning Web services both an exciting and a strange experience. Our intention is to teach you how to incorporate Web services into JSP. We will remove the confusion that surrounds Web services and give a clear path to learning the basics. This book will show the various elements that constitute a Web service.

On the Structure of the Book

The book is divided into four parts. Part I is designed to introduce you to each of the technologies exemplified throughout this book. Part II drills deeply into the various tools for each of these technologies. Part III shows how to successfully combine all these technologies to make your project easier and faster to implement. Part IV contains appendixes that provide reference material.

Part I: Data, XML, and Web Services Introduction

This part is intended to ground you. We do not assume that you already know a great deal about JSP, XML, or Web services; these three topics are introduced in Chapters 1–3.

Chapter 1: Integrating JSP and Data

This chapter shows how to use JSP and a database together. The chapter serves to ground you in JSP and show you how to perform basic database connectivity.

Chapter 2: Introduction to XML/XSL

This chapter is a whirlwind tour of XML and XSL. It introduces each of the major concepts that are needed for XML and begins teaching XSL and XPath.

Chapter 3: Understanding Web Services

Chapter 3 introduces the concepts of Web services. Web services are a confusing topic, and the chapter focuses on the basic concepts you will need to use them.

Part II: Integrating JSP and XML

Part II is a review of the tools, APIs, and logic required to successfully implement XML and Web services. These chapters introduce the various concepts of Web services and the various parsers for XML. Once you've studied these chapters, you will have enough knowledge to begin using XML and Web services successfully.

Chapter 4: A Quick Start to JSP and XML Together

This chapter gives you a quick start to mixing JSP and XML together. The chapter reviews the basic XML APIs and works through some examples of merging JSP and XML.

Chapter 5: Using DOM

This chapter teaches the important aspects of the DOM API. The DOM is the standard supported by the W3C for working with an XML file programmatically.

Chapter 6: Programming SAX

This chapter teaches you the ins and outs of the SAX API. SAX is probably the most common API used to read in an XML file. Most of the time, SAX is used automatically by other XML APIs. However, this chapter is very important because understanding SAX is critical for handling more complicated XML-based processes.

Chapter 7: Successfully Using JSP and XML in an Application

This chapter introduces the other major Java XML APIs: JDOM and dom4j. This chapter produces an integrated example showing how to work with JSP, XML, and a database. The goal of this chapter is to begin walking you through the integration of XML in a natural way within your JSP application.

Chapter 8: Integrating JSP and Web Services

Chapter 8 examines how to use a Web service within your JSP site. This chapter covers two important Web services topics. The first is using a Web service; the chapter shows the most efficient way to use a Web service within your JSP application. The second topic is building a Web service; the chapter walks through the creation of a Web service that can be used by other applications.

Chapter 9: Advanced JSP and XML Techniques

This chapter explores XML concepts that aren't discussed in other chapters. Topics include accessing a Web service from an HTML page, XML encoding issues, ways of processing large XML documents, and XML tag libraries.

Part III: Building JSP Sites to Use XML

Building a JSP site requires far more than just knowing how to use JSP. It requires the ability to think in terms of building a Web application. Web application design is a fine art that involves integrating many different tools as a seamless unit within a JSP project. To this end, Part III covers the implementation of XML and Web services from an application point of view. The chapters in this part cover many topics, from Web service security to building XML reporting systems. We show many different facets of Web application design, from the server to the often-overlooked browser client.

Chapter 10: Using XSL/JSP in Web Site Design

This chapter examines what is possible by going back to the roots of JSP—or more specifically by using servlets. The goal of the chapter is to examine generic XML handling. This means that the initial processing of an XML document can happen at the application level rather than at the page level. The chapter shows how to capture the processing of an XML page and route it directly to a servlet.

Chapter 11: Using XML in Reporting Systems

No matter what the Web application, it's a safe bet that there will be some reporting involved. This chapter examines how reporting systems can benefit from the appropriate placement and use of XML.

Chapter 12: Advanced XML in Reporting Systems

This chapter builds on the examples in Chapter 11. Additional concepts and topics to enhance an XML-based reporting system are shown in this chapter's examples. Among the examples is one that shows how to create reports that show a one-to-many relationship in the database.

Chapter 13: Browser Considerations with XML

JSP developers often overlook client-side XML processing. This is a serious oversight, as browsers are a growing and improving XML client-side tool. This chapter examines how using the browser can enhance handling of XML data and reduce Web server load.

Chapter 14: Building a Web Service

In this chapter, we build a Web service system for news delivery. The code within this chapter is based on a Web service within a production environment. The goal is to show the design and full integration of a complete Web service.

Chapter 15: Advanced Application Design

This chapter covers two topics. First, we'll show you how to build JSP pages that update themselves. This advanced capability permits JSP sites to be more flexible and to expand what is possible with XML, Web services, and JSP. The second main topic is security; the chapter examines how to secure your Web services.

Appendixes

The appendixes support the material presented in the main part of the book. Their contents are briefly described here.

Appendix A: Setting Up

This appendix covers basic information about setting up the JSP container and introduces NetBeans for the creation of all your JSP pages.

Appendix B: Introduction to JSP and How Things Work

For new JSP users, this appendix offers a crash course on JSP and how it works.

Appendix C: Tag Library

This book uses JSP tag libraries as much as possible. For users who are new to JSP, this appendix quickly covers how to build and use a JSP tag library.

Appendix D: XSL Reference

XSL is used extensively in this book. Appendix D is a reference to the most commonly used XSL tags and XPath functions.

A Word about Source Code

All the source code from the listings and programs included in this book is available via download from the Sams Publishing Web site at `www.samspublishing.com`.

Throughout the book, we create sample class files and JSPs and then build on them later in the same or another chapter. Whenever we do so, we clearly indicate where the original file can be found. Lines of code that should be added or changed are indicated in boldface type.

How to Use the Book

As we mentioned earlier, this book is geared toward new and intermediate JSP programmers. How you use the book, and where you begin reading, will depend on your experience level. Here are a few tips to get you started.

For All Users

If possible, we recommend coding the examples. In programming, the best way to learn is by coding, and the examples have been geared to enable you to do so. If you have any questions about initially setting up the JSP container or NetBeans to create JSPs, refer to Appendix A. Otherwise, the first time a specific component is used, it will be referenced for installation at that time.

In many respects, coding the examples is very important because this book explores many different concepts. If you don't write the code, many of the concepts are likely to slip by or not sink in as deeply as they should. We also encourage you to expand and tweak the examples. Try to break the code and find out why it breaks. As programmers, we learn best by coding and by fixing broken code. Coding is best learned by experience; don't shy away from this reality.

For New JSP Users

We are not going to assume that you already know JSP like the back of your hand. Someone with little or no JSP experience can pick up this book and learn how to use JSP and XML. The code and topics are built in a logical and easy manner to help show what is required in using XML within your JSP projects. Beginning JSP programmers will want to study the chapters in Part I closely. The examples are simple enough that they will be a great learning aid. New JSP readers will also benefit from reading Appendix B.

For Intermediate JSP Users

The best starting place will depend on your skills. For users who are inexperienced in XML or Web services, Part I is still your best bet. Otherwise, we recommend skimming the first section, as there is quite a bit of information within each chapter. These chapters have some information that can benefit more experienced readers. However, if you find that you already know the Part I material, skip ahead to Part II.

Conventions Used in This Book

The following typographic conventions are used in this book:

- Code lines, commands, statements, variables, and any text you type or see onscreen appears in a `mono` typeface.
- Placeholders in syntax descriptions appear in an *`italic mono`* typeface. Replace the placeholder with the actual filename, parameter, or whatever element it represents.
- *Italics* highlight technical terms when they're being introduced and defined.
- The book also contains Notes to help you spot important or useful information more quickly.

A Final Note

This book was written as a reference for JSP, XML, and Web services. Learning this material on our own was a long process, and our goal is to help give JSP developers some insights into building JSP Web applications. The fact is, XML and Web services are both fast becoming essential tools to most JSP applications. The problem is trying to learn everything at once. Our goal was to provide integrated examples of practical JSP, XML, and Web service implementations. We hope that you benefit from reading the book as much as we benefited from writing it.

PART I

Data, XML, and Web Services Introduction

IN THIS PART

1 Integrating JSP and Data

IN THIS CHAPTER

- Using JSP with a Database
- Other Considerations
- Basic Design Concepts

One of the most important concepts in building any application is the concept of data. Our applications are driven by data, and the tools that specialize in the handling of data form a central part of any application. XML is a specification that is geared to handle data. However, in using XML, it quickly becomes important to have access to several other tools. Usually a database is the first tool that will be used alongside XML. Oftentimes, the data for our XML files will come directly from a database. In addition, it will be important to import data from an XML file into a database. Using a database is important enough that this first chapter is dedicated to showing how to access and submit data to a database.

This chapter has two goals. The first is to show you how to access a database from JSP. If you are already familiar with using a database within JSP, it's advisable that you proceed to Chapter 2, "Introduction to XML/XSL." It's important to note that several chapters in this book will use a database in the examples. This makes setting up a test database very important. Instructions for setting up the MySQL test database used in all the examples can be found in Appendix A, "Setting Up."

The second goal is to ensure that newer JSP programmers have a chance to get more familiar with JSP before moving further into the book. This chapter is intended to be extremely accessible to newer JSP programmers regardless of their current skill level. This means that the chapter is very basic; more advanced JSP programmers will only want to skim this chapter quickly. Programmers who are just starting to learn about JSP are encouraged to first read Appendix B, "Introduction to JSP and How Things Work."

Using JSP with a Database

This section will not cover how to build or maintain a database. In addition, due to the vast number of databases, it would be impossible to cover special database-specific details. This means the examples here will be kept as generic as possible to help ease the process of porting code from database to database. The examples in this chapter will be using the MySQL database.

To make life simple, we are going to build several examples. The first example will be used to enter data into the database. The second example will be used to view the data in the database. The logic in these examples assumes that the BannerAds table has been created according to the instructions for setting up the MySQL database found in Appendix A.

Entering the Data

The actual process of entering data should be split across several JSP pages. One page will be a data input page. This page will only concern itself with gathering the data. The second page will be an action page that will run on the JSP server to process the results created through the input page. It's a good idea to split logic across several JSP pages. This is a perfect example of a case in which this is true. It's possible to build a single page to perform all the tasks of the input and action pages. Using one page would leave the code entangled and difficult to maintain with too much happening for a single page. This is especially true with more complicated database pages. Using two pages makes the logic more closely match the process and makes it easier for other programmers to understand what is going on within the pages.

The input page, shown in Listing 1.1, gathers data from the user and should be saved as `webapps/xmlbook/chapter1/UpdateTableForm.jsp`.

LISTING 1.1 UpdateTableForm.jsp

```
<%@page contentType="text/html"%>
<html>
<head><title>Update Table Form</title></head>
<body>

<form action="UpdateTableAction.jsp" method="post" name="update">
    <table>
        <tr>
            <td>Name</td>
            <td><input type="text" name="name" value="" size="40"/></td>
        </tr>
        <tr>
            <td>LinkText</td>
```

LISTING 1.1 Continued

```
            <td><input type="text" name="linktext" value="" size="50"/></td>
        </tr>
        <tr>
            <td>Link</td>
            <td><input type="text" name="link" value="" size="50"/></td>
        </tr>
        <tr><td> Action </td>
            <td>
             <input type="radio" name="Action" value="update" /> Update
             <input type="radio" name="Action" value="delete" /> Delete
             <input type="radio" name="Action" value="new" checked /> New
            </td>
        </tr>
        <tr><td><input type="SUBMIT" value="Submit" /> </td>
        </tr>
    </table>
</form>
</body>
</html>
```

This doesn't need to be a JSP page. It could be kept as a straight HTML page. However, we've kept it as a JSP page out of habit. Typically, an input page such as this would have other active features such as security validation, which would require it to use some JSP processing.

Now it's time to build an action page. This page, whose code is shown in Listing 1.2, will receive the data from the input page and then update the database. Save this file as `webapps/xmlbook/chapter1/UpdateTableAction.jsp`.

LISTING 1.2 UpdateTableAction.jsp

```
<%@page import = "java.sql.*" %>

<%
    /* Step 1) Get the data from the form */
    String ls_name     = request.getParameter("name");
    String ls_link     = request.getParameter("link");
    String ls_linktext= request.getParameter("linktext");
    String ls_action  = request.getParameter("Action");

    /* Step 2) Initialize Variables */
```

LISTING 1.2 Continued

```
String ls_result   = "Database was updated";
String ls_query    = "";
String ls_dburl    = "jdbc:mysql://localhost/xmlbook";
String ls_dbdriver = "org.gjt.mm.mysql.Driver";

/* Step 3) Create a query  */
if (ls_action.equals("new"))
{   ls_query  = " insert into BannerAds (name,link,linktext)";
    ls_query += " values (";
    ls_query += "'" + ls_name + "',";
    ls_query += "'" + ls_link + "',";
    ls_query += "'" + ls_linktext + "')";
}

if (ls_action.equals("delete"))
{
    ls_query  = " delete from BannerAds where name = ";
    ls_query += "'" + ls_name + "'";
}

if (ls_action.equals("update"))
{   ls_query  = " update BannerAds";
    ls_query += " set link= "      + "'" + ls_link     + "',";
    ls_query += " set linktext= " + "'" + ls_linktext + "'";
    ls_query += " where name = "   + "'" + ls_name     + "'";
}

/* Step 4) Make a database connection */
Connection l_dbconn = null;

try
{
     Class.forName(ls_dbdriver);
    /*  getConnection(URL,User,Pw) */
     l_dbconn = DriverManager.getConnection(ls_dburl) ;

    /*create a SQL Statement */
    Statement l_statement = l_dbconn.createStatement();

    l_statement.execute(ls_query);
}
```

LISTING 1.2 Continued

```
    catch (ClassNotFoundException e)
    {   ls_result  = " Error creating database drive class!";
        ls_result += " <br/>" +  e.toString();
    }
    catch (SQLException e)
    {   ls_result  = " Error processing the SQL!";
        ls_result += " <br/>" +  e.toString();
    }
    finally
    {
        /* We must close the database connection now */
        try
        {   if (l_dbconn != null)
            { l_dbconn.close(); }
        }
        catch (SQLException e)
        {   ls_result  = "Error in closing connection.";
            ls_result += " <br/>" +  e.toString();
        }
    }
%>

<html>
<head><title>Updating a Database</title></head>
<body>

The following query was submitted:
    <br/><br/>
    <%=ls_query%>
    <br/><br/>

The Result was:
    <br/><br/>
    <%=ls_result%>
    <br/><br/>

<a href="UpdateTableForm.jsp">Enter another value</a>

</body>
</html>
```

Now it's time to run everything and then discuss what's happening behind the scenes. First, let's launch the UpdateTableForm.jsp page to start the data entry process, as Figure 1.1 shows.

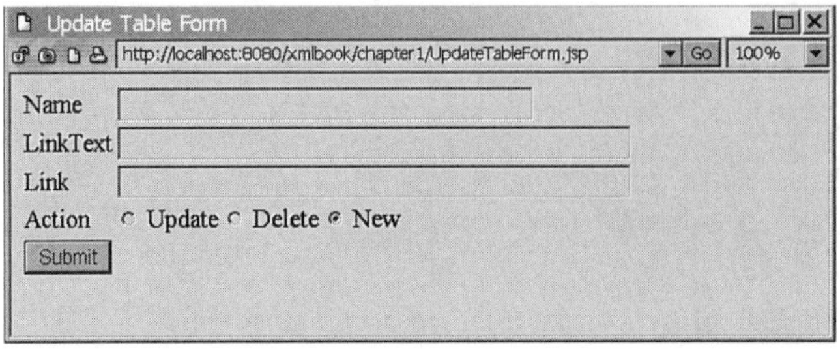

FIGURE 1.1 Running UpdateTableForm.jsp.

Let's go ahead and enter some data. As sample data, the examples here are using the following values: site1, JSP Site, and `www.jspinsider.com`. Once this page is submitted it will trigger the `UpdateTableAction.jsp` action page to produce the results shown in Figure 1.2.

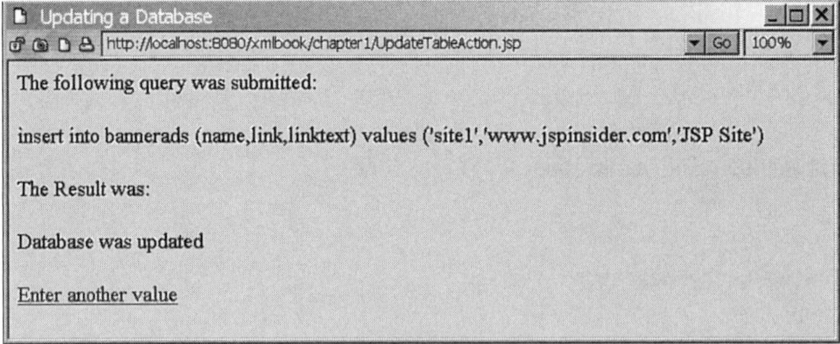

FIGURE 1.2 Results from UpdateTableAction.jsp.

Reviewing the Code for Entering Data

It's time to review and examine the UpdateTableAction.jsp page. The first step is to import the JDBC classes:

```
<%@page import = "java.sql.*" %>
```

Then the page needs to gather up the results from the UpdateTableForm.jsp page. Notice that the user request for this page comes as a result of clicking the Submit button on UpdateTableForm.jsp. This submits the form and puts the results in the

HTTP header. In JSP, the `request` implicit object can be used to gather these values. The `getParameter` method is used to collect the value of the name/value pair. Each name/value pair contains the name of the form element and the value that was submitted with that element. This code grabs the value of the form element named `name` and puts it into the string variable `ls_name`.

```
String ls_name     = request.getParameter("name");
```

The next major step is to initialize the JDBC setting information. The code will need the URL at which the database is open for client connections and the JDBC driver used to connect with the database. Note that `xmlbook` in the following line of code represents the database name. The values for our example are

```
String ls_dburl    = "jdbc:mysql://localhost/xmlbook";
String ls_dbdriver = "org.gjt.mm.mysql.Driver";
```

The next few lines are where the code creates a SQL statement to be executed by the database. In this example, several different SQL commands exist since entering, modifying, and deleting data require slightly different SQL statements. For example, the following code generates an update statement for when it is required to edit an existing record:

```
if (ls_action.equals("update"))
{   ls_query  = " update BannerAds";
    ls_query += " set link= "     + "'" + ls_link     + "',";
    ls_query += " set linktext= " + "'" + ls_linktext + "'";
    ls_query += " where name = "  + "'" + ls_name     + "'";
}
```

Now the fun stuff happens; we get to connect and use the database. The first step in using a database is creating a `Connection` object:

```
Connection l_dbconn = null;
```

The `Connection` object is our door into the database. Within the context of the `Connection`, the SQL statements will be executed and the results returned to us for our use.

All functions of connecting and using a database should be enclosed within a Java `try-catch` block. A lot can go wrong when working with a database. This means that the code needs to be ready to handle any exceptions that might happen. Notice that the `Connection` object is created before the `try-catch` block. We have a subtle reason behind our timing in declaring our `Connection` object. Database connections are both expensive in processing and precious in that they are usually limited in quantity. This means that database resources are often managed by a Web application. A database connection should always be closed after the code is finished with the connection. The best place to close a database connection is within the `finally` block of the `try-catch` block. In this example, the following code exists to perform the closing task:

```
finally
{
    /* We must close the database connection now */
    try
    {   if (l_dbconn != null)
        { l_dbconn.close(); }
    }
    catch (SQLException e)
    {   ls_result  = "Error in closing connection.";
        ls_result += " <br/>" +  e.toString();
    }
}
```

The example only attempts to close the connection if it was actually created. If it wasn't opened, it would still be `null` and nothing would happen. The advantage of using the `finally` block to close the database connection is that the database will still close even when an error happens within the `try-catch` block.

Okay, back to the example. After the connection object is created, the next step is to load the JDBC driver:

```
Class.forName(ls_dbdriver);
```

The act of loading the JDBC driver has the effect of registering the driver with the `DriverManager` object. This means that once the JDBC driver is loaded, it's possible to create the connection to the database:

```
l_dbconn = DriverManager.getConnection(ls_dburl);
```

The `getConnection` function is overloaded and has several formats. In this example, the database doesn't need a user or a password to log in successfully. However, most of the time a database will require an account. When this is the case, the following code can be used to connect to the database:

```
l_dbconn = DriverManager.getConnection(databaseURL,User,Password);
```

The code will apply SQL statements to the database through this connection. To do so, a `Statement` object is required to run the actual SQL statement that we have:

```
Statement l_statement = l_dbconn.createStatement();
```

The Statement object is used to execute queries and get any returning data (also known as a ResultSet) from the query. It's important to note that a Statement can only have one open ResultSet at any one moment. The code needs to be written so that only one thread will be using a Statement object at a given moment. The code in this example is effectively thread safe.

The last step is to actually execute the SQL statement:

```
l_statement.execute(ls_query);
```

JDBC will take the SQL statement and execute it against the database. In the preceding code snippets, the data is only being put into the database. This means that we don't need to capture a ResultSet.

One last piece of JDBC code to review involves catching the exceptions:

```
catch (SQLException e)
{ ls_result  = " Error processing the SQL!";
  ls_result += " <br/>" +  e.toString();
}
```

As stated earlier, database interactions are prone to many types of errors. This means that capturing exceptions is especially important in JDBC interactions. As a rule, a programmer should always capture SQLExceptions. The choice should be made to either handle the error, or at the very least report the exception to the user. It is a poor programming practice to disregard errors, as they happen fairly regularly.

The rest of the page is straightforward HTML. The only new piece of code we haven't used yet is the JSP expression statement:

```
<%=ls_query%>
```

The JSP expression is a handy shortcut method for dumping the string value of an object to the output stream. This is no different from using an out.print statement. As to which method is better, it comes down to which method is most convenient at the time of use within the code.

Viewing the Data

The first example built a page to enter data into the database. Now it's time to build a page to view this data. This example is called UsingACursor.jsp. The name reflects the fact that the code will loop through a database using a cursor. Ironically, you won't see any mention of a cursor in the code, since the code will default to a forward only cursor. What all this means is that when we get the data, we need to loop through the ResultSet one row at a time. Since it is a forward only cursor, it's only possible to move forward; the cursor can't go back to a record once it has moved to the next record. There are several different types of cursors, but forward only cursors are the easiest and fastest type to use. Armed with this brief explanation, let's plow forward and write the example page, as shown in Listing 1.3. This file should be saved as `webapps/xmlbook/chapter1/UsingACursor.jsp`.

LISTING 1.3 UsingACursor.jsp

```
<%@page import = "java.sql.*" %>
<%  /* Step 1) Initialize Variables */
    String ls_result   = "Nothing Happened";
    String ls_query    = "select name,link,linktext from BannerAds";
    String ls_dburl    = "jdbc:mysql://localhost/xmlbook";
    String ls_dbdriver = "org.gjt.mm.mysql.Driver";

    /* Step 2) Make a database connection */
    Connection dbconn = null;
    try
    {    Class.forName(ls_dbdriver);
         dbconn = DriverManager.getConnection(ls_dburl);

        /*create a SQL Statement */
        Statement statement = dbconn.createStatement();

        if (statement.execute(ls_query))
        {   /* Step 3) If we have a result lets loop through
                       to get the data */
            ResultSet           results   = statement.getResultSet();
            ResultSetMetaData   metadata  = results.getMetaData();

            /* validate result. Note switch to while loop if
               we plan on multiple results from query */
            if(results != null )
            {
            /* Use ResultSetMetaData object to determine the columns */
            int li_columns = metadata.getColumnCount();

            ls_result  = "<tr>";
            for ( int i = 1; i <= li_columns; i++)
            {ls_result += "<td>" + metadata.getColumnLabel(i) + "</td>";}
            ls_result += "</tr>";
```

LISTING 1.3 Continued

```
        /* Loop through the columns and append data to our table */
        while(results.next())
        {   results.getRow();
            ls_result += "<tr>";
            for ( int i = 1; i <= li_columns; i++)
            {
            ls_result += "<td>" + results.getObject(i).toString() + "</td>";
            }
            ls_result += "</tr>";
        }
        }
    }
  }
  catch (ClassNotFoundException e)
  {   ls_result  = " <tr><td> Error creating database drive class!" ;
      ls_result += " <br/>" +  e.toString() + "</td></tr>";
  }
  catch (SQLException e)
  {   ls_result  = " <tr><td> Error processing the SQL!";
      ls_result += " <br/>" +  e.toString()+ "</td></tr>";
  }
  finally
  {  /* We must close the database connection now */
      try
      {   if (dbconn != null)
          { dbconn.close(); }
      }
      catch (SQLException e)
      {   ls_result  = " <tr><td> Error in closing connection.";
          ls_result += " <br/>" +  e.toString() + "</td></tr>";
      }
  }
%>
<html>
<head><title>Viewing a Database Table</title></head>
<body>
The Result was:
  <table border="1">
      <%=ls_result%>
  </table>
</body>
</html>
```

This page is very similar to UpdateTableAction.jsp, but instead of launching a query to modify the database, it launches a query to retrieve data. The hard work is just looping through a `ResultSet` object (the cursor) . As the code loops through the data, the example will convert the data into a string to be displayed on the HTML page.

The page produces the results shown in Figure 1.3.

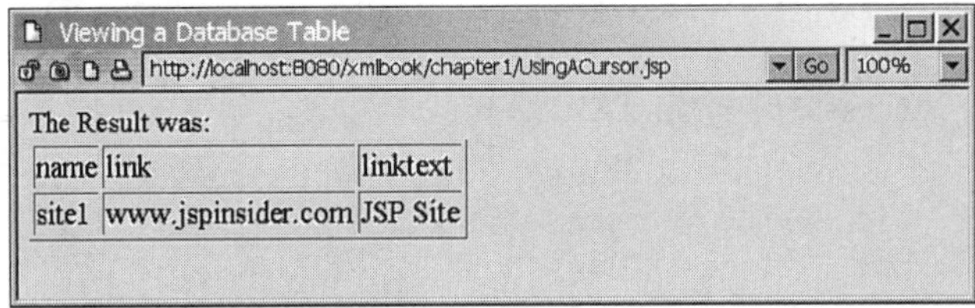

FIGURE 1.3 Results from UsingACursor.jsp.

We are only reviewing the sections of the page that differ from the UpdateTableAction.jsp page found in Listing 1.2.

This example runs a very different style of SQL:

```
String ls_query    = "select name,link,linktext from BannerAds";
```

This select statement will return all of the data from the BannerAds table stored in the xmlbook database. It begins by using the keyword select and listing the field names to be selected. Then the table name after the from keyword tells the statement which table to use.

Later, the code executes the SQL against the database:

```
if (statement.execute(ls_query))
```

In this call, the code checks to see whether a `ResultSet` is created upon execution of the SQL. If the statement is true then there exists a `ResultSet` (the results from the SQL query).

```
ResultSet           results    = statement.getResultSet();
ResultSetMetaData   metadata   = results.getMetaData();
```

The next important step is to grab both the `ResultSet`, which has our data from the SQL query, and the `ResultSetMetaData` object, which contains the data that describes the `ResultSet`. First, the `ResultSetMetaData` will be examined to determine how many columns are in the returned dataset. Notice that we know the number of columns because we explicitly selected particular columns in the query statement earlier. We are including this process to demonstrate how to do it when the number of columns returned is unknown:

```
int li_columns = metadata.getColumnCount();
```

Once the number of columns has been determined, it becomes easy to loop through and build a list of the column names:

```
ls_result  = "<tr>";
for ( int i = 1; i <= li_columns; i++)
{ls_result += "<td>" + metadata.getColumnLabel(i) + "</td>";}
 ls_result += "</tr>";
```

Notice that the code wraps the results with HTML. It does this so that when the string result is sent out to the browser, it will be formatted as an HTML table.

Once the column headers have been created, the next step is to loop through the results and create rows for each record. This string will be put into the `ls_result` table string:

```
while(results.next())
{   results.getRow();
ls_result += "<tr>";
    for ( int i = 1; i <= li_columns; i++)
    {
    ls_result += "<td>" + results.getObject(i).toString() + "</td>";
    }
ls_result += "</tr>";
}
```

The `results.next()` statement shows how to move through the data one row at a time. As long as this statement evaluates to a true result, there is a new row to process. Also notice that when actually pulling the data out of the result, we don't always know right away what type of data is being returned. Since we want a string to display, this code uses a shortcut by getting the data as type `object`:

```
results.getObject(i).toString()
```

Then we use the `toString()` function to easily convert it to a `String` in the same call.

Finally, in the HTML portion of the JSP page, the preformatted result string is placed into a table:

```
    <table border="1">
        <%=ls_result%>
    </table>
```

Overall, this example illustrates the basic steps of pushing data into and out of a database. After this, the next step is determining what to do with the data. In later chapters, we'll write some examples that convert data to XML from a database resultset.

Other Considerations

We need to quickly cover a few more issues in this chapter. These are things that programmers may not learn unless they are lucky enough to have well-trained coworkers, or have been burned on a project.

Connection Pooling

The code examples didn't use connection pooling. As a rule, connection pooling should be used to speed up database access and reduce the number of database connections used by any Web application. It turns out that one of the more expensive operations you can perform in terms of time and resources is simply connecting to the database. Each connection to a database takes time to perform and resources to manage. If a site had 10,000 users, it would be impractical to use 10,000 connections. Instead, it's better to pool the connections and reuse them on a need only basis. This prevents the overhead of creating and destroying connections repeatedly. Instead, they remain open and are available for use through connection management.

For example, if a project has 10,000 users, it might only need 500 connections at any one moment. Connection pooling software tends to be simple to use within a project. Most J2EE application servers will offer some form of connection pooling. For smaller JSP projects, you can find connection pooling from several resources. One good open source project to check out is PoolMan, which can be downloaded at `http://www.codestudio.com`. In addition, in JDBC 3.0, the drivers can be built to include connection pooling to make it transparent to the programmer.

Testing Components

In JSP, a programmer has many opportunities to use prebuilt components. As a rule, however, you should never assume that a component is perfect. If you are seeing strange behavior within your code, always perform a reality check to make sure that the component is working as expected. This holds true for any component, including JDBC drivers.

A Story of a Driver

This story will illustrate why early testing is important when using any component in a Java project.

On this project, we were using the Sybase SQL Server Database and Sybase JConnect, a free JDBC driver. The driver was installed and everything worked perfectly. That is, at first it did. Everything worked well for the initial simple SQL queries. As soon as the queries began to get larger, though, the application began to have problems.

The code was using a scrolling cursor and the query speed was pathetic. A SQL query that should run in a minute was taking the code 15 minutes to process. This was a problem. In investigating the problem, we closely reexamined the documentation for clues. Fortunately, the problem was listed in the documentation. The problem was that for large cursors, a scrolling cursor could have poor performance and cause crashes due to memory usage. Because this project had extra large cursors, this was a serious problem.

At this point, the options were to find a new driver that handled scrolling cursors better or rebuild the logic. Since budget was an issue, we chose to keep the JConnect driver and update the code to use a more limited forward cursor. After we rewrote the code, the program worked well enough for the project to move onward again. Then we began to notice a string of mysterious packet dropping errors.

After doing some research on the Sybase listserv, we discovered that other users were having the same problem and that it was a networking issue with the driver and NT. Luckily for us, the project was developed under NT, but deployed on Unix. Thankfully, the problem was specific to NT and never occurred on the Unix box.

The project taught us some important lessons. The most important was that one shouldn't assume that a JDBC driver or any other component will always work as expected. Nothing is bug free, and budgeting time and resources to deal with unexpected problems will in the end save money and permit the timely delivery of projects.

Testing for Scale

A common mistake made with database use in a project is to neglect to fully test load your application. Usually, smaller test databases are used to build a system. This makes life simple for initial building. However, SQL is easy to write and not always easy to optimize. As an example, on one project we had some SQL that worked fine on the test database and ran in under a minute. Once we moved the SQL to use production data, the same SQL took over 2 hours to run against the several million rows of data. The problem was fixed with some SQL optimization and some sweat, ending up with runtimes around 5 minutes. In this case, you should focus on the consequence, not the actual problem, because it's the lesson that is important. Always test at some point with data that closely matches the size load of your project. It's easy to build a system to work with small datasets. However, the large final dataset will always clobber your system if you haven't prepared for it.

This lesson also applies to using XML datasets. In fact, this lesson is probably more critical when dealing with XML. While databases are finely optimized to work with large datasets, the same cannot be said about all XML parsers, and especially our own hand written logic. When using small amounts of data, most everything works fine. Once we get into larger XML files or databases, the rules change and every ounce of performance can make or break a project.

Basic Design Concepts

As a rule of thumb, JSP should be used as a presentation layer. This means that the logic within a JSP page should be geared towards only generating the actual formatting of the output. All reusable or modular logic should be pushed into a JavaBean or a tag library. Generally, these modular objects are also referred to as business objects. The term *business object* is used because business logic should generally be placed into JavaBeans. The reason for this is that moving code into a lower level, such as a JavaBean, makes it reusable across many pages. The other benefit is that the final code in the JSP page will be modular and easier to update and maintain. We will demonstrate this by using a readily available database tag library. If you are interested in learning how to build and use your own tag library, check out Appendix C, "Tag Library."

Conversely, you should avoid putting presentation level logic (any logic used to create the display) into lower components such as JavaBeans or tag libraries. The reason pertains to flexibility; placing presentation logic in a lower level object forces the object into only producing a certain type of formatted output. As an example, if you built an object that produced hard-coded HTML, it would be difficult to use the same object to produce an XML document. If you look back to the UsingACursor.jsp example, the code from the result would only work for an HTML table. It would be awkward to recode everything in order to change the format or to add special formatting.

Using a Tag library

Generally, data presentation and data processing should be kept separate. In the UsingACursor.jsp page, we kept everything as a single JSP page to illustrate the coding of the JDBC logic. However, from a practical point of view this code should be built as a reusable JavaBean or tag library. The nice thing about JSP is that many people are already writing tag libraries that can be used with little extra effort. In fact, we can go ahead and use a prebuilt tag library to quickly recode the page.

The Jakarta project has a collection of open source tag libraries for anyone to freely use within a project. The one tag library we are interested in is the DBTags custom tag library. This library has a series of prebuilt functions to both read and write to a database. The actual description and code can be downloaded from http://jakarta.apache.org/taglibs/doc/dbtags-doc/intro.html.

After downloading the DBTags tag library, you will need to perform the following steps:

1. Copy the .tld (tag library descriptor) file into the xmlbook/WEB-INF directory.
2. Copy the tag library's JAR file into the xmlbook/WEB-INF/lib directory.
3. Modify the xmlbook/WEB-INF/web.xml file. Add the following lines between the <web-app></web-app> tags.

```
<taglib>
  <taglib-uri>http://jakarta.apache.org/taglibs/dbtags</taglib-uri>
  <taglib-location>/WEB-INF/dbtags.tld</taglib-location>
</taglib>
```

4. Restart Tomcat. This will permit Tomcat to find and register the database tag library.

Now we are ready to build a JSP page to view the data. Save the file shown in Listing 1.4 as webapps/xmlbook/chapter1/ViewTable.jsp.

LISTING 1.4 ViewTable.jsp

```
<%@ taglib uri="http://jakarta.apache.org/taglibs/dbtags" prefix="sql" %>

<html>
<head><title>Using Tags For DataBase Access</title></head>
<body>

<%-- Step 1) Make a database connection --%>
<sql:connection id="connect">
  <sql:url>jdbc:mysql://localhost/xmlbook</sql:url>
  <sql:driver>org.gjt.mm.mysql.Driver</sql:driver>
</sql:connection>

<%-- Step 2) Create a query --%>
<table border="1">
<sql:statement id="statement" conn="connect">
  <sql:query>
    select name,link,linktext from BannerAds
  </sql:query>
  <%--  Step 2a) loop through the query result --%>
```

LISTING 1.4 Continued

```
    <tr>
      <td>Name</td>
      <td>Link</td>
      <td>LinkText</td>
    </tr>
  <sql:resultSet id="data">
    <tr>
      <td><sql:getColumn position="1"/></td>
      <td><sql:getColumn position="2"/></td>
      <td><sql:getColumn position="3"/></td>
    </tr>
  </sql:resultSet>
</sql:statement>
</table>

<%-- Step 3) Close the Database Connection --%>
<sql:closeConnection conn="connect"/>

</body>
</html>
```

Running this page will produce results similar to Figure 1.4.

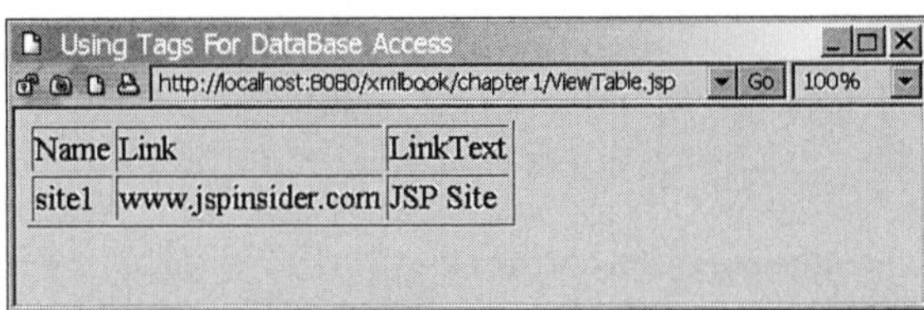

FIGURE 1.4 Results from ViewTable.jsp.

Let's review what happened in this page.

The first line tells the JSP container where to find the tag library. Tomcat looks up the URI (uniform resource identifier) reference in the web.xml file and obtains a prefix to use when referencing the database tags:

```
<%@ taglib uri="http://jakarta.apache.org/taglibs/dbtags" prefix="sql" %>
```

The prefix means that in this example, any tag starting with `<sql:` will resolve to the DBTags custom tag library.

The code follows a path of logic almost identical to that of the database examples. The difference is that the custom tags are performing the JDBC logic. All a programmer needs to do is provide the custom tags with the connection and SQL information. Following the logic, the next step is to tell the tag library where to make the database connection:

```
<sql:connection id="connect">
  <sql:url>jdbc:mysql://localhost/xmlbook</sql:url>
  <sql:driver>org.gjt.mm.mysql.Driver</sql:driver>
</sql:connection>
```

Then the code tells the tag library which connection to use and which SQL statement to apply to the database:

```
<sql:statement id="statement" conn="connect">
  <sql:query>
   select name,link,linktext from BannerAds
  </sql:query>
```

After we have the SQL statement loaded, it is possible to use a result tag to loop through and extract the data. In this example, the code puts the data into a table row, but it could just as easily put the data into an XML file or another format:

```
  <sql:resultSet id="data">
    <tr>
      <td><sql:getColumn position="1"/></td>
      <td><sql:getColumn position="2"/></td>
      <td><sql:getColumn position="3"/></td>
    </tr>
  </sql:resultSet>
```

Finally, notice that the code still has to close the database connection:

```
<sql:closeConnection conn="connect"/>
```

The custom tag library we are using is still young. At the time of this book's publication, it didn't have a method to extract the field names. Therefore, the example page had the column names hard-coded:

```
    <tr>
      <td>Name</td>
      <td>Link</td>
      <td>LinkText</td>
    </tr>
```

A future release of this tag library will probably include a method to extract field names. However, we can add this functionality ourselves if we want to. This particular tag library is open source, which means that anyone can add his or her own tags to the library, including one to resolve field names. Also, if any of the included custom tags don't work the way your project requires, it's possible to recode the tags to better suit your needs. This is one of the benefits of open source tag libraries.

Summary

This chapter has reviewed some of the basics of JSP and how to connect to a database. Keep in mind that using a database is a subject that could fill an entire book on its own. We intentionally kept the code and information presented in this chapter simple and brief. The goal was to give just enough information to get you started down the road to using a database. You should walk away knowing how to connect, update, and retrieve data from a database. With this starting knowledge, you can now begin to learn XML. Throughout the book, we will create examples that use both XML and a database at the same time (in most real-world projects, using a mixture of XML and a database will be a given). This will be especially true in Chapter 11, "Using XML in Reporting Systems," where we will create an automatic system to populate the database with thousands of records to test a sample reporting system.

Now, the book gets into the fun stuff. The first step will be to review XML. The next chapter will introduce XML, XSL, and XPath. It covers most of the basics of using XML and includes quite a bit of information. so get a cup of coffee and enjoy the ride.

2 Introduction to XML/XSL

IN THIS CHAPTER

The goal of this chapter is to walk you through the basics of XML and XSL. If you have never used XML or XSL before or know only a little bit about them, consider this your whirlwind course to get you on your feet.

One of the wonderful aspects of XML is its simplicity. It really doesn't take much to get up and running with XML. Therefore, this chapter is geared to race through the basics of XML. We will cover enough XML to enable you to use the rest of this book with confidence. After discussing XML, we will plunge into XSL. If you are already comfortable with XML, don't hesitate to skip ahead to the XSL section.

What Is XML?

XML is the Extensible Markup Language. It's called *extensible* because the modular nature of its structure enables you to make modifications easily by changing or adding data features. More importantly, XML is actually a "meta-language." That is, XML is really a specification that dictates how to describe languages and data.

XML's design gives us the following powerful features:

- XML simplifies communication because it is self-describing. When an XML document is created, the structure has also been created. It is this structure that describes the data therein. This permits programs to easily query an XML document for specific data without having to perform difficult parsing. The self-describing nature of XML makes it simple to share XML data between people and applications. XML permits you to create custom markup (your own tags). This permits XML to represent a limitless number of documents.

NOTE

Document is the term used for a single collection of XML data. A document can be stored as a file, as an object, or within a database. It is not where the document is stored, but rather the collection of data constituting the document that is the defining feature of an XML document.

- Data can be stored and arranged in a way that is customizable for your needs. Documents may be organized exactly how you want them.
- Unicode (an international standard for text) is the standard character set for XML and thus an immense number of languages and characters are supported. Documents can be created in nearly any language.
- XML is based on simple character text, which makes it easy to transport an XML document between systems or across the Internet.
- Document structure and quality can be checked. This means it is possible to validate the overall document, syntax, and data types before the data is processed by an application. Therefore, it is possible to add more robust and complete error detection within an application.
- XML can easily be mixed with stylesheets to create almost any output desired. An XML document should only consist of data. You can reuse the data in many different ways. It is easy to reuse a single set of data and reformat the data to display differently just by swapping stylesheets. In addition, once a stylesheet is built, it can be reused against many different XML documents as long as they have the same structure. Later in the book we will show the full power of stylesheets as we build some reports.
- Virtually any type of data can be expressed as an XML document. XML merely provides the rules that tell how to describe the data. The data itself is usually easily expressible using XML's rules.

When combined, these features create a means of describing data that is independent of any language or system. This permits us to reuse XML data across systems and businesses. It all comes down to a set of very simple and well-thought-out rules.

Rules of XML

To help explain XML, we've created the sample XML file shown in Listing 2.1.

LISTING 2.1 Sample XML Document shows.xml

```
<?xml version="1.0"?>
<SHOWS>
     <PERFORMANCE>
          <TITLE>Fairy Princess</TITLE>
          <AUTHOR/>
          <DESCRIPTION>
               Scratch sound with emphasis on color, texture.
          </DESCRIPTION>
          <DATE status="canceled">09/11/2001</DATE>
     </PERFORMANCE>
</SHOWS>
```

Use a text editor to create this file and save it to your hard disk as shows.xml. Over the next few sections we will refer back to this file to illustrate the structure of XML. Later, this file will be used for showing examples within a browser.

Tags and Elements

All XML markup consists of tags. Here is a sample tag:

```
<PERFORMANCE>
```

Tags are used to build an element. Here is a sample element:

```
<PERFORMANCE></PERFORMANCE>
```

An XML file author creates tags to describe the data that the file contains. These tags are very similar to HTML tags. Elements are the foundation of XML documents.

Tag and Element Basics

First, let's cover three commonly used terms with regard to tags. The terms are *opening tag, closing tag,* and *empty tag*. An *opening tag* is the first tag of a pair; in our sample element in the preceding section, `<PERFORMANCE>` is an opening tag. The *closing tag* is the end tag of a pair; in our sample element, `</PERFORMANCE>` is the closing tag. Finally, an *empty tag* is a standalone tag that has no data, and looks like this:

```
<PERFORMANCE/>
```

An *element* consists of an opening tag, a closing tag, and everything in between. All data within an XML document is expressed with tags. Elements can contain other elements, data or text, or can be empty and contain nothing between the tags. Elements can also contain a mix of data and other elements.

```
<PERFORMANCE>
    Marks Bros. Theater
    <TITLE>Fairy Princess</TITLE>
</PERFORMANCE>
```

Here are the basic rules for using tags:

- Tags are case sensitive. This means that <NAME> and <Name> are different tags. Take care to ensure that the case of opening and closing tags match.
- No whitespace is permitted at the beginning of a tag. An example of disallowed whitespace would be < NAME>. However, whitespace at the end of tags is allowed, as in <NAME >.
- The tag name must start with either a letter or an underscore.
- The tag name may contain any of the following: letters, numerals, hyphens (-), periods (.), or underscores (_).
- Each tag must be closed. This means that, where an opening tag is created, there must eventually be a closing one of the same name. When a tag contains no data, you can either close it immediately after opening it (<AUTHOR></AUTHOR>, for example) or use an empty tag (for instance, <AUTHOR/>).
- Each element must be appropriately nested before another tag is opened. Unlike HTML, which is tolerant of inappropriately nested tags, XML has strict nesting rules. In XML, if a tag is opened inside an element, it must be closed inside that element also. For example, in HTML the following will work:

  ```
  <B><FONT color="red">text here</B></FONT>
  ```

  However, in XML this is not valid because the font tag is opened within the bold tag and is closed after the end of the bold tag. This violates the rule that a tag must be closed within the same element in which it was opened. In this case, the font tag was not closed within the bold element. A correct version would look like this:

  ```
  <B><FONT color="red">text here</FONT></B>
  ```

Root Element

Every XML document must have one and only one *root element,* also known as the *document element.* This is an author-defined element that contains the rest of the XML document. Only two types of statements can reside outside the root element: A document declaration (which is always the first line of the XML document) and processing instructions.

In the shows.xml example document (see Listing 2.1) the root element is `<SHOWS>`. Notice that `<SHOWS>` is the first tag that is neither an XML declaration in the document nor a processing tag, and the closing tag `</SHOWS>` is the last. Finally, note that every other tag is inside the `SHOWS` element.

Attributes

Attributes are another important part of XML documents. An attribute is a name/value pair that can be found in an opening tag. Attributes provide additional information to a particular element. Embedded in a tag, an attribute looks like the following:

```
<DATE status="canceled">09/11/2001</DATE>
```

Attributes are useful for providing properties of an element. In the preceding code snippet, notice that the property name/value pair is `status="canceled"`. This is relevant to the date of the performance—if the information regarding that performance were requested, it would be important to note that it had been canceled. Many times, attributes and elements can be interchangeable in their functionality. That is, data expressed as an attribute could also be expressed as an element. In XML, it just doesn't make a difference because data is data. However, it will make a difference when you are processing an XML document. Here is a simple set of guidelines:

- Any data that needs to be displayed should be stored as an element.
- Any data meant to modify the way an element displays should be stored as an attribute.

Keep in mind that these are just guidelines. With experience, you will get a sense of whether data would be best stored as an attribute or an element.

Several rules exist regarding attributes:

- Attributes consist of a property name, an equal sign, and the property value in quotation marks (for instance, `status="canceled"`).
- The property name is case sensitive. An attribute named `Status` is not the same as one named `status`.
- There can never be two properties of the same name in any one tag.

- There can be more than one attribute per tag.
- There must be quotation marks around the value of an attribute. Either single quotes or double quotes may be used. If you need to use single quotes or double quotes within the actual value (for example, `owner="bill 'slim' jones"`), use the other type of quotation marks to contain the value.

The XML Declaration

Let's take a closer look at shows.xml (see Listing 2.1). The first line is called the *XML declaration* and looks like this:

```
<?xml version="1.0"?>
```

This line exists to tell the XML processor that this is indeed an XML file. It tells us that the file is based on version 1.0 of the XML specification. Notice that the version property name/value pair is an attribute that follows the earlier rules.

Some of the more useful properties of the document declaration are listed here:

- `version`—Sets the version of the XML specification being used by the XML document. Currently there is only one version of the specification (version 1.0). However, by declaring this property, you can ensure that the XML processor will know which version of the specification the XML document uses when the next version is released and thus maintain backwards compatibility.
- `encoding`—Defines the character encoding. The default is UTF-8. This is the character set used within the XML document. The character set defines the numeric value of each character in a file.
- `standalone`—Declares whether or not the XML document has other files that must be processed, such as an external stylesheet or document type definition (DTD). When you are working with a standalone XML document, you will see a performance gain in document processing when you use the `standalone` attribute.

Here are two document declaration examples:

```
<?xml version="1.0" encoding="UTF-8" ?>

<?xml version="1.0" standalone="yes" ?>
```

Document Type Declaration

The beginning of an XML file may contain other things after the XML declaration. The document can specify entity declarations, the root element, instructions to XML parsers, or the *document type definition (DTD)* that should be used to validate the XML document.

The DTD describes the structural requirements of an XML document. This means that a DTD can define the following:

- The elements and attributes that can appear in a document
- Which elements are child elements and what number, order, and placement they must have
- The default values for elements and attributes

It is used to ensure that each XML document follows a specific document model, and thus is in the exact format required for whatever processing may come its way.

Listing 2.2 shows a DTD for the shows.xml file found in Listing 2.1.

LISTING 2.2 External DTD File shows.dtd for shows.xml

```
<?xml version="1.0" encoding="UTF-8"?>
<!ELEMENT SHOWS (PERFORMANCE*)>
<!ELEMENT PERFORMANCE
(TITLE?, AUTHOR?, DESCRIPTION?, DATE?)+ >
<!ELEMENT TITLE (#PCDATA)>
<!ELEMENT AUTHOR (#PCDATA)>
<!ELEMENT DESCRIPTION (#PCDATA)>
<!ELEMENT DATE (#PCDATA)>
<!ATTLIST DATE status (canceled) #IMPLIED>
```

A DTD begins with the XML declaration. Then it starts defining the required structure of the XML document through the use of element declarations like the following:

```
<!ELEMENT TITLE (#PCDATA)>
```

The content of each element declaration begins with the element name it's defining. In this case, it's the `TITLE` element. Then it describes the content that is permitted therein. In our sample code snippet, the element `TITLE` may contain `#PCDATA`.

Possible values for contents include

- A list of other elements
- The keyword EMPTY (no contents)
- The keyword ALL (anything possible)
- The keyword #PCDATA (parsed character data only)
- Any reasonable mix of the above

This brings us to the question of how to combine these elements in a way that the DTD understands. They can be combined using the following operators:

- The comma (,) is used as an and operator. An example is (TITLE, AUTHOR). The element being described must have one TITLE element and one AUTHOR element as children.
- The pipe (|) is used as an or operator. An example is (TITLE | AUTHOR). The element being described must have either a TITLE or an AUTHOR child element.
- The question mark (?) means that the element is optional. An example is (AUTHOR, TITLE?). The element being described must have a child AUTHOR element and may also have a child TITLE element.
- The plus sign (+) is used to signify one or more. An example is (TITLE+). The element being described must have at least one TITLE child element.
- The asterisk (*) is used to signify that any number may exist. An example is (TITLE*). The element being described can have any number of child elements named TITLE.
- Parentheses are a way to force processing. For example, (A | (B, C)) means that the element being described must have either an A child element or both B and C child elements.

Attributes, like elements, can be defined within a DTD. The syntax is similar except that the tag looks like this:

```
<!ATTLIST DATE status (canceled) #IMPLIED>
```

Again, the contents begin with the name of the element whose attributes we are describing. Next, we list the name of the attribute, and then we define either its data type or a list of literal values that it can have. Last, we describe the behavior of the attribute.

Some possible data types and values used to describe attributes are

- An enumerated list of values that may be in the name/value pair. For example, `( canceled | onschedule )` indicates that the value of the attribute being described is either `canceled` or `onschedule`.
- `CDATA`—This is governed by the same rules regarding content as text data found within elements.
- `ID`—This type of attribute gives an element a label guaranteed to be unique in the document.

Next, we have several values that can be used in the DTD to describe the behavior of the attribute:

- When a string in quotes is given, it becomes the default value. If the user doesn't include the attribute, it will be created with the default value in the document structure when it is parsed.
- `#IMPLIED`—The attribute is optional.
- `#REQUIRED`—The attribute is required, and no default value is assumed.

For more information regarding DTDs and how to build them, check out `http://www.xml101.com/dtd/`, which offers some very helpful tutorials.

In order for the XML document to be validated against the DTD when the DTD is contained within another file, we have to add a DTD reference to the XML document.

The DTD can be an external file that is referenced by the XML document, or it can be completely included within the document.

Listing 2.3 adds a DTD reference (see boldface print) to the shows.xml file from Listing 2.1.

LISTING 2.3 shows.xml with DTD Reference Added

```
<?xml version="1.0"?>
<!DOCTYPE SHOWS SYSTEM "shows.dtd">
<SHOWS>
     <PERFORMANCE>
          <TITLE>Fairy Princess</TITLE>
          <AUTHOR/>
          <DESCRIPTION>
               Scratch sound with emphasis on color, texture.
          </DESCRIPTION>
          <DATE status="canceled">09/11/2001</DATE>
     </PERFORMANCE>
</SHOWS>
```

The contents of this reference begin with the root element to which the DTD applies; in this case it is `SHOWS`. Then the `SYSTEM` keyword is used to state that the DTD is unpublished and that the location of the following file is the DTD for this XML document. The other option is to use the keyword `PUBLIC` in place of `SYSTEM` and the Uniform Resource Identifier (URI) . The `PUBLIC` keyword means that the DTD is available to the public for validating documents. This option is usually used when XML documents are being passed between companies—it enables them to make sure that their XML documents have the expected structure.

Schemas

Many programmers feel that DTDs aren't flexible enough for current programming needs. Fortunately, schemas will replace DTDs in most Web applications. Schemas are much like DTDs in that they define the legal building blocks of an XML document. Unlike DTDs, however, schemas are written in XML and thus are extensible to future additions. They can also handle namespaces and data types.

Schemas have the following advantages over DTDs:

- Schemas are XML documents themselves; they can be validated and programmatically extended.
- Schemas have the ability to describe the data type of element text data.
- Unlike DTDs, which describe an entire XML document, a schema describes elements and attributes. This means that adding elements to the validated XML document won't break the validation provided they are of a different namespace.

Character Entities

Some characters may not appear in any data part of an XML document, or within an attribute value. This is due to the fact that they are delimiters to the XML parser. One example of a delimiter is the less than character (<), which is used as the opening of a tag. Consider this example:

```
<TITLE> less than : < </TITLE>
```

The text in this example will cause the parser to report errors. The parser will believe that the extra < is an opening tag and will be confused when it isn't closed.

To get around this problem, there is a special solution: You can replace single characters that serve as delimiters with their character entities. The *character entity* is the name for the character. The characters not permitted in XML documents and their replacements are shown in Table 2.1.

TABLE 2.1 Replacement Character Entity Names

Character	Name
<	<
&	&
>	>
'	'
"	"

So, in our last example, the code should be rewritten with the character entity value

```
<TITLE> less than : &lt; </TITLE>
```

This is also true for attribute values. If an attribute value contains &, >, or <, the value should be replaced with the replacement characters found in Table 2.1.

CDATA Sections

Sometimes it can be tedious to replace characters with their character entities. This is especially true when dealing with large blocks of text data. This is where the CDATA sections come in handy.

CDATA sections are areas in which the parser doesn't process the XML data. The parser knows that this part of the document contains no markup, just text. Therefore, the parser can handle characters that would normally delimit markup because it's not looking for any markup.

CDATA sections are delimited as follows:

```
<![CDATA[ your data ]]>.
```

All characters inside the innermost square brackets are treated as text with no markup. This means that the sequence of characters]]> cannot be a part of the text in a CDATA section. This sequence instead can be represented by]]>.

Here is an example of an element with a CDATA section:

```
<EQUATION><![CDATA[ x > y && z < x & z > y ? ]]></EQUATION>
```

CDATA sections are very useful when there is text in the document that needs to be passed through the parser unprocessed. This is especially true when XML is being used to send output to a browser, as it offers a simple way to prevent the parser from reacting to offending characters in JavaScript.

Comments

Comments may be put anywhere in the document, except for the first line, which is always reserved for the document declaration, and inside tags. XML comments have the same form as HTML comments. Here's an example of an XML comment:

```
<!--  comment goes here -->
```

The following rules apply for XML comments:

- `<!--` starts a comment, and `-->` ends a comment.
- Comments may not be nested.
- Double dashes (`--`) cannot be used within a comment because this is the delimiter that tells the processor that the comment is finished.

  The following example will cause an error:

  ```
  <!--  --the extra dashes in this comment will cause an error--  -->
  ```

Well-Formed and Validated Documents

XML gives you an immense amount of power to create custom markup languages and elements. This flexibility could wreak havoc on XML parsers if there weren't enough syntactical rules regarding markup. XML documents that follow all the XML syntax rules are referred to as "well-formed" documents. Following all the rules outlined in the previous sections of this chapter will ensure that your XML is well-formed. In brief, a well-formed document has

- A single root element
- Properly nested tags
- Properly closed tags
- Attribute values within quotation marks
- Only one value per attribute
- No offending characters

All XML documents that are processed must be well-formed, but they may also have to be valid. A valid XML document is one that conforms to the DTD or schema written to describe its structure. That is, the valid XML document meets all of the requirements declared in the DTD or schema.

On to Using XML

We've just given you a very brief introduction to XML. The preceding section introduced elements, attributes, nesting, and offending characters. Later, there will be more coverage of other specifics of XML. For now, however, let's start processing the XML that we have.

Processing

Once we have an XML document, we're ready to use the data. We might want to display it in a browser or have our JSP process some of the data. Let's look at what happens when you load an XML file into a browser.

No matter what the purpose of an XML file may be, it is parsed immediately upon being loaded. If any part of the file is in violation of a well-formed document rule, an error will be prominently displayed.

If the XML parser is a *validating* parser, it will read the DTD or schema associated with the XML document to determine whether the XML document conforms to it. If it conforms, all is well and processing will continue. However, if it does not conform, an error will be displayed and, depending upon the parser, the processing will cease.

If the parser is *non-validating,* it is able to read the DTD or schema, but cannot check to make sure that the XML document conforms to it.

You may find the pickiness of some parsers to be downright frustrating. However, in the long run this pickiness is very helpful because it prevents errors further down the software chain. It's much better that the parser finds errors early on, instead of later when your XML document has been sent to another business or application.

Let's work with an example now. This example will use the shows.xml file from Listing 2.1. Start Netscape and open the XML document by using the Open option in the File menu. Netscape will display the output shown in Figure 2.1.

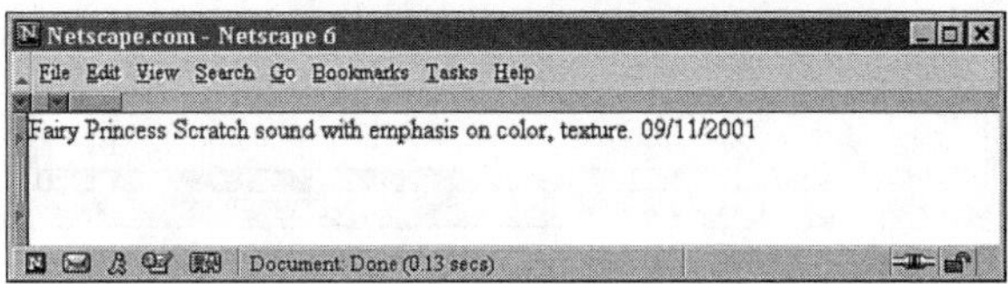

FIGURE 2.1 Netscape 6.1 displaying shows.xml.

Notice that only the data within the XML elements is displayed. This is because Netscape reads the XML tags as markup, much like HTML. The difference is that these tags are undefined markup for the browser.

At this point, we would like to comment on a difference between Internet Explorer (IE) and Netscape. IE has more built-in XML support and thus will display some things differently. It will display the entire XML file, tags included, because it recognizes that it's indeed XML (see Figure 2.2).

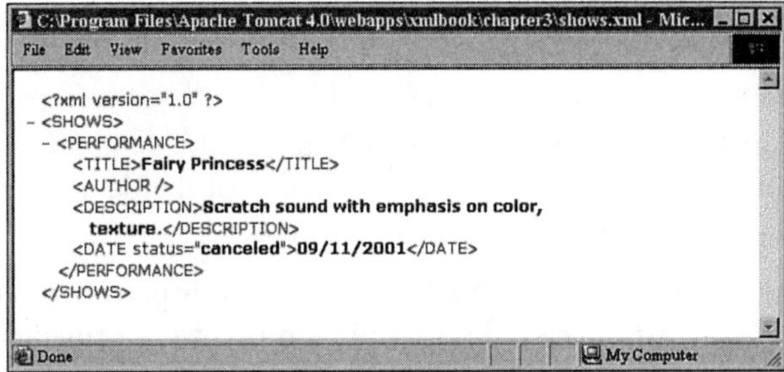

FIGURE 2.2 IE 6.0 displaying shows.xml.

If shows.xml were renamed shows.html, Internet Explorer would display the same output as shown in Figure 2.1.

Now let's see what happens when your XML isn't well-formed. Let's take the shows.xml file, open it in a text editor, and introduce a mistake. Change the text case of one of the tags, save it, and refresh Netscape. An error will be prominently displayed with information about the offense, as shown in Figure 2.3.

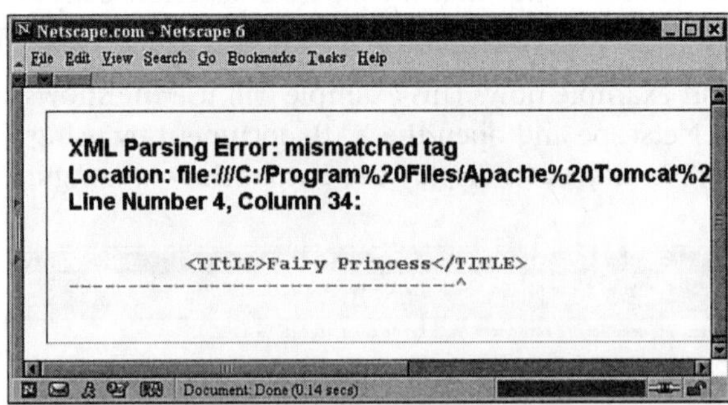

FIGURE 2.3 Netscape 6.1 displaying an error from shows.xml.

Loading an XML document into a browser is a quick way to check its structural integrity, and fix it if necessary.

The internal parser for Netscape is parsing the XML document. Internet Explorer and Netscape both have XML parsers included in their browsers to make XML easier to use. This is great, but how do we make XML display in the way we want? We'll see how in the next section.

XSL

XSL stands for Extensible Stylesheet Language. This language is what we'll use to transform an XML source into what we want. With the data we could output any format: HTML, more XML, or anything else. It is important to note that XSL is based on XML. This means that XSL must follow the same well-formed rules as XML: There are quotation marks around all attribute values, all tags are case sensitive and must be properly nested, and data must not contain the markup characters listed in Table 2.1. In the following examples, we are going to format some XML as HTML using XSL Transformations (XSLT).

Stylesheet Linking

First, we are going to add another processor instruction to the top of the XML file that we created. Add the following line after the document declaration in the shows.xml file and save it as shows2.xml. This will become the second line of the XML document.

```
<?xml-stylesheet type='text/xsl' href='shows.xsl'?>
```

Let's look at this more closely. This stylesheet processing instruction informs the XML processor where to find the associated stylesheet for the XML document. It contains the type of the associated stylesheet through the type name/value pair (or attribute). If, for example, the stylesheet were a cascading stylesheet (CSS), this value would be `text/css`. Next, this processing instruction indicates where to find the corresponding stylesheet using the `href` attribute. In our case, it can be found in the same directory as the XML file, and the filename will be shows.xsl. This association causes the XML to be transformed relative to the instructions of shows.xsl.

Listing 2.4 contains the shows.xsl file. Save the file to the same directory as shows2.xml. The line numbers have been added to aid in the following stylesheet analysis.

LISTING 2.4 Example Stylesheet shows.xsl

```
<xsl:stylesheet version="1.0"
     xmlns:xsl="http://www.w3.org/1999/XSL/Transform">
<xsl:template match="/">
<HTML>
```

LISTING 2.4 Continued

```
<HEAD>
<TITLE>First Performance Stylesheet</TITLE>
</HEAD>
<BODY>
<xsl:for-each select="SHOWS/PERFORMANCE">
    <FONT color="red">
    <B><xsl:value-of select="TITLE" /></B> -
    <I><xsl:value-of select="AUTHOR" /></I>
    </FONT>
    <xsl:value-of select="DATE" />
    <xsl:value-of select="DESCRIPTION" />
    <BR/>
</xsl:for-each>
</BODY>
</HTML>
</xsl:template>
</xsl:stylesheet>
```

This example takes each `PERFORMANCE` element found within a `SHOWS` element and displays the `TITLE`, `AUTHOR`, `DATE`, and `DESCRIPTION` formatted with HTML. The output is shown in Figure 2.4:

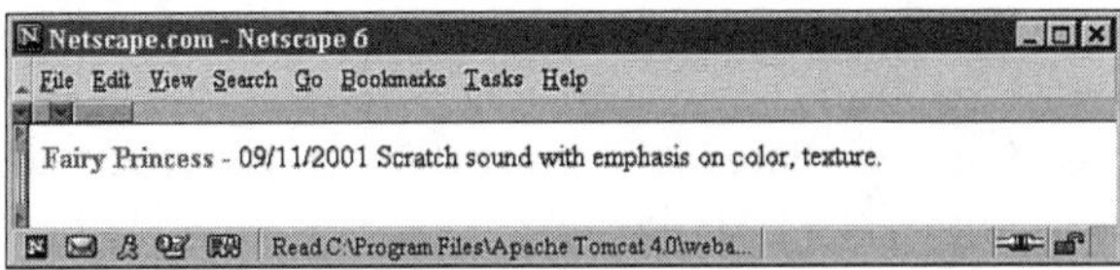

FIGURE 2.4 Output with stylesheet shows.xsl applied.

The stylesheet starts out with the root element spanning two lines:

```
<xsl:stylesheet version="1.0"
     xmlns:xsl="http://www.w3.org/1999/XSL/Transform">
```

The `xsl:stylesheet` element is always the first tag of any XSL stylesheet. The entire content of the stylesheet will reside within this element. The `version` attribute tells the processor which XSLT version to use. Currently the only option is `1.0`, but in the future this may change. Next, the attribute `xmlns:xsl` is listed. This attribute is called a namespace.

Namespaces

A *namespace* is a group of elements and attributes that are recognizable by their prefix. A namespace is declared so that all elements and attributes of that namespace are validated against the correct DTD, and can be distinguished from tags of the same name from a different source. Namespaces become very important when the content of one XML document comes from various sources.

For example, let's assume company A has an `author` element that requires a first name, last name, and date of birth, and company B has an `author` element that doesn't require anything. If these companies combined their data using XML, there could be collisions when validating these elements. Using namespaces with the DTDs would permit each company to validate its own `author` elements properly.

In Listing 2.5, notice how the tags are prefixed with placeholders such as `coA:`. The prefixes are linked to the full names using the attribute names starting with `xmlns:` found in the element `authors`. Notice that the full namespaces are URLs. The URLs don't actually point to anything—they are used to ensure that the namespaces are unique.

LISTING 2.5 XML Document with Two Namespaces Defined

```
<?xml version="1.0"?>
<coB:authors xmlns:coA="http://www.companyA.com/books"
             xmlns:coB="http://www.companyB.com/">
    <coA:author>
        <coA:fname></coA:fname>
        <coA:lname></coA:lname>
        <coA:dob></coA:dob>
    </coA:author>
    <coB:author>
        <coB:ssn/>
    </coB:author>
</coB:authors>
```

Getting back to our shows.xsl stylesheet from Listing 2.4, we find our one namespace is `xsl`. It is used to differentiate between data elements and elements that are used for processing XML. All elements for processing data in the stylesheet contain the prefix `xsl`, then a colon, and then the tagname. This `xsl` namespace will always be present in XSLT stylesheets, as it is the namespace for the processing tags.

Templates

Next, in Listing 2.4 we find the beginning of the XML processing with this XSL markup:

```
<xsl:template match="/">
```

This uses the xsl namespace, and is a template tag. A template element makes formatting and transformation possible. The template element's match attribute or property tells the XSL stylesheet which elements of the XML document to match, and thus to format or transform. A single stylesheet can contain many template elements. In this case, the match attribute is matching with the forward slash (/) expression. The forward slash indicates the root of the XML document. Therefore, starting at the root, the entire XML document will pass into this template as one unit.

Next we see some HTML:

```
<HTML>
<HEAD><TITLE>First Performance Stylesheet</TITLE></HEAD>
<BODY>
```

This HTML will be output to the browser. (Except for XSL markup, any characters encountered in a stylesheet will be directly output to the browser.)

Next, there is more XSL markup:

```
<xsl:for-each select="SHOWS/PERFORMANCE">
```

This xsl:for-each tag is used to select each element of a repeated structure. The value of the select attribute indicates what repeated patterns to choose. In our example, all PERFORMANCE elements within the SHOWS element will be selected in turn and processed within the body of the xsl:for-each element. In our example file, there is only one path like this. All content found within the PERFORMANCE element will be processed according to the contents of the xsl:for-each tag.

The next XSL markup found is the following:

```
<xsl:value-of select="TITLE" />
```

This tag selects the data from the current element and displays it. The value of the select attribute determines the source from which to select the data. In our example, this tag will select the data from the TITLE element, whose value is Fairy Princess. The select attribute can also select the data from an attribute. It does so by including an at sign (@) before the case-sensitive attribute name surrounded in quotes. Notice that the xsl:value-of tag has no content. That is, it is an empty tag. You may use separate opening and closing tags; however, everything in between will be replaced with the data from the selected XML element or attribute.

Next, we find the closing xsl:for-each tag. This tag closes the body of XSLT against which the chosen attributes and elements will be processed. Again, these elements and attributes are chosen through the expression found in the `select` attribute of the opening `xsl:for-each` tag. Then the template tag is closed. After this point, elements of the XML document are no longer matched against anything. This is because there is no longer a template element against which to match.

Finally, the stylesheet itself is closed.

The final output of the transformation of the XML and XSL will appear as follows:

```
<HTML>
<HEAD>
<TITLE>First Performance Stylesheet</TITLE>
</HEAD>
<BODY>
<FONT color="red">
<B>Fairy Princess</B> - <I></I>
</FONT>
09/11/2001
Scratch sound with emphasis on color, texture.
</BODY>
</HTML>
```

NOTE

If you look at the source as given by the browser through the View Source menu option, you will only see the original XML document. This is because viewing the source displays the original buffer that was sent to the browser, which is the XML document, and not the final output that is stored elsewhere.

This is similar to creating DHTML elements dynamically on the client side and not seeing those HTML elements when using the browser to view the source.

Notice how the data from the XML file replaces the `xsl:value-of` tags of the XSL stylesheet. Also notice that the other data, the dash and HTML markup, were output to the browser. With XSL stylesheets, XML data can be formatted and output with HTML with the appropriate placement of the text.

Repeating Patterns

Add the following XML fragment to the shows2.xml file:

```
<PERFORMANCE>
    <TITLE>Hamlet</TITLE>
    <AUTHOR>William Shakespeare</AUTHOR>
    <DESCRIPTION>Themes of youth, power, greed and deceit.</DESCRIPTION>
    <DATE>09/15/2001</DATE>
</PERFORMANCE>
```

This fragment should go within the SHOWS element, after the PERFORMANCE element. Refresh the browser and you will see the output in Figure 2.5.

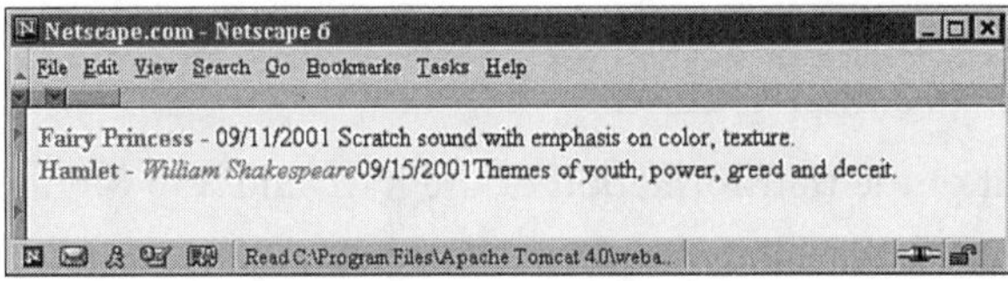

FIGURE 2.5 Output from shows2.xml with a repeating structure.

Notice how both PERFORMANCE elements were formatted and displayed using the same XSL stylesheet. This is a result of the for-each tag choosing each element of PERFORMANCE nested within the SHOWS element. In this case, there were two XML fragments that satisfied this requirement.

Stylesheet Errors

Now is a good time to demonstrate what happens when there is an error in the stylesheet. Delete the dash in the xsl:for-each tag in the shows.xsl stylesheet. Save the file and refresh the browser. Figure 2.6 shows the result.

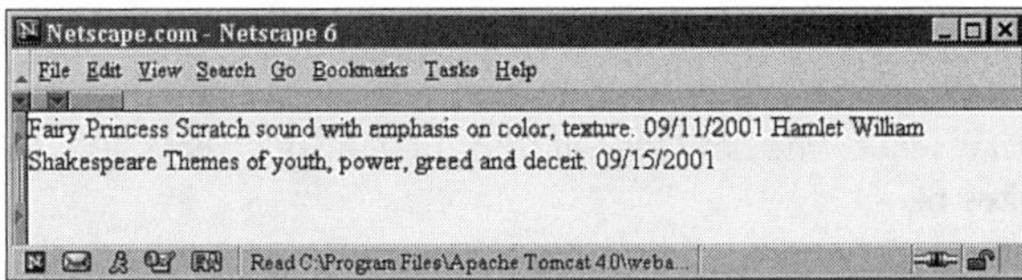

FIGURE 2.6 Output of shows2.xml with a stylesheet error.

Notice that all formatting that the stylesheet applied is missing. If there is an error in the stylesheet, it will fail parsing just as an XML document that is not well-formed will. Remember, an XSLT stylesheet has to follow the same rules as an XML file. When a stylesheet can't be parsed, there is a simple way of checking to see what the problem is. Instead of opening the XML document, open the shows.xsl file in a browser, as shown in Figure 2.7.

We found it! In our example, the browser output clearly shows a problem with the xsl:for-each tag. If all formatting is lost from an XSLT stylesheet linked from an XML document, load the stylesheet into the browser and fix the errors found.

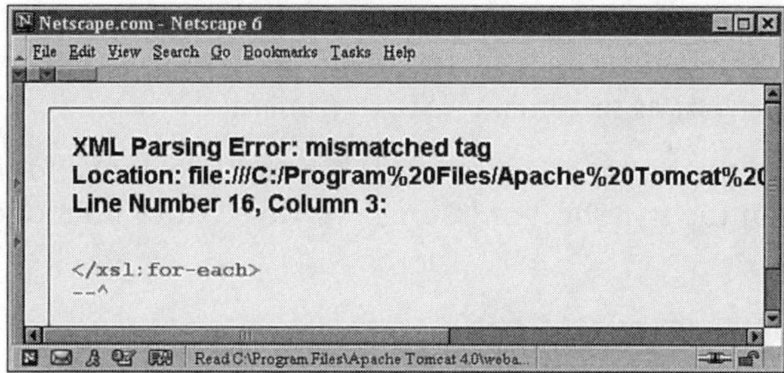

FIGURE 2.7 Output of a stylesheet error found in shows.xsl.

Whitespace and Encoding

We need to add some spacing after the AUTHOR element data and the DATE element data. XML strips out whitespace that is present outside of element data. So how do we add whitespace? We will answer that question shortly, but first a little background is in order.

XML was designed to support most languages. It does this through the use of an international 31-bit encoding system called ISO 10646, which can handle a huge number of different languages and symbol sets.

A *character* is any piece of text or signal that can be represented as one position in the character encoding system used. When text is typed on a keyboard, the letters and symbols on the screen are translated into numbers. The mapping of characters and symbols to numeric values creates a *character set*. XML allows multiple sets of characters to be used so that XML can be used with any language. The default encoding used by XML is UTF-8. This is an 8-bit character encoding.

NOTE

If you'd like to learn more about character encoding as it relates to XML, check out the excellent tutorial at `http://skew.org/xml/tutorial/`.

Also, you can find a table of characters and their octal encodings at `http://www.htmlhelp.com/reference/charset/latin1.gif`. This table only contains the Latin subset of the UTF-8 encoding used by default with XML. (This is the only encoding subset that we will be using here.)

The code 160 is a non-breaking space. We can use that character code within our XML and XSL and it will be output properly as a space. The addition of the leading ampersand (&) indicates that it is a character entity to be translated and displayed, and the pound sign (#) indicates that it is a number representing a character code. If we wanted to use hexadecimal numbers instead, we would use an x after the pound sign and before the numeric value. 160 converted to hexadecimal is A0, so ` ` would become ` ` as seen in an XML document.

Add ` ` after the `value-of` tag selecting the `DATE` element and the `AUTHOR` element found in the stylesheet of Listing 2.4. Those three lines of code will now look like this:

```
<I><xsl:value-of select="AUTHOR" /></I> 
</FONT>
<xsl:value-of select="DATE" /> 
```

Save the file and refresh the browser. There will now be a space after the `AUTHOR` and `DATE` element data. The output will now look like Figure 2.8.

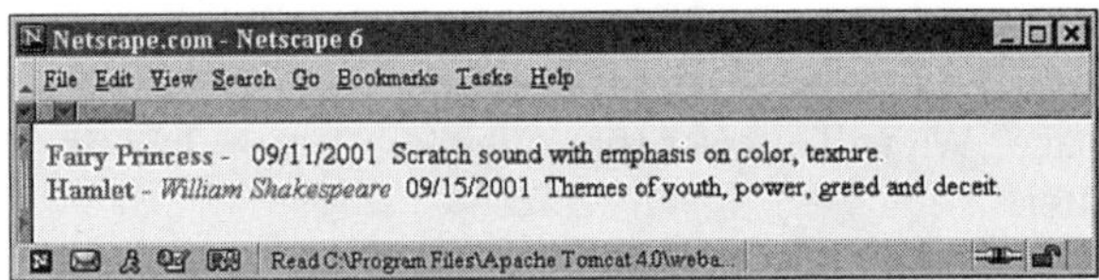

FIGURE 2.8 Output of shows2.xml with whitespace added.

Entity Declarations

Another way to add spaces or other characters is by using an entity declaration. An *entity declaration* is a statement found in the DTD that states that a particular sequence of characters should be replaced upon parsing. The character entity is replaced with the declared replacement string throughout the XML document or stylesheet. Entity declarations are useful in that they may improve readability.

NOTE

If you have done any HTML authoring, you might be familiar with the entity ` `. If this is easier to remember than the encoding for a space, you can declare it in the DTD and then use it throughout the document.

The document type declaration for a character entity is as follows:

```
<!DOCTYPE xsl:stylesheet [<!ENTITY nbsp " ">]>
```

This declaration starts with the literal string `<!DOCTYPE`, then declares the root element to which this declaration should be applied (in this case it is the root element of the stylesheet). Each entity must then be declared in the following

format, where name is the entity to be replaced and value is the string with which to replace it:

```
<!ENTITY name "value" >
```

The replacement string, like the entity name, can be anything. Place this command at the very top of the stylesheet, before the root element. If we were to use our document type declaration example, the character entity nbsp could be used throughout the document and it would be replaced by the parser with the actual sequence   to properly display spaces in the browser.

It is important to stress that for this replacement, the entity name nbsp can be anything. For example, the declaration string could be space. Let's build an example where we add our own arbitrary entity called tname. The tname entity will be replaced with some text. The declaration will then look like this:

```
<!DOCTYPE xsl:stylesheet [
<!ENTITY space " ">
<!ENTITY tname "Replacement text for the 'entity tname'">
]>
```

Add this to the beginning of the shows.xsl file. Then replace those Unicode spaces with the entity reference &space; and add &tname; after the closing xsl:for-each tag. Save and refresh the browser. The XSL stylesheet with changes is shown in Listing 2.6.

LISTING 2.6 shows.xsl with Entity Declarations Added

```
<!DOCTYPE xsl:stylesheet [
<!ENTITY space " ">
<!ENTITY tname "Replacement text for the entity 'tname'">
]>
<xsl:stylesheet version="1.0" xmlns:xsl="http://www.w3.org/1999/XSL/Transform">
<xsl:template match="/">
<HTML><HEAD><TITLE>First Performance Stylesheet</TITLE></HEAD>
<BODY>
<xsl:for-each select="SHOWS/PERFORMANCE">
     <FONT color="red">
     <B><xsl:value-of select="TITLE" /></B>&space; - &space;
     <I><xsl:value-of select="AUTHOR" /> &space;</I>
     </FONT>
     <xsl:value-of select="DATE" />
     <xsl:value-of select="DESCRIPTION" />
     <BR/>
```

LISTING 2.6 Continued

```
</xsl:for-each>
&tname;
</BODY>
</HTML>
</xsl:template>
</xsl:stylesheet>
```

The result of running the stylesheet is shown in Figure 2.9.

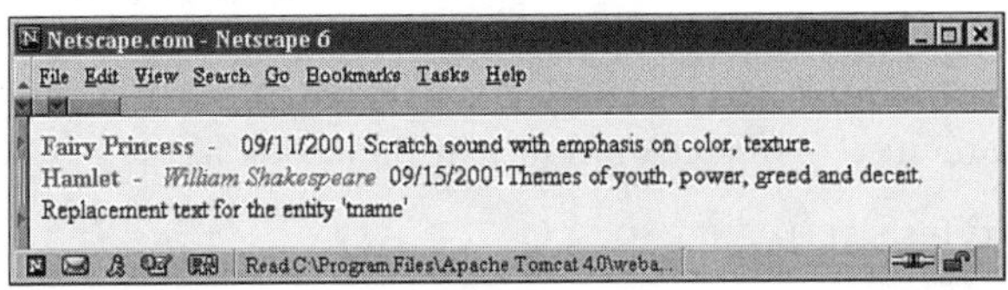

FIGURE 2.9 Output from shows.xsl with entity declarations.

Notice the replacement text and the spaces.

Trees, Nodes, and Family

Before we can begin to understand XML, XSL, and XPath, it is very important to establish some vocabulary for describing the positions of elements relative to each other. In more complex XML documents, these relationships quickly become impossible to describe with the limited vocabulary that we currently have. That's where tree structures, nodes, and the familiar family relationships become very useful.

Tree Structures

In thinking about an XML document in terms of a tree and branches, we begin with the root element. The root element is the starting point, and therefore the essential part of this tree structure. Each element found within the root element creates a branch from the root. Other elements in turn branch from the elements that contain them. For example, let's look at the following XML fragment:

```
<TITLE>
    <AUTH>
        <LNAME/>
    </AUTH>
    <AUTH/>
</TITLE>
```

In this code, each AUTH element is nested directly within the TITLE element. This is reflected in the tree diagram shown in Figure 2.10. In the same way, LNAME is nested directly within the AUTH element, and indirectly within the TITLE element. Notice that this structure also exists in the tree diagram. The LNAME element is branched directly from the AUTH element. Also, notice that the LNAME element is indirectly branched from the TITLE element. The XML document and the tree diagram contain the same information, but when dealing with more complicated XML, it is much simpler to think of it in terms of a tree structure.

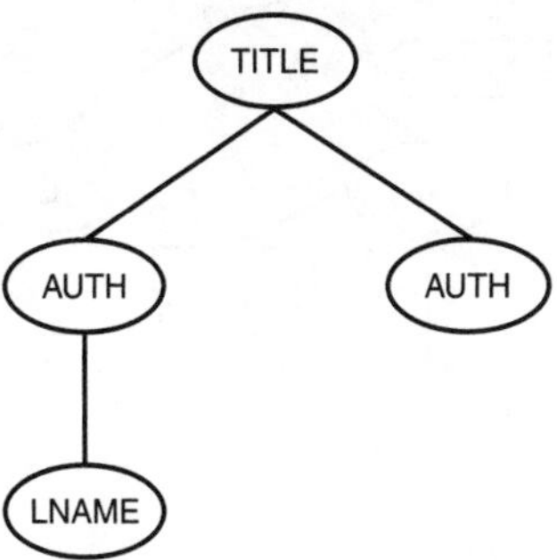

FIGURE 2.10 Example of XML document tree structure.

Nodes

A *node* is any one of the circles in the tree diagram shown in Figure 2.11. In the previous example, all the nodes are elements. However, that isn't always the case. Several other parts of XML can be drawn as nodes in a tree diagram. These include text data and attributes. Elements are always nodes, and will have lines drawn between them and other nodes.

Family

When describing the treelike structure of an XML document, it is helpful to be able to concisely describe relationships between elements in that structure. These relationships are defined in the same way as the structure of families. The common terms used are parents, children, descendants, ancestors, and siblings. You probably already know what most of these relationships mean. Now all we have to do is see how they apply to XML documents.

Descendants are your children, grandchildren, and so forth. In XML, a descendant is any element A nested within another element B. This means that every element of an XML document is a descendant of the root element. In the following example, element A is a descendant of B, but more specifically, it is a child of element B because no other elements exist in between; A is directly nested in B.

```
<B>
    <A>
        <D/>
    </A>
    <C></C>
</B>
```

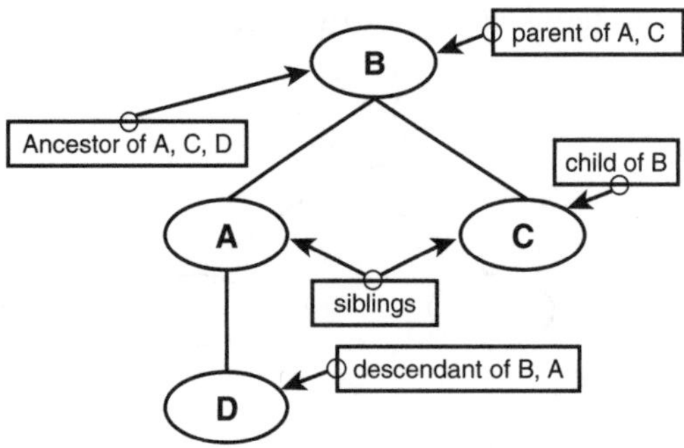

FIGURE 2.11 Tree diagram of XML family relationships.

Ancestors are your parents, grandparents, and so on. In XML, the ancestors are all the elements in which an element is nested (either directly or indirectly). Along the same lines, all elements that are nested within other elements have ancestors—namely, those elements in which they are nested. Let's go back to the previous example to clarify. In this example, element `B` is an ancestor of element `A`. (More specifically, element `B` is the parent of element `A` simply because the relationship between them is direct; there aren't other elements between them.) All elements within an XML document have the root element as an ancestor, except for the root element itself.

XPath

XPath is a language used for the identification of parts of the input XML document to be processed. XPath provides the mechanism for matching and then outputting selected parts of an XML document. Those parts can be a single element, one element and everything within it, a single attribute, several attributes of different elements, or any combination thereof.

XPath can also be used for numeric calculations, string manipulation, or testing Boolean conditions.

In some ways the addressing that XPath uses to select parts of documents is similar to the way in which file system paths select files and folders. When a folder is selected in a file system, all files within that folder are selected as well. With XPath, when one element is selected, all elements within it are also selected. Basically XPath provides a way of selecting parts of an XML document based on various criteria.

Selection Statements

Selection statements are the foundation of XPath. They are the logical syntax used to select which nodes are processed.

For the remaining examples in this chapter, we will be using the XML file shown in Listing 2.7. Type this into a text editor and save it as xpath.xml. Note that three elements (besides the root element) are used throughout this document. They are creatively named AA, BB, and CC.

LISTING 2.7 xpath.xml

```
<?xml version="1.0"?>
<?xml-stylesheet type='text/xsl' href='xpath.xsl'?>
<ROOT>
    <AA property="no">AA element within the ROOT
        <BB property="YES">BB element within AA
            <CC property="no">CC element within BB and AA
            </CC>
        </BB>
    </AA>
    <AA property="yes">2nd AA element within the ROOT
        <BB>2nd BB element within 2nd AA
        </BB>
        <CC property="NO">CC element within 2nd AA
        </CC>
    </AA>
    <BB property="NEVER">BB element within ROOT
        <CC>CC element within BB element
        </CC>
    </BB>
</ROOT>
```

This XML document has three children in the ROOT element. Two of them are AA elements and the other is a BB element. Notice that both AA elements have BB children. The first CC element in the document is a child of a BB element, and the second CC element is a sibling of a BB element. It is important to notice the various nesting levels of these elements. Knowledge of the relationships between the elements will aid you in understanding which elements will be selected and processed for output.

Next, type the code from Listing 2.8 into a text editor, and save it as xpath.xsl. This file will be constantly changing as we walk through the remaining examples in this chapter. Note that if you downloaded the code, the file allxpath.xsl will contain each of the xpath expressions found throughout this chapter.

LISTING 2.8 xpath.xsl; Absolute XPath Expression

```
<xsl:stylesheet version="1.0"
     xmlns:xsl="http://www.w3.org/1999/XSL/Transform">
<xsl:template match="/">
<HTML><HEAD><TITLE></TITLE></HEAD>
<BODY>
<!-- select each element BB child of element AA child of element ROOT -->
XPath is: /ROOT/AA/BB <BR/>
<xsl:for-each select="/ROOT/AA/BB" >
    <xsl:value-of select="." /><BR/>
 </xsl:for-each>
<BR/>
</BODY>
</HTML>
</xsl:template>
</xsl:stylesheet>
```

This stylesheet is very similar to our first XSL example. The main difference is that only part of the XML document is selected for output. With XPath, there will be times when the nodes selected for output will not appear to be directly related to each other. However, their relationship is simply that they each satisfy the XPath selection statement.

Let's review the logic of our example and what is happening behind the scenes. The group of elements that are selected with the XPath statement will constitute a set. This set is created according to the XPath statement found in the value of the `select` attribute of the `xsl:for-each` tag. Once this set is created, each element in turn will be used to walk through the body of the `xsl:for-each` element and will be processed accordingly.

The next line of interest is the line that selects the current element combined with an HTML break tag:

```
    <xsl:value-of select="." /><BR/>
```

The `select` attribute of the `xsl:value-of` tag chooses the current element. The dot notation (.) simply means to select and output the data that is currently passing this line of code—that is, each element of the set that the XPath selection statement has chosen, one at a time, followed by an HTML line break.

In this particular example, the XPath statement is selecting each `BB` element descending from an `AA` element. The `AA` element in turn must be descending from the `ROOT` element. The notation looks like this: `/ROOT/AA/BB`.

The beginning forward slash (`/`) indicates that the path is *absolute*. The path defined starts from the root of the document (in this case, the `ROOT` element). Note that the forward slash is the same as the `match` attribute of the `xsl:template` tag used in line 3 of Listing 2.8.

Once this node-set has been selected with the XPath expression, each node in turn is processed according to the body of the `xsl:for-each` element. The only processing we find in this body is the `xsl:value-of` element. This tag selects the current node being processed in the body. This is done with the dot notation (`.`), which is equivalent to saying "select the current item of the set selected by the XPath statement."

Figure 2.12 shows the output from this selection.

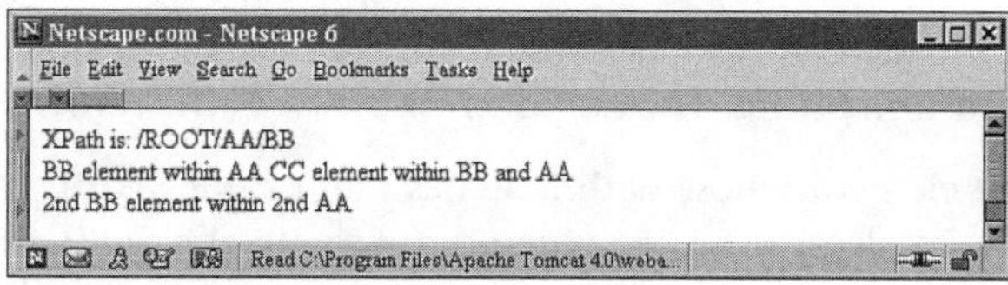

FIGURE 2.12 Display of xpath.xml rendered with the xpath.xsl stylesheet.

The first line of the output is text that we wrote in the stylesheet. Next out are two distinct elements that match the selection statement. (It's simple to see that they are distinct because they have an HTML break between them.)

The elements from Listing 2.7 that matched the selection criteria are noted in boldface type here:

```
<ROOT>
    <AA property="no">AA element within the ROOT
        <BB property="YES">BB element within AA
            <CC property="no">CC element within BB and AA
            </CC>
        </BB>
    </AA>
    <AA property="yes">2nd AA element within the ROOT
        <BB>2nd BB element within 2nd AA
        </BB>
```

```
        <CC property="NO">CC element within 2nd AA
        </CC>
    </AA>
    <BB property="NEVER">BB element within ROOT
        <CC>CC element within BB element
        </CC>
    </BB>
</ROOT>
```

When an element is selected through XPath, all child elements are also selected. The first `BB` element is selected, as is its child element, `CC`. This is why both the text data from within the first `BB` element and that from `BB`'s child element are output on one line. This is equivalent to loading only the following XML without a stylesheet:

```
<BB property="yes">BB element within AA
    <CC property="no">CC element within BB and AA
    </CC>
</BB>
```

In Figure 2.1, we loaded an XML document without a stylesheet, and the text was displayed without formatting. The output in this case is the same.

Next, the second element whose path matches that of the XPath statement is output. We put a break tag after each item output with the `xsl:value-of` tag. This is to make clear the distinction between each fragment meeting the XPath selection requirements, and those elements that are children of elements selected. When a new line is displayed, the next item in the set that met the requirements is being output. In this case, the `BB` element does not have any children and only the text of that element is output.

Let's do another example. We will again be using xpath.xsl. In this file, change lines 6–8 as shown in Listing 2.9 and save the file.

LISTING 2.9 xpath.xsl; Another Absolute XPath Statement

```
1    <xsl:stylesheet version="1.0"
2        xmlns:xsl="http://www.w3.org/1999/XSL/Transform">
3    <xsl:template match="/">
4    <HTML><HEAD><TITLE></TITLE></HEAD>
5    <BODY>
6    <!-- select each element BB in ROOT -->
7    XPath is: /ROOT/BB <BR/>
8    <xsl:for-each select="/ROOT/BB" >
9        <xsl:value-of select="." /><BR/>
```

LISTING 2.9 Continued

```
</xsl:for-each>
<BR/>
</BODY>
</HTML>
</xsl:template>
</xsl:stylesheet>
```

Notice that in changing this stylesheet file, we only really changed one line of XSL. The other changes are text data that will help us to see what our XPath selection statement is when we load the file in a browser and a code comment briefly explaining the XPath selection statement.

When you refresh your browser, the output shown in Figure 2.13 will appear.

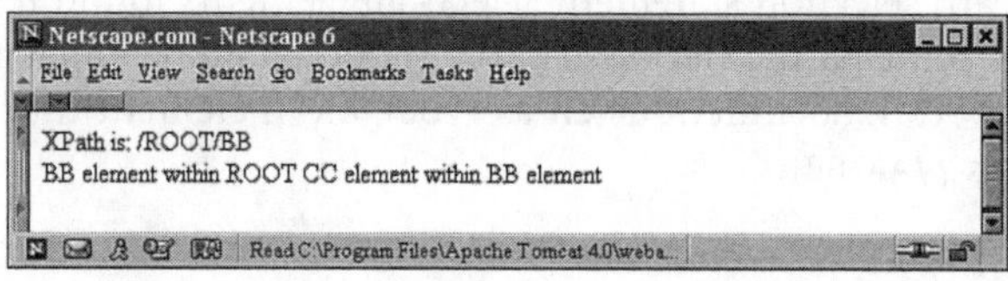

FIGURE 2.13 Output from an absolute XPath expression.

The first line is text data found in the stylesheet. Then the one element that was selected with the XPath statement is output. In this case it is each `BB` element found within the `ROOT` element. The line starts with the forward slash that denotes an absolute path. Then the root element is selected, followed by the `BB` elements contained therein. Only one element of xpath.xml matches this selection statement; it is noted in boldface print here:

```
<ROOT>
    <AA property="no">AA element within the ROOT
        <BB property="YES">BB element within AA
            <CC property="no">CC element within BB and AA
            </CC>
        </BB>
    </AA>
    <AA property="yes">2nd AA element within the ROOT
       <BB>2nd BB element within 2nd AA
       </BB>
       <CC property="NO">CC element within 2nd AA
       </CC>
```

```
    </AA>
    <BB property="NEVER">BB element within ROOT
        <CC>CC element within BB element
        </CC>
    </BB>
</ROOT>
```

Relative Paths

Relative paths are those that don't have a specific starting point. Rather, they are a set of conditions under which elements are selected. Any elements that satisfy the path criteria are selected with the use of double forward slashes (//). For example, we could search for all folders named "sherbet" in a file system. The resulting set would include every folder with that name. It wouldn't matter where the folder was found. There could be one in the root of the C: drive, and another one ten folders deep.

The relative XPath selection statement selects all elements found in an XML document that meet some path criterion. That criterion could be an element name found anywhere in the XML document (such as //BB), or an element that is a child of an element (such as //AA/BB).

Let's look at an example. Change lines 6–8 from Listing 2.8 to match the example shown in Listing 2.10 and save the file as xpath.xsl.

LISTING 2.10 xpath.xsl; Relative XPath Statement

```
1    <xsl:stylesheet version="1.0"
2         xmlns:xsl="http://www.w3.org/1999/XSL/Transform">
3    <xsl:template match="/">
4    <HTML><HEAD><TITLE></TITLE></HEAD>
5    <BODY>
6    <!-- select each BB element found anywhere -->
7    XPath is: //BB <BR/>
8    <xsl:for-each select="//BB" >
9        <xsl:value-of select="." /><BR/>
10   </xsl:for-each>
11   <BR/>
12   </BODY>
13   </HTML>
14   </xsl:template>
15   </xsl:stylesheet>
```

Refresh your browser and you will see the output shown in Figure 2.14. (The output order may depend on whether you use Netscape or IE due to XML processor differences.)

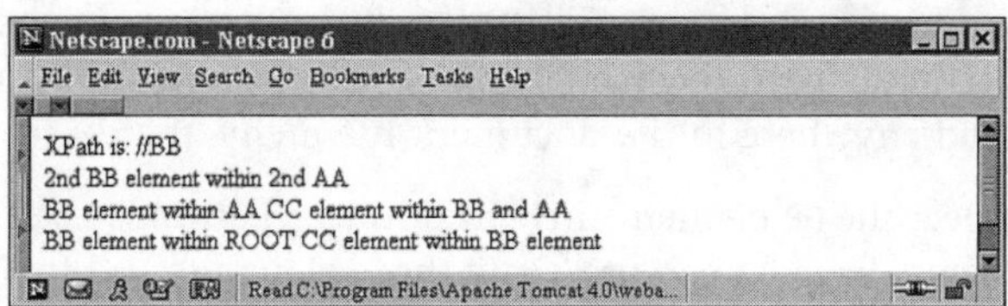

FIGURE 2.14 Output with a relative XPath expression.

Three elements meet the selection criteria (any element named BB found anywhere in the XML document hierarchy). The double forward slashes (//) mean that the selection match can start anywhere in the document. The processor will look at each element in turn to see whether it matches the path.

The selected parts of the xpath.xml document from Listing 2.7 are noted in boldface print here (all BB elements and their descendants are selected and output):

```
<ROOT>
    <AA property="no">AA element within the ROOT
        <BB property="YES">BB element within AA
            <CC property="no">CC element within BB and AA
            </CC>
       </BB>
    </AA>
    <AA property="yes">2nd AA element within the ROOT
       <BB>2nd BB element within 2nd AA
       </BB>
       <CC property="NO">CC element within 2nd AA
       </CC>
    </AA>
    <BB property="NEVER">BB element within ROOT
       <CC>CC element within BB element
       </CC>
    </BB>
</ROOT>
```

Let's look at another example. For the rest of the examples in this chapter, we are not going to display the entire stylesheet. Instead, we are only going to show you the code that will replace existing lines of the stylesheet.

Replace lines 6–8 from Listing 2.8 with the following lines and resave the file.

```
6    <!-- select CC element child of any BB element -->
7    XPath is: //BB/CC <BR/>
8    <xsl:for-each select="//BB/CC" >
```

Notice that the selection statement is `//BB/CC`. It starts out as a relative path with `//`. Then it has an absolute path to each `CC` child of `BB`. This XPath statement selects any element `CC`, found anywhere in the document hierarchy, that has a parent `BB`.

This does not select the `BB` elements involved in this path. Instead, it only requires that the `CC` elements have `BB` parents. Only those elements and their descendants that are listed last in the path are actually selected for output. The rest of the path denotes requirements for those elements that are finally output.

The elements of xpath.xml noted here in boldface print are selected:

```
<ROOT>
    <AA property="no">AA element within the ROOT
        <BB property="YES">BB element within AA
            <CC property="no">CC element within BB and AA
            </CC>
       </BB>
    </AA>
    <AA property="yes">2nd AA element within the ROOT
       <BB>2nd BB element within 2nd AA
       </BB>
       <CC property="NO">CC element within 2nd AA
       </CC>
    </AA>
    <BB property="NEVER">BB element within ROOT
       <CC>CC element within BB element
       </CC>
    </BB>
</ROOT>
```

As expected, the output consists of the elements shown in Figure 2.15. (There are other `BB` elements and `CC` elements in the document that were not selected because they are siblings and don't have the parent-child relationship required by the `select` statement.)

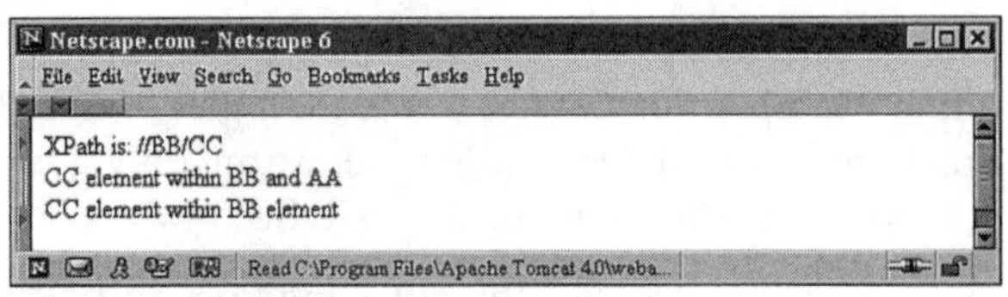

FIGURE 2.15 Output from a second relative XPath expression.

Asterisks and Elements

Now that you have an understanding of absolute and relative paths, let's see what the asterisk (*) can do. The asterisk means, in essence, "match all, no matter the name." This means that we can write selection statements that use every element meeting a requirement, even though the element name might not be used.

For example, change lines 6–8 of the stylesheet in Listing 2.8 to the following. Resave the file and refresh the browser.

```
6    <!-- select each grandchild element CC of any element -->
7    XPath is: /*/*/CC <BR/>
8    <xsl:for-each select="/*/*/CC" >
```

Wherever there is an asterisk in the selection statement, any element name can match it as long as the rest of the path is satisfied. The single forward slash found at the beginning of this statement indicates that it is an absolute statement. The forward slash signifies that this XPath is starting from the root. Then there is an asterisk that matches all. (In this case, it can only match the root element because there are no other tags at the root level.) Next, the statement has another forward slash, indicating a child of the previously matched elements. The following asterisk matches any child of the `ROOT` element no matter what the element name. The `select` statement ends with the element `CC`. This statement selects any grandchild element named `CC` starting from the XML document root.

The selected elements of xpath.xml are noted in boldface print here:

```
<ROOT>
    <AA property="no">AA element within the ROOT
        <BB property="YES">BB element within AA
            <CC property="no">CC element within BB and AA
            </CC>
        </BB>
    </AA>
    <AA property="yes">2nd AA element within the ROOT
       <BB>2nd BB element within 2nd AA
       </BB>
       <CC property="NO">CC element within 2nd AA
       </CC>
    </AA>
    <BB property="NEVER">BB element within ROOT
       <CC>CC element within BB element
       </CC>
    </BB>
</ROOT>
```

Note that the first CC element found in this document was not selected. This is because it is a great-grandchild of the ROOT, and not a grandchild. The selection statement is absolute, not relative; therefore, only grandchild elements can be selected.

The output looks like Figure 2.16.

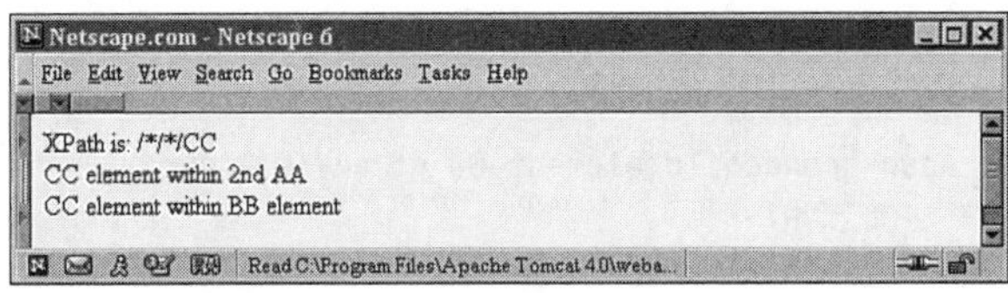

FIGURE 2.16 Output from an XPath expression with an asterisk.

Here is another example using the asterisk. Replace lines 6–8 of the stylesheet in Listing 2.8 with the ones that follow, save the file, and refresh the browser.

```
6    <!-- select each element that is a child of AA found within ROOT -->
7    XPath is: /ROOT/AA/* <BR/>
8    <xsl:for-each select="/ROOT/AA/*" >
```

This is another path using the asterisk, but this time we are going to select each element, no matter the name, that meets the other parts of the selection requirements as stated in the XPath statement. The statement starts off as an absolute path again with the forward slash. Then it matches each child element AA found in the ROOT element. Once that has been done, the forward slash and asterisk select every child element found therein. There is another way to read this statement: Select each grandchild element no matter what the element name, as long as its parent is an AA element and its grandparent is the ROOT element.

```
<ROOT>
    <AA property="no">AA element within the ROOT
        <BB property="YES">BB element within AA
            <CC property="no">CC element within BB and AA
            </CC>
       </BB>
    </AA>
    <AA property="yes">2nd AA element within the ROOT
       <BB>2nd BB element within 2nd AA
       </BB>
       <CC property="NO">CC element within 2nd AA
       </CC>
    </AA>
```

```
    <BB property="NEVER">BB element within ROOT
        <CC>CC element within BB element
        </CC>
    </BB>
</ROOT>
```

Three items satisfy this selection statement (see the boldface code lines). Notice that the sibling elements BB and CC that satisfy this XPath statement are separate items.

The output is shown in Figure 2.17.

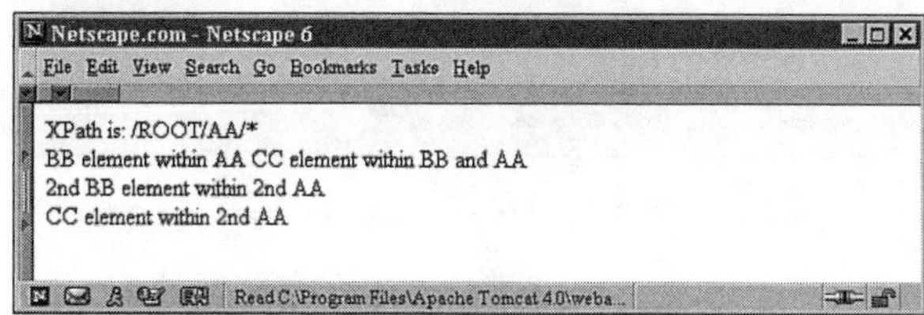

FIGURE 2.17 Output from an absolute XPath expression with an asterisk.

Expressions in Square Brackets

Square bracket expressions found within XPath statements can further specify which elements or attributes to select. These expressions act much like filters for those items already selected.

A number in the square brackets gives the position of the element to select. For example, suppose three siblings named GG are nested within the root element:

```
<ROOT>
    <GG/>
    <GG/>
    <GG/>
</ROOT>
```

The statement /ROOT/GG[2] would select only the second GG element. The statement /ROOT/GG[1] would only select the first GG element.

The last() function can also be used within square brackets to specify the last of some same-named siblings. This function will also select an element that is an only child, because it is not followed by any same-named siblings. For a demonstration of the last() function at work, replace lines 6–8 of Listing 2.8 with the following code, save it, and refresh the browser.

```
<!-- select each BB element that is the last -->
XPath is: //AA[last()] <BR/>
<xsl:for-each select="//AA[last()]" >
```

We know that this is a relative expression because of its starting double forward slashes. The statement begins by selecting each AA element found anywhere within the XML document. However, the selection is narrowed down by the filter expression in the square brackets. That expression is the method `last()`. This statement selects the last AA element of each AA sibling set.

Notice that in the output shown in Figure 2.18 there is only one selected item.

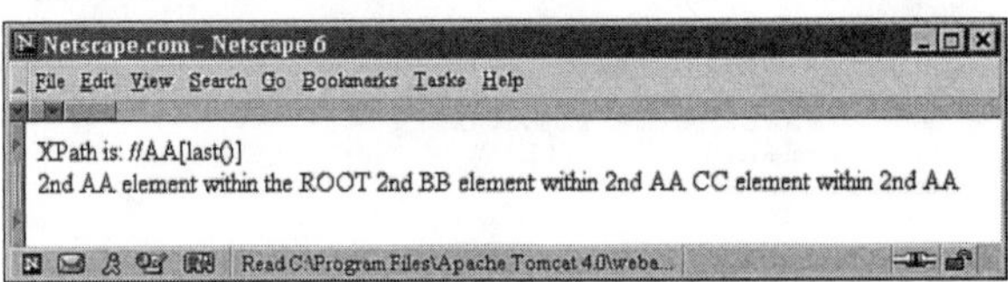

FIGURE 2.18 Output from a relative XPath expression with square brackets.

This is because there are only two AA elements, and they are siblings. This selection statement chooses the last of those two elements.

If there had been other AA elements in the XML document that were not siblings of the previously selected elements, they would have been selected and output. However, if there had been more than one AA sibling, only the last one would have been output.

Notice in xpath.xml that only the second AA element (see the boldface print) is selected:

```
<ROOT>
    <AA property="no">AA element within the ROOT
        <BB property="YES">BB element within AA
            <CC property="no">CC element within BB and AA
            </CC>
       </BB>
    </AA>
    <AA property="yes">2nd AA element within the ROOT
       <BB>2nd BB element within 2nd AA
       </BB>
       <CC property="NO">CC element within 2nd AA
       </CC>
    </AA>
```

```
    <BB property="NEVER">BB element within ROOT
        <CC>CC element within BB element
        </CC>
    </BB>
</ROOT>
```

With regard to the xpath.xml document structure, the statement `//AA[2]` is equivalent to the statement `//AA[last()]`. This is because the last sibling of the `AA` sibling set is also the second sibling. It is very important to be able to select a particular sibling from a set of siblings sharing the same name.

Selecting Attributes

We can select attributes in much the same way as elements. They can be selected using relative paths, absolute paths, or asterisk notation. The only difference is that we must use the at sign (`@`) before the attribute name to indicate that we are referring to an attribute.

Here's another example. Replace lines 6–8 of the stylesheet from Listing 2.8 with the following, and save the file.

```
6    <!-- select each attribute named property found anywhere -->
7    XPath is: //@property <BR/>
8    <xsl:for-each select="//@property" >
```

This relative path statement selects each value of the attribute named `property` found anywhere in the XML document. It's just the same as selecting all `AA` elements with the statement `//AA`, except that we are selecting attributes.

Notice in the output, shown in Figure 2.19, that each property value is on its own line. Each attribute value is selected and added to the set of items that satisfy this statement. Then they are output one at a time.

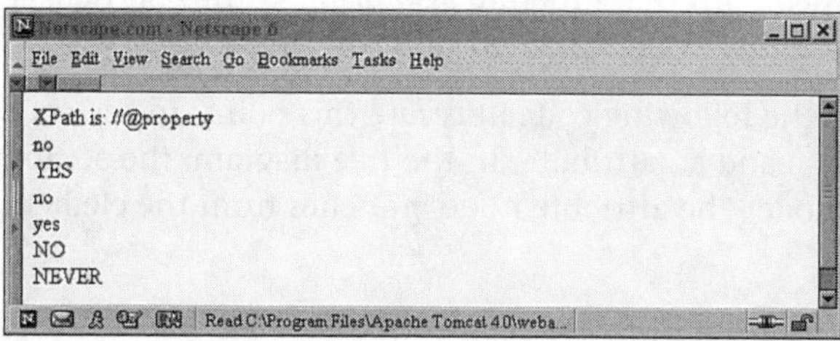

FIGURE 2.19 Output from an XPath expression selecting attributes.

Asterisks and Attributes

The asterisk notation that we've already used with elements can also be used with attributes. By putting an asterisk after the at sign (@), we are selecting all attributes, no matter what their name, that satisfy the rest of the XPath selection statement.

Change lines 6–8 of the xpath.xsl file from Listing 2.8 to the following, save the file, and refresh the browser.

```
6    <!-- select each attribute of each CC element that has an attribute -->
7    XPath is: //CC/@* <BR/>
8    <xsl:for-each select="//CC/@*" >
```

This selection statement begins by selecting every `CC` element in the XML document with the statement `//CC`. Then it further selects each attribute contained within those `CC` elements using `@*`. Figure 2.20 shows the output.

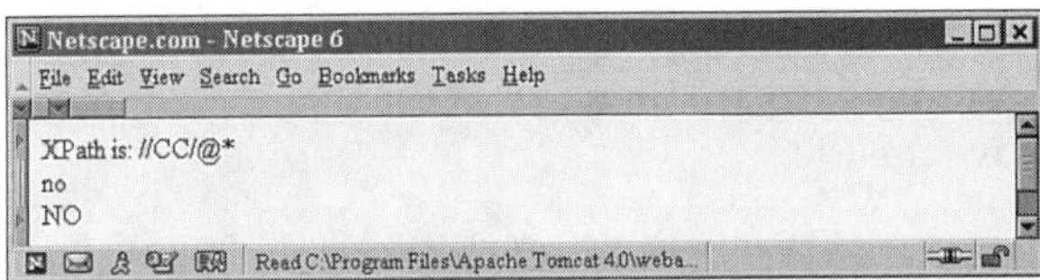

FIGURE 2.20 Output from an asterisk XPath expression selecting attributes.

You may have noticed that there is a forward slash (/) between the element selected and the attribute value of that element. Considering that we previously used the forward slash to signify a parent-child relationship between elements, it may be confusing to see one used between an element and the attributes of that element.

The explanation is simple: The treelike structure that is used to represent XML's document structure shows attributes as branching from the element node in which they are contained. This tree structure also displays the text data contained within an element as another node branched from the element node.

Figure 2.21 and the following code illustrate this point. In the code, the `BB` element contains text data and an attribute. In the tree diagram, the attribute name/value pair is its own node. The attribute node branches from the element node, as does the text data.

```
<ROOT>
    <AA/>
    <BB att='y'>text</BB>
</ROOT>
```

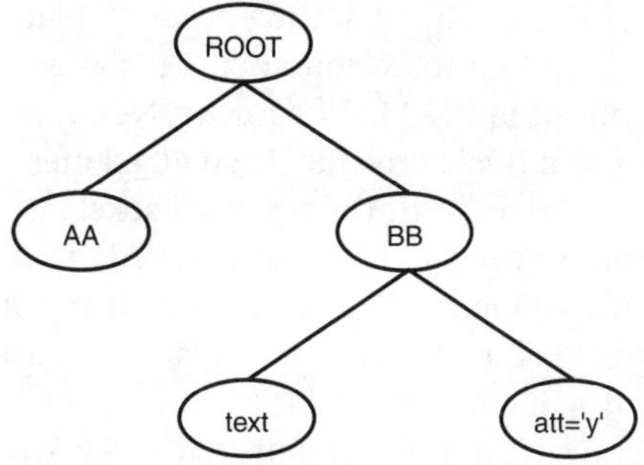

FIGURE 2.21 Tree/node diagram of attributes and text data.

Every element in a tree diagram can be thought of as the root of another subtree. With this in mind, look at the BB element in the tree diagram. If this element were separated from the rest of the XML document, it would become the root element, and the attribute and text data would be the only two branching nodes.

When writing `select` statements, you must use the forward slash to address the attribute node that branches from the element node.

The next example combines the things you've learned so far. We will use relative paths, square bracket statements, attributes, and asterisks. Change lines 6–8 in the stylesheet from Listing 2.8 to read as follows:

```
6    <!-- select each CC element that does not have any attributes -->
5    XPath is: //CC[not(@*)] <BR/>
7    <xsl:for-each select="//CC[not(@*)]" >
```

Boolean Values

The only Boolean values are `true` and `false`. Sometimes when writing XPath statements, we use a logical condition. This is a test that, if successful, will resolve to (or be evaluated as) `true`. If the test is unsuccessful, it will resolve to `false`. With XPath, all of the items selected at this point are used in the statement to see whether each resolves to `true` or `false` for that item. If it resolves to `false`, that item is no longer a member of the set of items selected by the XPath statement.

Square bracket statements can resolve to either a number or a Boolean value. When a statement resolves to a number, that number indicates which numbered sibling to select. For example, the statement `//AA[2]` selects the second AA element of siblings found anywhere in the XML document.

When a square bracket statement resolves to a Boolean value, the value tells whether the item will continue to be selected or not. If the value is `true`, the item will continue to be selected. Otherwise, it will be discarded from the selected set.

In the most recent change to Listing 2.8, the `select` statement starts out with the relative path indicator (`//`), then the element `CC`. This effectively selects each `CC` element found within our sample XML document. Next, we have a square bracket expression that resolves to a Boolean value. Each `CC` element must be checked to see whether it has an attribute. The `@*` in the square brackets is asking, Does the element have an attribute, no matter the name? If the answer is `true`, the `not()` method will reverse the value, and the element will be discarded. If the `CC` element does not have any attributes, the answer will be `false`, and the `not()` method will reverse it to `true`. Then that element will continue to be selected. Notice in our output, shown in Figure 2.22, that there is only one `CC` element that meets this condition. Every other `CC` element has at least one attribute.

Save the file and refresh the browser to see the output.

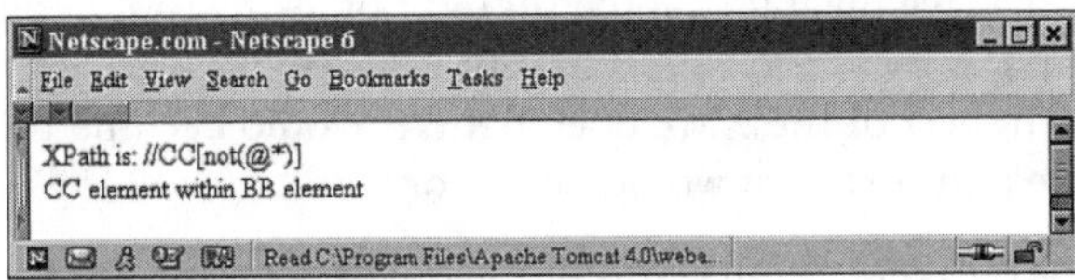

FIGURE 2.22 Output from a Boolean XPath expression.

You may be wondering why the statement wasn't written like this: `//CC/[not(@*)]`, with an extra forward slash. After all, we're looking at the attribute node, which is branched from the element node. That forward slash is not needed because when we are resolving square bracket statements we have access to all the nodes that are branched from the current element. This includes the text data and each attribute.

Next, we are going to write a selection statement that uses a square bracket statement within it, before the end of the statement. Update lines 6–8 of the xpath.xsl file from Listing 2.8 to match this, save it, and refresh the browser.

```
6    <!-- select each attribute of each CC element that has an attribute -->
7    XPath is: //BB[@property='YES']/CC/@* <BR/>
8    <xsl:for-each select="//BB[@property='YES']/CC/@*" >
```

This statement starts out by selecting every `BB` element found in the document. Next, the square bracket statement is resolved for each currently matched item in turn. The Boolean statement is asking, Does the current item have an attribute named `property` whose value is `'YES'`? There is only one `BB` element that resolves this statement to `true`, and thus will remain selected. Next, the statement matches the `CC` child element of the currently selected item. Then it outputs the value of each attribute of each selected `CC` element. In this case, there is only one `CC` element that has a `BB` parent with a `property` attribute equal to `'YES'`.

Figure 2.23 shows the output.

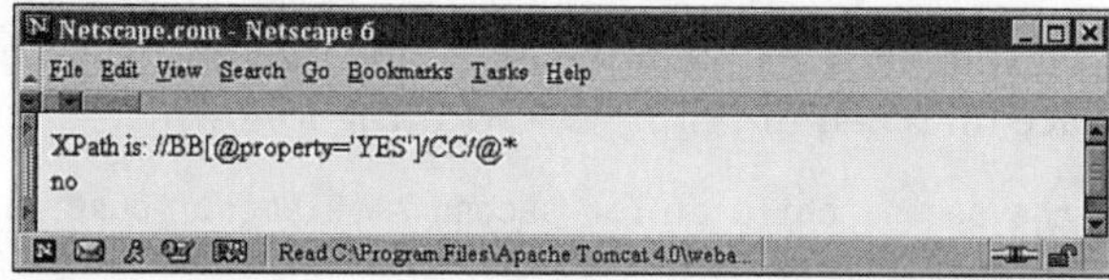

FIGURE 2.23 Output from an XPath expression that tests attribute values.

Next, we have another example with a square bracket statement. This one uses the `count()` function and a new Boolean operator.

Just as we have square bracket statements evaluate to a Boolean, we can have multiple statements do the same. We do so by using the logical `and` to connect the two statements. Then each item will have to meet all the selection criteria to be selected. The following example demonstrates the use of the `and` within a square bracket statement. Replace lines 6–8 of Listing 2.8, save the stylesheet, and refresh the browser.

```
6    <!--select each element that has only one BB child and one CC child -->
7    XPath is: //*[count(BB)=1 and count(CC)=1] <BR/>
8    <xsl:for-each select="//*[count(BB)=1 and count(CC)=1]" >
```

Figure 2.24 shows the output.

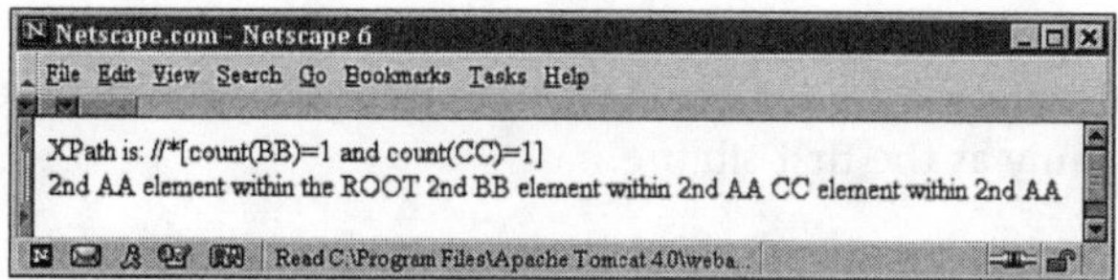

FIGURE 2.24 Output from an XPath expression using the `and` operator.

Only one item is selected and output in this example. Let's walk through the XPath statement. The statement begins with a relative path selecting all elements using the asterisk. Those elements are then filtered using the square bracket statement.

In this statement, we are selecting those items that have one child element named `BB` and one child element named `CC`. Notice how the two statements are connected with the logical `and`. If both resolve to `true`, the item is selected and output.

We can also connect two square bracket statements with a logical `or` using the pipe character (`|`). When you place a pipe character between two statements, the item will be selected if either statement resolves to `true`. Only if both statements resolve to `false` will the item be discarded from the selection.

Here is one more example. This example uses sibling counting, an absolute path, and an asterisk. Replace lines 6–8 in Listing 2.9 with the following:

```
6   <!-- select the second child of the second AA element found in ROOT -->
7   XPath is: ROOT/AA[2]/*[2] <BR/>
8   <xsl:for-each select="ROOT/AA[2]/*[2]" >
```

Save the file and refresh the browser. The output is shown in Figure 2.25.

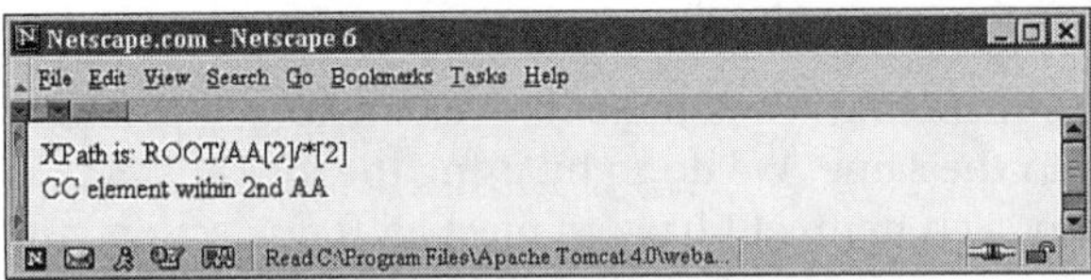

FIGURE 2.25 Output from an XPath expression with multiple square brackets.

This XPath statement begins by using an absolute path. It selects each `AA` element found within the `ROOT` element using `ROOT/AA`. Then it uses the square bracket to select only the second sibling of the `AA` elements already selected. Next, the path selects the second child of the selected `AA` elements no matter the element name. It does this by using an asterisk to select all children of the previously selected item, then using the square bracketed number 2 to select only the second siblings. Note that the second sibling, when selected with an asterisk, doesn't have to have the same element name as the first sibling.

In this case, there is only one element that meets the criteria, and it is output as shown in Figure 2.25.

Summary

This chapter gave you a solid introduction to XML, XSL, and XPath. If you are interested in learning more about XSL and XPath, refer to Appendix D, "XSL Reference," for more information.

In the next chapter, we will examine Web services. We will see how XML has created an entirely new way to do business by allowing the exchange of data over the Internet in a new way.

3 Understanding Web Services

IN THIS CHAPTER

The first revolution with the Internet was all about delivering information to people. We are now in the second revolution, which focuses on delivering information to systems. XML is the tool that makes this new revolution a reality, and Web services are the methods with which businesses will drive system-to-system communication.

This chapter will introduce the Web services concept and teach the basic facts behind both Web services and the various APIs that power it. The goal of the chapter is to introduce most of the major initiatives, standards, APIs, and toolsets that make up Web services. This will help reduce the confusion that arises when too many letters are strung together in meaningless names, a problem that plagues Web services. We will walk you through expanding the development environment that was set up in Chapter 1, "Integrating JSP and Data," to use Web services. Finally, the chapter will show some basic coding examples to get your feet wet with the Web services concept.

What Is a Web Service?

Let's start with the simplest definition. In the purest sense, a Web service is a product in the form of a reusable function built by one company that is exposed on the Internet for another company to use.

You can already find Web services on the Internet. A simple example is the automated site search service provided by Atomz. For a demonstration, use the search engine at `www.jspinsider.com`; the search request happens at the JSP Insider site, but the actual search occurs at another site hosting the search service. The Web service concept is growing and an exciting new model of business is evolving. What we now have is a situation where the Web service concept is exploding into new territory and expanding in its capabilities. The basic high-level goal of Web services is to further distributed computing (where application logic is separated into logical pieces and runs across many machines). The practical reason to build a Web service is to permit businesses to provide small, reusable, and self-describing computing methods to each other. A Web service by itself is just a piece of code that can be called by other applications or remote processes; however, if a programmer in the near future could pull together enough Web services, he or she could stitch together most of the features needed to support an entire Web application. The practical goal of a Web service is to permit a business to concentrate only on its core business needs and call up prepackaged "Web services" to complement the core business.

At the time of this writing, Web services are new enough that all of this is still not a reality. However, networks such as Microsoft's .NET Passport are being built on this Web services concept. As the Web services networks are built, we have the chance to watch as they are cobbled together into realistic systems. In many respects, this situation is very similar to when the Internet first began to open up to the commercial world in the 1990s.

The definition given at the beginning of this section applies to a Web service in the broadest sense of the term. The fact is that, at the beginning of 2002, there really wasn't a standard definition of a proper Web service. Every expert would give you a slightly different answer. For this book, a Web service is a remote Internet service that is capable of sending and receiving data over an HTTP network within a well-defined XML package. The difference between a Web site and a Web service is the use of XML to finely define and control the data being sent to and from a Web service. This brings up an interesting point: Unlike XML, which has the W3C to control and define XML, currently no single organization exists to define the nature of a Web service. Instead, a Web service is defined by the collection of tools and specifications a programmer uses to build it. What makes it all work is that nearly everyone is using the same set of standard specifications. Over time, this confusion will be resolved, and some large organization such as the United Nations (see the section titled "ebXML" later in this chapter) or W3C will take control of the larger Web services definition.

It is important to note that in this general discussion of Web services we are discussing both the creation of a Web service and the use of one. The creation of a Web service includes writing, exposing, and registering it for all authorized users to see and use. The use of a Web service includes finding and interfacing with the Web service in a stable, predictable manner.

At this point, it would be appropriate to define the terms *client* and *server*. A *server* is a computer or device that manages resources. According to this definition, a Web service server is any machine or device that responds to requests. This server manages resources by controlling the output of information through Web service responses. A *client* is any application that relies on a server to perform some operations. In this case, the Web service requestor is the client, as it is relying on the Web service server for information through responses.

Key features of creating and using Web services are listed here:

- They are accessible using standard Internet protocols such as HTTP or SMTP.
- They are distributed, which means that a Web service will usually reside on a different server than the applications that use the service.
- They can be centralized to a single source. This means that you can code once and access many times from many projects. In other words, Web services allow increased code reuse.
- A single Web service isn't a full application, but rather a standalone function that can be called by many different applications.
- A Web service can be self-describing. This enables businesses and applications to find and use Web services through automated processes and Internet registries (an electronic yellow pages to let other programs find the service).

All of these features add up to make a Web service a reusable component that can broadcast its functionality across an Internet network.

The advantages of creating and using a Web service come from the distributed nature of the overall system. They include the following:

- Logic can be broken into smaller reusable pieces of code.
- The code can be used by many different applications. For example, a Web service written in ASP.NET can be accessed by a JSP page.
- The code can be registered so that many different organizations can use a single Web service. As a result, the builder of a Web service doesn't need to communicate with every customer.
- Web services can describe themselves to the world through special registries.
- Standard protocols, APIs (standard code), and tools (coding development packages) are evolving to allow programmers to build and access Web services. In the future, these tools will allow for the automatic creation of a Web service. This will open the creation of Web services to developers of all skill levels, as they won't need to know the underlying mechanics.

The disadvantages of Web services include the following:

- You will need to create another software tier to utilize Web services. This new layer means that you must give careful consideration to application and service architecture in systems that utilize a Web service.
- Accessing Web services over the Internet causes both security and speed concerns for an application designer. However, you can increase the security of a Web service at the expense of speed.
- Automated tools such as Microsoft's Visual Studio .NET or Sun's Forte that support Web services are currently young and few. This means that in order to successfully build a Web service, you must clearly understand an entire set of protocols and APIs.
- Web services are new within the programming community. Solid and proven design patterns still need to be established for them. As a result, very few practical online resources exist to help a struggling programmer learn how to successfully implement a Web service.

As is often the case in the computer industry, it takes several iterations to get things right. In the case of Web services, this is especially true, as Web services are truly another iteration of older ideas. Their design aids in the reduction of development time and promotes code reuse.

Crystal Ball Readings

Web services are rapidly changing, and represent different things to different people. Because of this, it is important to give you an idea of what to expect in the future in order to place what you are learning in proper perspective. The goal is to show the probable direction of Web services. Of course, by the time you read this section, some of these predictions will have been realized or will no longer be possible, which means that you should take these predictions with a grain of salt.

So what can we expect for the future from Web services?

- The year 2002 will be marked with as many failures as successes with regard to Web services. The failures will result from trying to replace more traditional business models with Web services. Successful Web service implementations will be systems that start small or integrate Web services into existing business practices. This means that most failures will be due to projects pushing the Web services paradigm too fast and too hard.
- Web service implementation will become stabilized and by mid-2002 most J2EE servers will implement an easy front end to make using Web services more transparent.

- Web service tools will be divided primarily between Microsoft's .NET Framework and Java J2EE implementations. Since Web services are product independent, this doesn't pose a problem. Developers will chose to build Web services using the tool that best matches their business needs.
- Web service design structure will become more stable. By the end of 2002, the influence of successes and failures will establish practical business design guidelines for building successful Web services.
- The initial market for Web services in 2002/2003 will be smaller than what the 2001 hype portrays. New technologies very rarely live up to the hype, and the slow economic realities of 2001 will only slow Web services.
- Ironically, Web services will be most effectively used internally, providing a place to centralize and reuse business logic across many different Web applications for larger companies and state organizations. For some Java shops, this will be a method to avoid using EJBs. Enterprise JavaBeans are distributed Java objects (they are not JavaBeans, which are basically standalone Java objects). Most shops will tie EJBs and Web services closely together for their business. This in effect will create two different styles of Web service implementation for Java programmers: EJB-based Web services and JSP/Servlet/JavaBean-based Web services. The difference between the two styles will be a reflection of the framework being implemented by a project. Systems using J2EE systems will usually implement EJB-based Web services, while smaller projects based solely on JSP/servlets will use Web services based on JSP, servlet, and JavaBean technologies.
- In 2003, Web services will begin to be included in Web application design. This means that Web services will be used not by early user pioneers, but by businesses.
- The development of Web services can be highly automated and most Web service development will be through these automated tools. The first solid tools will be available in 2002. However, it won't be until 2004 that these tools will be fully mature and in widespread general use.
- Many implementations of Web services will fail as programmers experiment with the boundaries of Web service design. This will be similar to the trend of implementing EJB designs when simpler designs would have been quicker, cheaper, and simpler to build.
- Finally, expect that Web applications of the future will only use a handful of commercial Web services. The Web services market will be similar to the COM market for building Microsoft-based solutions. People will use public domain or commercial Web services to complement their applications for a few tasks, but the majority of programmers will build their own for specialized tasks.

These predictions are based on the authors' experiences with various technology implementations over the past 15 years. This isn't a scientific study of consumer need, but rather is based on similarities between Web services and other products.

All of this leads to the conclusion that, due to the slippery and constantly changing nature of Web services, the majority of programmers should not rush into using them. Instead, we suggest that you carefully and slowly enter into the Web services marketplace. Start with small implementations to gain experience. Once you've reached an understanding of Web services and the major tools have matured to the point at which they're acceptable for your business needs, jump in with both feet. Due to the small and distributed nature of a Web service, taking a slow and controlled approach is very practical.

This book has three chapters that pertain specifically to Web services:

1. This chapter provides an introduction to the various APIs that a Web service might use in its implementation.
2. Chapter 8, "Integrating JSP and Web Services," demonstrates how to implement Web services in a JSP-only environment. This book will not examine how to use Web services within a J2EE application server.
3. Chapter 14, "Building a Web Service," will cover the basics needed to get you to a point at which you can implement a Web service that others can access through an UDDI registry. Web services should be simple enough to build and use without much fuss.

The ABCs of Web Services

While building a Web service might be simple, getting started is very confusing. There exists an entire universe of initiatives, products, and APIs to sort through. If as a new user you are confused by this alphabet soup muddle, don't despair; things are getting better and more concise in the Web services development arena. The best news is that as a developer, you will only have to know a few critical pieces to make things work.

As stated earlier, much of what it takes to build a Web service will be automated in the future. In addition, higher-level APIs that hide the complexity of Web service infrastructure are being developed. Your programming style will determine when you should consider building Web services. For programmers who want full control and need to know the entire picture, now is the time to dive in. If you are more of a business-level programmer (concentrating mainly on your business requirements), you can wait a few months for the tools to catch up so that you can concentrate mainly on the business logic rather than the lower-level details of Web services.

First, let's look at how things work when everything is in action. Figure 3.1 gives an overview.

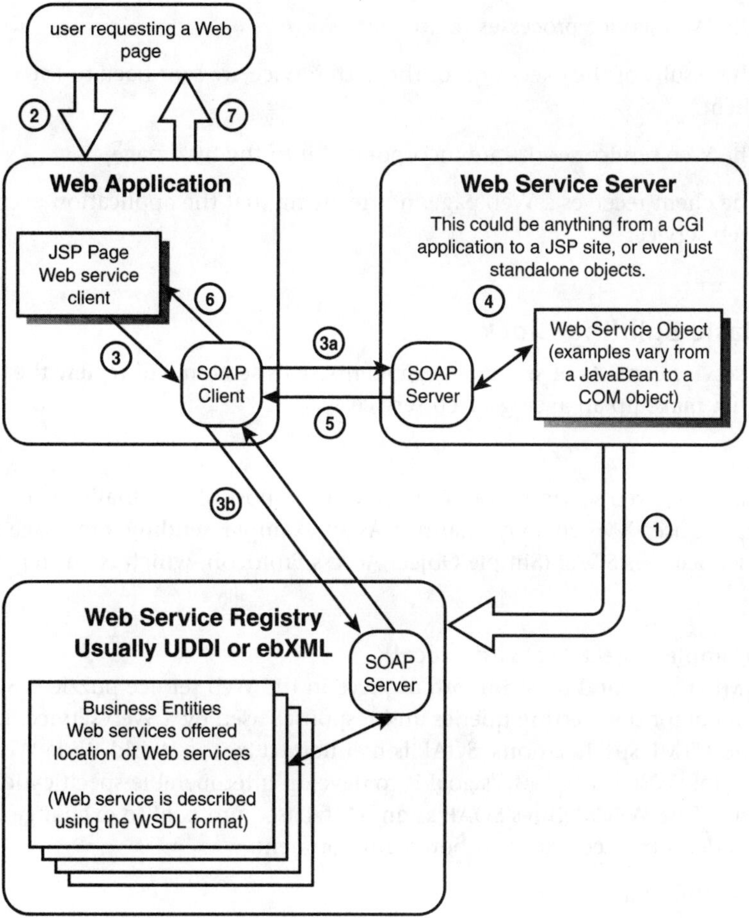

FIGURE 3.1 Overview of a Web service.

Let's review the steps involved in using a Web service, as shown in Figure 3.1.

1. A Web service provider registers a Web service. This can be done either manually or automatically through code.
2. A user requests a Web page.
3. The Web application accesses a Web service. If the service client already knows about the Web service, it directly accesses the Web service (step 3a). However, if

the Web service cannot be found, the service client can query to discover/rediscover an appropriate Web service to use (step 3b). Once done, the client can requery a Web service with the revised information.

4. The Web service processes the request.
5. The results of the execution of the Web service are sent back to the requesting client.
6. The Web service results are incorporated into the final page.
7. The client receives a Web page, not realizing that the application ever used a Web service.

The Basic Building Blocks

A Web service consists of several components. This section will review the components that make up an average Web service.

XML

Without XML, Web services would not have been possible. Virtually every aspect of a Web service uses XML in some manner. As an example, sending a message to invoke a Web service uses SOAP (Simple Object Access Protocol), which is entirely built on top of XML.

SOAP (Simple Object Access Protocol)

After XML, the second most important piece in the Web service puzzle is SOAP. This is a protocol for transferring queries and responses used by a Web service. Like the XML and HTML specifications, SOAP is maintained by the World Wide Web Consortium (W3C). The W3C's goal is to develop interoperable specifications and guidelines. The W3C defines SOAP as an XML-based protocol to exchange information in a decentralized and distributed environment.

SOAP has three parts:

1. The first part is an envelope in which a message is contained. This envelope is important as it does more than just hold a message.

   The envelope also

   - Describes what is in the message (sounds like XML, doesn't it? Self-describing envelopes...)
   - Contains rules on how to process the message
   - Includes information on which Web service should respond to the message

- Contains information that indicates whether responding to the message is optional or mandatory

The SOAP envelope gives quite a bit of information to the receiving Web service. With the data received, a Web service is able to determine whether it should process a SOAP service request or not.

2. SOAP also has a set of encoding rules to define special Web service–defined data types. This feature is helpful, as it allows the definition of unique data types for a service. Any data that can be described as an XML structure can be embedded and used within a SOAP message.

3. SOAP includes rules for describing the exposed methods of a Web service. This includes a structure for the description of the calls and responses of a Web service.

SOAP allows a program to invoke a service through the interchange of messages. It permits entities to invoke each other's exposed methods regardless of the programming language or network used to build and host the entities. An entity is anything that invokes a SOAP call, such as an application, a Web service, or any program.

SOAP can use any combination of other protocols for transporting messages between Web services. However, HTTP (Hypertext Transfer Protocol) is the protocol of choice for delivering messages. HTTP is the underlying protocol used by the World Wide Web. It defines how messages are transmitted and formatted and what actions Web servers should take in response. HTTP is favored due to its widespread availability and its ability to navigate through obstacles such as firewalls.

A simple SOAP message might appear as in Listing 3.1.

LISTING 3.1 A Simple SOAP Message

```
<SOAP:Envelope
  xmlns:SOAP="http://schemas.xmlsoap.org/soap/envelope/"
  SOAP:encodingStyle="http://schemas.xmlsoap.org/soap/encoding/">
   <SOAP:Body>
       <EXAMPLE:getBookPublisher xmlns:EXAMPLE="Example-URI">
           <title>JSP and XML</title>
       </EXAMPLE: getBookPublisher >
   </SOAP:Body>
</SOAP:Envelope>
```

In this example, the element `<SOAP:Envelope>` encloses the entire message, which is contained within the `<SOAP:Body>` element. Also note that in the envelope tag, the

SOAP:encodingStyle attribute indicates the encoding specification of the message. That is, when a SOAP server validates this message, it can refer to the schema found at http://schemas.xmlsoap.org/soap/encoding/ to find the rules with which this message was encoded. For this example, we are accessing a fictitious Web service method called getBookPublisher. For this method, the example passes the value JSP and XML into the <title> element, which acts as a return parameter called title.

To complete this example, let's imagine that a Web service responded to the example message. A response might look like the one in Listing 3.2.

LISTING 3.2 A SOAP Response Message

```
<SOAP:Envelope
  xmlns:SOAP="http://schemas.xmlsoap.org/soap/envelope/"
  SOAP:encodingStyle="http://schemas.xmlsoap.org/soap/encoding/">
   <SOAP:Body>
       <EXAMPLE:getBookPublisherResponse xmlns:EXAMPLE="Example-URI">
           <name>SAMS Publishing INC.</name>
       </EXAMPLE:getBookPublisherResponse >
   </SOAP:Body>
</SOAP:Envelope>
```

The routing of the SOAP message is handled by another protocol. This example doesn't demonstrate the protocol with which the message is transported. As stated earlier, HTTP is the preferred protocol for transferring SOAP messages.

SOAP has clients and servers. A SOAP server is an application waiting to process requests from a SOAP client. The SOAP server will interpret incoming SOAP requests and convert them into a format that the receiving process can use. Any request that the server cannot process will be rejected. A SOAP client is any application or piece of code sending a SOAP message to be processed by the server.

Another important term within SOAP is RPC (Remote Procedure Calls). RPC is a method of writing the procedure calls and responses that are found in SOAP messages. RPC enables a client to invoke a procedure call on a server. The client program sends a message to the server with the appropriate arguments for the method being called. Then the server returns a message containing the results of the program executed. In essence, RPC is a format through which these procedure calls and responses must be made. While we could just use SOAP to send messages between applications and act on the messages, using SOAP RPC gives a well defined method of declaring parameters and methods to be accessed over a SOAP message.

To use SOAP, we will need a server or API that implements the SOAP protocol. The Java API section of this chapter will go into more detail on two common SOAP tool implementations.

Before concluding our discussion of SOAP, we need to discuss security. SOAP frequently uses text-based XML and HTTP. This effectively means that any message transported with SOAP is exposed for the world to view. Currently, two simple solutions exist to protect sensitive data placed within a SOAP envelope.

1. Use SSL (Secure Sockets Layer) to transmit the messages back and forth. SSL is a protocol designed to transfer private documents over the Internet. The disadvantage of SSL relates to performance considerations. Simply put, security comes at the price of speed. Also, sometimes system architecture can have security ramifications for an SSL solution.
2. Encrypt the data that is wrapped within the SOAP message. The disadvantage of this method is that a Web service must be expecting the encrypted data and therefore can only be used with specific Web services designed to use encryption.

An in-depth security discussion is beyond the scope of this chapter. However, you should consider the following piece of advice: If you need high security in your Web service transactions, the security needs to be addressed at the start of your project.

For more information on SOAP refer to the SOAP Web site at `http://www.w3.org/TR/SOAP`.

WSDL (Web Service Description Language)

WSDL is an XML-formatted language for describing Web services. WSDL is a standard maintained by the W3C, and was originally proposed by Ariba, IBM, and Microsoft. The strength of WSDL lies in its ability to describe a Web service in a standard way. While we can use SOAP to access and query a Web service, we still need a way to determine the capabilities of the Web service. WSDL performs this task. By querying a Web service registry, we can obtain the WSDL document stored there. Through this document, we can retrieve information regarding the Web service in question. It is this information that will allow the client to determine what methods to call, how to use them, and where to direct those requests.

The real meat of WSDL is the document definition of the standard XML document used to describe the Web service. So let's look at an example WSDL file and review the high points of the document. The example WSDL file used here will be from a Web service that we will access later in the chapter. The WSDL definition can be found at the XMethods Web site (`http://www.xmethods.net/`). This site has a simple registry that publishes a list of Web services. From this list, the service selected is called "TemperatureService" and is geared at getting the current temperature at a zip code. The WSDL document for this service appears in Listing 3.3.

LISTING 3.3 XMethods TemperatureService WSDL File

```
<?xml version="1.0" ?>
<definitions name="TemperatureService"
          targetNamespace="http://www.xmethods.net/sd/TemperatureService.wsdl"
          xmlns:tns="http://www.xmethods.net/sd/TemperatureService.wsdl"
          xmlns:xsd="http://www.w3.org/2001/XMLSchema"
          xmlns:soap="http://schemas.xmlsoap.org/wsdl/soap/"
          xmlns="http://schemas.xmlsoap.org/wsdl/">

<message name="getTempRequest">
       <part name="zipcode" type="xsd:string" />
</message>

<message name="getTempResponse">
     <part name="return" type="xsd:float" />
</message>

<portType name="TemperaturePortType">
     <operation name="getTemp">
              <input message="tns:getTempRequest" />
              <output message="tns:getTempResponse" />
     </operation>
</portType>

<binding name="TemperatureBinding" type="tns:TemperaturePortType">
  <soap:binding style="rpc" transport="http://schemas.xmlsoap.org/soap/http" />
  <operation name="getTemp">
     <soap:operation soapAction="" />
     <input>
       <soap:body use="encoded" namespace="urn:xmethods-Temperature"
                 encodingStyle="http://schemas.xmlsoap.org/soap/encoding/" />
     </input>
     <output>
       <soap:body use="encoded" namespace="urn:xmethods-Temperature"
                 encodingStyle="http://schemas.xmlsoap.org/soap/encoding/" />
     </output>
  </operation>
</binding>

<service name="TemperatureService">
     <documentation>Returns current temperature in a given U.S. zip code
     </documentation>
```

LISTING 3.3 Continued

```
    <port name="TemperaturePort" binding="tns:TemperatureBinding">
      <soap:address
       location="http://services.xmethods.net:80/soap/servlet/rpcrouter" />
    </port>
</service>
</definitions>
```

Now let's walk through this XML document to highlight the various sections of a WSDL service document. This discussion is just a brief introduction to a few critical elements needed to translate the information from a WSDL document for use in a Web service invocation.

The initial high-level definition of the Web service is placed within the `service` element:

```
<service name="TemperatureService">
```

The document subelement gives us a description of the service:

```
        <documentation>Returns current temperature in a given U.S. zipcode
        </documentation>
```

The port subelement defines where the service resides. Each port will have a unique name and binding attribute. The binding attribute must match to a previous binding element:

```
        <port name="TemperaturePort" binding="tns:TemperatureBinding">
```

The location attribute gives us the URL to access this service:

```
        <soap:address
        location="http://services.xmethods.net:80/soap/servlet/rpcrouter" />
    </port>
</service>
```

Next, we need a way to specify the messages being sent around. The `binding` element defines the SOAP message format, protocols (SMTP, HTTP, and so on), messages the service will use (typically a request and response). The `soap:binding` subelement binds a SOAP envelope format to match to the Web service. Since we are using SOAP, the `soap:binding` element is a required element. To summarize, the binding takes the abstract information required for the calls to and from the Web service and produces a real physical model of the messages to be sent to and from the service.

Here's how the binding element works:

```
<binding name="TemperatureBinding" type="tns:TemperaturePortType">
```

The transport attribute indicates the protocol to use, in this case HTTP:

```
  <soap:binding style="rpc" transport="http://schemas.xmlsoap.org/soap/http" />
```

An operation matches to each method the Web service exposes for use:

```
      <operation name="getTemp">
```

The soapAction is an HTTP header the client sends when invoking the service:

```
         <soap:operation soapAction="" />
```

The message the Web service expects to receive to initiate this method is defined within the input element:

```
         <input>
```

The namespace is a unique URI used to reference the service method:

```
       <soap:body use="encoded" namespace="urn:xmethods-Temperature"
                  encodingStyle="http://schemas.xmlsoap.org/soap/encoding/" />
     </input>
```

The message the Web service sends back out from this method is defined within the output element:

```
     <output>
       <soap:body use="encoded" namespace="urn:xmethods-Temperature"
                  encodingStyle="http://schemas.xmlsoap.org/soap/encoding/" />
     </output>
      </operation>
  </binding>
```

Now let's look at how WSDL defines what methods are available from a Web service. The portType element defines a collection of all methods that the Web service exposes to the world. (Each operation matches a method.) In relation to SOAP, all operations have an input and output message that needs to be defined for use. Finally, the binding element shown previously will further define the operations first referenced in portType:

```
  <portType name="TemperaturePortType">
         <operation name="getTemp">
```

```
            <input message="tns:getTempRequest" />
            <output message="tns:getTempResponse" />
        </operation>
</portType>
```

The final piece to examine is how to define the parameters being sent back and forth within the messages. The `message` element, shown in the following code, defines the parameters that must be embedded within a message. For us, this translates to the method arguments and return values.

The first thing to notice is that the name matches a message attribute defined with the `portType`:

```
<message name="getTempRequest">
```

This message has a parameter called `zipcode` of type `string`:

```
        <part name="zipcode" type="xsd:string" />
</message>
```

This message also returns a value of type `float`:

```
<message name="getTempResponse">
        <part name="return" type="xsd:float" />
</message>
```

The key to learning and understanding WSDL is just working through the WSDL document specification. For more information, you can refer to the WSDL Web site at `http://www.w3.org/TR/wsdl`.

Service Management Initiatives

Once you've built a Web service, oftentimes you also want a way to let others know about it. This section will review the current options for listing a Web service for public access.

UDDI

Universal Description, Discovery, and Integration (UDDI) is a distributed directory that allows businesses to list themselves on the Internet. This directory is found on the Web, and, like the white and yellow pages of a phone book, enables businesses to find each other.

UDDI was started by Ariba, IBM, and Microsoft. The UDDI framework defines what Web-based services a business offers and creates a global registry specifically geared towards business-to-business electronic commerce. The core of the UDDI business registration is an XML file describing a business and any Web service it might provide. UDDI acts as an electronic phone book that provides information in three sections:

- Green pages—The green pages provide technical data about a business's services. The information found in the green pages includes pointers to technical information and URLs with more information about each service. It is interesting to point out here that while UDDI is advertised as primarily registering Web services, the actual index will permit any type of service to be indexed in the registry.
- White pages —The white pages consist of addresses and other contact data for business registrations. This is the basic identification information for a business registering to provide services.
- Yellow pages— The yellow pages are sorted by industrial categorizations to make searching for a business easier. The categories are based on several standard business coding systems such as SIC (Standard Industrial Classification) and the NAICS (North American Industry Classification System).

The overall UDDI registry is hosted across many sites. Currently both IBM and Microsoft are hosting UDDI registries. Information from each of these registries is duplicated so when you register at one site your business information is replicated across the entire UDDI registry.

Businesses can access UDDI either through a Web interface or through automated programming methods. Any company using the registry can have automated methods to query and find an appropriate service for their customers. In addition, your own services can automatically update themselves within the registry, so the UDDI registry always reflects current information.

It should be noted that UDDI by itself only provides basic searching features. More advanced features such as searching by price of service or geographic region are not part of the UDDI framework. Instead, UDDI permits others to add a new layer on top of the current framework to provide such features. In the future, various third parties will create search engines for querying the UDDI registry for the general business community. This evolution will end up having similarities to the current search engine marketplace for indexing Web sites.

From a technical point of view, the UDDI APIs are built on top of SOAP. A programmer can use the information supplied by the UDDI registry to directly query a Web service. The UDDI APIs are broken into two major sections. The first set is the Inquiry APIs. These are used to query the UDDI registry. The second set is the Publish APIs for creating and updating a UDDI registry entry.

The UDDI is not currently a standard. However, there are plans to submit UDDI to become a standard sometime in 2002. Currently UDDI is managed by dozens of companies.

For more information, you can refer to the UDDI Web site at `http://www.uddi.org`.

ebXML

ebXML (e-business XML) is a specification for standardizing XML globally to aid in trade between organizations of any size. It provides a standard method to exchange business messages written in XML.

This is a huge project that has many subgoals and groups working towards promoting electronic business. ebXML will become a formal standard using XML to provide a framework for messages and services for businesses and consumers.

The ebXML project is noteworthy because it is backed by the United Nations (UN). This project seeks to encourage enterprises around the world to conduct business with each other. More importantly, the goal is to create a single global electronic marketplace where anyone can engage in business. The other organization behind ebXML is OASIS. This organization consists of over 170 members, including many of the large technology companies. The primary goal of OASIS is to promote standards in XML to improve electronic business. Between the UN and OASIS, ebXML has the backing to become a rock solid specification. ebXML will bring with it a set of tools, APIs, and registries to empower businesses to exchange information with each other.

At the time of this writing, ebXML is new enough that it doesn't impact the way we currently build Web services. It isn't practical to cover an example of ebXML yet; it is just too new. The question then becomes When will ebXML become mature enough that ebXML standards will be used by our Web services? The answer to this is unclear; however, you needn't reexamine ebXML until late 2002 at the earliest.

For more information you can refer to the ebXML Web site at `http://www.ebxml.org/geninfo.htm`.

The Difference Between UDDI and ebXML

At first glance, UDDI and ebXML appear to be doing the same thing. However, while there is an overlap between the two initiatives, there is a difference between market focus and scope. ebXML is a much larger system aimed at general business-to-business communication. ebXML is designed to be a complete business-to-business solution while UDDI focuses on serving as a simple index and a place for companies to integrate Web services relative to each other.

Why do we need different service registries? The simple fact is that the marketplace will perceive a need for many different types of registries. From a technical point of view, ebXML is flexible enough with its structure to support most businesses, and this will reduce the need for more registries to appear in the marketplace. However, due to human nature and the mechanics of business, we can expect more registries to appear and disappear over time. Organizations will want their own system or someone will see a way to profit in making a new system. UDDI and ebXML are here to stay. Only time will tell what other registries will appear.

Finally, it should be noted that both ebXML and UDDI are supported by many of the same industries. This means that, over time, these two initiatives will end up complementing each other rather than competing with each other.

Java APIs

To make our lives easier, several Java applications and quite a few Java APIs exist to help us implement Web services. This section will discuss several of these projects.

Apache SOAP

`http://xml.apache.org/soap`

The Apache SOAP API is probably the most widely used Java SOAP implementation. Apache SOAP was built on top of the IBM SOAP4J API library. IBM donated the library to get a solid open source–based SOAP implementation out for the development community. The code examples in this book use Apache SOAP.

AXIS

`http://xml.apache.org/axis`

AXIS is the next generation of a Java-based SOAP implementation (at the time of this writing, it is in the alpha stage). AXIS replaces the Apache SOAP API. AXIS is much faster than Apache SOAP due to design considerations such as using XML tools like SAX over DOM (we will cover SAX and DOM in future chapters). The drawback of AXIS is that the API is still in alpha release and as such is still too young to use in production environments.

JAXM (Java API for XML Messaging)

`http://java.sun.com/xml/jaxm/index.html`

JAXM implements SOAP 1.1. A programmer can use JAXM to enable a JSP page or Java object to send SOAP messaging. JAXM hides much of the lower level programming so a programmer can concentrate on sending a message. Eventually, JAXM will expand the messaging capabilities so that it offers functionality that SOAP cannot provide.

JAXM is listed as JSR-67 at the Java Community Process Web site. The Java Community Process is a community-based approach Sun takes to expand and improve upon Java. Whenever a new tool or feature for Java is required, a small team of programmers and companies is formed to oversee and develop the specifications and code.

JAXR (Java API for XML Registries)

`http://java.sun.com/xml/jaxr/index.html`

This API will be a valuable one for many programmers. The JAXR API will define a standard Java interface to access any Web service registry whether it is based on ebXML, UDDI, or another standard. It is important to understand that this API doesn't define a registry, but rather is purely a one-stop shopping interface to access any registry. While at the time of writing it was too early to use it, sometime in 2002 this API will be ready for prime time. The API currently uses ebXML to establish a baseline of required functionality; however, it is being expanded as needed for additional functionality. Currently, it supports only ebXML and UDDI specifications (version 0.6 at the time of writing). JAXR will use JAXM to communicate between the registry and a client.

JAXR is listed as JSR-093 at the Java Community Process Web site.

JWSDL (Java API for WSDL)

This API is designed to simplify using WSDL. JWSDL can represent and manipulate a service described by a WSDL document. Currently, JAXP is the best way to access and use a WSDL document. However, later in 2002, when JWSDL has become an established Java API, it will be the quickest and easiest API to use for WSDL documents. This API is really meant more for the tool builders—programmers building the tools to access and use Web services. The average Web developer building a Web service will never need to access this API.

JWSDL is listed as JSR-110 at the Java Community Process Web site. At the time of this writing, no reference implementation of JWSDL has been released to the public.

How to Use a Web Service

Now that we have introduced Web services, let's play around and use one. To make life easy, let's go about this in a step-by-step process. These steps will be broken up between two sections.

1. "Using SOAP"—The first example is all about getting SOAP installed on our machines. We will set up a SOAP server to work alongside the Tomcat JSP Web server. We're using the SOAP server component of the Apache SOAP 2.2 Java API. Once we have this server up, we will build a very simple Web service to run on the local machine.

2. "Roaming the Internet"—The second example will show how to call up a Web service that isn't on the local machine.

Using SOAP

SOAP is really the core of Web services. In these examples, HTTP is the communication tier and Apache SOAP is the application handling the messages. We will use SOAP in two ways: firstly as a SOAP server to listen and process SOAP requests and secondly as a SOAP client to make requests. While many projects will only need to have a SOAP client, we will use both a client and a server to illustrate the full workings of SOAP.

Step 1: Installing a SOAP Server and Client

We need access to a Java implementation of SOAP. For this book, we will use the Apache SOAP API version 2.2. This software is open source and can be freely downloaded from `http://xml.apache.org/soap/index.html`. In this book we are using a nightly build of the SOAP application. The nightly builds can be found at `http://xml.apache.org/dist/soap/nightly/`. The nightly build has a few security features that are not found in the main 2.2 release. We recommend using either a recent nightly build or SOAP 2.3 when it is released in 2002.

Apache SOAP requires the following tools:

- An XML Parser—We are using Xerces, which is currently included with the Tomcat server.
- JAF (JavaBeans Activation Framework)—Simply defined, JAF is a framework for handling the transfer and use of data. Since SOAP is all about moving data back and forth, it makes logical sense that Apache SOAP would use JAF to simplify the internal coding. Sun defines JAF as "a set of standard services to determine the type of an arbitrary piece of data, encapsulate access to it, discover the operations available on it, and to instantiate the appropriate bean to perform said operation(s)." Fortunately, we really don't have to know anything about how to use JAF ourselves as it's used behind the scenes by Apache SOAP.

  JAF can be found at `http://java.sun.com/products/javabeans/glasgow/jaf.html`.

  To install JAF, all that you need to do is place activation.jar within your system's classpath so the Java Virtual Machine can find the JAF classes.
- JavaMail—JavaMail is a high-level Java API used to simplify the coding of e-mail applications. JavaMail is used by Apache SOAP to enable SMTP as a transport mechanism for SOAP messages.

  The JavaMail APIs can be found at `http://java.sun.com/products/javamail/index.html`.

  To install JavaMail, place the mail.jar within your system's classpath.

Once we have these tools, we are ready to install Apache SOAP. To use SOAP, we need to set up the SOAP client. This is required to permit our JSP container to reach out and talk to SOAP servers. To do this, Tomcat will need access to the soap.jar file that comes along with Apache SOAP. Place the soap.jar file into your classpath. Besides writing the code for the client request, this is the only step required for installing a SOAP client.

For this book, we placed the activation.jar, mail.jar, and soap.jar all in the Tomcat `lib` directory.

We also need a SOAP server to be up and running to process Web service requests. Within the Apache SOAP installation, you will find a soap.war file. Place this WAR file into your Tomcat `webapps` directory. This WAR contains a simple but complete Web application that functions as a SOAP server.

In the interest of conserving space, we won't repeat the general installation and testing examples that come with Apache SOAP. However, instead of installing SOAP at the root classpath level, we are having SOAP work through Tomcat. This will work for the examples in this book since we are going to use Tomcat and JSP for all the SOAP access (this *is* a JSP and XML book, after all). This means that all we really need to do is place the soap.jar, activation.jar, and mail.jar files into the Tomcat `lib` directory and install the soap.war file in order to have Apache SOAP run through Tomcat. One disadvantage of doing this, of course, is that you will not be able to run the SOAP examples from the Java command line. However, this will make setting up your classpath simple.

Once these files are in place, stop Tomcat and then restart it. Tomcat will install the SOAP server for you.

Let's write a quick test file, shown in Listing 3.4. (Save this file as `webapps\xmlbook\chapter3\ShowClients.jsp`.)

LISTING 3.4 ShowClients.jsp

```
<%@page contentType="text/html"
        import="java.net.*,
                org.apache.soap.server.*"
%>
<html>
<head><title>List Current Clients</title></head>
<body>
Listing Current Clients on Local Server:<br/>
<%
    URL l_url = new URL ("http://localhost:8080/soap/servlet/rpcrouter");
    ServiceManagerClient l_soap_client = new ServiceManagerClient(l_url);
```

LISTING 3.4 Continued

```
    String l_test[] = l_soap_client.list();
    for (int i=0; i < l_test.length; i++)
    {  out.print(l_test[i] + "<br/>"); }
%>
</body>
</html>
```

This file replaces the command-line client test that is in the Apache SOAP documentation. That example validates the services that are running on the server. It works by creating a `ServiceManagerClient` object with which we can query a SOAP server. In our case, we are using this object to query the status of our local SOAP server. In this example, it queries the URL `http://localhost:8080/soap/servlet/rpcrouter`.

If you have just installed the SOAP server, this page will only return an empty listing. After all, we haven't installed any Web services yet. We need to build a Web service so we can have something to test.

Step 2: Building a Simple Service

You will be amazed at how simple this will be. The first thing we need to do is create a JavaBean. After all, from our viewpoint a Web service is just a Java object (JavaBean) with a fancy front end (Apache SOAP server). This means we will create the Web service under the SOAP Web application we installed in the previous step. In our case, the JavaBean will look like Listing 3.5. (Save this file as `webapps\soap\WEB-INF\classes\xmlbook\chapter3\firstservice.java`.)

LISTING 3.5 firstservice.java

```
package xmlbook.chapter3;
import java.beans.*;
public class firstservice extends Object implements java.io.Serializable
{   public firstservice() {}

    public String testService ()
    { return("First Test Service");}
}
```

The Web service is called `firstservice` and it has one method called `testService`. The only thing this service does is return a string. Not very exciting, but we intentionally kept it simple so we can test everything quickly. Let's compile the Java file and move on to creating the SOAP deployment descriptor. (After compiling, stop and restart Tomcat so the firstservice.class file is registered within the SOAP server classpath.)

Once we have a Java object to use as a service, we must register the object with the SOAP server. Apache SOAP server uses an XML file called DeploymentDescriptor.xml to track the information of a Web service. The SOAP deployment descriptor is just an initialization file containing the basic service information. Let's go ahead and create this file. It turns out that the Apache SOAP server has a tool that permits us to type in the information and Apache SOAP automatically creates the deployment descriptor file. Point your browser to `http://localhost:8080/soap/admin/index.html`.

Select the Deploy service option. This will bring up an empty data entry screen. For our example, we can fill it in as shown in Figure 3.2.

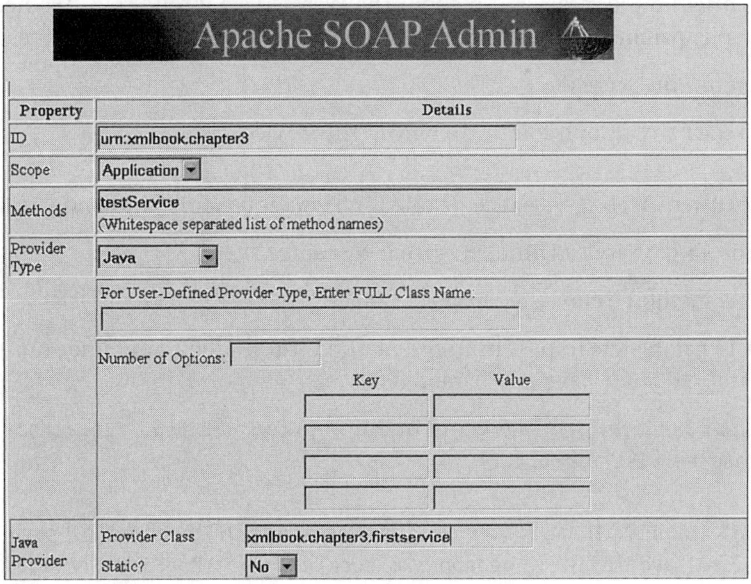

FIGURE 3.2 Deploying a Web service on Apache SOAP server.

Note that this screen extends on for a bit, but for this example, we only need to enter the information shown in the screenshot.

Click the Deploy button at the bottom of the data entry frame (not to be confused with the Deploy button on the sidebar!) when you are done.

To prove that everything is working so far, let's run the first test file, ShowClients.jsp. As shown in Figure 3.3, this will demonstrate that our new service is indeed up and running and that it's available for access from outside the SOAP server.

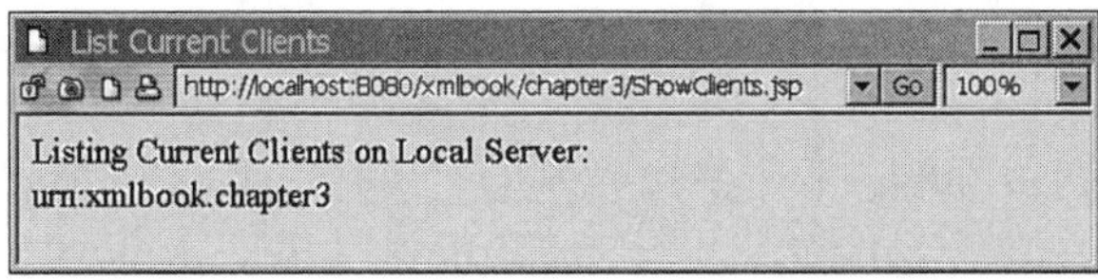

FIGURE 3.3 Running ShowClients.jsp.

Step 3: Using a Service

Now that we have a service, the next trick is to show how to invoke the Web service. We are going to write a client to access the service. To write this client we need to do the following:

- Gather up the information about the Web service in question. We need the name, parameters, and various other details about the service to track it down.
- Invoke the service.
- Extract any response sent back from the service.

For our current Web service, the detailed information we need to know is listed here:

- The Target Service URI (`urn:xmlbook.chapter3`)
- The method to invoke (`testService`)
- Any parameters to pass in to the method (there aren't any, since our first service doesn't have any parameters)
- The URL of the SOAP server in question (for us it's `http://localhost:8080/soap/servlet/rpcrouter`)

Now back in our XML book Web site it's time to add in the client JSP page shown in Listing 3.6. (Save this file as `webapps\xmlbook\chapter3\RunFirstService.jsp`.)

LISTING 3.6 RunFirstService.jsp

```
<%@page contentType="text/html"
        import="java.net.*,
               org.apache.soap.*,
               org.apache.soap.rpc.*" %>


<%
    String ls_result = "";
    Call call = new Call ();
```

LISTING 3.6 Continued

```
    call.setTargetObjectURI("urn:xmlbook.chapter3");
    call.setMethodName ("testService");
    call.setEncodingStyleURI(Constants.NS_URI_SOAP_ENC);

    URL url = new URL ("http://localhost:8080/soap/servlet/rpcrouter");

    Response resp = call.invoke (url, "");
    if (resp.generatedFault())
    {   Fault fault=resp.getFault();
        ls_result = " Fault code: " + fault.getFaultCode();
        ls_result = " Fault Description: " +fault.getFaultString();
    }
    else
    {   Parameter result = resp.getReturnValue();
        ls_result = (String) result.getValue();
    }
%>
<html><head><title>Running a Local Web Service</title></head>
<body>
The result of the Web service call is <br/>
<%= ls_result %>
</body>
</html>
```

In this example, the JSP page is acting as the client. When it is executed, it can successfully invoke `firstservice`, the service we created in a previous example. The result will look like Figure 3.4.

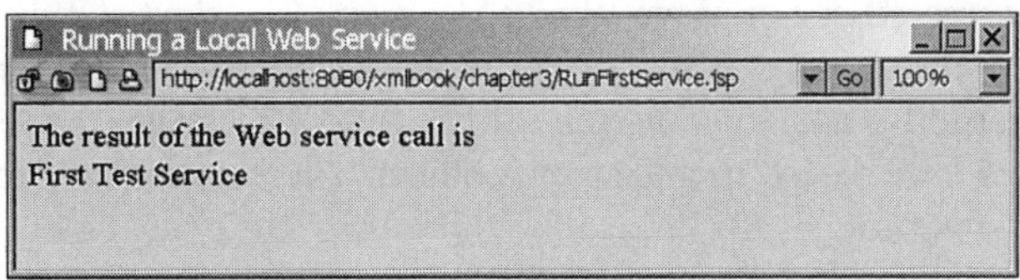

FIGURE 3.4 Running RunFirstService.jsp.

Now it's time to figure out what is happening. To do this, let's review the important sections of the RunFirstService.jsp example.

In the first section, the code of interest is the `import` statement. The classes of `java.net.*` are required for access to the URL object. The `org.apache.soap` classes were imported to access the Apache SOAP client APIs.

```
<%@page contentType="text/html"
        import="java.net.*,
                org.apache.soap.*,
                org.apache.soap.rpc.*"
%>
<%
    String ls_result = "";
```

Next, we use the `Call` object within Apache SOAP to access a Web service. The `Call` object represents the actual RPC call that is occurring. I personally think of it as my SOAP client because it's the object that is used to call the Web service. In fact, the `Call` object is the representation of the message to be sent to a Web service:

```
Call call = new Call ();
```

Once we have the `Call` object we need to initialize it with the Web service data (the identification data we supplied when creating the Web service on our SOAP server). The interesting thing to note here is that we are using `Constants.NS_URI_SOAP_ENC` to tell Apache SOAP to use the standard SOAP encoding. Most of the time, this will be the encoding value you will need to use. The URL object is storing the address of the SOAP server to access for the service:

```
    call.setTargetObjectURI("urn:xmlbook.chapter3");
    call.setMethodName ("testService");
    call.setEncodingStyleURI(Constants.NS_URI_SOAP_ENC);
    URL url = new URL ("http://localhost:8080/soap/servlet/rpcrouter");
```

Once we have created our message (the `Call` object), the next step is to send the message. This is also known as invoking the service and we use the `invoke` method. The `invoke` method is a client-side only call to send a message to a service. The results of the call are placed in a `Response` object. The `Response` object represents the message sent back from an RPC call:

```
Response resp = call.invoke (url, "");
```

Once we have the `Response` object, we need to check the return message to see what has happened. First, we check for any errors. If something went wrong, we will query the response for the details of the error:

```
   if (resp.generatedFault())
    {   Fault fault=resp.getFault();
```

```
        ls_result = " Fault code: " + fault.getFaultCode();
        ls_result = " Fault Description: " +fault.getFaultString();
    }
```

If everything is fine, we read the return value embedded within the message. In our case, we know that the Web service is only returning a `String` object, so we immediately type the return object to a `String`. In some cases, the logic to parse out the return value would be more robust to handle a complicated object or multiple values:

```
    else
    {   Parameter result = resp.getReturnValue();
        ls_result = (String) result.getValue();
    }
```

The rest of the page is just an HTML document to display the results.

The code to access the Web service is relatively simple. Half the battle is getting the information of the Web service to call. The other half Apache SOAP takes care of for us in the sending and receiving of the message. All we are doing is creating a message object, receiving a message object, and querying the results.

Roaming the Internet

This section concentrates on using a remote Web service; we will build an example to access a publicly available Web service from the XMethods Web site. For a Web service, this example will use the TemperatureService service shown in Listing 3.3.

Choosing a Web Service

This example needs the parameters to call the service and that means it's time to go back to Listing 3.3 and the WSDL file. From this file, it is possible to get the information we need to access the Web service. The pieces of data we need are

- The Target Service URI—This is read from the namespace attribute of the `soap:operation` element. For this example, it works out to be `urn:xmethods-Temperature`.
- The Web service method being invoked by our program—This information is based on the `operation` element. For this service, we are using `getTemp`.
- Any parameters needed for the Web service to run successfully—These were stored in the message element. From this we find `<part name="zipcode" type="xsd:string" />`.

  This translates into one input parameter called `zipcode` of type `String`.

- The URL of the SOAP server in question—For us it's stored in the `soap:address` element, within the location attribute, which gets us a value of `http://services.xmethods.net:80/soap/servlet/rpcrouter`.

Using these values, we can now write a quick JSP page to access this Web service. The code is shown in Listing 3.7. (Save this file as `webapps\xmlbook\chapter3\AccessService.jsp`.)

LISTING 3.7 Accessing the XMethods TemperatureService Web Service

```
<%@page contentType="text/html"
        import="java.net.*,
                java.util.*,
                org.apache.soap.*,
                org.apache.soap.rpc.*"
%>

<% String ls_result  = "";
   String ls_zipcode = (String) request.getParameter("zip");

if (ls_zipcode == null || ls_zipcode.length() == 0 || ls_zipcode.length() > 5)
{ ls_zipcode = "07931";}

   Call call = new Call ();
   call.setTargetObjectURI("urn:xmethods-Temperature");
   call.setMethodName ("getTemp");
   call.setEncodingStyleURI(Constants.NS_URI_SOAP_ENC);

   /* Create the parameters to pass to the Web service */
   Vector params = new Vector ();
   params.addElement (new Parameter("zipcode", String.class,ls_zipcode, null));
   call.setParams (params);

  URL url = new URL ("http://services.xmethods.net:80/soap/servlet/rpcrouter");
  Response resp = call.invoke (url, "");

   if (resp.generatedFault())
   {   Fault fault=resp.getFault();
       ls_result = " Fault code: " + fault.getFaultCode();
       ls_result = " Fault Description: " +fault.getFaultString();
   }
   else
```

LISTING 3.7 Continued

```
    {   Parameter result = resp.getReturnValue();
        ls_result  = result.getValue().toString();
    }
%>

<html>
<head><title>Accessing a Remote Service</title></head>
<body>

The result of the Web service call is <br/>
The temperature at <%= ls_zipcode %> is currently: <%= ls_result %>

<form  method="post" action="AccessService.jsp">
    <input type="text" name="zip" id="zip" value="<%= ls_zipcode %>" />
    <input type="submit" value="Enter New Zip Code" />
</form>

</body>
</html>
```

When this JSP page is accessed, it will produce a page that looks like Figure 3.5.

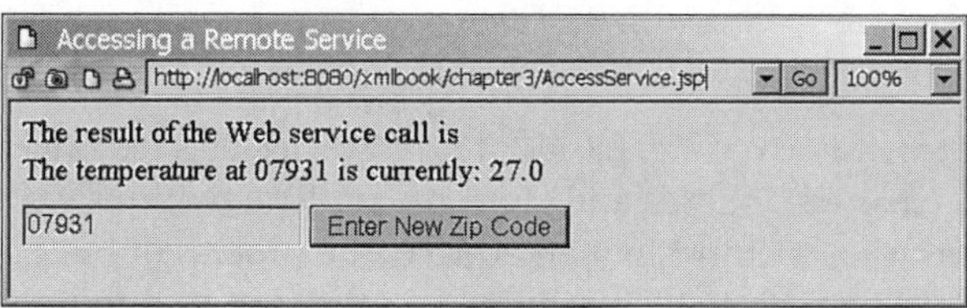

FIGURE 3.5 Running AccessService.jsp.

Let's review the example. Most of the code in this example is identical to the RunFirstService.jsp example. The only difference is that this remote Web service is using parameters and our first example didn't need any parameters (because the service didn't use any). This shows that from a programming viewpoint the location of the Web service (local versus Internet) doesn't make much of a difference. From a practical viewpoint, running a remote service might incur additional overhead depending on the location of the Web service. However, those are design issues we will examine in a later chapter.

Let's look at the differences in the code.

While the JSP page is a little more complicated in that we use an HTML form on it (to submit a zip code back to ourselves), we only want to focus on the Web service differences. The only difference from a Web service point of view is the addition of parameters.

Usually, to use parameters we need to use a `Vector` object to place the parameter arguments:

```
Vector params = new Vector ();
```

Once we have the `Vector`, we place the arguments into our local copy of the `Vector` object:

```
params.addElement (new Parameter("zipcode", String.class,ls_zipcode, null));
```

Once we've finished adding parameters to the `Vector`, we append the `Vector` to the `Call` object.

```
call.setParams (params);
```

Everything else is as before—we invoke our `Call` object and receive a response.

Calling a service isn't especially hard—all the pain is in setting the service up and getting the tools together.

Summary

In this chapter, we reviewed the basics of Web services. As we saw, the larger picture is confusing, as many standards and software implementations exist. Ironically, despite the confusion within the marketplace, the process of building and using a Web service is simple. While Web services and the surrounding tools are still very young, it is a very promising technology for the future.

In future chapters, we will delve into details of implementing a JSP-based Web service. At the JSP Insider Web site (`http://www.jspinsider.com`), we have a bimonthly newsletter called the JSPBuzz. This newsletter is created with a combination of XML and JSP. We will use the data and examples from the JSPBuzz newsletter as a real-world example of using JSP and XML together. More importantly, we will apply Web services to the JSPBuzz to expose it to the world. We will show how the JSP Insider is building remote services that you can use to access the information stored in the JSPBuzz newsletter.

We've finished the last of the introductory chapters. These first three chapters were a concise review of the information needed to give newer programmers a basic level of understanding of JSP and XML. Now we are ready to dig into the meat of JSP and XML. The next chapter starts the fun part—learning how to practically combine JSP and XML in your everyday projects.

PART II

Integrating JSP and XML

IN THIS PART

4

A Quick Start to JSP and XML Together

IN THIS CHAPTER

- The Relationship Between XML and JSP
- Java XML/XSL APIs

The goal of this chapter is to throw you right into the JSP/XML mix. This chapter will show you how easy it is to mix XML and XSLT together within a JSP. A second goal is to introduce the various APIs that enable you to use XML within Java.

The approach this chapter takes is to start with a brief discussion of how XML and JSP relate. Then the chapter will introduce the reader to three basic APIs: JAXP, Xerces, and Xalan. Using these Java coded libraries, we will expand what we learned from Chapter 2, "Introduction to XML/XSL," and put it into practice with a JSP environment. After discussing the code from these simple examples, we can turn up the heat and show a fuller example of building a newsletter processor that creates a weekly news page. Finally, the chapter shifts focus to describing the other APIs that a JSP/XML programmer will find in common use.

The Relationship Between XML and JSP

Using JSP and XML together makes quite a bit of sense. JSP is all about character-based output and XML is all about character-based data; mixing the two together ends up producing a natural match. Simply understanding XML is not enough, because XML is about marking up the data, not about moving the data around. JSP allows us to move data into and out of an XML data source. To use XML successfully in a project, we must understand how to pull and push character data around within a JSP. Several common ways of using JSP and XML together are listed here:

- The data is stored within an XML file. Using JSP, the data is imported and then converted to an HTML-based page to be viewed by a user with a browser.
- The data is stored within a database. A Java process is built to read the data from the database and convert it to an XML document. Once the data is stored as XML, either the data is shipped to the user as an XML file, or the XML file is transformed to another format such as an HTML page to be viewed by a user.
- Data is stored within an XML file. Java is used to parse the file and format the data for database insertion. Once the data is in the database, a JSP is used to access and view the data.
- Web application initialization information is stored within an XML file. The JSP reads the file and changes application behavior based on what it finds in the file.
- Data is transferred between two systems in an XML-formatted file. JSP is used as a front-end interface to initiate the process of sending or receiving the data.

These examples point out that data is being pushed and pulled around and converted to various formats. It's important to learn to use JSP as a layer to facilitate the transport of data using either XML or some other means.

A Warning

This is the appropriate time to give a warning regarding XML. XML is a wonderful creation, and it can do amazing things. However, be warned that it is not the appropriate solution to a number of problems. Used appropriately, it can improve performance and save time. Misused, XML *will* slow down Web applications, waste development time, and cost money.

Reporting systems are generally good places to use XML and XSL because of the filtering and formatting that can be implemented on the same datasets to achieve different reports. Examples of this can be found in Chapter 11, "Using XML in Reporting Systems," and Chapter 12, "Advanced XML in Reporting Systems." Also, data stored as XML within a Web page can be used to allow the client to reorganize the data in the reports without needing the server again. Examples of this can be found in Chapter 13, "Browser Considerations with XML."

In addition, XML gives an abstraction layer between business logic and presentation logic. This means that changing a report only requires updating an XSL stylesheet while the data generation level remains untouched by changes. Likewise, if the business objects generating the report change, it's possible to still generate the same XML, so the presentation layer still works. The XML layer ends up working like a rubber gasket that permits your Web application to flex with less effort.

As stated earlier in the book, XML is not designed to be a replacement for a database. While XML files can be used to store data, they are best used for initialization files or small data stores. Using XML to store and retrieve large amounts of data is a slower method of data storage than using a database. Databases provide additional features, such as transaction management, that are not part of XML. When designing larger systems using XML, you should balance the design relative to XML strengths and weaknesses. XML doesn't replace a database; rather, it complements a database. Our system designs should reflect and use each technology to the benefit of the other. In later chapters, we will demonstrate blending the two technologies together.

There are times when using XML as a data store may be a valid choice. Say, for instance, you need to enable many clients to view unchanging data without requiring either a database or network connection. A very simple system could be developed relatively quickly that would use a browser, XML, and some stylesheets to achieve this goal.

Sometimes projects convert data to XML just to use XML. This is a bad idea, because the process of creating and using XML adds another layer of processing to a project. This will both increase costs due to development time and slow down processing. Data should only be converted to XML when the use of XML can be shown to provide the best solution.

The basic rule to use is this: You should never transform data into XML format if the data isn't being packaged for a purpose. Don't use XML for XML's sake.

JAXP, Xerces, and Xalan

Many tools exist for the processing and transformation of XML. Each has strengths and weaknesses for differing circumstances. However, you have to start somewhere, so we will evaluate the APIs that are most commonly used with JSP. This translates into writing an example using the JAXP API. This API will use the Xerces Java parser and the Xalan stylesheet processor. If you haven't yet placed the xerces.jar and xalan.jar files in the `lib` directory found in the root of your Tomcat installation, do so now. Download locations follow.

Xerces (XML Parser)

Simply described, Xerces is an XML parser and generator. Named after the Xerces Blue butterfly, it implements the W3C XML and DOM (Levels 1 and 2), as well as the SAX standard.

Xerces is included with Tomcat, and therefore you will not need to install it. However, there may be times when the newest version is necessary for newly added functionality. Use the following URL to download the newest version of Xerces: `http://xml.apache.org/xerces2-j/index.html`. To date, Tomcat has been keeping pace with Xerces.

DOM and SAX are different ways in which to process XML and will be discussed in Chapter 5, "Using DOM," and Chapter 6, "Programming SAX." Simply put, DOM is the creation of a tree-like structure in memory that can be programmatically manipulated. SAX is a sequential event-driven XML reader.

This book uses Xerces version 1.4.3.

Xalan (XSLT Processor)

Xalan is an XSLT stylesheet processor. Named after a rare musical instrument, it implements the W3C XSLT and XPath recommendations. Sadly, Xalan is not included with Tomcat, so we must install it. Download Xalan from `http://xml.apache.org/xalan-j/index.html`. Place the xalan.jar file in the `lib` directory found under the Tomcat installation. Stop and restart the server so that Tomcat registers the new classes.

The examples in this book use Xalan version 2.2.d10.

JAXP (Generic XML Processing)

JAXP is technically an API for XML processing. More accurately, it's an abstraction layer because it contains no parsing functionality. JAXP is a single API through which to access the various supported XML and XSL processors. It's a lot like JDBC for XML parsers. It does not provide any new functionality to XML processing, except that it provides a common way to use different XML processor implementations. Through JAXP, several of the industry standard XML processor implementations may be used, such as SAX and DOM.

In order to use JAXP effectively, it's important to use its API only, and avoid directly using any of its underlying implementation-dependent APIs. The reason for this comes from the fact the JAXP layer is an abstraction layer. Any direct calls to the underlying XML APIs defeats the purpose of having the generic layer. This rule is especially important if your application will be deployed in different situations and if each deployment needs to use a different underlying XML processor. JAXP enables your application to be XML processor independent.

JAXP was created to facilitate the use of XML on the Java platform. It does this through the common interface to whichever XML processor is chosen.

JAXP comes bundled with the Tomcat server, and therefore requires no installation. If you want to review the source of JAXP or check the details of the latest version, check out `http://java.sun.com/xml/jaxp.html`.

This book uses JAXP version 1.1.

An Example with JAXP, XSL, and XML This example simulates the randomly generated banner ads that are seen all over the Web. The difference is that this version is simplified to use only text. In Chapter 1, "Integrating JSP and Data," we created a similar example using various methods. This version's data will be stored in a static XML file. Using JAXP we will apply an XSL stylesheet to the XML document and output the results. As a simple starting point, the example in this section will display all the data contained in the XML file. Then in the example in the next section, the code will randomize which link is displayed.

Let's begin with the XML data file, shown in Listing 4.1. This and all files throughout this chapter should be saved in the Tomcat `webapps` directory with the path `webapps/xmlbook/chapter4/BannerAds.xml`.

LISTING 4.1 BannerAds.xml; XML Data File for JAXP Example

```
<?xml version="1.0"?>
<BANNERS>
    <BANNERAD>
        <NAME>JSPInsider</NAME>
        <LINK>http://www.jspinsider.com</LINK>
        <LINKTEXT>JSP News</LINKTEXT>
    </BANNERAD>
    <BANNERAD>
        <NAME>Sun</NAME>
        <LINK>http://www.sun.com</LINK>
        <LINKTEXT>The Home of Java</LINKTEXT>
    </BANNERAD>
    <BANNERAD>
        <NAME>SAMS</NAME>
        <LINK>http://www.samspublishing.com</LINK>
        <LINKTEXT>Java Books</LINKTEXT>
    </BANNERAD>
    <BANNERAD>
        <NAME>Jakarta</NAME>
        <LINK>http://jakarta.apache.org</LINK>
        <LINKTEXT>Kewl Tools</LINKTEXT>
    </BANNERAD>
</BANNERS>
```

Notice that this file has four groups of data, each of which contains information for a banner link. Each group of data is properly nested under the root element `BANNERS`.

Next, the XSL stylesheet, shown in Listing 4.2, needs to be built to apply the formatting to the XML file. Briefly, this stylesheet creates a table row for each child `BANNERAD` found within the root element `BANNERS`. Then the text data found at various nodes is selected and placed within table cells.

LISTING 4.2 BannerAds.xsl; XSL Stylesheet for JAXP Example

```
<xsl:stylesheet version="1.0" xmlns:xsl="http://www.w3.org/1999/XSL/Transform">
<xsl:template match="/">
<HTML>
<HEAD><TITLE>Banner Ads With JAXP</TITLE></HEAD>
<BODY>
    <TABLE border="1">
    <TR>
        <TH>Name</TH>
        <TH>Link</TH>
        <TH>LinkText</TH>
    </TR>
    <xsl:for-each select="BANNERS/BANNERAD">
    <TR>
        <TD><xsl:value-of select="NAME" /></TD>
        <TD><xsl:value-of select="LINK" /></TD>
        <TD><xsl:value-of select="LINKTEXT" /></TD>
    </TR>
    </xsl:for-each>
    </TABLE>
</BODY>
</HTML>
</xsl:template>
</xsl:stylesheet>
```

This XPath `select` statement begins by selecting all `BANNERAD` children of the root element `BANNERS`.

```
<xsl:for-each select="BANNERS/BANNERAD">
```

This causes the body of this `for-each` element to be processed for each element that is matched through the `select` expression.

Now it's time to build the JSP that uses JAXP to apply the stylesheet transformation to the XML file. The code is shown in Listing 4.3.

LISTING 4.3 BannerAds_JAXP.jsp; JSP for JAXP Example

```
<%@ page
  import="javax.xml.transform.*,
          javax.xml.transform.stream.*,
          java.io.*"
%>
```

LISTING 4.3 Continued

```
<%
String  ls_path = request.getServletPath();
        ls_path = ls_path.substring(0,ls_path.indexOf("BannerAds_JAXP.jsp")) ;

String  ls_xml  = application.getRealPath(ls_path + "BannerAds.xml");
String  ls_xsl  = application.getRealPath(ls_path + "BannerAds.xsl");

StreamSource xml = new StreamSource(new File(ls_xml));
StreamSource xsl = new StreamSource(new File(ls_xsl));
StreamResult result = new StreamResult(out);

TransformerFactory tFactory = TransformerFactory.newInstance();
Transformer transformer = tFactory.newTransformer(xsl);
transformer.transform(xml, result);
%>
```

This page begins by declaring those packages used by the code. The first package, `javax.xml.transform.*`, is the package that contains the `Transformer` and `TransformerFactory` classes. These classes transform a source tree, the XML and XSL, into a result tree. The next package declared, namely `javax.xml.tranform.stream.*`, is used for the `StreamResult` and `StreamSource` classes. The `StreamSource` is the XML source being handled. It makes no difference to us whether it is a file being read in a stream of data or an existing representation of the XML data. The `StreamSource` takes care of the details for us in this matter. The `StreamResult` represents where we want to send our final XML document. These classes serve as holders for the XML and XSL files before transformation, and for the final output after processing. Last, we have the `java.io.*` package, which handles external file management.

The JSP then requests the path to itself. This path check is performed so that we can be sure that we are using the proper path when we grab the XML and XSL files. Once we have the path, we use it to put the XML and XSL files into the `StreamSource` objects that serve as holders. The `StreamResult` object is built to send the results of the transformation. In this page, the example just needs to send the output directly to the JSP's output, or the `out` implicit object of type `javax.servlet.jsp.JspWriter`.

All of the work we've done so far just sets up everything for the XML/XSLT transformation to occur. At this point, the code creates an instance of the `TransformerFactory` object. Factories are used to create specific transformations. A factory sets up all the reusable information, which the XML process will need later when we perform the actual XSL transformation of the XML data. We use the `TransformerFactory` to create a specific `Transformer`. Each `Transformer` created handles a single XSL file. If we had five different XSL files to process, we would create five transform instances, or reinitialize a single `Transformer` five times. So when creating the `Transformer` object, we tell it which XSL file to use. Then we call the transform method to process an XML document. This requires that we know which XML file to process (which `StreamSource` object) and also where to send the output (the `StreamResult`). The overall transformation only used a few lines of JAXP. Figure 4.1 shows the results.

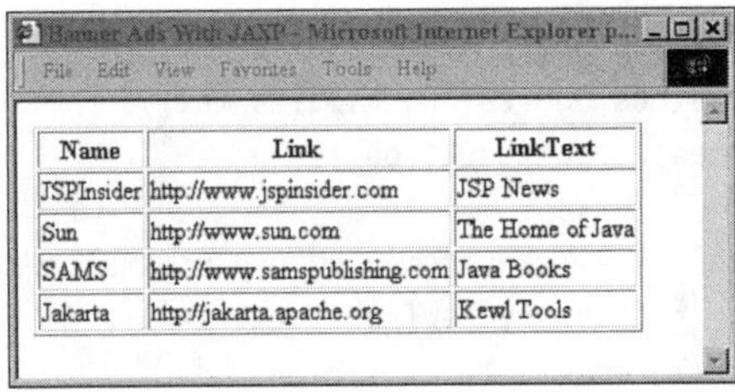

FIGURE 4.1 Results of JAXP transformation.

The ability to display an XSLT transformation is very powerful, but let's expand our example to have some more functionality. A real banner ad system would only display one randomly selected banner ad at a time. We'll modify our example to accommodate this behavior.

An Example with XSL Parameters We will begin by adding a parameter tag to the XSL stylesheet. This tag will create a parameter that will tell the stylesheet which banner ad to display. The value of this parameter will be set through our JSP (more specifically, through JAXP). Listing 4.4 shows the new stylesheet with the changes noted in boldface print.

LISTING 4.4 BannerAds_Param.xsl; Externally Set Parameter

```
<xsl:stylesheet version="1.0" xmlns:xsl="http://www.w3.org/1999/XSL/Transform">
<xsl:param name="Choose"/>
<xsl:template match="/">
<HTML>
<HEAD><TITLE>Banner Ads With Parameter</TITLE></HEAD>
<BODY>
    <TABLE border="1">
    <TR>
        <TH>Name</TH>
        <TH>Link</TH>
        <TH>LinkText</TH>
    </TR>
    <xsl:for-each select="BANNERS/BANNERAD[$Choose]">
```

LISTING 4.4 Continued

```
    <TR>
        <TD><xsl:value-of select="NAME" /></TD>
        <TD><xsl:value-of select="LINK" /></TD>
        <TD><xsl:value-of select="LINKTEXT" /></TD>
    </TR>
    </xsl:for-each>
    </TABLE>
</BODY>
</HTML>
</xsl:template>
</xsl:stylesheet>
```

Within the `stylesheet` element we've added a parameter element named `Choose`.

```
<xsl:param name="Choose"/>
```

This parameter element has global scope for the entire stylesheet because it was placed outside an `xsl:template` tag. Normally when a parameter is declared it is also set to a default value with the `select` attribute. We chose not to use a default value; if we had used one, it would look like this:

```
<xsl:param name="Choose" select="2" />
```

The other place that parameters may be declared is in the beginning of a template. In this case, the parameter scope is limited to within the template in which it resides.

The next changed part of the original stylesheet from Listing 4.2 is the `select` statement of the `for-each` loop.

```
<xsl:for-each select="BANNERS/BANNERAD[$Choose]">
```

This XPath `select` statement still begins by selecting all `BANNERAD` children of the root element `BANNERS`. Now, however, only the `BANNERAD` element whose position number matches our parameter in the square brackets will continue into the `for-each` loop. This is, in effect, only selecting one of all the possible options to be output through code found within this loop.

NOTE

To reference a parameter anywhere within its scope, use a dollar sign before the case-sensitive parameter name.

Finally, we have a new JSP, shown in Listing 4.5. This page still contains the original code from Listing 4.3 with some added processing. We now need to find out how many banner ads are contained within the XML file, and then randomly choose a number within that range. Once that number is chosen, we have to set the parameter in the XSL stylesheet so only that data is displayed.

LISTING 4.5 BannerAds_Param.jsp; Elements and XSL Parameters

```
<%@ page
  import="javax.xml.transform.*,
          javax.xml.transform.stream.*,
          java.io.*,
          javax.xml.parsers.*,
          org.w3c.dom.*"
%>

<%
String  ls_path = request.getServletPath();
        ls_path = ls_path.substring(0,ls_path.indexOf("BannerAds_Param.jsp")) ;

String  ls_xml  = application.getRealPath(ls_path + "BannerAds_Param.xml");
String  ls_xsl  = application.getRealPath(ls_path + "BannerAds_Param.xsl");

DocumentBuilderFactory factory = DocumentBuilderFactory.newInstance();
factory.setValidating(false);

DocumentBuilder builder = factory.newDocumentBuilder();
Document doc = builder.parse(new File(ls_xml));

NodeList nodes = doc.getElementsByTagName("BANNERAD");
int intNodeLength = nodes.getLength();

int intRandom = 1 + (int) (Math.random() * intNodeLength);

StreamSource xml = new StreamSource(new File(ls_xml));
StreamSource xsl = new StreamSource(new File(ls_xsl));

StreamResult result = new StreamResult(out);

TransformerFactory tFactory = TransformerFactory.newInstance();
Transformer transformer = tFactory.newTransformer(xsl);
```

LISTING 4.5 Continued

```
transformer.setParameter("Choose", new Integer(intRandom));

transformer.transform(xml, result);
%>
```

In this new JSP we added two packages. The first package, `javax.xml.parsers.*`, gives us access to the JAXP DOM builder implementations and thus allows us to create a tree-like structure in memory using the `DocumentBuilder` and `Document` classes. The other package is `org.w3c.dom.*`. This package allows us to access the DOM definition of the W3C. Through this we can create a set of chosen nodes using the `NodesList` object.

At this point we create an instance of the `DocumentBuilderFactory` object. Once created, this object will be used to create a `Document` object into which we will parse the XML. Notice the line

```
factory.setValidating(false);
```

This line is important, as it determines whether an XML file is validated as it loads or not. Because this file doesn't have a DTD or schema, we will leave validation off.

In short, validation means that we are comparing the XML document structure to a definition of that structure. If they are the same, the document is valid.

Now that the XML file has been loaded into the `Document` object, we are ready to figure out how many banner ads' worth of data exists in the XML file:

```
NodeList nodes = doc.getElementsByTagName("BANNERAD");
int intNodeLength = nodes.getLength();
```

In looking at the XML file shown in Listing 4.1, we see that each `BANNERAD` element contains information for one banner ad. We create a `NodeList` and select only the elements called `BANNERAD`. This `NodeList` now contains a single node for each banner ad. Using `getLength()` in this list returns the total number of banner ads.

NOTE

At this point we would like to mention that counting child elements is a bad idea when large amounts of data are involved. It is fine for the XML documents we are using because they are small. However, when working with large XML documents, loading the entire document into memory just to count elements would result in a huge performance hit.

Using the length of the list, it is possible to use the random method with that number as a scaling factor to obtain a random number:

```
int intRandom = 1 + (int) (Math.random() * intNodeLength);
```

Then the code sets the parameter in the stylesheet:

```
transformer.setParameter("Choose", new Integer(intRandom));
```

We are setting the parameter named Choose within the XSL stylesheet to the random number from the last step. It's this number that will select which banner ad to display.

This is just the beginning. Using similar techniques, we could determine which data a user gets to see based upon the user's login security rating. It is also possible to pass in parameters that change the way an XSL stylesheet formats reports or that change sorting order dynamically. You will learn how to implement these options later when we begin to delve into the realm of creating XML documents based on data obtained from a database.

Figure 4.2 shows the output produced by this JSP. The output, of course, is random, so you will not see the same thing each time the JSP is executed.

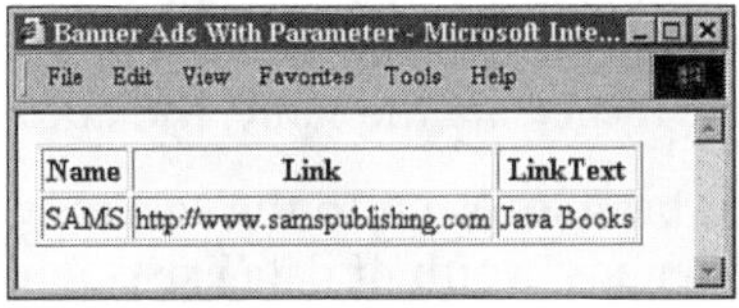

FIGURE 4.2 Results of random banner ad.

Outputting Transformations to a JSP File There may be times when processing XML and XSL files is redundant because the same output is created repeatedly. An example of this would be a newsletter. Let's say we have a Web site that posts a newsletter. The contents of that newsletter, which are in XML, change once a week, but the rest of the time they remain the same. In this case, it would be a waste of processing power to transform the XML with the XSL stylesheet each time a user requested the page. Instead, we should output the transformation results into another JSP file and have the user request the preprocessed page. This way, we can make the transformation happen only when the XML source file has changed by calling the processing page.

Now, let's look at a JSP that processes an XML and XSL file and places the results into another JSP. The processing page is called CreateNewsLetter.jsp and the results are placed in NewsLetter.jsp. This example is loosely based on the JSPBuzz newsletter, which is published at the JSP Insider Web site.

The flow of logic is shown in Figure 4.3.

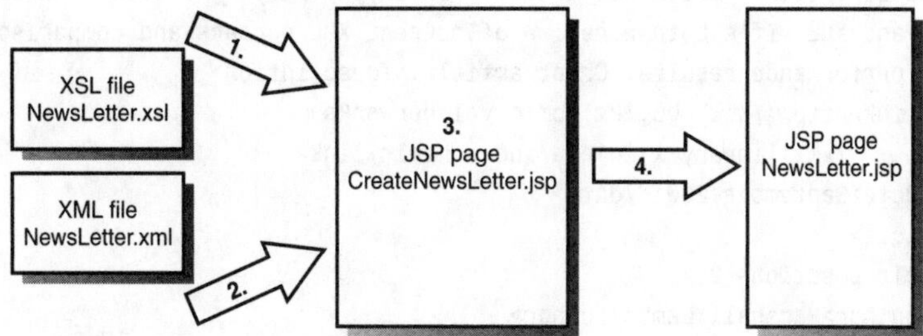

FIGURE 4.3 Creating a new file from output.

The steps illustrated in Figure 4.3 are as follows:

1. CreateNewsLetter.jsp loads the XSL document.
2. CreateNewsLetter.jsp loads the XML document.
3. The XML and XSL are transformed into the results.
4. The results are put into Newsletter.jsp and the file is closed.

The code will create a newsletter from an XML data source and an XSL stylesheet. The newsletter will have articles and links related to Java and XML. We will output the results from the processing JSP to another JSP file so that the transformation won't be called repeatedly and reprocessed redundantly. Using this design, the links in the Web site can point to the output file instead of the processing file.

We will begin with a new XML file found in Listing 4.6. This XML file has header information and content information. Save this file as `webapps/xmlbook/chapter4/NewsLetter.xml`.

LISTING 4.6 NewsLetter.xml; Data for Newsletter Example

```
<?xml version="1.0" encoding="UTF-8"?>
<newsletter volume="II" issue="15">
    <header>
        <title>Newsletter Example</title>
        <description>Demonstrate XML/XSL Transformation Output
        Into JSP File</description>
        <date>12.14.2001</date>
    </header>
    <article position="1">
        <author>Dennis M. Sosnoski </author>
        <title>XML in Java : Document models, Part 1: Performance</title>
```

LISTING 4.6 Continued

```
        <description>A must read article for anyone playing around with Java
          and XML. It's both a review of current XML parsers and comparison on
          performance results. Great article.</description>
        <link>http://www-106.ibm.com/developerworks
              /xml/library/x-injava/index.html</link>
        <date>September 2001</date>
    </article>
    <article position="2">
        <author>Marshall Lamb</author>
        <title>Generate dynamic XML using JavaServer Pages technology</title>
        <description>A good article describing how to use JSP to create dynamic
         content beyond HTML, such as XML.</description>
        <link>http://www-106.ibm.com/developerworks/library/j-dynxml.html</link>
        <date>December 2000</date>
    </article>
    <links position="1">
        <title>Tomcat Home Page</title>
        <link>http://jakarta.apache.org/tomcat/index.html</link>
    </links>
    <links position="2">
        <title>W3C XML Home Page</title>
        <link>http://www.w3.org/XML/</link>
    </links>
    <links position="3">
        <title>Java Tutorial</title>
        <link>http://java.sun.com/docs/books/tutorial/</link>
    </links>
</newsletter>
```

Next we have the XSL stylesheet. This file, shown in Listing 4.7, should be saved in `webapps/xmlbook/chapter4/NewsLetter.xsl`.

LISTING 4.7 NewsLetter.xsl; Newsletter Stylesheet

```
<?xml version="1.0" ?>
<xsl:stylesheet  version="1.0" xmlns:xsl="http://www.w3.org/1999/XSL/Transform">
<xsl:output method="html"/>

<xsl:template match="/">
    <html><head><title>Example Newsletter</title></head>
    <body bgcolor="#ECFCEA">
```

LISTING 4.7 Continued

```
    <center><font size="4pt"><b>
        <xsl:value-of select="newsletter/header/title" /><br/>
        Volume <xsl:value-of select="newsletter/@volume" /> #
        <xsl:value-of select="newsletter/@issue" /><br/>
        <xsl:value-of select="newsletter/header/date" /><br/>
        <xsl:value-of select="newsletter/header/description" />
    </b></font></center>
    <table border="0" width="100%">
        <tr>
            <td bgcolor="#9EC49A">
                <b><font color="#000000">Table of Contents</font></b>
            </td>
        </tr>
        <tr>
            <td><br/><a href="#article">Articles of Interest</a>
                <ul>
                <xsl:for-each select="newsletter/article" >
                    <li><a href="#article{@position}">
                        <xsl:value-of select="title"/></a>
                    </li>
                </xsl:for-each>
                </ul>
            </td>
        </tr>
        <tr>
            <td><a href="#article">Useful Links</a>
                <ul>
                <xsl:for-each select="newsletter/links" >
                    <li><a href="#links{@position}">
                        <xsl:value-of select="title"/></a>
                    </li>
                </xsl:for-each>
                </ul>
            </td>
        </tr>
    </table>
    <table width="100%"><tr>
        <td bgcolor="#9EC49A"><a name="article">
            <font color="#000000"><b>Articles of Interest</b></font></a>
        </td></tr>
    </table>
    <xsl:apply-templates select="newsletter/article" />
```

LISTING 4.7 Continued

```
    <table width="100%"><tr>
        <td bgcolor="#9EC49A"><a name="links">
            <font color="#000000"><b>Useful Links</b></font></a>
        </td></tr>
    </table>
    <xsl:apply-templates select="newsletter/links" />
    </body>
    </html>
</xsl:template>
<xsl:template match="newsletter/article">
    <table style="border-style:groove;border-width:2px;" width="100%">
        <tr><td>
            <table border="0" width="100%">
                <tr><td colspan="2">
                    <a href="{link}" name="article{@position}">
                    <xsl:value-of select="title"/></a>
                    </td>
                </tr>
                <tr>
                    <td width="50%"><xsl:value-of select="author"/>
                    </td>
                    <td><xsl:value-of select="date"/></td>
                </tr>
                <tr>
                    <td colspan="2"><xsl:value-of select="description"/></td>
                </tr>
            </table>
        </td></tr>
    </table><br/>
</xsl:template>

<xsl:template match="newsletter/links">
    <table border="0" width="100%">
        <tr>
            <td><a href="{link}" name="link{@position}">
                <xsl:value-of select="title"/></a>
            </td>
        </tr>
    </table>
</xsl:template>
</xsl:stylesheet>
```

More on XSL Templates This stylesheet uses most of the same elements introduced in Chapter 2, "Introduction to XML/XSL." However, there are a couple of new things that we need to go over. The first of these is the use of templates. In Chapter 2, we introduced templates. Again, templates provide the means by which we match and extract data from an XML document. The `template` tag's `match` attribute determines what of the XML document will make it into the template element to be matched. Here's an example:

```
<xsl:template match="/">
```

This template tag, found near the beginning of Listing 4.7, selects the root of the XML document using `"/"`. The entire XML document will make it into this template to be processed.

However, templates can be defined that only format or transform a select part of an XML document. Notice that an XPath statement is used in a template's `match` attribute to determine which part of an XML document will be selected into the template. This means that we can be as specific or as general as XPath expressions allow in selecting which XML elements will be matched into a template.

In the stylesheet in Listing 4.7, we have created three templates. The first one is discussed earlier in this section, and selects the entire XML document. The other two each format only the `article` and `links` child elements of the root. These templates are defined towards the bottom of the listing. The article template looks like this:

```
<xsl:template match="newsletter/links">
    <table border="0" width="100%">
        <tr>
            <td><a href="{link}" name="link{@position}">
                <xsl:value-of select="title"/></a>
            </td>
        </tr>
    </table>
</xsl:template>
```

Notice that the `select` attribute of this template tag only chooses those `links` elements that are children of the root element `newsletter`. Templates are very helpful in keeping large stylesheets organized and modular. Using a different template to format specific elements makes it easier to find and quickly update or change formatting rather than searching through a single large template.

NOTE

If there are no templates that match parts of an XML document, the unmatched parts of the document will be output as text data without the markup. This is because the default template for elements discards the tags and outputs the text. Imagine, for example, the stylesheet from Listing 4.7 without the first template that matches the root. If you'd like to see what this looks like, once we have our JSPs running (later in the chapter), comment out the first template and see what happens.

The first part of the XML document output will be the text data from the elements unmatched in any templates. In this example, that is the `header` element and children. (This text is output first because processing occurs from start to finish in the order of the source XML file when there are no templates that match the root.) Next, the `links` and `article` elements, which match the remaining templates, are formatted accordingly.

Finally, let's look at another new template-related tag:

```
<xsl:apply-templates select="newsletter/article" />
```

This element provides a way to state at a particular point within another template that you'd like to apply the template that formats those elements indicated by the value of the `select` attribute of this tag. In this case, it's calling the template that formats the `article` children of the root `newsletter` element. In Listing 4.6 these are used to output the result of the called template in the appropriate place.

More on Accessing XML Element Data Now we need to change gears away from templates to discuss another new syntax that is used in Listing 4.7. Let's say an HTML page is being created from the XML/XSL transformation. How can we select XML text values from a tag to place within the `href` attribute of HTML? Well, we can use the `value-of` tag, right? That would create something looking like this:

```
<a href="<value-of select="elementname" />">
```

Do you see the problem with this? It is not valid XML because the tags are not properly nested, or more specifically, a tag is opened inside another tag. We need a way around this. It turns out that we have a shorthand notation that uses curly braces to delimit the node that needs to be selected. This notation is used in the stylesheet in Listing 4.7 and looks like the following:

```
<td><a href="{link}" name="link{@position}">
```

The shorthand is used twice in the above code snippet. The value of the `href` attribute of the anchor tag becomes the text data from the currently selected `link` element of the XML document. The name of the anchor tag is the combination of the string `link` and the value of the `position` attribute found in the XML document. Isn't that clever?

Now that we understand the XML and XSL files, let's move on to the JSP. This page is very similar to the JSPs found in Listings 4.3 and 4.5. The only difference is that instead of putting the result of the transformation into the output buffer through the `StreamResult` object, we are going to put it into another JSP file.

Listing 4.8 shows the source code for the JSP file that will transform the XML with the XSL stylesheet. The differences between it and Listing 4.3 are noted in boldface type. Save this file as `webapps/xmlbook/chapter4/CreateNewsLetter.jsp`.

LISTING 4.8 CreateNewsLetter.jsp; Outputting to File

```
<%@ page
  import="javax.xml.transform.*,
          javax.xml.transform.stream.*,
          java.io.*"
%>

<%
    String  ls_path = request.getServletPath();
            ls_path = ls_path.substring
                 (0,ls_path.indexOf("CreateNewsLetter.jsp")) ;

    String  ls_JSPResult   = application.getRealPath
            (ls_path + "NewsLetter.jsp");
    String  ls_xml  = application.getRealPath(ls_path + "NewsLetter.xml");
    String  ls_xsl  = application.getRealPath(ls_path + "NewsLetter.xsl");

    FileWriter l_write_file = new FileWriter(ls_JSPResult);

    StreamSource xml = new StreamSource(new File(ls_xml));
    StreamSource xsl = new StreamSource(new File(ls_xsl));

    StreamResult result = new StreamResult(l_write_file);

    TransformerFactory tfactory = TransformerFactory.newInstance();
    Transformer transformer = tfactory.newTransformer(xsl);
    transformer.transform(xml, result);

    l_write_file.close();
%>
<jsp:forward page="NewsLetter.jsp"/>
```

This file starts out the same way as the other JSP built in this chapter. We get the path to the JSP file itself and then use that path to create a string that states where each of the XML, XSL, and result JSP files resides. This assumes that all files will reside in the same directory. The difference this time is that we are creating an extra string for the result JSP file:

```
String  ls_JSPResult   = application.getRealPath(ls_path + "NewsLetter.jsp");
```

Next, we create a `FileWriter` object that will be used to write a character file, namely our result file called NewsLetter.jsp:

```
FileWriter l_write_file = new FileWriter(ls_JSPResult);
```

Then `StreamSource` objects are again used to hold the XML and XSL. The `TransformerFactory` object is used to create the transformer that will apply the stylesheet to our XML file and put the result into our `StreamResult` object, which is outputting to the JSP file.

Now that the transformation is complete, we need to close the JSP file that contains the results:

```
l_write_file.close();
```

And last but not least, we will perform a page forward so that we can see the results. Using the following JSP action element will redirect the server to a different file to send to the requesting Web browser:

```
<jsp:forward page="NewsLetter.jsp"/>
```

Normally, we will be using the JSP file named NewsLetter.jsp to view our newsletter. This file doesn't perform any transformations; rather, it is the result of that transformation. After running the CreateNewsLetter.jsp file, go and look at the source of NewsLetter.jsp. This is a flat HTML file that has the result of the transformation and looks like Figure 4.4 in a browser.

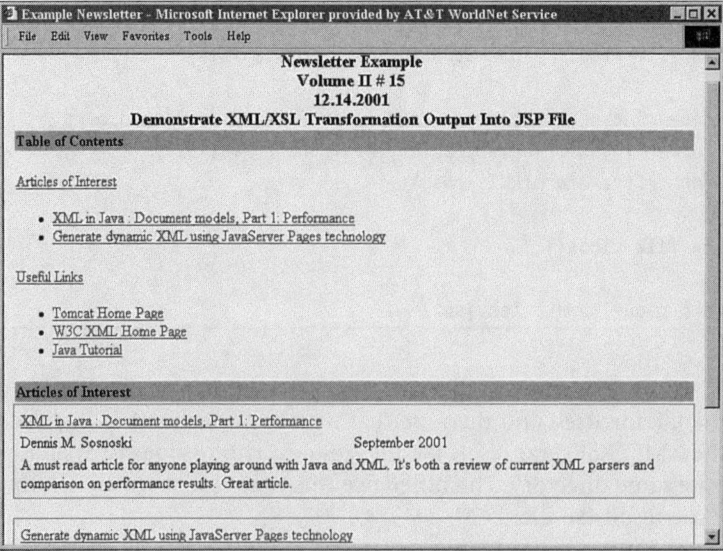

FIGURE 4.4 Result of running CreateNewsLetter.jsp.

Now you may ask why we output the result as a JSP, when this example only has HTML? Typically, there will be other processing that has to happen on the destination JSP. As an example, on the JSPBuzz newsletter where a similar process occurs, the final output page has special JSP include and footer files to deal with our standard site header and footers. The advantage of this system is that the newsletter only performs the processing that has to happen on every call, and the actual XML/XSL transformation only happens once every two weeks with the publication of the newsletter.

Lots of XML and XSL and Not Much JSP Now we need to spend some time discussing the bigger picture of what we just covered. You may wonder why we are spending so much time with what goes on within the XML and XSL. In fact, the JSP part of this chapter seems quite minimal. The fact is that JSP can be viewed as glue that holds everything together.

A typical JSP/XML page requires only a little bit of JSP code to hold everything together, and requires lots of XML and XSL to produce the results. So coverage of XML and XSL is as important as JSP, since in these examples the XML and XSL really constitute the majority of the work that needs to be performed. The true secret of JSP design is the knowledge of how to weave together the many elements before they are sent to a client. The JSP logic in most JSP applications is actually the smallest portion of your logic.

Most of the logic on any JSP is distributed to other processes such as the database, XSLT transformations, JavaBeans, Web services, and other external processes. JSPs are used just to hold it all together. The fact is that the JSP element is the simplest part of the learning equation. The first big step toward becoming a great JSP programmer is realizing that your skills are more about all the different technologies being brought together and being able to weave them to produce an output for the client. You might say that the best JSPs are the ones that contain the least JSP code and have the greatest modularity.

JSP and XML: An Overview

Where do we stand? Earlier in this chapter we examined JAXP and JSP. JAXP lets us easily access XML and apply XSL to the XML files. JAXP will also allow event-driven types of XML processing. However, we need to begin peeling away the layers of the processing that we performed in the examples.

First, we have XML, which is a language used to create documents. These documents are a mixture of data and the markup used to describe the stored data. Then JSPs are used as a scripting template for running code on the server side.

The problem is that a JSP and an XML document are not in the same place at the same time. In the code, it looks as though it's all in one place. However, the JSP is a process being executed in memory, while the XML file is stored in another location.

This means that JSP never directly works on an XML file. Rather, we must create a *representation* of the XML data and use it for the code to access. A document representation is a logical construct of the XML document, which resides in memory. We have several options in the types of representations we can use, but in the end, all are based on some model representation of the data.

JAXP is wonderful in that it permits us to easily transform an XML file with XSLT. In all of our earlier examples, the main effort was geared towards supporting these XSLT transformations to an XML file. However, what do we do when we need to modify the XML file? Or what happens when we want to build some output by using Java logic rather than an XSLT transformation? In these cases we need to scratch the surface of JAXP and look at what is happening underneath the JAXP polish.

In one example, the code actually obtained some specific data from the XML file and then appended it to the XSL document. However, the code didn't explain what was happening behind the scenes to get to the data. In this case, we were accessing other APIs more directly to examine the XML files. This leads us to our next discovery: when we dig deeper, we find a whole alphabet soup of APIs that we can use to accomplish different tasks with XML. You may wonder whether it's really necessary to know all the APIs. We only need to know about the major APIs, but each one brings a solution to a different problem. This means that we should examine the primary APIs that are available for our use.

Java XML/XSL APIs

This section covers the Java APIs that we haven't yet discussed. In later chapters, we will use several of these APIs to make life easier for XML users.

DOM (XML Document Object Model)

The DOM will be covered in detail in Chapter 5, "Using DOM." The DOM represents the standard W3C representation of an XML document. The advantage that the DOM offers is that it's a standard, and the same DOM methods that work within Java code will work within a Web browser using JavaScript, or within a C application. The DOM is very widely understood and has extensive support in the user community.

The biggest problem that the DOM has is that it creates large in-memory representations of XML documents. This makes it slow and often impractical when dealing with large XML documents because the entire XML document has to be parsed before processing can begin. This large footprint was a driving force in the creation of many of the other XML APIs because a definite need exists to handle larger documents.

The most common Java DOM parser is Xerces. Another frequently encountered DOM parser is Crimson. However, Xerces 2.0 is considered the replacement DOM parser for Crimson. As mentioned earlier, Xerces 1.4.3 forms the best baseline to use as a DOM parser for this book. This is due to the fact that Tomcat 4.0 uses version 1.4.3 of Xerces. Xerces 2.0 is still very much in development at the time of this book's writing.

The home page for the DOM specification is `http://www.w3.org/DOM/`.

SAX (XML Parser)

The Simple API for XML (SAX) is a tool for event-driven XML parsing. SAX is widely used, and it will be covered in detail in Chapter 6, "Programming SAX."

Briefly, SAX enables programmers to parse through an XML document by defining *events*. An event is a callback from the SAX parser when certain conditions are met while the SAX parser is reading sequentially through an XML document. Users can take any action they desire on the callback, from reading the data in the XML file to acting on the data. In the end, it's the programmer's decision whether to create the callbacks. Also, it is up to the programmer to determine what action to take upon receiving a callback from SAX. SAX is quickly becoming a lower level API. This means that while many programmers will use SAX, it will be indirectly through another tool or API such as JAXP. Using SAX directly is a lot of work, but it is fast and efficient. Many of the other APIs will use SAX as a quick way to read in an XML file. In fact, many XML tools will use SAX as the default XML parser because of speed considerations. However, you should always check your tool's documentation to be sure, as the default parser can vary from tool to tool.

The home page for SAX can be found at `http://www.saxproject.org/`.

JDOM (XML Document Representation)

JDOM is a method of creating a Java representation of an XML document.

JDOM has several classes that permit it to use SAX or the DOM to read XML data into its own Java representation. JDOM supports many of the commonly found features that the DOM supports. Unlike many of the other APIs discussed in this section, which use Java interfaces to define the Java representation, JDOM uses concrete classes to define the Java representation. This approach has the advantage of making JDOM simpler to use out of the box than either SAX or the DOM. It also gives JDOM the disadvantage of limited flexibility in implementation. This gives JDOM a different flavor than most of the other APIs. One result is that you won't see factory objects within JDOM.

JDOM makes heavy use of the Java `Collection` API, especially the `List` and `Map` Java interfaces, to define its representation. This means that a programmer can use standard Java structures to navigate around the JDOM representation.

JDOM doesn't offer XML parsing; instead, you must use SAX or read in a DOM representation. JDOM offers several classes that make it easy to use SAX or the DOM as a data source.

JDOM is listed as JSR-102 at the Java Community Process Web site.

The JDOM project can be found at `http://www.jdom.org/`.

dom4j (XML Document Representation)

dom4j is an open source project that has a set of Java APIs used for handling XML, XSLT, and XPath.

This API is similar to JDOM in the sense that it creates a Java-based XML document representation. However, it also differs as it uses Java interfaces. Using interfaces offers advantages (a flexible and expandable design) and disadvantages (you have several extra layers to learn) to the dom4j API. This API permits the use of Java `Collection` objects, which makes navigating the XML structure easy for an experienced Java programmer.

With dom4j it's easy to use the DOM standard while also providing an easy-to-use Java document representation. Also, dom4j is able to easily integrate with JAXP, as is SAX and DOM. An extremely nice feature of dom4j is the fact that it incorporates an event-based model for the processing of XML documents. This permits a dom4j parser to handle large XML files in sections rather than as a single document. This means that an entire XML document doesn't need to be in memory (a plus when dealing with a huge XML file). We will use this feature in Chapter 14, "Building a Web Service."

The dom4j project can be found at `http://dom4j.org/`.

JAXB (Parser and XML Document Representation)

Java Architecture for XML Binding (JAXB) is used to automate mapping between XML documents and Java. JAXB's unique angle is to use the XML schema (currently the DTD, and in future releases the XML schema) to build an optimized Java class to perform the parsing of the XML document representation. This permits JAXB to automatically use these customized Java classes to process an XML document faster than SAX, while giving a document representation of the XML data structure, which is similar to DOM. The drawback is that the resultant XML document representation is only functional against the XML schema it was generated to match. JAXB uses a binding language to permit the programmer to optimize the resulting XML document representation relative to the schema and design needs.

JAXB is a solution that works best when you need a document representation that requires fast content validation, and the XML document is stable in format.

At the time of writing, this is still a young project. However, it will most likely end up being one of the standard APIs to use in XML document handling.

The JAXB project can be found at `http://java.sun.com/xml/jaxb/`.

JAXB is listed as JSR-031 at the Java Community Process Web site.

Summary

This chapter gave you a first taste of using XML and JSP together. JAXP makes it easy to combine an XML file and an XSL stylesheet to produce new pages. However, XSLT is only part of the picture in using XML and JAXP. In exploring what else we can do, it quickly becomes apparent that there are many APIs available. Each API offers unique features, advantages, and disadvantages. While on paper we could discuss the merits of each, it's within the code that we will find out the benefits of the various tools. In the next chapters, you will learn how to programmatically examine, modify, and act upon an XML document in detail.

In working with JAXP, we discovered a few surprising facts about JSPs. The first is that the secret to using JSPs is more about weaving multiple technologies together than about using JSPs. The second is that solid JSP design is about modularity and a JSP is really just a glue or template to connect the modules together.

5

Using DOM

IN THIS CHAPTER

- What Is the DOM?
- Nodes and Tree Structure
- Programming with DOM
- JDOM, dom4j, and Deferred DOM

XML is a great way to represent data in certain situations. However, there needs to be a way in which to access this data and document structure in an intuitive way. Without this access, XML is virtually useless. The two most prevalent APIs for accessing this data are the DOM and SAX. DOM will be covered here, and SAX will be covered in Chapter 6.

This chapter will discuss the Document Object Model (DOM), which is an in-memory representation of a well-formed document. After a walk-through of the basics of DOM, we'll show examples of the various ways that the DOM structure can be traversed and manipulated. We'll move, delete, and copy parts of documents. After that, we'll expand an example of creating a document using DOM programmatically from scratch to import parts of other DOM documents. Toward the end of this chapter, we will demonstrate an example of traversal methods. Finally, we will present an introduction to ranges and their uses.

What Is the DOM?

The Document Object Model (DOM) is a garden-variety tree structure consisting of a hierarchy of nodes stored in memory. This structure is used to represent the content and model of an XML document. Once a document is parsed using DOM, that tree-like structure will exist in memory, and can then be processed in various ways.

The DOM is a standard issued by the W3C, just like the XML specification. This specification is unrelated to any one programming language, and therefore isn't designed for use with Java specifically. Instead, various bindings of the DOM specification exist for the various programming languages that implement it.

The DOM binding for Java provides APIs that facilitate the manipulation of nodes. Through these manipulations, nodes may be created, modified, deleted, selected, or even removed from one document and added to another.

In this chapter, DOM will be used specifically with XML documents. However, DOM can represent other types of documents, such as HTML.

Strengths of DOM

DOM is the most prevalently used API for processing XML documents. The reasons for this include the following:

- The tree structure created by DOM is easy to use once you understand its hierarchy and structure.
- The entire content of any document is always available. This means that repeated access and movement through the document is relatively simple.
- The selection of nodes, located anywhere within the document structure, is simple.
- Once you have established an understanding of DOM in one language, using it in another language is very easy. The methods and structure are the same within *any* language.
- In the Java language binding, all node types are the same. This enables each node to be accessed and coded in the same manner, with only minor exceptions.

Weaknesses of DOM

Although DOM has many advantages, many times it isn't the perfect choice for processing XML documents. Reasons for this include the following:

- DOM requires memory proportional to the size and complexity of the XML document being parsed. This is because the entire document is available in memory during processing.
- Before an XML document is usable through the DOM, the entire document must be parsed and added to the DOM model in memory.
- Some ways in which DOM is implemented in Java can be confusing to a Java programmer. This is because DOM's specification is language neutral. As a result, some Java language features, such as method overloading, are not utilized. This is because other programming languages that implement DOM do not have this feature.

Nodes and Tree Structure

A tree structure in memory is the foundation of DOM. The DOM tree is composed of nodes, each of which represents a part of the parsed XML document. The arrangement and types of the nodes form the tree structure that represents a parsed document.

Nodes are represented through the `org.w3c.dom.Node` interface. Other interfaces are extended from this interface to more specifically represent the various types of nodes required to describe an XML document. An example of this is the `org.w3c.dom.Element` interface extending the node implementation. This allows methods to be defined that are more relevant to each specific type of node.

For each component of an XML document, a node of the correct type is created and properly placed in the hierarchy in memory. The most commonly recognized node is one of type `Element`. Descending from each `Element` node are all the nodes that combine to make up the contents of that element. If the element only contains text data, there will only be a single child `Text` node descending from the `Element` node.

By using the functionality available within the base `Node` interface, all nodes can be treated in a similar way. Also, methods such as `getChildNodes()` and `getParentNode()`, which are part of the `Node` interface, make navigation around the DOM tree easy.

Each different node type also contains methods that are directly relevant to that specific node type. For example, the `Attr` (attribute) node contains methods relevant only to attributes, such as `getOwnerElement()`.

The Document Node

When a document is parsed, the entire document is available to be processed through a `Document` node. Descending from this node are the contents of the entire document represented as nodes. This includes one `Element` node that directly descends from the `Document` node and represents the root element of the XML document structure. If the document has a DTD associated with it then it will also have a single `DocumentType` node that represents the `DOCTYPE` component. Also, if processing instructions or comments exist at this level, they too will be modeled as either a `ProcessingInstruction` or `Comment` node, respectively, descending directly from the `Document` node.

If an image of an XML document comes to mind, you may be wondering what happened to the document declaration. It tells the version number and encoding, among other things. Remember, this is always the first line of an XML document. Shouldn't this node be one that directly descends from the `Document` node?

It would seem logical that the document declaration would be represented as a node descending from the Document node and would contain Attribute nodes for each of the properties therein. However, this is not the case.

The document declaration is not a processing instruction, and as such, the information contained therein should not be available outside the parser. (At least, this is the logic that the W3C used.) On some levels this makes sense. However, to anyone who has ever had to parse, process, and serialize an XML document, this is a big problem. The encoding attribute value is very important when the document needs to be serialized or processed in some manner specific to the correct encoding.

Currently, the W3C is working on the DOM Level 3 specification, which resolves these issues. The solution is the creation of methods such as getEncoding() and getVersion() invoked on the Document node. While this does not conform to the strict node and tree structure, it will enable access to this vital information when it is implemented.

Many other new methods have been created in the new DOM Level 3 specification besides those just mentioned. At the time of this writing, this specification hasn't been ratified yet, and as such, these methods are not yet implemented in the various language bindings. They will be available soon enough, so keep your eyes open.

In the XML document found in Listing 5.1 there are elements, text data, attributes, processing instructions, and entity references. Each of these components will become a single node, descending from the appropriate parent. Reproduce this file and save it as webapps\xmlbook\chapter5\House.xml. This XML document will be used throughout this chapter for examples.

LISTING 5.1 House.xml

```
<?xml version="1.0" encoding="UTF-8"?>
<!DOCTYPE HOUSE [
<!ENTITY newroom "project room">
]>
<HOUSE>
    <UPSTAIRS sqfeet="200">
        <ROOM>bedroom</ROOM>
    </UPSTAIRS>
    <?color blue?>
    <DOWNSTAIRS sqfeet="900">
        <ROOM>bathroom</ROOM>
        <ROOM>kitchen</ROOM>
        <ROOM>living <![CDATA[ room ]]></ROOM>
        <ROOM>&newroom;</ROOM>
    </DOWNSTAIRS>
</HOUSE>
```

Figure 5.1 shows a representation of the DOM tree structure created in Listing 5.1.

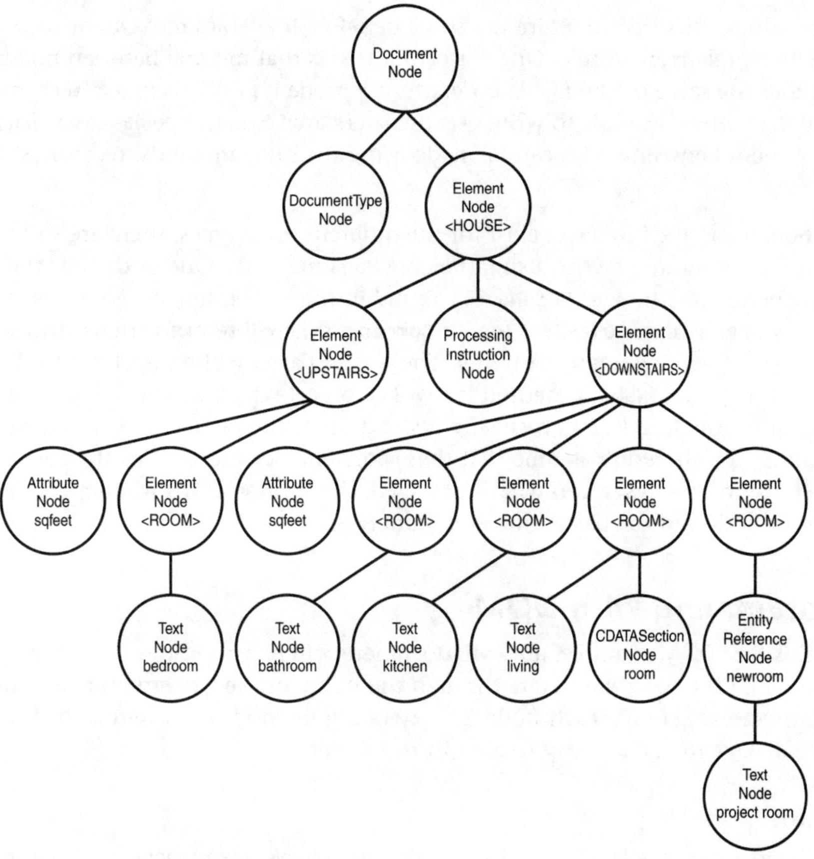

FIGURE 5.1 DOM representation of House.xml.

Note that the tree structure is followed in every sense. `Text` nodes are children of `Element` nodes when an element has text content. `Element` nodes are children of `Element` nodes when elements are nested. Instead of there being methods invoked on an `Element` node that return the contents found therein, a `Text` node contains that text and descends from it. This is true of all other components found within elements, such as `CDATA` sections, entity references, processing instructions, and comments.

Notice also in Figure 5.1 that the entity reference is descended from the element in which it is contained. This makes sense considering that text data of an element is also descended from its element. However, there is another node descending from the entity reference node. This is a text node that contains the entity character data. Again, the tree structure is enforced in every sense.

This rather strict tree structure has some benefits. It enables movement within the tree to be relatively simple. One reason for this is that moving between nodes requires the same method calls no matter the node types. This makes recursive tree-walking methods simple to write because there aren't many special cases. Each movement between nodes can be made using the same methods, regardless of node types.

Although specific interfaces exist for the different node types, there are still some things to be aware of when using the core `Node` methods. One of these is the seemingly benign method `getNodeName()` found in the `Node` interface. For nodes whose type is one of `Text`, `CDATASection`, or `Comment`, this will return various strings that are garbage, depending upon the parser. The Xerces parser will return the literal `#text` when the `getNodeName()` method is invoked on a `Text` node. On the other hand, it will return the target of a processing instruction or the tag name of an element. The point is, you shouldn't assume that these convenience methods of the core `Node` interface will always return what's expected. What they return will depend on the type of node and the parser implementation being used.

Programming with DOM

In this first DOM example, an XML document will be parsed into a DOM representation. Then the code will iterate through the nodes of the tree structure and output information regarding each node. This iterating method will be embedded within the JSP page to make it easy to alter in this chapter.

NOTE

Our examples serialize DOMs to the output. These examples are only intended to demonstrate the workings of DOM in Java. If you need a production-grade serializer, check out the `XMLSerializer` class found in the Xerces parser.

The complete JSP page is shown in Listing 5.2 and should be saved as `webapps\xmlbook\chapter5\DOMExample.jsp`.

LISTING 5.2 DOMExample.jsp

```
<%@ page
  import="org.w3c.dom.*,
          org.apache.xerces.parsers.DOMParser"
%>
<html>
```

LISTING 5.2 Continued

```
<head><title>DOM Parser Example</title></head>
<body>
<%
try{
    DOMParser parser = new DOMParser();

    String  path = request.getServletPath();
    path = path.substring(0,path.indexOf("DOMExample.jsp"));
    String  xml  = application.getRealPath(path + "House.xml");

    parser.parse(xml);
    Document doc = parser.getDocument();

   listNodes(doc.getChildNodes(), out, "");
}
catch (Exception e){
    out.print("<br/><br/><font color=\"red\">There was an error<BR>");
    out.print (e.toString() + "</font>");
}
%>
</body>
</html>
    <%!
    private void listNodes(NodeList nlist, JspWriter out, String spacer)
    throws Exception{
        try{
            for(int i = 0; i < nlist.getLength(); i++){
                out.print(spacer + "[");
                out.print(" " + nlist.item(i).getNodeName());
                out.print(" type:" + nlist.item(i).getNodeType());
                out.print("<font color=\"green\"> "
                   + nlist.item(i).getNodeValue() + "</font> ");
                out.print("]<BR>");
                if(nlist.item(i).getChildNodes().getLength() > 0)
                    listNodes(nlist.item(i).getChildNodes(), out,
                        spacer + "      ");
                //if the node is of type Element then create closing string
                if(nlist.item(i).getNodeType() == 1)
                   out.print(spacer + "[/ " + nlist.item(i).getNodeName()
                      + "]<BR>");
```

LISTING 5.2 Continued

```
            }
        }
        catch(Exception e){out.print( "<font color=\"red\">" +
            e.toString() + "</font>");}
    }
    %>
```

The JSP page begins with the import statements necessary for our code and then some static HTML to create a page title. Next, a `try` block is used to catch any and all `Exceptions` created.

The only DOM-specific exception that can be thrown while using the DOM methods in these examples is `DOMException`. When an operation is impossible to perform for logical reasons or due to loss of data, this exception will be thrown. In general, however, DOM methods return specific error values in ordinary processing situations, such as `NullPointerException` when trying to process a node that doesn't exist.

```
<%@ page
  import="org.w3c.dom.*,
          org.apache.xerces.parsers.DOMParser"
%>
<html>
<head><title>DOM Parser Example</title></head>
<body>
<%
try{
```

Next, a `DOMParser` instance is created and into it are passed the path and filename of the XML document to be parsed. This instance will use the Xerces parser by providing the Xerces class. If you haven't yet placed the Xerces.jar file in the `lib` directory found in the root of the Tomcat installation, place it there now and restart the server.

```
    DOMParser parser = new DOMParser();

    String  path = request.getServletPath();
    path = path.substring(0,path.indexOf("DOMExample.jsp"));
    String  xml  = application.getRealPath(path + "House.xml");
```

After the parsing is complete, the code obtains a reference to the `Document` node through the `getDocument()` method invoked on the parser. We now have access to the DOM for this XML file.

It may seem as though it would be better for the parser to return the DOM reference upon the invocation of the parse() method. However, this returns void so that it can be consistent when parsing with SAX, as described in the next chapter. This means that the code should explicitly get the Document node from the parser with the getDocument() method, as shown here:

```
parser.parse(xml);
Document doc = parser.getDocument();
```

With access to the DOM model, we take the children of the Document node and pass them into our method. This will begin the traversal of the tree, and the outputting of the information contained in each processed node.

The method being used is called listNodes() and is shown in Listing 5.2. This method will indent the output strings to demonstrate the current depth of the nodes being processed in the DOM hierarchy. Due to this, the parameters used are a NodeList, the out that is of type javax.servlet.jsp.JspWriter, and the String that will be used to determine the indentation of those Nodes passed in.

After each of the Nodes found in the NodeList argument is processed, listNodes() is again invoked on the children of the node that was just processed. The listNodes() method recursively walks the DOM tree and enables the output of properly indented strings for each node.

This method begins by performing some actions within a try block. This permits the catching and handling of any exceptions that may occur. However, this chapter only briefly discusses exceptions with regards to the DOM. The catch block of the try block outputs the Exception in string format and colors it red.

The next step is to use a for loop to step through the NodeList. The NodeList is a creation of the W3C specification, and as such does not take advantage of the language-specific implementations for collections. Due to this, iterators cannot be used on NodeLists. Instead, the methods item() and getLength() must be used to step through the NodeList.

Once each node has been accessed, the code outputs the results of getNodeName(), getNodeType(), and getNodeValue(). These return a String, a short, and a String, respectively. What should the value of an Element node be? Or what about the name of a Text node? In the case of the value of an Element node, a null is returned due to its having no value. The String returned when invoking the getNodeName() method on a Text node is the unexpected string literal of #text mentioned earlier.

After the preceding output and some HTML markup, we continue by invoking the getChildNodes() method on the node being processed. This will return the NodeList that contains all the children of this node. If there are child nodes as determined by getLength() then code will take the NodeList and re-call listNodes() on them. In this case, however, whitespace is going to be added to the `spaces` parameter to create a deeper indention than the parent node has.

Next, a string emulating a closing tag will be output to show that the descendants of an `Element` node have all been processed. By obtaining the node type through `getNodeType()` we can determine whether it's an `Element` node, and thus output a closing string that emulates the closing tag of an XML document.

Now it's time to see the output of DOMExample.jsp and House.xml. It will have the same structure as Figure 5.1, but won't be as visually oriented, as Figure 5.2 shows.

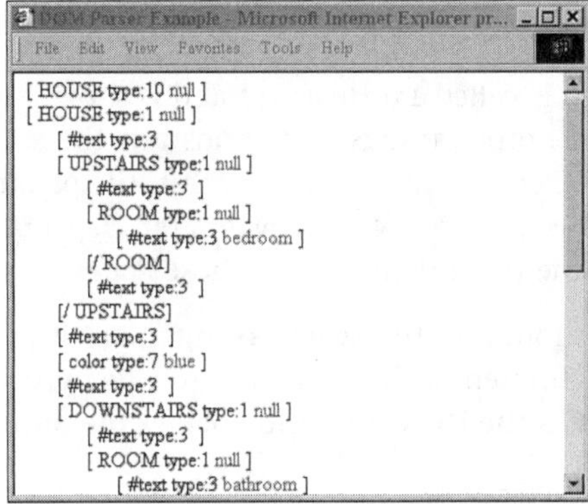

FIGURE 5.2 Output of DOMExample.jsp and House.xml.

The first thing to examine is the difference between the output shown in Figures 5.1 and 5.2. Notice how in Figure 5.2 there are a number of additional `Text` nodes that have no string value. These extra `Text` nodes are a result of the whitespace found between elements. The parser has no way of knowing whether whitespace is text data or just blank space caused by indentations and such. Due to this, the parser will return each of these blocks of space as a `Text` node.

Attributes

We're missing a very large and important part of XML: The attributes of the XML document are nowhere to be seen. This seems strange considering the `Attr` interface is based on the `Node` interface, just like all the other types of nodes. But attribute nodes don't show up when you're invoking the `getChildNodes()` of any type of nodes, including `Element` nodes.

Attribute nodes don't follow the strict tree structure that the rest of DOM follows. They are not considered children of the element in which they are found. Instead, it is almost as if they are at the same level as the `Element` node. The relationship isn't clear. For this reason, attributes are only accessible from their parent `Element` node with the `getAttributes()`, `getAttribute()`, and `getAttributeNode()` methods. These methods return a `NamedNodeMap`, a `String` with the value of the attribute, and an `Attr` node, respectively.

A `NamedNodeMap` is a collection of nodes unrelated to `NodeList`. The difference between these two sets of nodes has to do with the differences between child elements and attributes. The order in which attributes are found within an element makes no difference, whereas order is important with element siblings. Another difference between these two collections of nodes has to do with the distinctness of attributes. There can never be two attributes with the same name within an element. However, two child elements that have the same name can exist. As a result, `NodeLists` maintain order among selected `Nodes` and can have `Nodes` that have all the same properties, while `NamedNodeMaps` do not.

We will now alter the code for the `listNodes` method from Listing 5.2 so that it will output attributes. The new JSP is shown in Listing 5.3. (Additions and changes from Listing 5.2 are noted in boldface.) Save this new file as `webapps\xmlbook\chapter5\DOMExampleAttr.jsp`.

LISTING 5.3 DOMExampleAttr.jsp

```
<%@ page
  import="org.w3c.dom.*,
          org.apache.xerces.parsers.DOMParser"
%>
<html>
<head><title>DOM Parser Example With Attributes</title></head>
<body>
<%
try{
    DOMParser parser = new DOMParser();

    String  path = request.getServletPath();
    path = path.substring(0,path.indexOf("DOMExampleAttr.jsp"));
    String  xml  = application.getRealPath(path + "House.xml");

    parser.parse(xml);
    Document doc = parser.getDocument();

    listNodes(doc.getChildNodes(), out, "");
}
catch (Exception e){
```

LISTING 5.3 Continued

```
    out.print("<br/><br/><font color=\"red\">There was an error<BR>");
    out.print (e.toString() + "</font>");
}
%>
</body>
</html>
    <%!
    private void listNodes(NodeList nlist, JspWriter out, String spacer)
    throws Exception{
        try{
            for(int i = 0; i < nlist.getLength(); i++){
                out.print(spacer + "[");
                out.print(" " + nlist.item(i).getNodeName());
                out.print(" type:" + nlist.item(i).getNodeType());
                out.print("<font color=\"green\"> "
                   + nlist.item(i).getNodeValue() + "</font> ");
                if(nlist.item(i).hasAttributes()){
                    NamedNodeMap attributes = nlist.item(i).getAttributes();
                    for(int j = 0; j < attributes.getLength(); j++){
                        out.print(" {");
                        out.print(" name:" + attributes.item(j).getNodeName());
                        out.print(" value:" + attributes.item(j).getNodeValue());
                        out.print(" }");
                    }
                }
               out.print("]<BR>");
               if(nlist.item(i).getChildNodes().getLength() > 0)
                   listNodes(nlist.item(i).getChildNodes(), out,
                       spacer + "      ");
               //if the node is of type Element then create closing string
               if(nlist.item(i).getNodeType() == 1)
                  out.print(spacer + "[/ " + nlist.item(i).getNodeName()
                      + "]<BR>");
            }
        }
        catch(Exception e){out.print( "<font color=\"red\">" +
            e.toString() + "</font>");}
    }
    %>
```

The modified code in Listing 5.3 checks to see whether the node being processed has attributes with the appropriately named method `hasAttributes()`. If it does, the code obtains `NamedNodeMap` by invoking the `getAttributes()` method. Once these attribute nodes are obtained, the `for` loop iterates through them and outputs their name and value. The `getNodeName()` and `getNodeValue()` methods are from the `Node` interface. The `Attr`-specific methods not used in this example that return the same results are named `getName()` and `getValue()`. To use the `Attr`-specific methods, the nodes would have to be cast to `Attr`, because a `NamedNodeMap` is a collection of `Nodes`, not `Attrs`. This example uses the more generic methods of the `Node` interface.

Now that attributes have been taken care of, let's look at the new output, shown in Figure 5.3. The attributes from the House.xml document are output just where they should be.

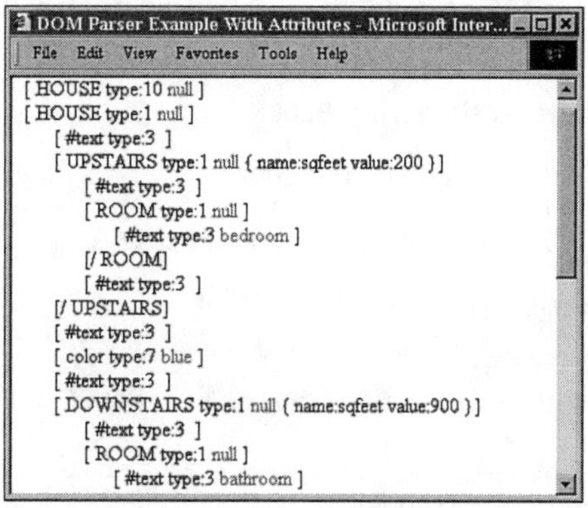

FIGURE 5.3 Output from addition of attribute-handling code.

Namespaces

Programmatically accessing any other part of an XML document is the same as in the previous examples. For instance, you can obtain namespace information through the use of the following methods found in the `Node` interface:

- `getNamespaceURI()`—returns the namespace in which the element resides. This only returns a `String` when the node is of type `Element` and the namespace has been declared. This means that either the default namespace or the namespace in which this element resides has been declared. Otherwise, this method returns `null`. In essence, if the namespace attribute that describes the element is not present, this will return `null`; otherwise, expect the value of the namespace attribute.

- getLocalName()—returns the Element name as a String with the namespace prefix removed. When no namespace is associated with an element, it returns the same String as getNodeName().
- getPrefix()—returns the namespace prefix found on an Element name. The method returns null when no prefix exists.

For example, let's look at namespaces using the following small XML document:

```
<?xml version="1.0" encoding="UTF-8"?>
    <BLOCK xmlns="http://www.default.com" xmlns:xo="http://www.xo.com">
        <xo:HOUSE/>
   </BLOCK>
```

When this is invoked on the Element node representing the BLOCK element, the following occur:

- getNodeName() returns the string BLOCK
- getLocalName() returns the string BLOCK
- getNamespaceURI() returns http://www.default.com
- getPrefix() returns null

However, when these methods are used on the <xo:HOUSE/> Element node, they return the following:

- getNodeName() returns xo:HOUSE
- getLocalName() returns HOUSE
- getNamespaceURI() returns http://www.xo.com
- getPrefix() returns xo

If the namespace declarations are removed

```
<?xml version="1.0" encoding="UTF-8"?>
    <BLOCK>
        <xo:HOUSE/>
   </BLOCK>
```

the preceding method results would be the same except for getNamespaceURI(), which would return null in both cases.

Now that we've discussed the behavior of these methods on `Element` nodes, let's touch on `Attr` (attribute) nodes. The return values of the methods are almost the same. The only difference is that even when a default namespace has been declared, `getNamespaceURI()` will not return that namespace when invoked on an attribute unless the attribute has been explicitly placed in that namespace (that is, it has a prefix). If an attribute has not been explicitly associated with a namespace, it's not considered part of that namespace even if a default namespace has been declared, as in the following:

```
xmlns="http://www.default.com"
```

The results of namespace methods differ depending on whether they are invoked on attribute nodes or `Element` nodes. Don't assume the same behaviors.

Removing a Node

Now that you've gotten the idea behind the methods available through the DOM implementation, let's modify a document. Continuing with the previous example, let's remove the `UPSTAIRS` `Element` node and child nodes.

We will do this in the next example, shown in Listing 5.4, with the addition of only four lines of code. (Additions from Listing 5.3 are noted in boldface type.) Save this file as `webapps/xmlbook/chapter5/DOMExampleRemove.jsp`.

LISTING 5.4 DOMExampleRemove.jsp with Additional Node Selection

```
<%@ page
  import="org.w3c.dom.*,
          org.apache.xerces.parsers.DOMParser"
%>
<html>
<head><title>Example Removing an Element with DOM Parser</title></head>
<body>
<%
try{
    DOMParser parser = new DOMParser();

    String  path = request.getServletPath();
    path = path.substring(0,path.indexOf("DOMExampleRemove.jsp"));
    String  xml  = application.getRealPath(path + "House.xml");

    parser.parse(xml);
    Document doc = parser.getDocument();
    NodeList list = doc.getElementsByTagName("DOWNSTAIRS");
```

LISTING 5.4 Continued

```
    Node downstairs = list.item(0);
    downstairs.getParentNode().removeChild(downstairs);

    listNodes(doc.getChildNodes(), out, "");
}
catch (Exception e){
    out.print("<br/><br/><font color=\"red\">There was an error<BR>");
    out.print (e.toString() + "</font>");
}
%>
</body>
</html>
    <%!
    private void listNodes(NodeList nlist, JspWriter out, String spacer)
    throws Exception{
        try{
            for(int i = 0; i < nlist.getLength(); i++){
                out.print(spacer + "[");
                out.print(" " + nlist.item(i).getNodeName());
                out.print(" type:" + nlist.item(i).getNodeType());
                out.print("<font color=\"green\"> "
                   + nlist.item(i).getNodeValue() + "</font> ");
            if(nlist.item(i).hasAttributes()){
                NamedNodeMap attributes = nlist.item(i).getAttributes();
                for(int j = 0; j < attributes.getLength(); j++){
                    out.print(" {");
                    out.print(" name:" + attributes.item(j).getNodeName());
                    out.print(" value:" + attributes.item(j).getNodeValue());
                    out.print(" }");
                }
            }

               out.print("]<BR>");
               if(nlist.item(i).getChildNodes().getLength() > 0)
                   listNodes(nlist.item(i).getChildNodes(), out,
                       spacer + "      ");
               //if the node is of type Element then create closing string
               if(nlist.item(i).getNodeType() == 1)
                  out.print(spacer + "[/ " + nlist.item(i).getNodeName()
                      + "]<BR>");
            }
```

LISTING 5.4 Continued

```
    }
    catch(Exception e){out.print( "<font color=\"red\">" +
        e.toString() + "</font>");}
}
%>
```

Any node can be removed using the `removeChild()` method. However, this method requires a reference of the node to be removed. This requires some programmatic traversal of the tree.

This example begins by obtaining a `NodeList` of all elements with the tag name `DOWNSTAIRS`, as shown in the boldface code in Listing 5.4. The XML document House.xml from Listing 5.1 only has one of these elements. You can obtain the reference to this particular `Node` by selecting the first `item` (index 0) in the `NodeList` returned from the `getElementsByTagName()` method.

Once you've obtained this reference, it is very simple to remove this node. All that you must do is invoke the method `removeChild()` on the parent node of the node being removed. A convenient method found in the base `Node` interface is `getParentNode()`. This method permits simple access to the parent node of any node that can be referenced. You can use this method to access the parent node and thus invoke the `removeNode()` method on the parent node of the node that is being removed, as in the last of the boldface lines in Listing 5.4.

The results are shown in Figure 5.4. Note that when this `DOWNSTAIRS` node is removed, all child nodes are also removed. This makes perfect sense and demonstrates the ease with which nodes can be removed using DOM.

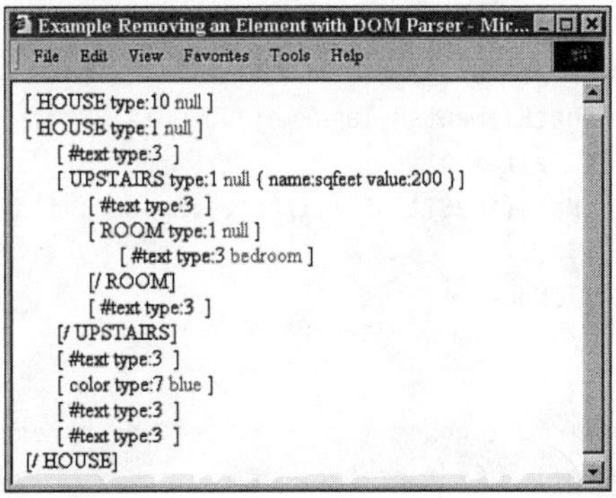

```
Example Removing an Element with DOM Parser - Mic...
File Edit View Favorites Tools Help
[ HOUSE type:10 null ]
[ HOUSE type:1 null ]
    [ #text type:3 ]
    [ UPSTAIRS type:1 null ( name:sqfeet value:200 ) ]
        [ #text type:3 ]
        [ ROOM type:1 null ]
            [ #text type:3 bedroom ]
        [/ ROOM]
        [ #text type:3 ]
    [/ UPSTAIRS]
    [ #text type:3 ]
    [ color type:7 blue ]
    [ #text type:3 ]
    [ #text type:3 ]
[/ HOUSE]
```

FIGURE 5.4 Results of removing the `DOWNSTAIRS` element subtree.

Moving Nodes

Now that we've seen how easy it is to remove nodes, let's move one around. In the following example, the DOWNSTAIRS element will be removed and placed as a child descending from the UPSTAIRS element.

The DOM provides us with a single method that will both remove a node and append it. This method is called appendChild() and takes as a parameter a reference to the Node being repositioned.

The differences between the previous JSP, which removes a node, and this listing appear as boldface text. Save this altered file, shown in Listing 5.5, as webapps/xmlbook/chapter5/DOMExampleAppend.jsp.

LISTING 5.5 DOMExampleAppend.jsp

```
<%@ page
  import="org.w3c.dom.*,
          org.apache.xerces.parsers.DOMParser"
%>
<html>
<head><title>Example Appending Node with DOM Parser</title></head>
<body>
<%
try{
    DOMParser parser = new DOMParser();

    String  path = request.getServletPath();
    path = path.substring(0,path.indexOf("DOMExampleAppend.jsp"));
    String  xml  = application.getRealPath(path + "House.xml");

    parser.parse(xml);
    Document doc = parser.getDocument();
    NodeList list = doc.getElementsByTagName("DOWNSTAIRS");
    Node downstairs = list.item(0);
    doc.getElementsByTagName("UPSTAIRS").item(0).appendChild(downstairs);

    listNodes(doc.getChildNodes(), out, "");
}
catch (Exception e){
    out.print("<br/><br/><font color=\"red\">There was an error<BR>");
    out.print (e.toString() + "</font>");
}
%>
```

LISTING 5.5 Continued

```
</body>
</html>
    <%!
    private void listNodes(NodeList nlist, JspWriter out, String spacer)
    throws Exception{
        try{
            for(int i = 0; i < nlist.getLength(); i++){
                out.print(spacer + "[");
                out.print(" " + nlist.item(i).getNodeName());
                out.print(" type:" + nlist.item(i).getNodeType());
                out.print("<font color=\"green\"> "
                    + nlist.item(i).getNodeValue() + "</font> ");
            if(nlist.item(i).hasAttributes()){
                NamedNodeMap attributes = nlist.item(i).getAttributes();
                for(int j = 0; j < attributes.getLength(); j++){
                    out.print(" {");
                    out.print(" name:" + attributes.item(j).getNodeName());
                    out.print(" value:" + attributes.item(j).getNodeValue());
                    out.print(" }");
                }
            }
               out.print("]<BR>");
               if(nlist.item(i).getChildNodes().getLength() > 0)
                   listNodes(nlist.item(i).getChildNodes(), out,
                       spacer + "      ");
               //if the node is of type Element then create closing string
               if(nlist.item(i).getNodeType() == 1)
                  out.print(spacer + "[/ " + nlist.item(i).getNodeName()
                      + "]<BR>");
           }
       }
       catch(Exception e){out.print( "<font color=\"red\">" +
           e.toString() + "</font>");}
   }
   %>
```

The second new line of code in this listing begins with the `Document` node variable named `doc`, and grabs all the `Element` nodes whose tag name is `UPSTAIRS`.

House.xml only has one of these nodes; therefore, it's obtained by indexing the first item (index 0) of the `NodeList` returned from `getElementsByTagName()`. Once a reference to the UPSTAIRS Element node is obtained, the node referenced by the downstairs variable can be appended through the invocation of the appendChild() method.

The appendChild() method will first check to see whether the node referenced by the downstairs variable already exists in the tree to which it is being appended. This information is obtained by comparing the Document node that they both descend from. If they are both Nodes from the same Document, this node and the subtree descending from it will be removed. At this point, this subtree will be appended as the last child of the Element node on which the appendChild() method is invoked.

This method can be very helpful if an XML document needs to be programmatically altered before using a stylesheet or some other processing occurs.

The results of our alteration to Listing 5.5 are shown in Figure 5.5. Notice that the DOWNSTAIRS element (along with all its contents) was removed as a sibling of UPSTAIRS and then added as the last child of the UPSTAIRS element.

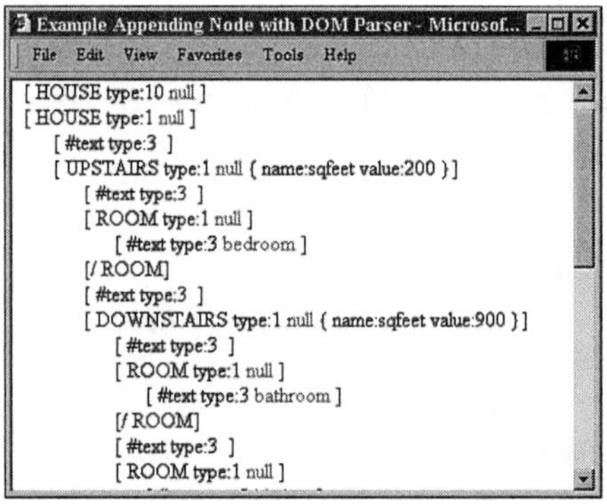

FIGURE 5.5 Results of appending the DOWNSTAIRS element.

Copying and Appending Nodes

What is required to copy an existing node and its descendants and then append them somewhere else in the same XML document? For example, perhaps we would like to still append the UPSTAIRS node in the same place, but without removing it from its original location.

In essence, the node must be copied, or cloned, and then appended somewhere else. Listing 5.6 does this.(Differences from the previous listing are noted in boldface type.) Save this file as webapps/xmlbook/chapter5/DOMExampleClone.jsp.

LISTING 5.6 DOMExampleClone.jsp; Copy and Append Node

```
<%@ page
  import="org.w3c.dom.*,
        org.apache.xerces.parsers.DOMParser"
%>
<html>
<head><title>Example Cloning and Appending Node with DOM Parser</title></head>
<body>
<%
try{
    DOMParser parser = new DOMParser();

    String  path = request.getServletPath();
    path = path.substring(0,path.indexOf("DOMExampleClone.jsp"));
    String  xml  = application.getRealPath(path + "House.xml");

    parser.parse(xml);
    Document doc = parser.getDocument();
    NodeList list = doc.getElementsByTagName("DOWNSTAIRS");
    Node downstairs = list.item(0);
    Node cloneDownstairs = downstairs.cloneNode(false);
    doc.getElementsByTagName("UPSTAIRS").item(0).appendChild(cloneDownstairs);

    listNodes(doc.getChildNodes(), out, "");
}
catch (Exception e){
    out.print("<br/><br/><font color=\"red\">There was an error<BR>");
    out.print (e.toString() + "</font>");
}
%>
</body>
</html>
    <%!
    private void listNodes(NodeList nlist, JspWriter out, String spacer)
    throws Exception{
        try{
            for(int i = 0; i < nlist.getLength(); i++){
                out.print(spacer + "[");
                out.print(" " + nlist.item(i).getNodeName());
                out.print(" type:" + nlist.item(i).getNodeType());
                out.print("<font color=\"green\"> "
                   + nlist.item(i).getNodeValue() + "</font> ");
```

LISTING 5.6 Continued

```
            if(nlist.item(i).hasAttributes()){
                NamedNodeMap attributes = nlist.item(i).getAttributes();
                for(int j = 0; j < attributes.getLength(); j++){
                    out.print(" {");
                    out.print(" name:" + attributes.item(j).getNodeName());
                    out.print(" value:" + attributes.item(j).getNodeValue());
                    out.print(" }");
                }
            }
               out.print("]<BR>");
               if(nlist.item(i).getChildNodes().getLength() > 0)
                   listNodes(nlist.item(i).getChildNodes(), out,
                       spacer + "      ");
               //if the node is of type Element then create closing string
               if(nlist.item(i).getNodeType() == 1)
                  out.print(spacer + "[/ " + nlist.item(i).getNodeName()
                      + "]<BR>");
           }
       }
       catch(Exception e){out.print( "<font color=\"red\">" +
           e.toString() + "</font>");}
   }
   %>
```

The new code, shown in boldface type, begins by creating a copy of the `DOWNSTAIRS` `Element` node with the `cloneNode()` method. The `boolean` parameter of this method determines whether the copy will include all the node's children or not. In our example, we are not including the entire subtree descending from the `DOWNSTAIRS` element. However, this shallow copy will include all attributes if the node being copied is of type `Element`.

The copy of the `DOWNSTAIRS` element and its children is then appended in the same manner as demonstrated in the previous example.

NOTE

Once a node is cloned using the `cloneNode()` method, that copy is editable regardless of whether or not the original document was read-only. Any changes to the copy will not affect the original document. They are completely unrelated and separate nodes.

The output is shown in Figure 5.6. Notice that the `DOWNSTAIRS` element and attributes were indeed copied and appended as the last child of the `UPSTAIRS` element. Also, notice that the original `DOWNSTAIRS` element, the sibling of the `UPSTAIRS` element, is still present.

```
Example Cloning and Appending Node with DOM Pars...
File Edit View Favorites Tools Help
[ HOUSE type:10 null ]
[ HOUSE type:1 null ]
  [ #text type:3 ]
  [ UPSTAIRS type:1 null { name:sqfeet value:200 }]
    [ #text type:3 ]
    [ ROOM type:1 null ]
      [ #text type:3 bedroom ]
    [/ ROOM]
    [ #text type:3 ]
    [ DOWNSTAIRS type:1 null { name:sqfeet value:900 }]
    [/ DOWNSTAIRS]
  [/ UPSTAIRS]
  [ #text type:3 ]
  [ color type:7 blue ]
  [ #text type:3 ]
  [ DOWNSTAIRS type:1 null { name:sqfeet value:900 }]
    [ #text type:3 ]
    [ ROOM type:1 null ]
      [ #text type:3 bathroom ]
    [/ ROOM]
```

FIGURE 5.6 Cloning and appending nodes.

Programmatically Creating an XML Document

Next, we will create an XML document in its entirety programmatically. This JSP page, shown in Listing 5.7, is almost the same as the one in Listing 5.6. The difference is the additional code for the programmatic creation of a DOM document. This code is noted in boldface type. The complete JSP page should be saved as `webapps\xmlbook\chapter5\DOMExampleProgram.jsp`.

LISTING 5.7 Complete JSP Page with Code to Create a DOM Document

```
<%@ page
  import="org.w3c.dom.*,
          org.apache.xerces.parsers.DOMParser"
%>
<html>
<head><title>Programmatically Using DOM to Create Document</title></head>
<body>
<%
try{

    //create new XML Document programmatically
```

LISTING 5.7 Continued

```
    DOMImplementation domImpl = new org.apache.xerces.dom.DOMImplementationImpl();
    Document newdoc = domImpl.createDocument(null, "TREEROOT", null);
    Element root = newdoc.getDocumentElement();
    Element firstEl = newdoc.createElement("FIRSTELEMENT");
    root.appendChild(firstEl);
    Element secondEl = newdoc.createElement("SECONDELEMENT");
    root.appendChild(secondEl);
    Text firsttext = newdoc.createTextNode("this is text data");
    firstEl.appendChild(firsttext);
    Text secondtext = newdoc.createTextNode("here is more text data");
    secondEl.appendChild(secondtext);

    listNodes(newdoc.getChildNodes(), out, "");

}
catch (Exception e){
    out.print("<br/><br/><font color=\"red\">There was an error<BR>");
    out.print (e.toString() + "</font>");
}
%>
</body>
</html>
    <%!
    private void listNodes(NodeList nlist, JspWriter out, String spacer)
    throws Exception{
        try{
            for(int i = 0; i < nlist.getLength(); i++){
                out.print(spacer + "[");
                out.print(" " + nlist.item(i).getNodeName());
                out.print(" type:" + nlist.item(i).getNodeType());
                out.print("<font color=\"green\"> "
                   + nlist.item(i).getNodeValue() + "</font> ");
            if(nlist.item(i).hasAttributes()){
                NamedNodeMap attributes = nlist.item(i).getAttributes();
                for(int j = 0; j < attributes.getLength(); j++){
                    out.print(" {");
                    out.print(" name:" + attributes.item(j).getNodeName());
                    out.print(" value:" + attributes.item(j).getNodeValue());
                    out.print(" }");
                }
            }
```

LISTING 5.7 Continued

```
            out.print("]<BR>");
            if(nlist.item(i).getChildNodes().getLength() > 0)
                listNodes(nlist.item(i).getChildNodes(), out,
                    spacer + "      ");
            //if the node is of type Element then create closing string
            if(nlist.item(i).getNodeType() == 1)
               out.print(spacer + "[/ " + nlist.item(i).getNodeName()
                   + "]<BR>");
        }
    }
    catch(Exception e){out.print( "<font color=\"red\">" +
        e.toString() + "</font>");}
}
%>
```

The code begins by creating an instance of the `DOMImplementation` interface. It does this by instantiating the implementing class constructor `DOMImplementationImpl()`:

```
//create new XML Document programmatically
DOMImplementation domImpl = new org.apache.xerces.dom.DOMImplementationImpl();
```

Once this is done, a DOM container is established and we can create an XML document from scratch. This container is required in order to avoid associating any of our newly created nodes with an already existing DOM. If the code did not use this container, the newly created `Nodes` would have to be associated with an already existing DOM.

Now that the container exists which permits the creation and positioning of nodes, let's begin. First, we need to create a `Document` node that can contain DTD information and the root element of our XML hierarchy, among other things.

The `createDocument()` method is invoked with three parameters. The first is the namespace URI that this element is associated with. There will not be any namespaces in this example. The next parameter is the root `Element` node of the XML document being created. This node will be referenced as `TREEROOT`. Last is the DTD parameter. If we were creating an XML document that had an associated DTD, this is where that `DocumentType` node would be passed in and associated with this XML document:

```
Document newdoc = domImpl.createDocument(null, "TREEROOT", null);
```

Armed with the `Document` node, the next step is to obtain the root element created in the `createDocument()` method earlier. We can do this using the familiar `getDocumentElement()` method invoked on the `Document` node.

```
Element root = newdoc.getDocumentElement();
```

From this point on, all we need to do is create various types of `Nodes` and append them in the desired place. The `Document` interface is filled with various methods for the creation of each type of `Node`:

```
Element firstEl = newdoc.createElement("FIRSTELEMENT");
root.appendChild(firstEl);
Element secondEl = newdoc.createElement("SECONDELEMENT");
root.appendChild(secondEl);
Text firsttext = newdoc.createTextNode("this is text data");
firstEl.appendChild(firsttext);
Text secondtext = newdoc.createTextNode("here is more text data");
secondEl.appendChild(secondtext);
```

Now let's output our results through the `listNodes()` method to see what we've got:

```
listNodes(newdoc.getChildNodes(), out, "");
```

The output shows the new DOM tree in Figure 5.7. Notice that the `Text` nodes are positioned as children within the `Element` nodes. This is because they were appended to the `Element` nodes, and not the root node.

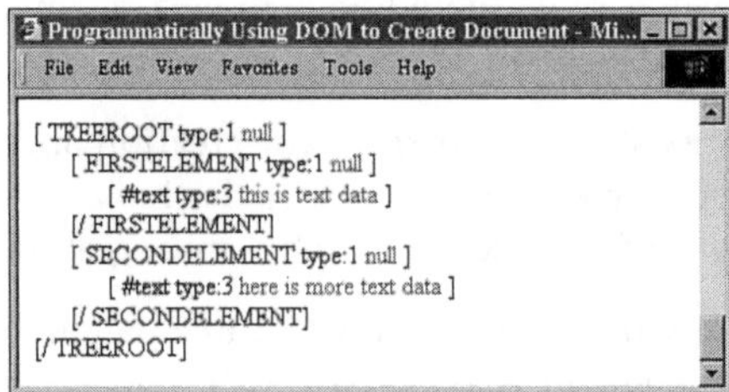

FIGURE 5.7 Output of the programmatically created XML document.

Creating any other type of node is as simple as in the previous example. The `Document` node has many methods for creating the various types of nodes. Methods also exist for creating namespace-aware elements and attributes. These methods are used in the exact same way as the non-namespace-aware methods used previously. The only difference is in the parameters. The methods `createElementNS()` and `createAttributeNS()` take the qualified element or attribute name (this is the tagname with the namespace prefix, or no prefix if the default namespace is used), and the namespace URI.

By using these methods when creating an XML document, we ensure that the other namespace-aware methods will work as expected.

NOTE

When a node has been created with an associated namespace, the namespace attribute node will not be automatically added to the root `Element` node. You must add it by hand. To obtain the proper namespace structure, create the appropriate `Attr` node and add it to the root element.

Moving Nodes Between Documents

What if a node from one XML document needs to be moved to another document? This is a relatively simple procedure and uses the same methods, such as `appendNode()`, that we used previously. However, you'll need to watch out for one particular error, as we'll explain in the following short example.

Continuing with the previous example, the code will move the `DOWNSTAIRS Element` node from one DOM to another. This node began as a result of the parsing of an XML file. The element is then appended to the DOM programmatically created in the previous example.

Save the JSP in Listing 5.8 as `webapps/xmlbook/chapter5/DOMExampleImport.jsp`. (Additions from the previous listing are shown in boldface type.)

LISTING 5.8 DOMExampleImport.jsp

```
<%@ page
  import="org.w3c.dom.*,
          org.apache.xerces.parsers.DOMParser"
%>
<html>
<head><title>Copying Node from One Document to Another</title></head>
<body>
<%
try{
    DOMParser parser = new DOMParser();

    String  path = request.getServletPath();
    path = path.substring(0,path.indexOf("DOMExampleImport.jsp"));
    String  xml  = application.getRealPath(path + "House.xml");

    parser.parse(xml);
    Document doc = parser.getDocument();
```

LISTING 5.8 Continued

```
    NodeList list = doc.getElementsByTagName("DOWNSTAIRS");
    Node downstairs = list.item(0);

    //create new XML Document programmatically
    DOMImplementation domImpl = new org.apache.xerces.dom.DOMImplementationImpl();
    Document newdoc = domImpl.createDocument(null, "TREEROOT", null);
    Element root = newdoc.getDocumentElement();
    Element firstEl = newdoc.createElement("FIRSTELEMENT");
    root.appendChild(firstEl);
    Element secondEl = newdoc.createElement("SECONDELEMENT");
    root.appendChild(secondEl);
    Text firsttext = newdoc.createTextNode("this is text data");
    firstEl.appendChild(firsttext);
    Text secondtext = newdoc.createTextNode("here is more text data");
    secondEl.appendChild(secondtext);
    Node importednode = newdoc.importNode(downstairs, false);
    secondEl.appendChild(importednode);

    listNodes(newdoc.getChildNodes(), out, "");

}
catch (Exception e){
    out.print("<br/><br/><font color=\"red\">There was an error<BR>");
    out.print (e.toString() + "</font>");
}
%>
</body>
</html>
    <%!
    private void listNodes(NodeList nlist, JspWriter out, String spacer)
    throws Exception{
        try{
            for(int i = 0; i < nlist.getLength(); i++){
                out.print(spacer + "[");
                out.print(" " + nlist.item(i).getNodeName());
                out.print(" type:" + nlist.item(i).getNodeType());
                out.print("<font color=\"green\"> "
                   + nlist.item(i).getNodeValue() + "</font> ");
            if(nlist.item(i).hasAttributes()){
                NamedNodeMap attributes = nlist.item(i).getAttributes();
                for(int j = 0; j < attributes.getLength(); j++){
```

LISTING 5.8 Continued

```
                out.print(" {");
                out.print(" name:" + attributes.item(j).getNodeName());
                out.print(" value:" + attributes.item(j).getNodeValue());
                out.print(" }");
            }
        }

            out.print("]<BR>");
            if(nlist.item(i).getChildNodes().getLength() > 0)
                listNodes(nlist.item(i).getChildNodes(), out,
                    spacer + "      ");
            //if the node is of type Element then create closing string
            if(nlist.item(i).getNodeType() == 1)
               out.print(spacer + "[/ " + nlist.item(i).getNodeName()
                   + "]<BR>");
        }
    }
    catch(Exception e){out.print( "<font color=\"red\">" +
        e.toString() + "</font>");}
}
%>
```

This is a rather straightforward example using techniques covered previously. However, if a node from one document is appended to another document, it will throw a strange error. It will simply report, "Wrong document."

The point is that the node must be imported into the target document before the appending action can occur. Any nodes that are moved among different DOMs must be imported to the proper document with the `importNode()` method and then appended. This method will create a copy of the node being imported, including the subtree of ancestor nodes and attribute nodes.

Notice that the `importNode()` method has two parameters. The first is the `Node` being imported. The second, a `boolean`, indicates whether the entire subtree descending from this node should also be imported. Previously, the code passed `false` into this method, and the entire subtree was not included:

```
Node importednode = newdoc.importNode(downstairs, false);
```

However, if we change this `boolean` value to `true`, it will cause only the `Node` being directly referenced and any attributes contained therein to be imported. All other nodes are discarded. If the node is not an `Element` node, it will be imported alone with the boolean value set to false. If it's an Element node, the attributes will also be imported.

In this example, we are importing the Node but not the children through the false parameter.

Now that the Node has been imported, it must be placed in the DOM representation hierarchy. This is done with the familiar appendChild() method from the previous example.

This brings up the situation where the node is imported, but never appended. If this occurs and the DOM is output or traversed, this node will not be there. It's almost there, but it doesn't exist in terms of the hierarchy.

Let's take a look at the output in Figure 5.8. Notice that the DOWNSTAIRS Element appears as the last child node of the SECONDELEMENT node. This includes the attributes found in the appended Element node but not the entire subtree descending from it.

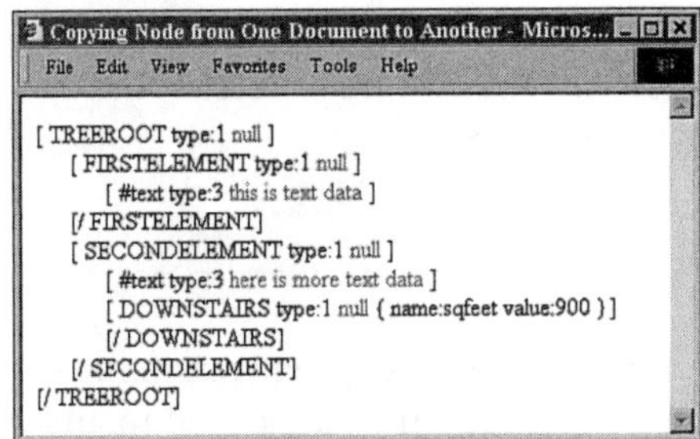

FIGURE 5.8 Output of node moved between documents without subtree.

The processes of altering and traversing DOMs are very easy. This is especially true when the structure of the document is known beforehand. However, there are other ways to traverse the tree when the structure of the document and the depth of a particular node are unknown. These classes for DOM traversal are found in the org.w3c.dom.traversal package.

TreeWalker

The first technique for altering and traversing a DOM involves the use of a TreeWalker.

TreeWalker objects are very powerful because they enable you to create a "view" on the XML document. This view is similar to database views, in that it is used to look at very specific parts of tables or combinations of tables.

With an XML document, a view can be used to look at the document with different types of nodes filtered out. In fact, you can pass an entire document through the `TreeWalker`, and only the nodes that meet particular requirements will be traversed.

This has the potential of making a tree structure change dramatically. For example, removing every `Element` node of an XML document leaves very little hierarchy in the document. This also causes all text nodes to be siblings of each other instead of being nested at various depths within particular elements.

The next simple example is designed to get you started using `TreeWalkers`. Save this file, shown in Listing 5.9, as `webapps/xmlbook/chapter5/TreeWalker.jsp`.

LISTING 5.9 TreeWalker.jsp; Example using a `TreeWalker`

```
<%@ page
  import="org.w3c.dom.*,
          org.apache.xerces.parsers.DOMParser,
          org.w3c.dom.traversal.*"
%>
<html>
<head><title>TreeWalker Example</title></head>
<body>
<%
try{
    DOMParser parser = new DOMParser();

    String  path = request.getServletPath();
    path = path.substring(0,path.indexOf("TreeWalker.jsp"));
    String  xml  = application.getRealPath(path + "House.xml");

    parser.parse(xml);
    Document doc = parser.getDocument();

    TreeWalker treewalker = ((DocumentTraversal)doc).createTreeWalker
        (doc.getDocumentElement(),
        NodeFilter.SHOW_ELEMENT, null, true);
    Node n = treewalker.firstChild();
    while( n != null){
         out.print(n.getNodeName() + "  Type: "
            + n.getNodeType() + "  Value: "
            + n.getNodeValue() + "<BR>");
         n = treewalker.nextNode();
    }
}
```

LISTING 5.9 Continued

```
catch (Exception e){
    out.print("<br/><br/><font color=\"red\">There was an error<BR>");
    out.print (e.toString() + "</font>");
}
%>
</BODY>
</HTML>
```

This example begins by importing the appropriate packages and then loads the XML document in the same manner as before. Once that has been completed, a `TreeWalker` instance is created on the `Document` node of the XML document to be traversed. Note that we need to cast the `Document` node (`doc`) to the `DocumentTraversal` type in order to invoke the `createTreeWalker` method on it.

The `createTreeWalker()` method has four arguments:

1. The `Node` after which the tree traversal will start. This causes the subtree formed under this node to be selected and traversed. All other `Nodes`, beyond those in this subtree, do not exist according to the `TreeWalker` and therefore cannot be returned using `TreeWalker` methods.
2. An `int` that indicates which nodes are filtered out from the subtree. This enables the exclusive traversal of one particular type of node present in the subtree. For example, if you use the `int` value 1, only nodes of type `Element` will be selected for traversal. The constants that make up the values of this `int` can be found in the `org.w3c.dom.traversal.NodeFilter` class.
3. A `NodeFilter` object that can be programmed to filter nodes found through the `TreeWalker` in any way possible using code. The user writes a class that will implement the `NodeFilter` interface and define the only method present: `acceptNode()`. Each node the `TreeWalker` is about to traverse will be passed into this method and processed according to the return value. If the `acceptNode()` method accepts the node with `FILTER_ACCEPT`, the `TreeWalker` will traverse it; otherwise, it will be skipped. Entire subtrees can be skipped if `acceptNode()` returns `FILTER_REJECT`. The return value is a `short` whose constants can again be found in the `NodeFilter` class.
4. A `boolean` that indicates whether entity references should be expanded.

You may have noticed that the `createTreeWalker()` method has two different ways of excluding `Nodes`. The distinction is subtle but important.

The first way to filter `Nodes` is through the `int` constant that is the second parameter of the `createTreeWalker()` method. As previously stated, this constant can be used to select which nodes are processed according to node type. You can choose to process either a specific type of `Node` or all `Nodes`. It is not possible to select only two types of nodes to process. This form of filtering is helpful, but not specific enough for all situations.

The second way to filter nodes can be as specific as you want. It involves the creation of a class that implements the `NodeFilter` interface. By definition, the `acceptNode()` method of this interface allows very specific nodes to be selected for processing. These nodes can be selected according to type, value, or position.

Before each node is processed with the `TreeWalker`, it is first passed into the `acceptNode()` method of the `NodeFilter` implementation class. The result of the method invocation on each node determines whether that node will continue to be processed and traversed with the `TreeWalker`.

In this example, we chose to use the static `SHOW_ELEMENT` to only allow nodes of type `Element` into the `TreeWalker`. Also, we did not define a `NodeFilter` implementation for the `createTreeWalker()` method and thus did not use the more specific filtering capabilities.

The results are shown in Figure 5.9. It is important to restate that this example doesn't demonstrate the full power of this tool. When the `TreeWalker` is created, one parameter is a `NodeFilter`. Our code passed `null` in this argument. The power of the `TreeWalker` lies in its ability to filter nodes through a `NodeFilter` implementation *before* the `TreeWalker` traverses it. The power of this feature is enormous.

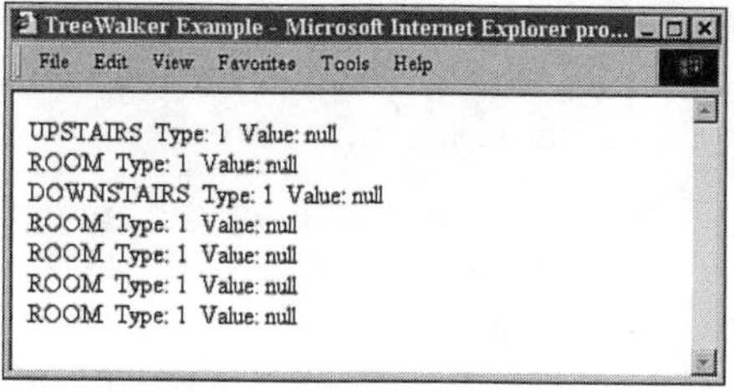

FIGURE 5.9 Results of the `TreeWalker` traversal.

Notice in the output that only nodes of type `Element` were output. `Element` nodes are indicated by the value 1.

NodeIterator

A `NodeIterator` is used in the same way as a `TreeWalker`. The only difference between a `NodeIterator` and a `TreeWalker` is that a `TreeWalker` maintains the tree structure of a document.

A `NodeIterator`, on the other hand, collapses the tree structure into a `NodeList` that you can step through and filter just like a `TreeWalker`. The order of this set is the same order in which the start tags occur in the text representation of the document.

The only other difference with a `NodeIterator` is that the `detach()` method should be invoked when the list of nodes returned by the `NodeIterator` is finished. This releases the set that it iterated over and frees other resources.

Ranges

Several modules were released in the DOM Level 2 specification. One of those was the DOM Level 2 Traversal module, which includes the `NodeIterator` and `TreeWalker` discussed previously. Another one is the DOM Level 2 Range module implemented in the `org.w3c.dom.ranges` package. The only reason we mention them is to give you some knowledge of their existence. This will permit you to delve deeper into them if the need arises.

A range is a set of `Nodes` in a DOM tree. It has nothing to do with values of nodes or numeric quantities. Rather, it is a way of indicating a grouping of `Nodes` that need to be labeled together as a collection and manipulated.

In some ways a range is similar to selecting a node and its descendants. However, a range isn't limited to a tree or subtree structure. It's possible to start a range at a node that is the child of the root element and end it at a great-grandchild descending from the starting element's sibling. All nodes that are between these two points are a part of that range, and that range isn't a tree.

This can be useful if the structure of the document is unknown, and it is necessary to remove or edit parts of it. Feel free to check out the JavaDocs and see the many things that you can do using ranges.

JDOM, dom4j, and Deferred DOM

Before closing, we should mention JDOM, dom4j, and deferred DOM. JDOM and dom4j are very similar to DOM except that they were designed and written only for Java. This allows users to overload methods and to use other features of the Java language to make these Java representations of documents more intuitive to an experienced Java programmer. Some examples of JDOM and dom4j can be found in Chapter 7, "Successfully Using JSP and XML in an Application."

Deferred DOM is an answer to the memory issues that large and complex DOM structures create. Through the use of deferred DOM, nodes are only created in memory when they are accessed. This is a feature that certain parsers, such as Xerces, support. This is a solution to memory problems in certain situations. If only a small portion of the document will be used, and that portion is nonsequentially accessed, deferred DOM is the way to go. If it's sequential, use SAX, which is covered in the next chapter and is a very fast way to sequentially access documents.

Summary

This chapter covered the vast majority of tasks that any programmer will have to do with DOM. These include copying, moving, and deleting nodes and subtrees.

Most of the chapter described the uses of the DOM Level 2 Core module and the DOM Level 2 Traversal and Range modules. The entire Level 2 specification was broken into modules due to its size. Four other modules of the DOM Level 2 specification exist. Also, there is a module that enables HTML documents to be manipulated in the same ways described in this chapter.

6 Programming SAX

IN THIS CHAPTER

- What Is SAX?
- The Workings of SAX

Now that we've covered DOM and the easier-to-visualize model of processing XML files, let's go in a different direction. This chapter has only one goal: to teach you what SAX is and how to use it to parse an XML file. As a result, the SAX coverage will be intense as we explore the richness of the features found in SAX.

After a walk-through introduction to SAX, we will dive into a non-validating parser example. This example will serve as a baseline and we will spend the rest of the chapter expanding and changing the original example to show additional features of SAX.

While focusing on examples, we will also illustrate how to avoid common problems that programmers find in using SAX.

After illustrating what is possible with SAX, we will show a simple example of how to take an XML document and format it for output as an HTML table.

This chapter covers quite a bit of detail, and you might find it useful to review it after you've read through it once.

What Is SAX?

The users of the XML-DEV mailing list originally developed SAX, the Simple API for XML, in 1998. Simply stated, SAX is an event-based model for accessing XML document contents. SAX invokes methods when certain conditions (such as start tags and end tags) are encountered as an XML document is sequentially read from start to finish.

The Workings of SAX

The DOM, covered in the previous chapter, creates a tree-like structure of the parsed XML document in memory. This structure is very memory consumptive, but is very easy to visualize and simple to use programmatically. SAX takes a completely different approach to processing XML documents.

In essence, the SAX parser reads the XML document sequentially from start to finish, and along the way will invoke various *callback* methods when particular events occur. A callback is a method registered with the parser, written to enable the code to respond to events of interest to the programmer.

An example of a callback is the `startElement()` method. The SAX parser will invoke this method whenever an opening element tag is encountered. This enables us to do something as a result of this event, such as outputting the tag name that invoked this event.

SAX Interfaces

SAX has four interfaces that contain all the callback methods. They are as follows:

- `ContentHandler`—Defines all the available methods pertaining to XML markup, such as `startElement()` and `processingInstruction()`.
- `ErrorHandler`—Defines the methods used for the three kinds of parsing errors.
- `EntityResolver`—Defines the methods used to customize handling of external entities; this includes a DTD reference.
- `DTDHandler`—Defines the methods used to handle unparsed entities found in the DTD.

SAX2 provides a convenience class called `DefaultHandler` that implements all four of these interfaces. All of our examples in this chapter will extend this convenience class so that we don't have to define all the methods of each interface. Of course, it is possible to define separate classes to implement each interface.

Implementing these interfaces and registering the newly created class or classes with the parser allows the parser to call back the appropriate method pertaining to the event that has occurred. By defining the body of these callback methods, we can do anything we want in response to the parsing events.

Each parsing event will invoke the appropriate method if it is defined and registered. All methods are synchronous, meaning that once an event-handler callback is invoked, the parser cannot report another event until that callback returns. On the same note, once a parser begins to parse an XML document, it cannot be used to parse another XML document until it returns from parsing the first document.

The advantage of the event-driven, serial-access mechanism is that the SAX parser only reads a small part of the XML document at any one time. This creates a means of processing XML documents that is very fast and has very low memory usage. This means that SAX is the parser of choice when dealing with large XML documents. Now you may ask, What defines a large XML file? There isn't a direct answer to this question. It depends on a series of factors, including how fast your machine is, how much memory the machine has, what JVM you are using, the optimization of logic, and so on. If you are using another parser with an XML file and are having performance problems, it might be time to switch to SAX.

Downsides to SAX

SAX is great, but it does have a few shortcomings. The negative aspects of SAX include the following:

- "Backing up" in an XML document is not possible because SAX is a read-forward process on the serial data stream.
- SAX is a read-only process. XML source documents cannot be directly modified using SAX. However, an XML document can be read and a modified version output. Using this modified output as a source for another SAX reader finally results in the processing of a modified version of the original XML source document.
- It takes a bit more programming to use SAX than it takes to use the DOM.
- Determining the position of elements in terms of hierarchy and sibling relationships requires more programming effort than with the other parsers.

Differences Between SAX1 and SAX2

The primary difference between SAX1 and SAX2 is the addition of namespace support for element and attribute processing. Through the use of SAX2 it is now possible to obtain namespace information. This improvement has caused several classes to be replaced and deprecated.

Also new to SAX2 is the creation of a standardized style of accessing properties and features of a SAX2 parser. Each property and feature is associated with a distinct URL, similar to namespace concepts. This prevents collisions in naming. This also permits any feature or property, including vendor-specific versions, to be accessed in a standardized way through the `setFeature()`, `getFeature()`, `setProperty()`, and `getProperty()` methods of the `XMLReader` interface.

In this book, we're using the term SAX to refer to the combination of SAX1 and SAX2.

First SAX Example

This example echoes the events that are called by the parser. We will start with a simple example and expand it as the chapter progresses. This will be used to demonstrate the various callbacks that are invoked and what causes the changes in their usage.

We will begin by creating an instance of a non-validating parser and registering our `SAX2Example` class for some of the event handling. Next, our parser will parse an XML document that contains a reference to an external DTD, all the while invoking our callbacks found in `SAX2Example`.

Let's begin with the XML file defined in Listing 6.1. Save this file as `\webapps\xmlbook\chapter6\Books.xml`.

You should notice several things about this file:

- Two namespaces are defined. The first is the default namespace because there is no prefix, and the second has the prefix `mac`.
- One processing instruction exists. The target is `color` and the data is `blue`.
- A DTD is associated with this XML document and is called, appropriately enough, Books.dtd. The source of this DTD can be found in Listing 6.2.
- An external entity reference called `info` exists in the `FOOTER` element.

LISTING 6.1 Books.xml

```
<?xml version="1.0" encoding="UTF-8"?>

<!DOCTYPE BOOKS SYSTEM "Books.dtd">
<BOOKS xmlns="http://www.samspublishing.com/"
       xmlns:mac="http://mcp.com/">
    <mac:BOOK pubdate="1/1/2000">
        <mac:TITLE>Rising River</mac:TITLE>
        <mac:AUTHOR>
            <mac:NAME>John Smith &amp; Garith Green</mac:NAME>
        </mac:AUTHOR>
    </mac:BOOK>
<?color blue?>
    <BOOK pubdate="5/5/1998">
        <TITLE>Timberland</TITLE>
        <AUTHOR>
            <FNAME>Chris</FNAME>
            <LNAME>Hamilwitz</LNAME>
```

LISTING 6.1 Continued

```
        </AUTHOR>
    </BOOK>
    <FOOTER>&info;</FOOTER>
</BOOKS>
```

Now that we have our XML document, let's take a look at the DTD associated with it. Save the DTD in Listing 6.2 as `\webapps\xmlbook\chapter6\Books.dtd`.

LISTING 6.2 Books.dtd; DTD for Books.xml

```
<?xml version="1.0" encoding="UTF-8"?>
<!ENTITY info "For more information contact Mary at mary@publish.com">
<!ELEMENT BOOKS (mac:BOOK*, BOOK*, FOOTER)>
<!ELEMENT BOOK (TITLE, AUTHOR)>
<!ATTLIST BOOK pubdate CDATA #REQUIRED>
<!ELEMENT TITLE (#PCDATA)>
<!ELEMENT AUTHOR (FNAME, LNAME)>
<!ELEMENT FNAME (#PCDATA)>
<!ELEMENT LNAME (#PCDATA)>
<!ELEMENT FOOTER (#PCDATA)>
<!ELEMENT mac:BOOK (mac:TITLE, mac:AUTHOR)>
<!ATTLIST mac:BOOK pubdate CDATA #REQUIRED>
<!ELEMENT mac:TITLE (#PCDATA)>
<!ELEMENT mac:AUTHOR (mac:NAME)>
<!ELEMENT mac:NAME (#PCDATA)>
```

There is nothing unusual about this DTD, but it will become very important as we change to a validating parser later in this chapter.

Next, we have our handler class, found in Listing 6.3. This is the class that defines those methods that the XML parser will invoke when particular events occur during the parsing of the XML document from Listing 6.1. Save this file as `\webapps\xmlbook\WEB-INF\classes\xmlbook\chapter6\SAX2Example.java`. Make sure to compile this class before using it and to restart Tomcat to make sure that it is registered. This applies to all classes throughout this chapter and will not be mentioned again.

LISTING 6.3 SAX2Example.java; SAX2 Content Handler Class

```
package xmlbook.chapter6;

import java.io.*;
import org.xml.sax.helpers.DefaultHandler;
import org.xml.sax.*;

public class SAX2Example extends DefaultHandler{
    private Writer w;

    public SAX2Example(java.io.Writer new_w)
    {   w = new_w;    }

    public void startDocument() throws SAXException{
        try{ output ("<br/><b>Start Document</b>"); }
        catch(Exception e){throw new SAXException(e.toString());}
    }

    public void endDocument() throws SAXException{
        try{ output ("<br/><b>End Document</b>");  }
        catch(Exception e){throw new SAXException(e.toString());}
    }

    public void startElement(String uri, String localName, String elemName,
                         Attributes attrs) throws SAXException{
        try{
            output ("<br/>Start Element: \"" + elemName + "\"");
            output (" Uri: \"" + uri + "\"");
            output (" localName: \"" + localName + "\"");
            if (attrs.getLength() > 0){
                output("<br/> ");
                for (int i = 0; i < attrs.getLength(); i++)
                {output ("  attribute: ");
                 output (attrs.getQName(i) + "=\"" + attrs.getValue(i) + "\"");
                }
            }
        }
        catch(Exception e){throw new SAXException(e.toString());}
    }

    public void endElement(String uri, String localName, String elemName)
    throws SAXException{
```

LISTING 6.3 Continued

```
        try{ output ("<br/>End Element: \"" + elemName + "\""); }
        catch(Exception e){throw new SAXException(e.toString());}
    }

    public void characters(char[] ch, int start, int length)
    throws SAXException {
        try
        {  String s = new String(ch, start, length);
           output("  <b>Characters encountered:</b> \""
           + s.trim()+ "\"");
      }
      catch(Exception e){throw new SAXException(e.toString());}
    }

    public void processingInstruction(String target, String data)
    throws SAXException{
        try
        { output("<BR>PROCESSING INSTRUCTION: target: "
                    + target + " data:" + data );
        }
        catch(Exception e){throw new SAXException(e.toString());}
    }
    private void output (String strOut) throws SAXException{
        try { w.write (strOut);   }
        catch (IOException e)
            {throw new SAXException ("I/O error", e);}
    }
}
```

Again, `DefaultHandler` is the class that extends all four of the interfaces that make up the handlers for the SAX2 parser. We chose to extend this class instead of each interface so that we were not required to define all the methods found in each interface.

In the handler class, a `Writer` object is passed to the constructor. When an instance of this class is created in our JSP, found in Listing 6.4, we will pass the implicit object `out` of type `javax.servlet.jsp.JspWriter` into the object. This will give the object the ability to write to the JSP output stream.

From this point on, all the methods defined, except for the `output` method that is listed last, are callbacks. These methods override only a small portion of those defined in the `DefaultHandler` class and they have several things in common.

The bodies of all the callback methods in this example simply respond with a string that echoes the method being invoked and the tag or text that prompted the call. This will provide us with output that will explain the sequence of events that occur when a document is being parsed by SAX2.

When the parser encounters a start tag or end tag, the name of the tag is passed as a `String` to the `startElement()` or `endElement()` method, as appropriate. When a start tag is encountered, any attributes found therein are also passed in an `Attributes` object.

Each of these methods is required by the interface to throw a `SAXException`. In order to provide a standard interface to the parsing behavior, this is the only type of exception that SAX events ever throw. These exceptions can also wrap other exceptions, such as an `IOException` if there is an error writing to the output stream. To get at the wrapped exception, use the `getException()` from the `SAXException` class.

There will be more on error handling with SAX later in this chapter. For now, notice that all `catch` blocks in our `SAX2Example` handler class throw exceptions back to the parser, which in turn throws it to where the parser was created. In our case, that's back to the JSP found in Listing 6.4. Eventually, we will be adding to our handler class to explore errors more.

Characters and Ignorable Whitespace

The `output()` and `characters()` methods found in our class need further explanation. The `characters()` callback is the method that will output any non-markup encountered anywhere in the XML document. At times this will include whitespace.

Why would `characters()` be called with blank space? Without a DTD or schema, the parser has no way of figuring out whether the blank space found before or after a tag is text data or not. It will simply call `characters()` every time anything that isn't markup is encountered. Remember, this parser can't see ahead to know the context of the blank space or characters that it's encountering. However, if a DTD or schema is present, the parser has the definitions of the elements, and can know whether text data is permitted within an element or not. The method `ignorableWhiteSpace()` will be invoked on any non-markup space that is undefined within the DTD or schema.

The final item to note is that the `output()` method in the `SAX2Example` class from Listing 6.3 was written specifically to handle `IOExceptions`, which can occur while writing. If we just used `out` directly within the callbacks, we would have no means of catching the `IOExceptions` that might result.

Next, in Listing 6.4, we have our JSP that will glue everything together. Save this file as `\webapps\xmlbook\chapter6\SAX2Example.jsp`.

LISTING 6.4 SAX2Example.jsp

```
<%@ page
  import="org.xml.sax.helpers.*,
  org.xml.sax.*,
  javax.xml.parsers.*,
  xmlbook.chapter6.*"
%>
<html>
<head><title>SAX2 Parser Content Handler Example</title></head>
<body>
<%

try{
    XMLReader reader =
        XMLReaderFactory.createXMLReader("org.apache.xerces.parsers.SAXParser");

    reader.setFeature("http://xml.org/sax/features/validation", false);

    //create instance of handler class we wrote
    SAX2Example se = new SAX2Example(out);

    //register handler class
    reader.setContentHandler(se);

    String  ls_path = request.getServletPath();
    ls_path = ls_path.substring(0,ls_path.indexOf("SAX2Example.jsp"));
    String  ls_xml  = application.getRealPath(ls_path + "Books.xml");

    //parse the XML document
    reader.parse(ls_xml);
}
catch (Exception e){
    out.print("<br/><br/><font color=\"red\">there was an error<BR>");
    out.print (e.toString() + "</font>");
}

%>
</body>
</html>
```

Examine the following lines from the listing:

```
XMLReader reader =
    XMLReaderFactory.createXMLReader("org.apache.xerces.parsers.SAXParser");
```

This creates an instance of an `XMLReader`. This instance will use the Xerces parser by providing the Xerces class. If you have not yet placed the Xerces.jar file in the `/lib` directory found in the root of the Tomcat installation, do it now and restart the server.

Once the JSP has the reader, the code sets the validation feature of the parser to false. This is done by telling SAX the distinct URL associated with the feature and the setting:

```
reader.setFeature("http://xml.org/sax/features/validation", false);
```

Our JSP next creates an instance of the `SAX2Example` handler found in Listing 6.3:

```
SAX2Example se = new SAX2Example(out);
```

Then the handler is registered with the `XMLReader` as the `ContentHandler` implementation:

```
reader.setContentHandler(se);
```

To conclude the code within the `try` block, this JSP finds the path to the current XML document and passes it into the reader to parse:

```
String  ls_path = request.getServletPath();
ls_path = ls_path.substring(0,ls_path.indexOf("SAX2Example.jsp"));
String  ls_xml  = application.getRealPath(ls_path + "Books.xml");

//parse the XML document
reader.parse(ls_xml);
```

Finally, the code ends with only the most basic error handling. The code will catch everything re-thrown by our `SAX2Example` class, and any error that may have occurred in the `try` block of this JSP. The error handling will be expanded in later examples.

The output is shown in Figure 6.1.

In looking at the result of the processing, several things stand out:

- Since this example uses namespaces, each opening tag causes the `startElement()` to be called with the following parameters: the namespace URI associated with the element, the literal tag string, and the tag name without the namespace prefix.

- The same parameters are available within the `endElement()` method, which is called when the parser encounters an end tag.
- The processing instruction data and target are available in the `processingInstruction()` method. Note that the XML declaration will not invoke this method. The XML declaration is for parsers only, not for applications.
- Although we aren't using a validating parser now, notice that the entity declaration `info` declared in Books.dtd and used in Books.xml was resolved in the output.

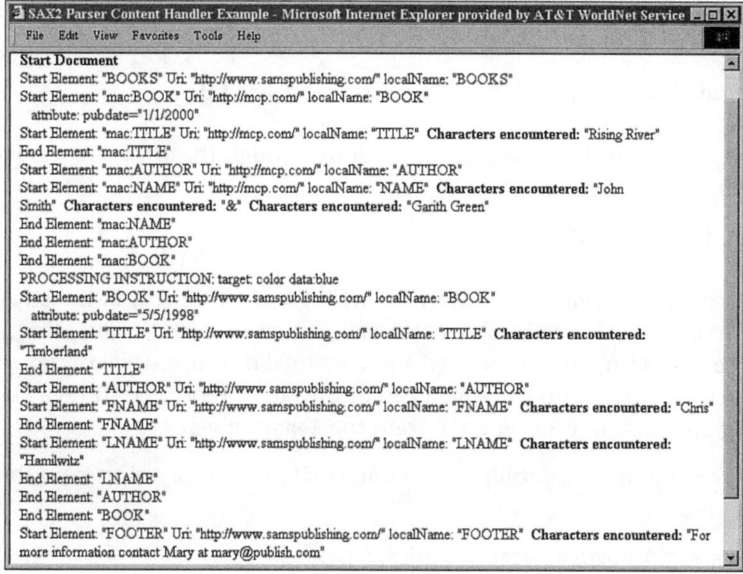

FIGURE 6.1 Output of SAX2Example.jsp.

Processing Versus Validation

Doesn't it seem strange that a non-validating parser would even look at the DTD? It turns out that if a DTD or a schema is present, it will be processed (but not validated) by SAX. This means that entity declarations will be resolved to their replacement values.

Also, if the XML file doesn't have a DTD or schema, whitespace is returned in the `characters()` method. Since this example references a DTD, the `characters()` method doesn't return whitespace. Instead, the `ignorableWhiteSpace()` callback is invoked by SAX. This is due to the DTD giving the parser enough information to know when to ignore the whitespace.

Characters Revisited

Unless you understand its behavior, the `characters()` method can cause you a great deal of heartache. Notice in the output shown in Figure 6.1 that the `characters()` method was called three times in a row for text data found in the single element `mac:NAME`. (See the eighth line of the output.) The number of times the `characters()` method will be invoked for text data found within one element varies. With that in mind, don't depend on there being only one invocation.

Another trap caused by the `characters()` method involves the parameters that are passed into the method:

```
public void characters(char[] ch, int start, int length)
```

The problem here is that when the code loops through the array as in the following line, problems will ensue:

```
for(int 1=0; i<ch.length; i++)
```

Do you see the problem with this? The code is using the length of the `ch` array to end the loop, not the `length` parameter that was given to us through this method. The `characters()` method is defined this way to allow lower-level optimizations, such as reusing arrays and reading ahead of the current location. It depends on the wrapping application to never go beyond the `length` given.

An easy way around this problem is to immediately create a string from the parameters, like this:

```
String s = new String(ch, start, length);
```

This will ensure that the `characters()` method doesn't cause problems in your application. On the other hand, it will create a new string object each time this method is called. With that in mind, this would be a good place to pool resources.

Another aspect of the `characters()` method that needs more analysis has to do with the timing of the invocations. We already mentioned that when there is no DTD present, it will be invoked every time any space that isn't markup is encountered. Let's demonstrate this.

Comment out the DTD declaration in the Books.xml file found in Listing 6.1, as shown here:

```
<!--  <!DOCTYPE BOOKS SYSTEM "Books.dtd">  -->
```

Save the file; the output is shown in Figure 6.2.

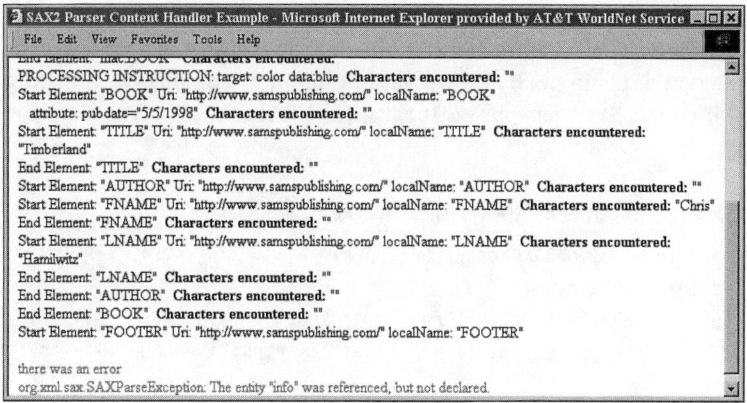

FIGURE 6.2 Output of SAX2Example.jsp with DTD commented out.

Look how many times `characters()` is called when the DTD is absent. The only reason we can't see exactly how much whitespace is passed into the method is because we trim the string upon output. The method `characters()` is also called after elements are closed, and anywhere else that spaces exist in the XML document. If these spaces are removed and the XML document becomes one long string, these calls won't happen, but that's not very practical.

Notice that there is an error at the bottom of Figure 6.2. This fatal error is a result of the inability to resolve the entity reference `info`. This makes sense considering that the declaration is in the DTD whose reference was just commented out.

Error Handling

SAX provides the `ErrorHandler` interface for handling three different types of parsing errors. Each of these callbacks is able to throw `SAXExceptions`. The reason is that the body of a method may cause exceptions, and the method needs a way to pass exceptions back up the hierarchy.

In addition to the `SAXExceptions`, SAX also provides for three different types of error events:

- `warning`: Related to document validity and DTDs.
- `error`: Recoverable errors that violate some portion of the XML specification. An `error` results if, for example, the wrong version number is found in the document declaration.
- `fatalError`: Nonrecoverable errors that may relate to an XML document not being well formed, the absence of a DTD when validation is turned on, or unrecognizable encodings.

Now that we've briefly covered the three error handling events, let's create a new class with some implementations of these methods. This new class will contain the complete code of Listing 6.3, and the additional methods shown in Listing 6.5. Save the combined code as `\webapps\xmlbook\WEB-INF\classes\xmlbook\chapter6\SAX2ExampleErr.java`.

LISTING 6.5 Additional Methods for SAX2ExampleErr Class

```
    public void warning(SAXParseException e)
    throws SAXException{
        output("<BR><font color=\"red\">warning: " + e.getMessage() + "  "
                + e.getSystemId() + " Line: " + e.getLineNumber() + "</font>");
    }

    public void error(SAXParseException e)
    throws SAXException{
        output("<BR><font color=\"red\">error: " + e.getMessage() + "  "
                + e.getSystemId() + " Line: " + e.getLineNumber() + "</font>");
    }

    public void fatalError(SAXParseException e)
    throws SAXException{
        output("<BR><font color=\"red\">fatalError: " + e.getMessage() + "  "
                + e.getSystemId() + " Line: " + e.getLineNumber() + "</font>");
    }
```

Remember to change the name of the class and the constructor from `SAX2Example` to `SAX2ExampleErr`, or the file will not compile. This applies to all classes in this chapter that are using code from a previous listing and will not be mentioned again.

Next, we need to make a JSP that will use the newly created error handling callbacks. This JSP, shown in Listing 6.6, has the same content as the one found in Listing 6.4 except for some minor changes. (These changes are noted in boldface print in the listing.) Save the code as `\webapps\xmlbook\chapter6\SAX2ExampleErr.jsp`.

LISTING 6.6 SAX2ExampleErr.jsp

```
<%@ page
  import="org.xml.sax.helpers.*,
  org.xml.sax.*,
  javax.xml.parsers.*,
  xmlbook.chapter6.*"
%>
```

LISTING 6.6 Continued

```
<html>
<head><title>SAX2 Parser Error Handler Example</title></head>
<body>
<%

try{
    XMLReader reader =
       XMLReaderFactory.createXMLReader("org.apache.xerces.parsers.SAXParser");

    reader.setFeature("http://xml.org/sax/features/validation", true);

    //create instance of handler class we wrote
    SAX2ExampleErr se = new SAX2ExampleErr(out);

    //register handler class
    reader.setContentHandler(se);
    reader.setErrorHandler(se);

    String  ls_path = request.getServletPath();
    ls_path = ls_path.substring(0,ls_path.indexOf("SAX2ExampleErr.jsp"));
    String  ls_xml  = application.getRealPath(ls_path + "Books.xml");

    //parse the XML document
    reader.parse(ls_xml);
}
catch (Exception e){
    out.print("<br/><br/><font color=\"red\">there was an error<BR>");
    out.print (e.toString() + "</font>");
}

%>
</body>
</html>
```

The first change is the reference to the handler class. Instead of using the old `SAX2Example` class, we will now be using the `SAX2ExampleErr` class with its error handling callback functions. Next, we need to register this class with the parser as the implementation of the `errorHandler`:

```
reader.setErrorHandler(se);
```

This will tell the parser to invoke the new methods from Listing 6.5 when any of the error classifications discussed earlier occur.

Once this is done, we need to turn validation on. This is done by changing the following line from Listing 6.4

```
reader.setFeature("http://xml.org/sax/features/validation", false);
```

to look like this in Listing 6.6:

```
reader.setFeature("http://xml.org/sax/features/validation", true);
```

Turning validation on means that the XML document structure will now be validated against the DTD. If for any reason the DTD cannot be found, or the structure is wrong, the new `error()` callback we just added will be invoked. Load SAX2ExampleErr.jsp and check out the results. If for some reason you have already uncommented the DTD declaration that we commented out, go ahead and comment it out again.

The results are shown in Figure 6.3.

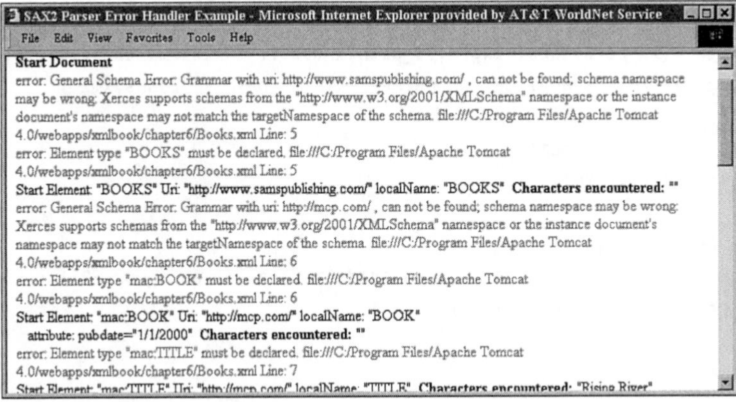

FIGURE 6.3 Validation errors resulting from the absence of the DTD.

Notice that the errors resulting from the absence of the DTD when using a validating parser are non-fatal errors. A fatal error results from the parser's inability to resolve the entity reference. This is a fatal error regardless of whether validation is turned on or off.

The specifics of your application will determine how to deal with the various errors that occur when parsing XML documents. In general, your application should log all warnings and nonfatal errors in some way, and hopefully recover from them in some manner that the user doesn't see. Fatal errors, on the other hand, should display a user-friendly error message and gracefully exit after releasing all resources used.

Ignorable Whitespace

This is a good time to introduce the `contentHandler` interface, which is where the `ignorableWhitespace()` method resides and is invoked when the parser is able to discern ignorable whitespace within an XML document. It has the same method structure as `characters()` and will be invoked any time that there is a schema or DTD present. Validation does not have to be turned on, only DTD or schema processing. This method is useful when it's necessary to process the whitespace of an XML document for output.

Entity References

Using SAX, it is possible to perform some extra processing with entity references. That's done through the `EntityResolver` interface. Each time the parser comes across an entity reference, it will pass the system ID and public ID for that entity to the `resolveEntity()` method defined. This method provides the ability to redirect the resolution of entities, an especially handy way to avoid the fatal entity reference errors shown in the earlier examples.

The method `resolveEntity()` will be invoked before any external reference, including a DTD reference, is used. When this method returns a new `InputSource`, it will be used in place of the original ID. If it returns `null`, the original entity reference ID is used to resolve the entity. Through this method, DTDs can be changed, and entity references resolved.

For example, take the DTD found in Listing 6.2 and replace the entity declaration so that it now looks like Listing 6.7. (The new declaration appears in boldface print in the listing.) Save this file as `\webapps\xmlbook\chapter6\Books2.dtd`.

LISTING 6.7 New DTD Books2.dtd for Books.xml

```
<?xml version="1.0" encoding="UTF-8"?>
<!ENTITY info "Let us help you find the information you were looking for.
              E-mail Mary at mary@publish.com">
<!ELEMENT BOOKS (mac:BOOK*, BOOK*, FOOTER)>
<!ELEMENT BOOK (TITLE, AUTHOR)>
<!ATTLIST BOOK pubdate CDATA #REQUIRED>
<!ELEMENT TITLE (#PCDATA)>
<!ELEMENT AUTHOR (FNAME, LNAME)>
<!ELEMENT FNAME (#PCDATA)>
<!ELEMENT LNAME (#PCDATA)>
```

LISTING 6.7 Continued

```
<!ELEMENT FOOTER (#PCDATA)>
<!ELEMENT mac:BOOK (mac:TITLE, mac:AUTHOR)>
<!ATTLIST mac:BOOK pubdate CDATA #REQUIRED>
<!ELEMENT mac:TITLE (#PCDATA)>
<!ELEMENT mac:AUTHOR (mac:NAME)>
<!ELEMENT mac:NAME (#PCDATA)>
```

Also uncomment the DTD reference in the Books.xml file.

Next, append the method shown in Listing 6.8 to the code from the `SAX2ExampleErr` class and save it as `\webapps\xmlbook\WEB-INF\classes\xmlbook\chapter6\SAX2ExampleRef.java`.

LISTING 6.8 Appended Method to Create SAX2ExampleRef Class

```
public InputSource resolveEntity(String publicId, String systemId)
throws SAXException{
   try{
       output("<br>publicID: " + publicId + " systemId: " + systemId);
       return new InputSource
       ("file:///TomcatPath/webapps/xmlbook/chapter6/Books2.dtd");
   }
   catch(Exception e){throw new SAXException ("Resolve Entity Error", e);}
}
```

Notice that you will have to substitute your Tomcat path in the sixth line of this listing.

Finally, we need to create another JSP that will register the new handler with the parser. This JSP, shown in Listing 6.9, has the same content as the one found in Listing 6.6 except for some minor changes. (These changes are noted in boldface print in the listing.) Save the code as `\webapps\xmlbook\chapter6\SAX2ExampleRef.jsp`.

LISTING 6.9 SAX2ExampleRef.jsp

```
<%@ page
  import="org.xml.sax.helpers.*,
  org.xml.sax.*,
  javax.xml.parsers.*,
  xmlbook.chapter6.*"
%>
```

LISTING 6.9 Continued

```
<html>
<head><title>SAX2 Parser Entity Resolver Example</title></head>
<body>
<%

try{
    XMLReader reader =
       XMLReaderFactory.createXMLReader("org.apache.xerces.parsers.SAXParser");

    reader.setFeature("http://xml.org/sax/features/validation", true);

    //create instance of handler class we wrote
    SAX2ExampleRef se = new SAX2ExampleRef(out);

    //register handler class
    reader.setContentHandler(se);
    reader.setErrorHandler(se);
    reader.setEntityResolver(se);

    String  ls_path = request.getServletPath();
    ls_path = ls_path.substring(0,ls_path.indexOf("SAX2ExampleRef.jsp"));
    String  ls_xml  = application.getRealPath(ls_path + "Books.xml");

    //parse the XML document
    reader.parse(ls_xml);
}
catch (Exception e){
    out.print("<br/><br/><font color=\"red\">there was an error<BR>");
    out.print (e.toString() + "</font>");
}

%>
</body>
</html>
```

Besides changing the handler class registered with the SAX parser, this JSP also registers the class as the entity resolver.

```
reader.setEntityResolver(se);
```

Load SAX2ExampleRef.jsp to see the results shown in Figure 6.4.

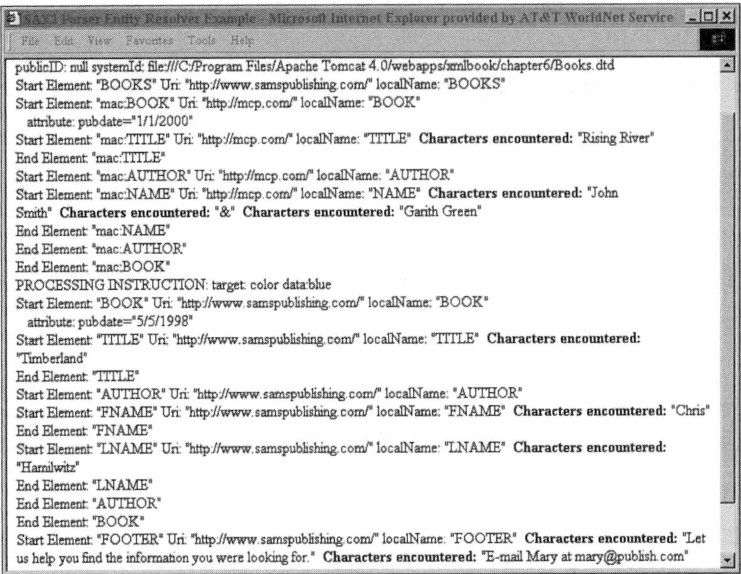

FIGURE 6.4 Results from replacement of the entity reference.

In this example we output the string that appears on the first line of the output shown in Figure 6.4 when `resolveEntity()` is invoked. It is at this point that the external entity, in this case the DTD reference, is replaced with our new DTD, books2.dtd (see Listing 6.7). Notice that the entity reference `info`, found at the bottom of the output, was resolved to the value that was defined in Books2.dtd.

This interface allows any external reference, including a DTD association, to be programmatically changed. For example, imagine an application that uses XML documents whose `PUBLIC` DTD is only available on the Internet. What would happen if the application could no longer access the Internet? Instead of having a document that couldn't resolve to an inaccessible DTD, it's possible to use the `resolveEntity()` method and replace entity references with local ones.

Entity references are not limited in any way. They can be images, XML fragments, and much more. They do not have to be strings or characters.

Generally, when multiple entities are being replaced through the `resolveEntity()` method, there may be Java `case` statements or nested `if` statements. Make sure that if an entity reference falls through these paths, a `null` is returned and not an `InputSource` that hasn't been properly created. If an `InputSource` that hasn't been properly created is returned from this method, expect unpredictable results.

The Document Locator

What happens when we need to know the line number or column at which some markup ends? SAX gives us the means of accessing the exact location of the parser when any callback event occurs. It does so through the use of a `Locator`. By creating a `Locator` variable in the `ContentHandler` class and registering it with the SAX parser through the `setDocumentLocator()` method, we have access to this information.

The `setDocumentLocator()` method is the very first callback to be invoked by a SAX parser upon parsing a new XML document. It's even before the `startDocument()` callback event. The parser passes a `Locator` object into the `setDocumentLocator()` callback event. Using the passed `Locator` object, it's possible to get location and ID information when any other callback is invoked by SAX. If parsing begins and the `setDocumentLocator()` callback is undefined, the `Locator` object will not be accessible from elsewhere in the code. For this reason, the next example will create a `Locator` variable inside the `ContentHandler` implementation. The example will then set the `Locator` instance through the `setDocumentLocator()` method. In this way, the example will be guaranteed access to the `Locator` object.

We will demonstrate this in our last SAX handler class. This new class will contain the majority of the code from the previous handler classes with some additions. (These changes are noted in boldface print in the listing.) Save the code from Listing 6.10 as `\webapps\xmlbook\WEB-INF\classes\xmlbook\chapter6\SAX2ExampleLoc.java`.

LISTING 6.10 SAX Document Locator Class

```
package xmlbook.chapter6;

import java.io.*;
import org.xml.sax.helpers.DefaultHandler;
import org.xml.sax.*;

public class SAX2ExampleLoc extends DefaultHandler{
    private Writer w;
    private Locator locator;

     public SAX2ExampleLoc(java.io.Writer new_w)
    {   w = new_w;     }

     public void setDocumentLocator(Locator locator){
       this.locator = locator;
    }
```

LISTING 6.10 Continued

```
    public void startDocument() throws SAXException{
        try{ output ("<br/><b>Start Document</b>"); }
        catch(Exception e){throw new SAXException(e.toString());}
    }

    public void endDocument() throws SAXException{
        try{ output ("<br/><b>End Document</b>");  }
        catch(Exception e){throw new SAXException(e.toString());}
    }

    public void startElement(String uri, String localName, String elemName,
                             Attributes attrs) throws SAXException{
        try{
            output ("<br/>Start Element: \"" + elemName + "\"");
            output (" Uri: \"" + uri + "\"");
            output (" localName: \"" + localName + "\"");
            if (attrs.getLength() > 0){
                output("<br/> ");
                for (int i = 0; i < attrs.getLength(); i++)
                {output ("  attribute: ");
                 output (attrs.getQName(i) + "=\"" + attrs.getValue(i) + "\"");
                }
            }
        }
        catch(Exception e){throw new SAXException(e.toString());}
    }

    public void endElement(String uri, String localName, String elemName)
    throws SAXException{
        try{
            output("<br/>End Element: \"" + elemName + "\"");
            output("<BR><font color=\"green\">line:" + locator.getLineNumber()
                    + " column: " + locator.getColumnNumber() + " system ID: "
                    + locator.getSystemId() + "</font>");
        }
        catch(Exception e){throw new SAXException(e.toString());}
    }

    public void characters(char[] ch, int start, int length)
    throws SAXException {
        try
```

LISTING 6.10 Continued

```
        {String s = new String(ch, start, length);
        output("  <b>Characters encountered:</b> \"" + s.trim()+ "\"");
        }
        catch(Exception e){throw new SAXException(e.toString());}
    }

    public void processingInstruction(String target, String data)
    throws SAXException{
        try
        { output("<BR>PROCESSING INSTRUCTION: target: "
                    + target + " data:" + data );
        }
        catch(Exception e){throw new SAXException(e.toString());}
    }

    private void output (String strOut) throws SAXException{
        try { w.write (strOut);   }
        catch (IOException e) {throw new SAXException ("I/O error", e);}
    }

}
```

The `setDocumentLocator()` method simply sets our local `Locator` variable to the `Locator` object that our parser is passing into this callback. Through this, we will have access to location and ID information of the parser in the XML document.

The last step is to add some code to the `endElement()` method found in our `SAX2ExampleLoc` class so that we can see the `Locator` in action. The additional lines of code simply output the parser's location information each time the `endElement()` callback is invoked. That information includes which file the parser is working against and where it is in the parsing process. These pieces of information become more useful when multiple files are used together.

Finally, we need to create another JSP that will use our new handler. This JSP, shown in Listing 6.11, has the same content as the one found in Listing 6.9 except for some minor changes. (These changes are noted in boldface print in the listing.) Save the code as `\webapps\xmlbook\chapter6\SAX2ExampleLoc.jsp`.

LISTING 6.11 SAX2ExampleLoc.jsp

```
<%@ page
  import="org.xml.sax.helpers.*,
  org.xml.sax.*,
  javax.xml.parsers.*,
  xmlbook.chapter6.*"
%>
<html>
<head><title>SAX2 Parser Document Locator Example</title></head>
<body>
<%

try{
    XMLReader reader =
       XMLReaderFactory.createXMLReader("org.apache.xerces.parsers.SAXParser");

    reader.setFeature("http://xml.org/sax/features/validation", false);

    //create instance of handler class we wrote
    SAX2ExampleLoc se = new SAX2ExampleLoc(out);

    //register handler class
    reader.setContentHandler(se);

    String  ls_path = request.getServletPath();
    ls_path = ls_path.substring(0,ls_path.indexOf("SAX2ExampleLoc.jsp"));
    String  ls_xml  = application.getRealPath(ls_path + "Books.xml");

    //parse the XML document
    reader.parse(ls_xml);
}
catch (Exception e){
    out.print("<br/><br/><font color=\"red\">there was an error<BR>");
    out.print (e.toString() + "</font>");
}

%>
</body>
</html>
```

The output of the additions is shown in Figure 6.5.

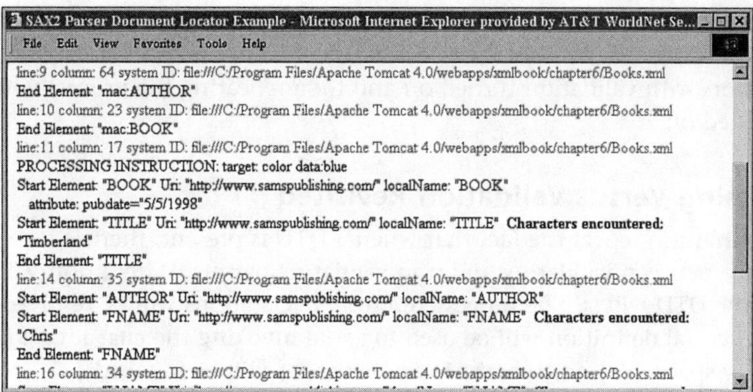

FIGURE 6.5 Output using the document locator.

We are only outputting the parser location during the `endDocument()` invocation. However, the information is available within every callback that is available in SAX.

The `Locator` should be reinitialized for each document parse. If the same parser is going to be used over and over again, which is possible, make sure that you don't hold a reference to the `Locator` outside the `ContentHandler` implementation. If a `Locator` reference is held outside, it will become meaningless as soon as SAX finishes parsing an XML document.

As already mentioned, all parsing is sequential. Each callback must return before the parser can invoke the next event handler. This is also true of parsers being reused to parse other XML documents. The parser may not be used again on another XML document until it has returned from parsing the current XML document. It's fine to reuse parsers, but don't put one in a loop structure unless it is finished parsing before it is used again.

Breaking the System to See How It Works

Now that we've looked at most of the handlers in SAX, let's break the system in various ways to see which type of error is called, and what the results are. Try the following one at a time:

- Change the version number of the XML document or DTD document found in the document declaration.
- Add an element or attribute that is undeclared in the DTD.
- Add an element in the DTD that is nonexistent in the XML document.
- Change the DTD filename so that it can't be found.

By breaking things and seeing how the validating parser reacts, it's possible to get a better understanding of how things work. It would be a good idea to try inducing these errors with validation turned on and then repeating the process with validation turned off.

Processing Versus Validation Revisited

It's important to repeat the fact that when a DTD is present, there is a very subtle difference between validating and non-validating parsers. With a non-validating parser, the DTD will still be processed. Entity declarations will be resolved, and the DTD structural definition will be used to avoid invoking the `characters()` method on empty space. Instead, `ignorableWhiteSpace()` will be invoked.

The only difference in using a validating parser is that the parser will compare the structure of the XML document to the DTD or schema. If the XML document does not maintain the structure defined in the DTD or schema, `error()` will be invoked. That is to say that if `error()` is undefined or its class is not registered as the `ErrorHandler`, *you will have no idea that your XML document is failing validation.* The failure of an XML document to validate is not considered a fatal error, and therefore, unless the error is caught correctly, will pass by unnoticed.

Using SAX to Output HTML

Now that we've had our crash course in SAX, we are going to introduce a short example that is slightly more realistic than simply outputting strings in response to events as we did earlier. In this example, we are going to create a new class that extends `DefaultHandler` to define the callbacks. This class is written specifically to handle the XML document that we defined in Listing 6.1.

The example will create a table to display book data. Upon encountering the processing instruction, we will change the color of the table contents from red to the value of the instruction, which is blue. All the while, we will be counting the rows and displaying the sum after the footer has been added to the table.

Let's begin with the JSP found in Listing 6.12. Save this file as `\webapps\xmlbook\chapter6\XMLTable.jsp`.

LISTING 6.12 XMLTable.jsp

```
<%@ page
  import="org.xml.sax.helpers.*,
  org.xml.sax.*,
  javax.xml.parsers.*,
  xmlbook.chapter6.*"
%>
```

LISTING 6.12 Continued

```
<html>
<head><title>Using SAX to Create a Table</title></head>
<body>

<%
try{
    XMLReader reader = XMLReaderFactory.createXMLReader
        ("org.apache.xerces.parsers.SAXParser");
    reader.setFeature("http://xml.org/sax/features/validation", true);

    //create instance of handler class we wrote
    XMLTable xmlt = new XMLTable(out);

    //register handler class
    reader.setContentHandler(xmlt);
    reader.setErrorHandler(xmlt);

    String  ls_path = request.getServletPath();
    ls_path = ls_path.substring(0,ls_path.indexOf("XMLTable.jsp"));
    String  ls_xml  = application.getRealPath(ls_path + "Books.xml");

    //parse the XML document
    reader.parse(ls_xml);
}
catch (Exception e){
    out.print("<br/><br/><font color=\"red\">there was an error<BR>");
    out.print (e.toString() + "</font>");
}
%>

</body>
</html>
```

This JSP is very similar to the one found in Listing 6.4. The only differences, which appear as boldface print in Listing 6.12, are as follows:

- HTML output title has changed.
- The handler class we are instantiating for parser events is different.
- The JSP for which we are finding the path has changed.

Next, the example needs a handler class as shown in Listing 6.13. Save this class as `\webapps\xmlbook\WEB-INF\classes\xmlbook\chapter6\XMLTable.java`.

LISTING 6.13 XMLTable.java; Converting from XML to a Table

```
package xmlbook.chapter6;
import java.io.*;
import org.xml.sax.helpers.DefaultHandler;
import org.xml.sax.*;

public class XMLTable extends DefaultHandler{
    private Writer w;
    private int intRowCount = 0;
    private String strColor = "red";

    public XMLTable(java.io.Writer new_w){
        w = new_w;
    }

    public void startDocument() throws SAXException{
        try{
            output("<table border=\"2\">");
            output("<tr><th>Pub Date</th><th>Book Title</th>");
            output("<th>Authors</th></tr>");
        }
        catch(Exception e){throw new SAXException(e.toString());}
    }

    public void endDocument() throws SAXException{
        try{
            output ("</table><br> Total Books Listed: " + intRowCount);
        }
        catch(Exception e){throw new SAXException(e.toString());}
    }

    public void startElement(String uri, String localName,
                             String qName, Attributes attributes)
    throws SAXException{
        try{
            if(0 == localName.compareTo("BOOK")){
                intRowCount++;
                output("<tr><td>");
                output(attributes.getValue("pubdate") ) ;
```

LISTING 6.13 Continued

```
            }
            if(0 == localName.compareTo("TITLE"))
                output("<td>");
            if(0 == localName.compareTo("AUTHOR"))
                output("<td>");
            if(0 == localName.compareTo("FOOTER")){
                strColor = "black";
                output("<td colspan=\"3\">");
            }
        }
        catch(Exception e){throw new SAXException(e.toString());}
    }

    public void endElement(String uri, String localName, String qName)
    throws SAXException{
        try{
            if(0 == localName.compareTo("BOOK"))
                output("</tr>");
            if(0 == localName.compareTo("TITLE"))
                output("</td>");
            if(0 == localName.compareTo("AUTHOR"))
                output("</td>");
            if(0 == localName.compareTo("FOOTER"))
                output("</td>");
        }
        catch(Exception e){throw new SAXException(e.toString());}
    }

    public void characters(char[] ch, int start, int length)
    throws SAXException{
        try{
            String s = new String(ch, start, length);
            output(" <font color=\"" + strColor + "\">" +
                s.trim() + "</font>");
        }
        catch(Exception e){throw new SAXException(e.toString());}
    }

    public void processingInstruction(String target, String data)
    throws SAXException{
        try{
```

LISTING 6.13 Continued

```
            if(0 == target.compareTo("color"))
                strColor = data;
        }
        catch(Exception e){throw new SAXException(e.toString());}
    }

    private void output (String strOut) throws SAXException{
        try {
            w.write (strOut);
        }
        catch (IOException e) {throw new SAXException ("I/O error", e);}
    }

    public void warning(SAXParseException e)
    throws SAXException{
        output("<BR><font color=\"red\">warning: " + e.getMessage() + "  "
                + e.getSystemId() + " Line: " + e.getLineNumber() + "</font>");
    }

    public void error(SAXParseException e)
    throws SAXException{
        output("<BR><font color=\"red\">error: " + e.getMessage() + "  "
                + e.getSystemId() + " Line: " + e.getLineNumber() + "</font>");
    }

    public void fatalError(SAXParseException e)
    throws SAXException{
        output("<BR><font color=\"red\">fatalError: " + e.getMessage() + "  "
                + e.getSystemId() + " Line: " + e.getLineNumber() + "</font>");
    }

}
```

This class is somewhat similar to the one in `SAX2Example`, which we created in Listing 6.3. The class has the event handlers we need to define for the parser. The details of this class are the same as in Listing 6.3; the difference lies in the fact that it will be writing HTML strings to the `Writer` upon encountering specific hard-coded XML markup.

Some highlights include the following:

- The HTML `font` tag color attribute changes to the color specified in the color processing instruction.
- The rows are counted through a variable incremented upon the `startElement()` invocation with the `BOOK` tag. Counters like this can be used in many different ways. In HTML reporting, counters can be used to add page breaks for printing purposes.
- The error handling for this class is incomplete and not usable in production systems.

The results produced by this example are shown in Figure 6.6.

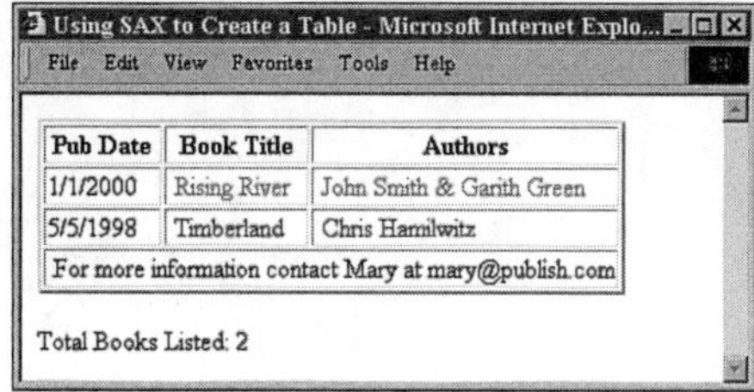

FIGURE 6.6 Output from XMLTable.jsp.

This example gives you a taste of what is possible using SAX, especially when using extremely large XML documents where the DOM memory print is an issue.

Summary

This chapter covered the three most commonly used interfaces of SAX and provided enough information to enable you to get a good start with using SAX. It also discussed various ways that a SAX programmer could get into trouble and how to avoid those problems. The chapter then showed how to use the various callback events that SAX provides for our use in parsing XML.

While the chapter showed the richness of SAX, it also demonstrated that using SAX isn't especially hard. The state of the current development in XML means that many JSP programmers will only use SAX indirectly through various interfaces found in JAXP, JDOM, dom4j, or other XML parsers. However, this chapter has shown that using SAX directly isn't something to fear. It's important as a JSP developer to keep SAX in your back pocket for the tough problems, such as when your business logic requires every ounce of power and speed to work through some XML data. In these cases, you should have nothing to fear from SAX; armed with the information you learned from this chapter, you should be ready to tackle tough XML parsing.

7

Successfully Using JSP and XML in an Application

IN THIS CHAPTER

- Using a Java Representation of an XML Document
- Why Not Just Use SAX or DOM?
- Installing JDOM and dom4j
- Why Both JDOM and dom4j?
- Common Ways to Use XML
- Using a Database with XML
- Pulling in XML Files

This chapter has two goals. The first is to help you begin walking through using XML in a natural way within your JSP application. The second is to show you how to create and use a Java representation of an XML document.

The chapter will start by introducing JDOM and dom4j. These two APIs enable a programmer to create and use a Java representation of an XML document. Once the XML data is conveniently stashed as a Java object, it then becomes simple to use standard Java techniques to manipulate the data. The other benefit of these APIs is that they have convenient helper classes that make performing common tasks easy with Java and XML.

After we've introduced these two APIs, we'll go through several examples of XML usage with a JSP application.

Using a Java Representation of an XML Document

One of the best features of Java is the object-oriented nature of the language. Objects are containers within which it is easy to store and then later access data. The first trick then is to get the data into the Java objects. In this book, we have shown how to use both SAX and DOM to read data into Java. However, these APIs have limitations. With SAX, you can quickly read the data, but you still need to customize and build your own special classes to handle the data. DOM provides classes to handle the data within Java; however, the data representation given in DOM is bulky and not written with an eye towards Java. This means that the next problem to solve is developing a standard way to represent the XML data within Java. Because XML is a standard method of describing data, it makes sense to create a repeatable method to represent an XML document within Java. The two APIs that have been developed to turn XML into a Java representation are JDOM and dom4j.

At this point, a quick explanation of the names JDOM and dom4j is in order. Because of trademark issues, neither stands for anything. The names are not acronyms. Rather, these are the full names of the two products.

Why Not Just Use SAX or DOM?

There are several different ways to read, write, and manipulate an XML document. Up to this point in the book, we have covered two major APIs: SAX and DOM. With these APIs, a Java programmer can do quite a bit with XML. However, each of these APIs has its weaknesses.

SAX is a very fast way to read in and process an XML document. However, SAX doesn't create a memory representation of the XML document. It instead permits us to stream through an XML document. SAX is a forward-only read process. This means that SAX is perfect when only a single pass through a document is required. However, it isn't always the right solution if the program needs to repeatedly access the same XML document. In cases where the data needs to be used more than once, it makes sense to use SAX to read in the data once and then use another process to work with the data. Finally, many programmers prefer to work against an internal document rather than against a stream process.

It turns out that when JDOM and dom4j are used, programmers will often still use SAX. This is because JDOM and dom4j are not XML parsers. The XML document still needs to be parsed and read into memory. SAX is a fast way to do this. Both JDOM and dom4j have builder classes that enable you to use SAX to quickly read an XML file into memory.

Now let's look at DOM for a moment. As shown in Chapter 5, "Using DOM," DOM is very complete; however, it isn't optimized from a Java coding viewpoint. This means that the Java interface to DOM can be awkward to a Java programmer. In addition, DOM is an extremely memory-intensive model. The large memory footprint of DOM is related to the fact that it's such a complete representation of the XML document. The final representation ends up consuming a very large amount of internal memory. JDOM and dom4j were created as a solution to these and other problems encountered when using DOM within Java.

Both JDOM and dom4j create a Java-optimized representation of an XML document. You can use either to represent the XML document in terms of a Java `Collection`. Thus, you can use the standard `List`, `Map`, and `Iterator` Java classes when working with the XML document. Note that *Java-optimized* doesn't necessarily refer to performance. In this case, we are referring to the ability to write and read the Java code in a simpler way. The best tool to use in terms of performance cannot be defined here. Performance depends on internal optimizations within the APIs, which are constantly improving between versions, and the manner in which an API is used in the code. Because these APIs are updated on almost a monthly basis, you have to test for yourself to ensure that the performance is acceptable relative to your project needs.

Installing JDOM and dom4j

This section will briefly cover downloading and installing the JDOM and dom4j APIs. Doing so will enable you to follow along with the examples in this chapter.

JDOM

The JDOM site is found at `http://www.jdom.org/`.

This book uses beta version 7 of JDOM. Once you have downloaded the JDOM zip file and installed the software, place the JDOM.jar file into your Tomcat's `lib` directory.

dom4j

The dom4j site is found at `http://www.dom4j.org/`.

This book uses version 1.1 of dom4j. Once you have downloaded the dom4j zip file and installed the software, place the dom4j.jar file into your Tomcat's `lib` directory. Of course, it should be noted that dom4j comes with several JAR files. Since we already have JAXP and Xerces installed to run with Tomcat, we only need to use the dom4j.jar file.

Notes

After installing both JDOM and dom4j, stop and restart Tomcat. Also, if you are using NetBeans, don't forget to add the dom4j and JDOM JAR files to the development environment.

Why Both JDOM and dom4j?

You don't really need both JDOM and dom4j since these APIs perform the same task. They both create a Java representation of an XML document. They differ, however, in the approach they take to creating the XML representation. JDOM is based on abstract classes, while dom4j is based on interfaces. In this chapter, we will discuss and use both APIs and will leave it to you to decide which Java XML representation you prefer. I personally use both APIs on the JSP Insider Web site. I just match each API to the particular task I am performing and choose the one that best fits my current needs.

Both JDOM and dom4j are good systems and each is an excellent choice for building a Java representation. The examples in this chapter will show how simple it is to use either API.

JDOM and dom4j: A Quick Comparison

While these APIs do the same thing, there are quite a few differences between the implementations. However, the APIs have the same roots. JDOM is an open source project, and the original dom4j code base is a fork from JDOM. A fork occurs in an open source environment when a project splits into two different projects due to differences in philosophy among its users. The developers of dom4j felt that there was a need for an interface-based version of JDOM, so they started their own project.

One sign that both of these APIs are well established is their inclusion in Sun Microsystems products. The next version of JAXP is slated to have a JDOM builder. JDOM is an active JSR within Java and is slated to be rolled into the Java package in late summer 2002. Meanwhile, JAXM is currently built around dom4j.

We can't give you a clear indication of which API is best to use for your own projects. The choice really just boils down to which API is closest to your needs. To determine this, visit each API's Web site and examine the current features.

Choose the API that comes closer to your needs in terms of its prebuilt features and general performance. At the time of this writing, the only published benchmark showed dom4j to be the faster of the two tools. In addition, dom4j has a few extra helper classes built in for XPath features. However, by the time this book is published, the reverse might be true. The two tools will dance around each other for the next few years. Each tool is growing and changing very rapidly. A feature-by-feature comparison list would be useless here, because such a list would be hopelessly out-of-date by the time the book is published. This means that each new build of one API will offer slightly different performance benefits over the other API. JDOM generally changes less rapidly than dom4j, but it has a larger following than dom4j. Because this book will use both APIs, you will have a chance to judge for yourself which one you prefer while working through the examples.

Common Ways to Use XML

Now it's time to begin mixing XML and JSP together. We will do this by building two main examples. While it's possible to show how to use XML piecemeal, the best way to demonstrate XML use is through larger integrated examples. The two examples in this chapter will show you how to use a database with XML and how to incorporate data from XML files into JSP pages.

Using a Database with XML

This first example is a series of smaller examples tied together. The goal will be to take the data from the BannerAds table discussed in Chapter 1, "Integrating JSP and Data," and store the results in a Java XML representation. Once we've stored the data as an XML representation, we can reuse the same data and JavaBeans for different processes throughout the book. For example, this chapter will show how easy it is to apply XSLT and XPath to create formatted output against data from the database. It would be a good idea to add some additional data to this table and to enter a few values for the `starttext` and `endtext` fields. Refer to Table 7.1 for the data entry values used in this example.

TABLE 7.1 Data Within the BannerAds Database Table

Name	Link	`linktext`	`starttext`	`endtext`
Sun	`http://www.sun.com`	The Home of Java		
SAMS	`http://www.samspublishing.com`	Java books	Find great	at SAMS
JSP Information	`http://www.jspinsider.com`	JSP Insider	Get inside your code.	
Jakarta	`http://jakarta.apache.org`	Kewl Tools	If you need some great JSP software, check out:	Jakarta is one of the best sites for JSP code around!

This first set of examples will use dom4j. We will walk through the following steps:

1. Use an XML initialization file to define the database parameters.
2. Design a special object to store and retrieve the database connectivity data.
3. Build a servlet listener file to import the database information to application memory.

4. Build a Java class to create a JDBC `ResultSet` and convert it to a dom4j `Document`.
5. Create a helper class to perform some common dom4j functionality. This class will be used to apply XSL stylesheets to the `Document`.
6. Construct a Java class to create and handle the actual banner ads.
7. Build a test JSP page to demonstrate everything we've created.

XML Initialization Files

Initialization files provide a time-honored method of data storage. Using an XML file is the best way to build an initialization file. Using XML ensures that the data in the file is in the correct format and is accessible to anyone editing the file.

A standard initialization file is typically used to store database connectivity information for a project. Such a file, named database.xml, is shown in Listing 7.1. Create this file and save it as `webapps/xmlbook/WEB-INF/database.xml`.

LISTING 7.1 XML Database Initialization File

```
<?xml version="1.0" encoding="UTF-8"?>
<database>
    <databasename>xmlbook</databasename>
    <driver>org.gjt.mm.mysql.Driver</driver>
    <url>jdbc:mysql://localhost/xmlbook</url>
    <username></username>
    <password></password>
</database>
```

Note that the file is stored in the `WEB-INF` directory, so only the Web application and administrators with direct access to the server machine can access it.

Storing the Initialization Data

To use data from the XML file, you will need to parse it into memory. To do this, just build a special Java class to store the parameters. Listing 7.2 shows a class file named DatabaseParameter.java. Save this file as `webapps/xmlbook/WEB-INF/classes/xmlbook/chapter7/DatabaseParameter.java`.

LISTING 7.2 Database Initialization Object

```
package xmlbook.chapter7;
import java.io.File;
import org.dom4j.Document;
```

LISTING 7.2 Continued

```
import org.dom4j.Element;
import org.dom4j.io.SAXReader;

public class DatabaseParameter extends Object implements java.io.Serializable {

    private String databaseName = "";
    private String driver       = "";
    private String url          = "";
    private String userName     = "";
    private String password     = "";

    public DatabaseParameter() {}

    public DatabaseParameter(String as_db,   String as_driver, String as_url,
                             String as_name, String as_password)
    {setDatabaseName(as_db) ;
     setDriver      (as_driver) ;
     setUrl         (as_url) ;
     setUserName    (as_name);
     setPassword    (as_password);
    }

    public DatabaseParameter(String as_xmlfile) throws Exception
    {   try
        {   SAXReader xmlReader = new SAXReader();
            Document  doc       = xmlReader.read(new File(as_xmlfile));

            Element root = doc.getRootElement();

            setDatabaseName ( root.element("databasename").getText());
            setDriver       ( root.element("driver").getText());
            setUrl          ( root.element("url").getText());
            setUserName     ( root.element("username").getText());
            setPassword     ( root.element("password").getText());
        }
        catch(Exception e)
        {throw e;}
    }

    public String getDatabaseName () {   return databaseName;   }
```

LISTING 7.2 Continued

```
    public String getDriver ()         {   return driver;    }

    public String getUrl ()            {   return url;    }

    public String getUserName ()       {   return userName;    }

    public String getPassword ()       {   return password;    }

    public void setDatabaseName (String as_data)  {databaseName = as_data; }

    public void setDriver (String as_data)        {driver = as_data; }

    public void setUrl (String as_data)           {url = as_data;}

    public void setUserName (String as_data)      {userName = as_data; }

    public void setPassword (String as_data)      {password = as_data;}
}
```

This class does more than just store the database parameters. It comes equipped with its own reader methods. Pass in the XML file and it can initialize itself:

```
public DatabaseParameter(String as_xmlfile) throws Exception
```

The code first creates a SAX reader. This object reads in the XML file and creates a dom4j `Document` object:

```
SAXReader xmlReader = new SAXReader();
Document  doc       = xmlReader.read(new File(as_xmlfile));
```

The `Document` object is the Java representation of the XML file. Once the code has the `Document`, it becomes simple to navigate around the XML data. Each tag within the XML document representation is represented using an `Element` object. The code will need access to the root element of the Document:

```
Element root = doc.getRootElement();
```

Once the root element is at hand, it's easy to drill down further into the dom4j `Document`. This example only requires two methods to query the `Document` elements. The `getText()` method returns the text data of an `Element`. The second method is `element`, which gives a handle to the first subelement that matches a given name:

```
setDatabaseName ( root.element("databasename").getText());
setDriver       ( root.element("driver").getText());
```

```
setUrl          ( root.element("url").getText());
setUserName     ( root.element("username").getText());
setPassword     ( root.element("password").getText());
```

This simple code snippet is all we need to use to read the data in from the XML file. In these few lines of code, it's easy to forget that there is so much happening. This is a multi-step process that entails reading the file, building a `Document` object, and then parsing through the Java representation. The code here is very simple because dom4j is doing all the work for us. For pure speed, it would be faster just to use SAX and build the events to deal with the data. However, in most cases, especially with smaller XML files, the runtime difference is very small, and the use of dom4j enables a programmer to achieve large time savings in design and programming. Just keep in mind that this isn't always the case. When each millisecond counts, it's time to build your own SAX handler, as discussed in Chapter 6, "Programming SAX."

Of course, this is only the start. Throughout this example, the code will illustrate other ways to use dom4j `Documents`.

Using a Listener to Store the `DatabaseParameter` Object

Two common options exist as to how to use the XML database file. The code can read the file as required, or read it once and reuse a cached version of the data. Since the information in this example will not change very often, it makes sense to read the data once and then cache the results.

The best way to do this is to build a listener class to initialize everything upon startup of the JSP application. The servlet specification supports several events within a JSP container against which a programmer can hang a listener event. A listener can be defined against state changes in the application (`ServletContext`) or the session (`HttpSession`) objects. In practice, this means that it's possible to listen for the creation or destruction of the application or session objects (known as life cycle events). It's also possible to listen for the creation, removal, or updating of attributes (attribute events) stored in the application or session. To create a listener, a class must implement an appropriate interface, as described in Table 7.2.

TABLE 7.2 Servlet Listener Interfaces

Interface	Purpose
`javax.servlet.ServletContextListener`	application life cycle
`javax.servlet.ServletContextAttributesListener`	application attributes
`javax.servlet.http.HttpSessionListener`	session life cycle
`javax.servlet.HttpSessionAttributesListener`	session attributes

Note that these interfaces are abstract, so a programmer must create all the methods declared within the interface. This example requires an event to be triggered when the application starts up. This means that the code will implement ServletContextListener.

This part of the example is all about building a listener. Such a file is shown in Listing 7.3. Save it as webapps/xmlbook/WEB-INF/classes/xmlbook/chapter7/DatabaseInitialization.java.

LISTING 7.3 Creating an Application Startup Listener

```
package xmlbook.chapter7;

import javax.servlet.ServletContext;
import javax.servlet.ServletContextEvent;
import javax.servlet.ServletContextListener;


public final class DatabaseInitialization implements ServletContextListener
{    public void contextInitialized(ServletContextEvent event)
    { ServletContext application = event.getServletContext();

      try
      { String  ls_xml  = application.getRealPath("WEB-INF/database.xml");
         DatabaseParameter dbdata = new DatabaseParameter(ls_xml);
         application.setAttribute("DatabaseParameter",dbdata);
      }
      catch (Exception e)
      { application.log("Problem encountered at Startup:" + e.toString());
      }
   }

   public void contextDestroyed(ServletContextEvent event)
   {}
}
```

The code in the listener is basic. The class determines the actual path to the database initialization XML file. Then it creates a DatabaseParameter object. The DatabaseParameter object is stashed in a ServletContext attribute. Once it is in the ServletContext, the object is accessible to every JSP page through the application implicit object.

The next step in building a listener object is to tell the `JSPContainer` about the listener. Listing 7.4 shows how to update the web.xml file located at `webapps/xmlbook/WEB-INF/web.xml`.

LISTING 7.4 Updating the web.xml File

```
<?xml version="1.0" encoding="ISO-8859-1"?>
<!DOCTYPE web-app
  PUBLIC "-//Sun Microsystems, Inc.//DTD Web Application 2.3//EN"
  "http://java.sun.com/j2ee/dtds/web-app_2_3.dtd">

<web-app>
    <listener>
         <listener-class>
          xmlbook.chapter7.DatabaseInitialization
         </listener-class>
    </listener>

    ... Your original web-app contents here!

</web-app>
```

NOTE

Make sure that the web.xml file is defined using version 2.3 of the DTD. (Listeners are a servlet 2.3 feature.)

The JSP container will register listeners in the order of definition within the web.xml file. Thus, the listeners are executed in order of placement. The listeners need to be defined before any servlets are declared within the web.xml file. No servlets are currently defined, so this isn't an issue for this example. Finally, the entries don't tell the JSP container the style of listener being deployed in the web.xml file. The Web container determines this from the interface the listener implements.

At this point, we must repeat our normal routine; it's time to restart Tomcat. A word of warning: An error in the listener class will prevent the Web application from being loaded as a Web application. If this happens, it will not be available for access. The error will be a general `The requested resource (/URL) is not available` message. In case of such a failure, double-check the log file. Within the Tomcat log file, you'll find the following message:

```
Error configuring application listener
```

Examine and solve the error posted in the log file. This error shouldn't happen, but if it does occur, it's disconcerting enough to earn this little warning.

The code we've built up to this point runs behind the scenes. It's time now to build the database portion of the example.

Using a Java XML Model

Let's expand the banner ad example from Chapter 1. This example will read the data from the database and generate a Java XML object representation of the data. Then the Java XML representation will be stored in memory for easy access to the data.

Now we'll build the files needed for the automated text banner system. The first class that we will create, shown in Listing 7.5, will translate a JDBC `ResultSet` to a dom4j `Document` object. Save this file as `webapps/xmlbook/WEB-INF/classes/xmlbook/chapter7/XMLFromResult.java`.

LISTING 7.5 XMLFromResult.java

```
package xmlbook.chapter7;

import java.sql.*;
import org.dom4j.Document;
import org.dom4j.DocumentFactory;
import org.dom4j.util.NonLazyDocumentFactory;
import org.dom4j.Element;

public class XMLFromResult
{   public XMLFromResult() {}

    private String rootName = "Statement";

    private String rowName  = "row";

    public String getRootName ()      {   return rootName;   }

    public String getRowName  ()      {   return rowName;    }

    public void setRootName (String as_data)  {rootName = as_data; }

    public void setRowName  (String as_data)  {rowName = as_data;  }

    public XMLFromResult(String as_root, String as_row)
    { setRootName (as_root);
```

LISTING 7.5 Continued

```
    setRowName  (as_row);
  }

  public Document createXML (DatabaseParameter dbdata, String as_query)
  throws Exception
  {   return createXML ( dbdata, as_query, false);  }

  public Document createXML (DatabaseParameter    dbdata,
                             String               as_query,
                             boolean              ab_embedmetadata)
  throws Exception
  {   String ls_dburl     = dbdata.getUrl();
      String ls_dbdriver  = dbdata.getDriver();
      Connection dbconn   = null;
      Document   resultxml= null;
      try
      {   Class.forName(ls_dbdriver);
          dbconn = DriverManager.getConnection(ls_dburl);

          Statement statement = dbconn.createStatement();

          if (statement.execute(as_query))
          {   ResultSet  results   = statement.getResultSet();
              resultxml =  CreateDocument(results,ab_embedmetadata);
          }
      }
      catch (ClassNotFoundException e)
      {   throw e;  }
      catch (SQLException e)
      {   throw e;  }
      finally
      {   try
          {   if (dbconn != null)
              { dbconn.close(); }
          }
          catch (SQLException e)
          {   throw e;  }
      }

     return resultxml;
  }
```

LISTING 7.5 Continued

```
    public Document CreateDocument(ResultSet a_result)
    { return CreateDocument(a_result, false);  }

    public Document CreateDocument(ResultSet a_result,boolean ab_embedmetadata)
    {DocumentFactory factory  = NonLazyDocumentFactory.getInstance();
     Document xmldoc          = factory.createDocument();

     Element root = xmldoc.addElement(getRootName());

        if(a_result != null )
        {   try
            {
             ResultSetMetaData  metadata  = a_result.getMetaData();
             int li_columns = metadata.getColumnCount();
             int li_rows    = 0;
                while(a_result.next())
                {   li_rows++;

                    Element row = root.addElement( getRowName())
                   .addAttribute( "rownum", String.valueOf(li_rows));

                   for ( int i = 1; i <= li_columns; i++)
                   {   if(a_result.getObject(i) == null)
                       {row.addElement( metadata.getColumnLabel(i) )
                           .addText("");
                       }
                       else
                       {row.addElement( metadata.getColumnLabel(i) )
                           .addText( a_result.getObject(i).toString() );
                       }
                   }
                }
             /* embed metadata if asked for */
             if (ab_embedmetadata)
             { Element mrow = root.addElement("metadata");
               /* embed row count */
               mrow.addElement( "rowcount" )
                      .addText( String.valueOf(li_rows) );
               /* embed column datatypes */
               for ( int i = 1; i <= li_columns; i++)
               {    mrow.addElement(metadata.getColumnLabel(i))
```

LISTING 7.5 Continued

```
                        .addText(metadata.getColumnTypeName(i));
                }
              }
            }
            catch(Exception e)
            { root.addElement( "error" ).addText(e.toString()); }
        }
    return xmldoc;
    }
}
```

Let's examine the points of interest within the `XMLFromResult` class. The first thing to notice is the `rootName` and `rowName` properties. These properties are important because the data being returned from the database isn't in XML format. Most importantly, the SQL results are missing a root element and the row element containing each row of data. When the logic goes to build the `Document` object, the code will need a name for the root element and the element containing data from each row.

The code for accessing the database is similar to the code described in Chapter 1. The new aspect of this object is the `CreateDocument` method. This method will loop through a `ResultSet` and create the actual `Document` object. Creating the actual `Document` only takes a few lines. The first step is to get a `DocumentFactory`; with this, it's possible to create an initial `Document`:

```
DocumentFactory factory  = NonLazyDocumentFactory.getInstance();
Document xmldoc          = factory.createDocument();
```

Once the `Document` object is created, it's a simple matter to add elements using the `addElement` method:

```
Element root = xmldoc.addElement(getRootName());
```

Then the code loops through and appends one row element at a time to the `Document`:

```
Element row = root.addElement( getRowName())
                  .addAttribute( "rownum", String.valueOf(li_rows));
```

Notice that this code will also append an attribute with the `addAttribute` method to each row to indicate the row number the element represents. While not necessary, this will ensure that the Document can return the data in the same order as the original SQL. Within each row element, the code will then add each column of data. The actual element name will be created to match the column name returned by the SQL statement. The only new method of note here is addText, which appends a string to serve as the text data within the element:

```
for ( int i = 1; i <= li_columns; i++)
                 {   row.addElement( metadata.getColumnLabel(i) )
                         .addText( a_result.getObject(i).toString() );
                 }
```

Note that after the data from the SQL statement is processed, the code has one additional step:

```
if (ab_embedmetadata)
{ Element mrow = root.addElement("metadata");
  /* embed row count */
  mrow.addElement( "rowcount" )
         .addText( String.valueOf(li_rows) );
  /* embed column datatypes */
  for ( int i = 1; i <= li_columns; i++)
  {     mrow.addElement(metadata.getColumnLabel(i))
                .addText(metadata.getColumnTypeName(i));
  }
```

The code creates an additional optional element called metadata to store important metadata. In this example, the code stores the row count and the column data types. This example could be easily expanded to store other metadata information. It's our way to embed additional data into the XML representation. The XML data is all string based; once it is placed within the Document, the data is stored as a String. The information from the metadata element makes it possible to recall the original data type and perform special logic when the need arises.

Threading Issues

In dom4j, the default implementation of Element (DefaultElement) can use lazy instantiation to avoid creating List instances. This can cause problems when a document object is shared among threads without being traversed. In a JSP application, it's likely that the code will share a Document object across threads, so we must put some thought into this potential problem. In the case of Listing 7.5, we don't know whether the document object will be accessed by multiple threads. The reason? This is a generic object for use in different processes. This means that the object needs to be designed with thread safety in mind. The code will use the NonLazyDocumentFactory to ensure that no lazy evaluation occurs. Thus, the Document object will be safe for read-only access across concurrent threads.

Keep in mind, additional logic will have to be implemented when this object is within a process that will use the `Document` object for concurrent modifications. For our purposes, concurrent modifications will not be an issue, as the code is used in a read-only capacity.

Getting the Row Count

One of the our goals is to display a random entry. This means that the code will need to get the count of banners. In this case, the code builds an XML file to match the `RecordSet`, so it's simple to count the rows while building the XML document.

While getting the row count is simple in our example, this wasn't always the case. Within JDBC, this seemingly simple task turns out to be more difficult than it appears. There isn't a method to directly count rows in JDBC. The reason? Databases can start returning rows as soon as they are available to output. This means that a count function could return inaccurate numbers as rows stream into the resultset.

A programmer has access to two standard methods to retrieve a row count from the `ResultSet`. One method is to use a `Count` within the SQL statement. Of course, this method has the problem that the count could change between the time of the count and the time of the SQL statement operation.

The second method is to perform the count once you've obtained the recordset. The problem here is one of speed. First, move to the last row using the `last()` method. Then, ask for the current row number using the `getRow()` method. Then, move back to the first row using the `first()` method. At this point, the code can continue its normal processing. This method is slow and at times can be extremely resource intensive.

Ironically, it's easier to perform the count once the data is stored in the `Document` object. Using dom4j, you can either perform an XPath statement (not the fastest way to count the data) or obtain a `List` of the elements from which you can get an element count.

Why get into the gory details of counting? This example illustrates that dom4j and JDOM introduce new tools. Programmers accustomed to logic using JDBC now have additional ways to view, examine, and modify data within a Java XML representation. Code and logic that used to be written exclusively for dealing with a JDBC `ResultSet` might at times be better written to work against the dom4j `Document` object.

XML and the `WebRowSet`

In Java 1.4, JDBC 3.0 will introduce the `WebRowSet`. This Java class is based on the `CachedRowSet` class. The nice thing about this class is that it can describe the data as an XML document. This means that we could simplify the code in Listing 7.5 using the `WebRowSet`. The `WebRowSet` isn't covered in this book, as the code is written using the Java 1.3 specification.

Building a dom4j Helper Class

Listing 7.6 contains a class that handles the dom4j `Document` object we created in the `XMLFromResult.java` class. Save this new class as `webapps/xmlbook/WEB-INF/classes/xmlbook/chapter7/ProcessDom4J.java`.

LISTING 7.6 ProcessDom4J.java, a Class to Process a dom4j `Document`

```
package xmlbook.chapter7;

import org.dom4j.Document;
import org.dom4j.io.DocumentResult;
import org.dom4j.io.DocumentSource;
import org.dom4j.io.*;

import java.io.*;
import javax.servlet.jsp.JspWriter;
import javax.xml.transform.Transformer;
import javax.xml.transform.TransformerFactory;
import javax.xml.transform.stream.*;

public class ProcessDom4J
{
public ProcessDom4J() {}

public void produceXML (JspWriter out, Document a_xmlresult) throws Exception
{   try
    {   OutputFormat format = OutputFormat.createPrettyPrint();
        XMLWriter writer = new XMLWriter( out, format );
        writer.write(a_xmlresult);
        writer.close();
    }
    catch (Exception e)
    {  throw e; }
}

public void applyXSL (JspWriter out,    Document a_xmlresult,
                      String    as_xsl) throws Exception
{       StreamSource xsl    = new StreamSource(new File(as_xsl));
        StreamResult result = new StreamResult(out);
```

LISTING 7.6 Continued

```
        Transformer transformer;

        TransformerFactory factory = TransformerFactory.newInstance();

        transformer = factory.newTransformer( xsl );

        // Creates a JAXP Source from the dom4j document
        DocumentSource source = new DocumentSource( a_xmlresult );

        // create the output stream from the xsl / document combo
        transformer.transform(source, result);
}
}
```

Listing 7.6 represents a helper class that makes it easy to manipulate a dom4j `Document`. Only a few functions are included here to demonstrate some basic capabilities.

The first method of note is `produceXML`:

```
public void produceXML (JspWriter out, Document a_xmlresult) throws Exception
{   try
    {   OutputFormat format = OutputFormat.createPrettyPrint();
        XMLWriter writer = new XMLWriter( out, format );
        writer.write(a_xmlresult);
        writer.close();
    }
    catch (Exception e)
    {  throw e; }
}
```

This method takes a `Document` object and applies the dom4j `OutputFormat` object against the `Document`. More specifically, the `createPrettyPrint` method is used to take the `Document` and transform it into a simple XML document.

The second method is called `applyXSL`. This method first reads in an XSL file:

```
{       StreamSource xsl    = new StreamSource(new File(as_xsl));
        StreamResult result = new StreamResult(out);
```

It then creates a `Transformer` object with which to apply the XSL stylesheet against a document:

```
Transformer transformer;
TransformerFactory factory = TransformerFactory.newInstance();
transformer = factory.newTransformer( xsl );
```

However, the XSL isn't applied directly to the dom4j `Document` object. Rather, the code creates a JAXP data source against the `Document` object through which to apply the XSL:

```
DocumentSource source = new DocumentSource( a_xmlresult );
```

Then, the code applies the source against the XSL and sends the data back to the output buffer:

```
transformer.transform(source, result);
```

Creating a Banner Handler

Listing 7.7 shows a class that handles the actual banners. Save this new class as `webapps/xmlbook/WEB-INF/classes/xmlbook/chapter7/BannerAdStore.java.`

LISTING 7.7 BannerAdStore.java, a Class to Create Banner Ads

```
package xmlbook.chapter7;

import java.util.Iterator;
import org.dom4j.Document;
import org.dom4j.Element;
import org.dom4j.Node;

public class BannerAdStore  implements java.io.Serializable
{
private  Document bannerData = null;

public void setBannerData(Document data) {bannerData = data;}

public Document getBannerData() {return bannerData;}

public BannerAdStore() {}

public BannerAdStore(Document data) {setBannerData(data);}

public BannerAdStore(DatabaseParameter dbdata)
```

LISTING 7.7 Continued

```
{   XMLFromResult result= new XMLFromResult("BANNERS","BANNERAD");
    try
    {  String ls_sql = "select name as NAME," +
                       "       link as LINK," +
                       "       linktext as LINKTEXT," +
                       "       starttext as STARTTEXT," +
                       "       endtext as ENDTEXT" +
                       "       from BannerAds";
       setBannerData(result.createXML (dbdata, ls_sql,true));
    }
    catch(Exception e)
    {  setBannerData(null);
    }
}

public String randomBannerLink()
{ int li_row = 1 + (int) (Math.random() * getCount());
  return produceBannerLink(li_row) ;
}

public String produceBannerLink (int bannerid)
{    String xpath = "//BANNERAD[" + bannerid + "]";
     Node bannernode  = bannerData.selectSingleNode( xpath );

     String link      = bannernode.valueOf( "LINK" );
     String linktext  = bannernode.valueOf( "LINKTEXT" );
     String start     = bannernode.valueOf( "STARTTEXT" );
     String end       = bannernode.valueOf( "ENDTEXT" );

     String ls_banner = " <a href=\"" + link + "\">" + linktext + "</a> ";
     return start + ls_banner + end;
}

public int getCount ()
{    Element root = bannerData.getRootElement();
     String ls_count = root.element("metadata").element("rowcount").getText();
     return Integer.parseInt(ls_count.trim());
}

public String[] bannerArray ()
```

LISTING 7.7 Continued

```
{   String links[] = new String[getCount()];

    Element root = bannerData.getRootElement();
    Iterator banner_iterator = root.elementIterator("BANNERAD");
    int li_count = 0;
    while(banner_iterator.hasNext())
    {
       Element bannerad = (Element)banner_iterator.next();

       String link      = bannerad.element("LINK").getText();
       String linktext  = bannerad.element("LINKTEXT").getText();
       String start     = bannerad.element("STARTTEXT").getText();
       String end       = bannerad.element("ENDTEXT").getText();

       String banner = " <a href=\"" + link + "\">" + linktext + "</a> " ;
       links[li_count]  = start + banner + end;
       li_count++;
    }
    return links;

}
}
```

The purpose of this class is to create and store a banner document. The banner document is a dom4j `Document` representation of every banner stored in the database. The class also has several access methods to randomly extract a banner and to pull out specifically requested banners.

The first property to examine is the current `Document` object containing all the latest banners from the database:

```
private  Document bannerData = null;
```

The class also has a constructor class to automatically create and store the `bannerData` `Document` object:

```
public BannerAdStore(DatabaseParameter dbdata)
{   XMLFromResult result= new XMLFromResult("BANNERS","BANNERAD");
    try
    { String ls_sql = "select name as NAME," +
                      "       link as LINK," +
                      "       linktext as LINKTEXT," +
```

```
                    "       starttext as STARTTEXT," +
                    "       endtext as ENDTEXT" +
                    "       from BannerAds";
    setBannerData(result.createXML (dbdata, ls_sql,true));
}
```

In this constructor, the code is geared to create an XML representation that will be compatible with the XSL stylesheet BannerAds.xsl created in Listing 4.2 of Chapter 4, "A Quick Start to JSP and XML Together."

Once this object is created, the code has several functions that produce a banner ad to be displayed. Notice the actual use of XPath. One advantage of using dom4j is the ability to use XPath statements to query the `Document` object. Using the `selectSingleNode` and `selectNodes()` methods, you can obtain a `Node` and `List` sorted relative to an XPath expression. This is a very powerful search technique for finding data within the `Document` object:

```
public String produceBannerLink (int bannerid)
{   String xpath = "//BANNERAD[" + bannerid + "]";
    Node bannernode  = bannerData.selectSingleNode( xpath );

    String link      = bannernode.valueOf( "LINK" );
    String linktext  = bannernode.valueOf( "LINKTEXT" );
    String start     = bannernode.valueOf( "STARTTEXT" );
    String end       = bannernode.valueOf( "ENDTEXT" );

    String ls_banner = " <a href=\"" + link + "\">" + linktext + "</a> ";
    return start + ls_banner + end;
}
```

In `produceBannerLink`, the code uses XPath to search for a particular banner within the `Document`. Once the node with the matching banner is obtained, the `valueOf` method can be used to extract the text data from the subelements within the node.

The class also has a function to produce a `String` array containing completed text banners of each banner. The `bannerArray` function will be used in the next chapter for the Web service methods. The `bannerArray` function differs from `produceBannerLink` in that it doesn't use XPath. Rather, it uses an `Iterator` to loop through the entire `Document`:

```
Element root = bannerData.getRootElement();
Iterator banner_iterator = root.elementIterator("BANNERAD");

while(banner_iterator.hasNext())
{
```

Once a row `Element` is obtained, the next step is simply to use the `element` and `getText` methods to get the banner data:

```
Element bannerad = (Element)banner_iterator.next();

String link      = bannerad.element("LINK").getText();
String linktext  = bannerad.element("LINKTEXT").getText();
String start     = bannerad.element("STARTTEXT").getText();
String end       = bannerad.element("ENDTEXT").getText();
```

The data is then used to build a link with surrounding text. This data is used to build the `String` array containing the text-based banners:

```
String banner = " <a href=\"" + link + "\">" + linktext + "</a> ";
links[li_count]  = start + banner + end;
```

The nice thing about `BannerAdStore` is that all of the code is specifically geared towards generating and retrieving a final banner. The actual object doesn't have any special methods or properties for dealing with data manipulation of the individual banner elements. By storing the data within a `Document` object, the class receives the benefit of pushing all of the assessor functions used for data control back towards the simple dom4j methods. As developers, we don't have to spend much time customizing the class for it to handle the data intelligently. The dom4j API takes care of this aspect of data manipulation for us.

Creating a Test JSP Page

The last step of this example is to build a JSP page to access a banner. In Appendix C, "Tag Library," we will show you how to build a tag library interface for these classes. In addition, Chapter 8, "Integrating JSP and Web Services," will show you how to build a Web service interface for this same code. Listing 7.8 builds a simple JSP page, which you should save as `webapps/xmlbook/chapter7/DisplayBannerText.jsp`.

LISTING 7.8 DisplayBannerText.jsp, Used to Display a Banner

```
<%@page contentType="text/html"
        import="xmlbook.chapter7.*,
                org.dom4j.Document"%>

<%DatabaseParameter dbdata;
  dbdata = (DatabaseParameter)  application.getAttribute("DatabaseParameter");
  BannerAdStore banners = new BannerAdStore(dbdata);
%>
<html><head><title>Using a complete banner</title></head><body>
```

LISTING 7.8 Continued

```
Calling the Banner 5 times for kicks
<div align="center">

<%
for (int i = 0 ; i < 5 ; i++)
{
    out.print("<p>" + banners.randomBannerLink() +  "</p>" );
}
%>
</div>
</body></html>
```

The code in this page is basic; it merely retrieves our database parameters stored in the application space, creates a `BannerAdStore` object, and has it return a few random banners from the XML document representation of the banner ad list from the database. The page will produce the result shown in Figure 7.1.

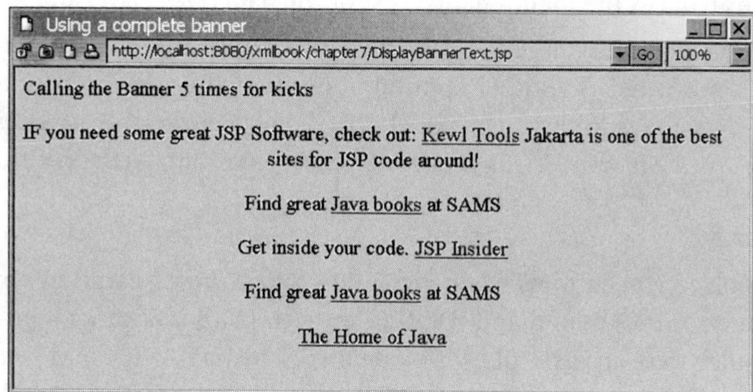

FIGURE 7.1 Results of running DisplayBannerText.jsp.

This example is basic. Using the XML representation hasn't gained us very much compared to using a straight database resultset. It all depends on how the code needs to use the data. The nicest aspect of using the XML representation is that the code is clean and easy to use. This makes these objects easy to expand and use for other purposes. In fact, in later chapters we will take this example and further demonstrate other concepts, such as how to build a tag library and implement a Web service.

You should cache `BannerAdStore` into memory to allow it to be reused by multiple pages. You can store the object in either the application or session space. Re-creating the `Document` object would be inefficient—it can be reused since the banners don't change frequently. The strength of this example comes from its use of a `Document` object. Let's examine what this will gain for us.

Using a Java Representation of an XML Document

One powerful technique of Java is to create an object representation of data used within an application. Any object that defines and stores data in this fashion is referred to as a datastore. One advantage of placing the data into a JDOM or dom4j `Document` object is that doing so gives us a standard way to describe data and create a datastore. This permits the use of the same methods and techniques across many different data objects created as `Documents`. The Java XML API becomes a common interface for most of the data objects needed within our code. This is an incredible boon, as it makes our life much easier by reducing the number of data interfaces we need to learn and use. Also, when a data object changes with time (which it will; that's the natural law of code entropy at work), the actual data interface doesn't change. This reduces the maintenance cost of the data object over the long term.

This technique doesn't replace the use of business objects to encapsulate data. Instead, it is presented as another method in our toolkit of practices for encapsulating data within a Java project. The benefits of using `Document`-based datastores are discussed in the "`HashMap` Versus Java XML Representation" section of this chapter.

Using JAXB

Several options are open to us when we build an XML-based datastore. In this chapter, the code uses dom4j and JDOM. However, JAXB is another consideration. If the data source were an XML file with a defined schema, JAXB could be an interesting choice for building a datastore. This API would be very fast and would automate most of the work involved in building our JavaBean object representation (JAXB could take the XML file and quickly create our Java object based on the XML schema). However, at the time of this writing, JAXB is still too young and incomplete. By time this book is published, JAXB should be close to final release. After you work through this chapter, we encourage you to also consider JAXB as another option in building the XML data blocks used within Java.

HashMap Versus Java XML Representation

Moving every piece of data into an XML datastore isn't always an appropriate solution. Some programmers think of using an XML representation as another layer of work. This extra layer is costly in terms of extra programming and data processing. For example, a very common method to store the data from the JDBC ResultSet involves pushing the data into a HashMap. This is a fast and reliable method for storing data within a Java application.

So the question now becomes Why use a Document representation when it's faster to use a HashMap? The advantage of using an XML datastore is that it offers some flexibility. The layer of XML abstraction makes it easy to reuse a common XML style interface over the data. This in itself isn't a compelling reason, as the HashMap also introduces a level of abstraction in storing the data. However, the XML Document introduces different ways to handle and manipulate the data. Once the data is stored in a JDOM or dom4j Document, we gain functionality, such as the ability to use XPath and XSLT. In addition, the data is very easy to translate to different XML formats. JDOM and dom4j offer direct access to XML data sources. This enables us to easily aggregate data from many sources. Also, when performing a task that requires the manipulation of data over time, using the XML representation is easier. The XML representation can be easily stored in memory and written out as a permanent XML file for long-term storage. Finally, a HashMap doesn't allow for duplicate keys, while XML allows for multiple elements of the same name.

An XML representation only allows the storage of String-based data. If you need to store Java objects, a HashMap is the way to go. You should also use a HashMap when the code needs speed. On the other hand, you should use a Java XML representation when you need long-term data access or flexibility for data access and manipulation.

Pulling in XML Files

Our second example will use JDOM. This example shows how to drive a JSP page from a collection of XML files. In this particular case, the code is based on the XML files of the JSPBuzz newsletter. The JSPBuzz is a bimonthly newsletter stored within an XML file. The goal of the example is to build an archive page that lists the contents of each issue of the JSPBuzz.

As more data is stored within XML files, it will become a common practice to mix and match various XML sources to produce different views to display to the user. The first thing that needs to be mentioned is that storing data within XML files is not as efficient as using a database. Another reality to consider is that XML files are like dust—over time, they will collect and gather into XML "file piles" around a Web application. For situations where the files are small and the usage load isn't overwhelming, it's quite acceptable to use the XML files directly. In these situations, the XML files are accessed directly as a data source.

If speed is of utmost importance, or if user load is beginning to drag the server down, you should quickly import the XML into a database.

Defining an XML File

First, we'll define an XML file for the example to use. Listing 7.9 uses a shortened version of an October issue of the JSPBuzz. Save the file as `webapps/xmlbook/chapter7/buzz_10_09_2001.xml`.

LISTING 7.9 Shortened Version of buzz_10_09_2001.xml

```
<?xml version="1.0" encoding="UTF-8"?>
<jspbuzz volumn="II" issue="19">
    <title>JSP Buzz - October 9th, 2001 - Misc Tidbits</title>
    <description>A Java Current Event Newsletter. </description>
    <buzzdate>10/9/2001</buzzdate>
    <sponsor>Amberjack Software LLC</sponsor>
    <sponsor_text> Sponsored by Amberjack Software LLC. </sponsor_text>
    <ramble position="1">
        <author>Casey Kochmer</author>
        <title>More on Web Services</title>
        <topicbody position="1">
                  <body>In continuing to play with Web services, I am amazed
                        at the simplicity of building a Web service. With
                        little experience and existing tools any programmer
                        can implement a Web service. The problems with Web
                        services isn't in building a Web service but with
                        everything else surrounding Web services. The problems
                        I see are:</body>
        </topicbody>
        <topicbody position="2">
                   <body>-The overall marketplace is in confusion with general
                          economic conditions.</body>
        </topicbody>
        <topicbody position="3">
                   <body>... The article continues on in the full version
                   </body>
        </topicbody>
    </ramble>
    <buzzlink type="news" numericdate="20011007" position="1">
```

LISTING 7.9 Continued

```
        <reference>Microsoft</reference>
        <title>Microsoft Plans Java Counterpunch for .NET</title>
        <link>http://www.theregister.co.uk/content/4/22088.html</link>
        <author>The Register</author>
        <date>October 7th, 2001</date>
        <body>Rumors of Java.Net (J#) from the land of Microsoft</body>
    </buzzlink>
    <buzzlink type="link" numericdate="20010925" position="1">
        <reference>Discussion</reference>
        <title>Succeeding as a Developer In Todays Economy </title>
        <link> http://theserverside.com/discussion/thread.jsp?thread_id=9215
               </link>
        <author>The ServerSide</author>
        <date>September 25th, 2001</date>
        <body>A discussion and article about the current marketplace and
                      the skills required to survive in the current and future
                      chaos. Well worth the time to read if you are nervous
                      about your job situation.</body>
    </buzzlink>
    <buzzlink type="link" numericdate="20011003" position="2">
        <reference>Article</reference>
        <title>Where are Web Services Today?</title>
        <link> http://www.webservicesarchitect.com/content/articles/mark01.asp
               </link>
        <author>Mark Waterhouse</author>
        <date>October 3rd, 2001</date>
        <body>A relatively positive article on Web services.  It reviews
                      some strengths and weaknesses of Web services.</body>
    </buzzlink>
    <buzzlink type="link" numericdate="20011001" position="3">
        <reference>Site</reference>
        <title>XMethods</title>
        <link>http://www.xmethods.com/</link>
        <author/>
        <date/>
        <body>A decent site with a listing of Web services to access and
                      some basic Web service information.</body>
    </buzzlink>
    <buzzlink type="link" numericdate="20010901" position="4">
        <reference>Article</reference>
        <title>XML in Java : Document Models, Part 1 </title>
```

LISTING 7.9 Continued

```
        <link> http://www-106.ibm.com/developerworks/xml/library/x-injava/
               </link>
        <author>Dennis M. Sosnoski</author>
        <date>September 2001</date>
        <body>A must read article for anyone playing around with Java
                  and XML. It's both a review of current XML parsers and
                  comparison of performance results. Great article.</body>
    </buzzlink>
    <buzzlink type="product" numericdate="20011007" position="1">
        <reference>JSP Container</reference>
        <title>Tomcat 4.0 Maintenance Release #1</title>
        <link>http://jakarta.apache.org/</link>
        <author>Jakarta</author>
        <date>October 7th, 2001</date>
        <body>Tomcat 4.0 maintenance release #1 is now available.</body>
    </buzzlink>
    <buzzlink type="product" numericdate="20011001" position="2">
        <reference>Build Tool</reference>
        <title>Ant Beta 1 Released</title>
        <link>http://jakarta.apache.org/ant/index.html</link>
        <author>Jakarta</author>
        <date>October 1st, 2001</date>
        <body>Various bug fixes for Ant 1.4 are in this release.</body>
     </buzzlink>
     <copyright> JSP Buzz Copyright 2001 Amberjack Software LLC.
                 All rights reserved.</copyright>
     <trademarks>Sun, Sun Microsystems, JSP and Java are registered
                 trademarks of Sun Microsystems, Inc. in the United States
                 and other countries. JSP Insider and JSP Buzz are
                 independent of Sun Microsystems, Inc. </trademarks>
</jspbuzz>
```

This XML file is unremarkable. It contains the links and data needed to create a JSPBuzz newsletter. The file contains no HTML markup. All presentation logic is performed through either XSL or Java programming logic. The JSPBuzz XML format uses attributes within elements to store metadata that aids in displaying the data. For example, any element for which display order is important has a `position` attribute to indicate the order in which the data is to be displayed. The other pieces of metadata stored within the XML file are the element names themselves. For example, header elements are always displayed before body elements and footer elements are displayed after body elements.

Pondering XML Design

One lesson learned from building the XML version of the JSPBuzz is the importance of a solid XML layout. The XML file layout is as important as any database design. Time and careful planning are required to build a suitable XML layout. The final design should meet three needs: storage of data, data design that complements coding requirements, and creation of metadata for special presentation needs.

The first purpose of the XML document is holding the data in an efficient manner. This idea is basic, since an XML file stores data. However, while data storage is the primary purpose of an XML document, it represents only one third of the design picture.

The second aspect of XML design is the consideration of how the data gets placed into the XML file. An XML schema with poor design can have a negative impact on how easy it is to create and maintain an XML document. This impact is due to the fact that XML layout is very flexible. It is possible to create many different variations of an XML file design to hold the same data. For example, data can be stored either as an attribute or as an element. Simple differences like this can impact how XSLT and Java processes are written to process an XML file. So in simple terms, make sure an XML design supports the way users and programmers will enter and extract data from the XML files.

The third consideration of XML design is producing a schema that supports a process using the XML-based data. It's important to remember that XML is not a database. Rather, XML is a bridge between processes. This means an XML dataset might need metadata to support the processes that use the XML dataset. Oftentimes XML data is used to drive presentations with the help of XSLT. This translates into a requirement to include some metadata to support presentation needs.

The JSPBuzz newsletter provides a quick example. Within the XML file, the JSPBuzz stores the story position. Without this information, the XSLT stylesheet would have no way to properly order the stories from the newsletter. This positional information has nothing to do with the news story data; it is purely for presentation purposes. This simple example shows that building an XML file can indeed be different from building a database dataset. XML serves different purposes, and driving presentation of data is one of those purposes. Be warned, the design of an XML file should minimize how much presentation data is stored within the XML file. The reason for this is that presentation data can be very arbitrary; it is subject to interpretation and changes over time. Building an XML file is at times a fine art that takes practice and time to learn.

Now, there will be XML programmers who disagree with the second and third statements. That's fine; there's plenty of room for debate. We make the points here to get you thinking about XML design. You should walk away with the understanding that XML is not a database, which also means that the design of an XML file doesn't necessarily follow the same rules as database design. Unfortunately, many programmers who have database experience automatically assume that XML file design should match database design. This assumption can cause problems.

Typically, you should plan and design XML files towards the end of the database design phase of a project. Just as changing a database design in mid-project necessitates reprogramming and extra work, the same is true for XML file formats. In fact, we would go so far as to say that a bad XML file design is harder to fix than a bad database design. The reason is one of scope. XML files typically are used to communicate between projects. An XML specification is released to many programmers outside the project. Releasing a bad design early on affects every related project. Sadly, we have seen projects delayed by months because of the premature release of XML specifications. Remember, not only does releasing a bad XML file make a project look bad, but chasing down everyone affected by a design change is very time-consuming.

A well-designed XML schema is an important first step in successfully using JSP and XML together within an application.

Reading XML Files and Creating New Output

Now let's build a class to take the XML data and convert it to a JSPBuzz table of contents listing. In building this example, we considered two options for generating the output:

- Use an XSL stylesheet and XPath. This has the advantage of being modular. Using a stylesheet would make it a simple matter to swap XPath statements around to change the processing of the JDOM `Document`. In addition, most of the logic already existed in the JSPBuzz stylesheet used to build the current newsletter page. The disadvantage is that the XPath solution generally would be the slower of the two options. In addition, a stylesheet doesn't have access to other data stored in the Web application, or the Java class libraries.

- Use Java logic to work through the JDOM `Document`. The advantage of this solution is that it uses the Java language directly. Our class would have all the resources available to a Java program and servlet.

The choice of an approach was a difficult one to make. In this case, speed was not an issue and most of the logic existed in a stylesheet already in use. However, the XML file didn't contain the location of the various JSP pages displaying the JSPBuzz newsletter. It was simpler to build the actual HTML links within a Java class. For this reason, we decided to use Java logic to work with the JDOM `Document`.

The class we used to convert the XML data to the JSPBuzz table of contents appears in Listing 7.10. Save this file as `webapps/xmlbook/WEB-INF/classes/xmlbook/chapter7/ProduceListing.java`.

LISTING 7.10 ProduceListing.java, Used to List the Contents of a Newsletter

```
package xmlbook.chapter7;

import java.io.File;
import java.io.IOException;
import java.util.Iterator;
import java.util.List;
import javax.servlet.jsp.JspWriter;
import org.jdom.Document;
import org.jdom.Element;
import org.jdom.JDOMException;
import org.jdom.input.SAXBuilder;

public class ProduceListing
{   public ProduceListing() {}

    public void listContent(String    as_site,
                            String    as_file,
                            String    as_path,
                            JspWriter out) throws JDOMException, IOException
    { try
      { // Use Sax to Read the File, Uses Builder as Defined in JAXP.
        SAXBuilder builder = new SAXBuilder();

        // Build the JDOM Document
        Document doc = builder.build(new File(as_path + "/" + as_file));

        // Get the Root Element
        Element root = doc.getRootElement();

       // Build a table to list all items.
       out.print("<table><tr>");
       out.print("<td align=\"center\" valign=\"bottom\" class=\"GreenBox\">");
```

LISTING 7.10 Continued

```
out.print("<a href=\"" + as_site + as_file + "\"/>");
out.print(root.getChild("title").getTextTrim());
out.print("</a></td></tr><tr>");
out.print("<td align=\"left\" valign=\"top\" class=\"OffWhiteBox\">");
out.print("<ul>");

/* first gather the links and re-sort them to the proper order*/
List buzzlinks = root.getChildren("buzzlink");
int  li_count = buzzlinks.size();
String[] news_links    = new String[li_count];
String[] general_links = new String[li_count];
String[] product_links = new String[li_count];

Iterator i = buzzlinks.iterator();

while (i.hasNext())
{   Element link = (Element) i.next();
    if (link.getAttributeValue("type").equals("news"))
    {int position =Integer.parseInt(link.getAttributeValue("position"));
     news_links[position] = link.getChild("title").getTextTrim();
    }
    if (link.getAttributeValue("type").equals("link"))
    {int position =Integer.parseInt(link.getAttributeValue("position"));
     general_links[position] = link.getChild("title").getTextTrim();
    }
    if (link.getAttributeValue("type").equals("product"))
    {int position =Integer.parseInt(link.getAttributeValue("position"));
     product_links[position] = link.getChild("title").getTextTrim();
    }
}

 /*first print out the news items */
 for (int loop = 0; loop < li_count; loop++)
 { if (news_links[loop] != null)
   out.print("<li>" + news_links[loop] +"</li>");
 }

 /* Then list the Ramble links */
 List buzztopics = root.getChildren("ramble");
 i = buzztopics.iterator();
 while (i.hasNext())
```

LISTING 7.10 Continued

```
        {   Element link = (Element) i.next();
            out.print("<li>" + link.getChild("title").getTextTrim() +"</li>");
        }

        /*Then print out the Links items */
        for (int loop = 0; loop < li_count; loop++)
        { if (general_links[loop] != null)
          out.print("<li>" + general_links[loop] +"</li>");
        }

        /*Then print out the products */
        for (int loop = 0; loop < li_count; loop++)
        { if (product_links[loop]!= null)
          out.print("<li>" + product_links[loop] +"</li>");
        }

        /* Then list the main topic links */
        buzztopics = root.getChildren("topic");
        i = buzztopics.iterator();
        while (i.hasNext())
        {   Element link = (Element) i.next();
            out.print("<li>" + link.getChild("title").getTextTrim() +"</li>");
        }

        out.print("</ul></td></tr></table>");
        }
        catch(Exception e)
        {   /* output nothing if something goes wrong */
            //out.print(e.toString());
            out.print("Archived copy of JSPBuzz not available.");
        }
    }
}
```

This class wasn't built to be reusable. It has one purpose, and that is to build a table of contents for a specified JSPBuzz newsletter. In addition, this class is only being used by a single JSP page, so no tag library interface will be built and the presentation logic will be embedded within the class. We have no reason to make this class any more complicated. If we ever want to use the code for other processes, we can re-factor it to be more efficient. However, it's very doubtful this will ever be the case.

Using JDOM

Let's examine what the code in Listing 7.10 does.

First, it uses SAX to read in the XML file and then has JDOM build a `Document` representation of the XML file:

```
SAXBuilder builder = new SAXBuilder();
Document doc = builder.build(new File(as_path + "/" + as_file));
```

JDOM comes with a variety of builders. A builder is a helper class used to create the actual JDOM `Document`. In this example, the code uses the `SAXBuilder` since this is currently the fastest way to read in the file. Over time, expect to see other builders emerge in JDOM that are faster than SAX. JDOM also has builders to support DOM and even an experimental builder to support translating a JDBC `ResultSet`. Chapter 11, "Using XML in Reporting Systems," will discuss using the JDOM `ResultSetBuilder`. As an interesting side note, it's easy for us as programmers to create JDOM builder classes. If JDOM doesn't support a builder class that meets your project needs (for example, a parser that translates comma-separated files into JDOM), it's a simple matter to create your own.

Once the code has the JDOM `Document`, the next step involves working with the data. In this example, the code will programmatically walk its way through the `Document`. To do this, the code will need to get a handle on the root `Element` of the `Document`:

```
Element root = doc.getRootElement();
```

The class then outputs the initial HTML to surround the XML data. After this, the code obtains a `List` containing all the `buzzlink` XML elements:

```
List buzzlinks = root.getChildren("buzzlink");
```

Now the code encounters an interesting problem. A `buzzlink` contains an attribute called `type` that defines the location in which to place the link within the newsletter. Also, the `buzzlink` element contains a `position` attribute to define placement relative to links of the same `type`. The XML document doesn't guarantee the placement of elements. The code must use these attributes to place the actual data correctly. It's a simple matter to use XPath to sort the data relative to these elements. However, XPath is not an option in this case. The code will need to perform an initial sorting phase to re-sort the data correctly:

```
int  li_count = buzzlinks.size();
String[] news_links    = new String[li_count];
String[] general_links = new String[li_count];
String[] product_links = new String[li_count];
```

The code uses three arrays to store the data in the proper order. As the logic works its way through the `List`, it sorts the data into the appropriate array:

```
while (i.hasNext())
{   Element link = (Element) i.next();
    if (link.getAttributeValue("type").equals("news"))
    {int position =Integer.parseInt(link.getAttributeValue("position"));
     news_links[position] = link.getChild("title").getTextTrim();
    }
```

Then, once the data has been processed, it is a simple matter to print out the sorted links:

```
/*first print out the news items */
for (int loop = 0; loop < li_count; loop++)
{ if (news_links[loop] != null)
  out.print("<li>" + news_links[loop] +"</li>");
}
```

This code demonstrates the ease with which you can navigate a JDOM `Document`. The actual XML data is represented using JDOM Java classes such as `Element`. Extracting the information is a simple matter of calling methods such as `getAttributeValue` (which returns data from an element's attribute) or `getTextTrim` (which returns the text of an element trimmed of all whitespace).

Building the Final JSP Page

We're ready to build the JSP page that will display the contents of the JSPBuzz newsletter (see Listing 7.11). Save this file as `webapps/xmlbook/chapter7/NewsletterArchive.jsp`.

LISTING 7.11 NewsletterArchive.jsp, Used to Display Newsletter Contents

```
<%@page contentType="text/html"
        import="xmlbook.chapter7.*"%>
<html>
<head><title>JSP Page</title>
<style>
    td { font-family: verdana, Arial, ; font-size: 10pt; border-style: groove;
         border-width:2px; border-color:#ffffff; padding:2px;}
.Clear{background:#ffffff;border-width:0px;padding-left:0px;padding-right:0px;}
.OffWhiteBox {background: #f5f5f5;}
.GreenBox {background: #aabbbb;}
</style>
```

LISTING 7.11 Continued

```
</head>
<body>

<% ProduceListing listing = new ProduceListing();
   String path = request.getServletPath();
          path = path.substring(0,path.indexOf("NewsletterArchive.jsp")) ;
          path = application.getRealPath(path);
%>
<table width="100%">
    <tr>
     <td width="33%" align="center" valign="bottom" class="clear">
        <% listing.listContent("http://www.jspinsider.com/jspbuzz/2001/",
                               "buzz_10_09_2001.xml",
                                path,
                                out); %>
     </td>
     <td width="33%" align="center" valign="bottom" class="clear">
        <% listing.listContent("http://www.jspinsider.com/jspbuzz/2001/",
                               "buzz_11_13_2001.xml",
                                path,
                                out); %>
     </td>
     </tr>
</table>

</body>
</html>
```

As with the ProduceListing.java file, NewsletterArchive.jsp has only one purpose and will not be reused. Thus, it's easiest and fastest to simply access the `ProduceListing` class directly on the page.

The `listContent` content method is passed the URL, file, and path of the XML file to be handled. Also, the `out` implicit object is given to allow the `ProduceListing` object to send the output directly to the buffer.

This page, when run, will produce the output shown in Figure 7.2.

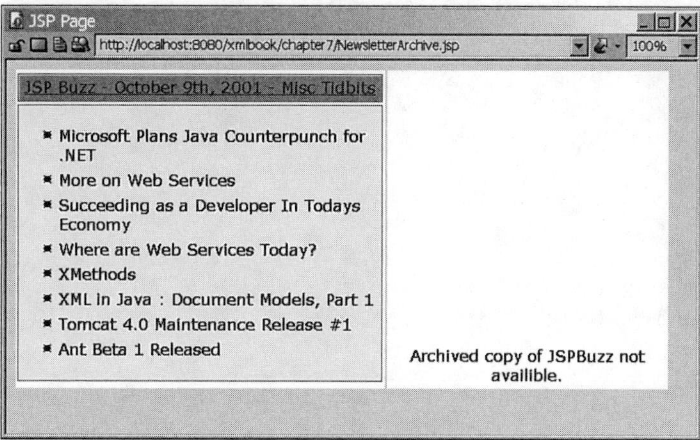

FIGURE 7.2 Results of running NewsletterArchive.jsp.

This example shows how easy it is to take data from a collection of XML files and add data to a JSP page. A slightly modified version of the code shown here drives the JSPBuzz section of the JSP Insider Web site (`http://www.jspinsider.com/jspbuzz/list.view`). Web traffic is light enough that nothing fancy is needed. If Web traffic were to become an issue, we have a simple solution to improve performance.

Back in Chapter 4, we discussed the ability to generate a new page from data. (Refer to Listing 4.8 and the CreateNewsLetter.jsp page.) The solution involves a two-step process. The first step is to set up a JSP page that the system calls on a need-only basis. This page polls the XML files and then creates an access JSP page that enables users to view the final collated results. The second step is to show the user the newly created page with the final data. In Chapter 15, "Advanced Application Design," we will show a fully integrated example of this type of processing.

Summary

In this chapter, we examined the use of JDOM and dom4j as APIs when working with XML. These APIs offer an interface that is easy to use with XML documents. More importantly, they give us a simple way to describe any data with an XML-centric set of Java objects.

We then examined several examples of using XML mixed into a JSP site. XML doesn't change the way JSP is used, but rather introduces new ways to handle data and import it into a JSP page.

The next chapter will jump back into Web services. We will get into the actual implementation of a Web service within a JSP application.

8

Integrating JSP and Web Services

IN THIS CHAPTER

- Thinking in JSP and Web Services
- Integrating a Web Service into a JSP Page
- When Should You Build Your Own Web Service?
- Building a Corporate Web Service
- Apache SOAP Help

In Chapter 3, "Understanding Web Services," we introduced the basic concepts of using a Web service. However, at that point of time, we merely looked at Web services, not how JSP and Web services can be used in harmony. Now it's time to go into high gear and begin integrating Web services into a JSP application.

This chapter is broken down into two major sections. The first section deals with how to integrate a Web service into a JSP project. This is a high-level discussion on when to consider using a Web service. More importantly, this section will review how to properly implement an external Web service call within a JSP page. The coding example of the first section is written in a relatively simple tone as an aid to newer JSP programmers. The goal is to show how to properly wrap a Web service into a JSP application.

The second section then details the actual design and building of a new Web service to work within a site. The example in the second section is geared toward an intermediate coding level. This section will

- Review the design issues of using a Web service within a JSP application.
- Take code from the previous chapter and wrap a Web service around it to demonstrate the techniques of building a Web service.

Thinking in JSP and Web Services

Web services shouldn't be thought of as a different outside toolset. Rather, Web services should be thought of as a new construct that JSP programmers have in their arsenal to implement. Over time, the concepts of using Web services will become as familiar as using tag libraries to a JSP programmer.

JSP programmers have six methods at their disposal with which to encapsulate their code:

1. Scriptlet in the JSP page
2. JavaBean object
3. Tag library
4. Web service
5. Servlet
6. Applet or client-side code

A JSP programmer can tackle any type of system with these six coding styles. From a programming point of view, a Web service is merely a distributed function the JSP programmer is accessing. Using a Web service is nothing new to a JSP programmer. It isn't much different than using a pre-made Java object. For us, this means that a Web service is implemented using a combination of JavaBeans (the actual service, or the call to access a remote service), servlets (our Apache SOAP service server), and plain old-fashioned Java programming (the actual code to use the service).

Back when I was taking advanced algebra, my college professor made the statement that even a student in third grade already knew most of the advanced techniques of abstract algebra. He then showed us, to our wonder, that abstract algebra wasn't anything new, but instead just a matter of how one thought about the math. This is the situation with Web services, in a sense. The concepts and tools are all the same; what's new is how to use the tools and integrate them into a project.

The question quickly becomes If using Web services is nothing new, then why use them at all? The answer is their capability to easily give the JSP programmer another location to distribute code processing. A Web service gives us the capability to move our programming logic out of our JSP application to another location. In addition, our Web service methods can be used easily by other applications outside of our JSP application.

A follow-up question to all this is When should I use a Web service? As with most things in JSP, the answer depends on many factors.

Using a Web service comes at a price. A Web service adds additional layers to a process call. These additional layers are usually outside of the current JSP application. The processing time for a Web service will typically be the greatest factor against using it, relative to the other programming styles available to a JSP programmer. From a practical viewpoint, programmers shouldn't build a Web service if a process is only geared towards a single project.

Keep in mind that most design practices tell programmers to always keep all business logic embedded within JavaBeans. This is so a single project can use tag libraries to expose the JavaBean for use within the project. However, if the need arises to create a Web service over time, it's easy to use the same JavaBeans to build a Web service. Case in point is our banner ad logic. In Chapter 7, "Successfully Using JSP and XML in an Application," a banner ad process was built to work for a single site. This chapter will expand the banner ad logic into a Web service. For this example, it's very easy to move the logic over and quickly build a Web service with minimal fuss. The key point is to keep any central business logic within JavaBeans or business objects.

Tag Libraries Versus Web Services

On a broader scale, you would use a Web service when thinking globally, and a tag library when thinking locally. Thinking locally means the logic will only be used internally within a JSP application. From a programming point of view, there exists an area of overlap where it would be practical to implement code as either a Web service or a tag library. It makes sense to use tag libraries to package code across many JSP Web applications when each instance of the tag library only produces local results relative to the project the tag resides within.

Tag libraries and Web services are vastly different constructs. However, there is some overlap in their functionalities. A tag library is a perfect tool with which to package code that will be used across many JSP projects. The ideal tag library is data- and project-independent. At their hearts, they're both processes, and it's in this sense that a Web service and tag library can be viewed as very similar entities.

Use a Web service if

- The destination Web applications are built in languages other than JSP. This is one of the best reasons to use a Web service. It doesn't make a difference if the client using the service is an ASP project or a CGI project! Compare this to a tag library, which will only work within a JSP project.
- You'd rather sell or package your product in a per-use model. The sales advantage of this is a higher profit margin and the prevention of pirated software from hurting sales. These are some of the reasons why Microsoft is switching to a service model in their software packages.

- Your organization needs to ensure everyone is using the exact same version of the code. Since a Web service is centrally controlled, there exists only one version of the code. Version control is very easy to maintain with Web services.

Use a tag library if

- You would rather sell or package your product as a component rather than on a per-use basis. Packaging software in component form is easier from a sales perspective, as currently it's a more commonly used model of business.
- The logic is similar between projects, but in reality is application-dependent. Many times code or a process ends up being project-specific. Therefore, the code will be similar from project to project, but the final code needs to be modified slightly for each project. When this is the case, build an initial tag library as a starting point. Distribute the tag libraries and let each project modify the tag library to meet the project-specific needs. If you take this option, make sure each project renames and places a unique identifier on the project variations of the tag libraries. This will help prevent confusion between the similar tag libraries.
- You want to keep the code as close to JSP as possible. Using a tag library keeps the code within the JSP project, without adding the additional overhead of learning the details of a Web service and the components required to make it all work.
- Connectivity issues to your central Web service exist. Although this is the age of the Internet, countless variations of setup exist, along with many accessibility issues. It's conceivable that a set of Web services may not be accessible to a particular JSP project; perhaps the JSP project resides on an intranet, with no access to the services server. In this case, using a tag library to package the service functionality makes sense.

All things considered, there will be some overlap, and at times you will find it equally valid to place your code either as a Web service or as a tag library as a means to distribute the code/process across projects. At the times when it seems both options are in balance, choose the paradigm you are more comfortable with maintaining. My personal philosophy is this: When possible, keep the code within a tag library to stay as close to the JSP framework, for simplicity reasons.

Using Tag Libraries to Access a Web Service

Now let's introduce a slight chaos factor to the mix. Many times it will make sense to use both constructs at the same time. Web services are external function calls. Usually it's bad design practice to place a service call straight into a JSP page. Instead, from a practical design viewpoint, the service call should be wrapped within a JavaBean or a tag library. It makes sense, as the tag library will create an easy interface to use the Web service logic within the JSP page. In this case, the tag library isn't performing a process; rather, the tag library is just a simple interface to access the Web service.

While it's simple to access a Web service directly on a JSP page, doing so has the following problems:

- Calling a Web service directly in a page creates a problem regarding how to cleanly handle problems. What happens if the service is unavailable? What happens if the service returns bad data? Because of these issues, a Web service call should be embedded within a JavaBean. It is possible to customize the JavaBean to handle any problems that might occur when calling the Web service.
- A call to a more complicated Web service would quickly become very messy to do within a JSP page. Code within a JSP page is not object-oriented, and more complicated service calls should be wrapped within objects to make the logic easier to maintain and handle.
- Ideally, a JSP page should be simple enough for Web designers to modify the page. Embedding a service call within a tag library gives all users a simple interface with which to access the Web service.

Now let's examine an example of how to cleanly implement a Web service within a JSP page.

Integrating a Web Service into a JSP Page

This section will expand the AccessService.jsp example shown in Listing 3.7 from Chapter 3. The AccessService.jsp page is a great example of why it isn't a good idea to call a Web service directly. The temperature service used in the example is merely a developer's example of a Web service. This service isn't going to always be up and running. From a development point of view, you should expect this service to be down as often as it is running. Also, developers should think of worst-case situations instead of perfect conditions. Programmers aren't considered saints if the application is running 98% of the time. The reality is that users will leave over time as the 2% failure rate slaps them in the face. Remember, it doesn't take much to get a tarnished reputation; it just takes one bad page to lose a customer. As an example, we will rebuild the AccessService.jsp page to handle the problem of an unavailable service.

Expanding the example will be a simple multiple-step process:

1. Create a custom exception class for handling service-based errors.
2. Create a JavaBean to encapsulate the Web service call.
3. Create a tag library as a JSP interface for the service call.

The first step is to build our own exception class to handle any problems that might occur. The new class, shown in Listing 8.1, should be saved as `webapps/xmlbook/WEB-INF/classes/xmlbook/chapter8/ServiceBookException.java`.

LISTING 8.1 Custom `Exception` Class to Handle Service Calls

```
package xmlbook.chapter8;

public class ServiceBookException extends Exception
{
    public ServiceBookException() {}

    /* Create a few specialized constructors */
    public ServiceBookException(int ai_error_level)
    {   setErrorSeverity(ai_error_level);  }

    public ServiceBookException(String as_note, String as_data, int ai_error)
    {   super(as_note);
        setDataRecieved(as_data);
        setErrorSeverity(ai_error);
    }

    /* Store any data received from the service */
    private String dataReceived = null;

    public String getDataReceived(){return dataReceived;}

    public void   setDataRecieved(String as_result)
    {dataReceived = as_result;}

    /* Store level of severity of the error */
    private int    errorSeverity = 0;

    public  int    getErrorSeverity(){return errorSeverity;}

    public  void   setErrorSeverity(int ai_error) {errorSeverity = ai_error;}
```

LISTING 8.1 Continued

```
    /* Override the toString function to include our extra data */
    public String toString()
    { String ls_newMessage =  super.toString()    + "\n";
      ls_newMessage        += "Error Level:"      + getErrorSeverity();
      ls_newMessage        += "\n Received Data:" + getDataReceived();
      return(ls_newMessage);
    }
}
```

The first thing to note is the customized `Exception` class. We have three options in how to approach handling both the data and the problems that occur when accessing the service. The first option is to build a special object to contain data being returned by the service. This object could also contain several parameters to store any error information that occurred during the process. The second option is to build a special `Exception` class to handle any problem encountered in using the Web service. The third option is to perform a combination of the first and second options.

We'll select the second option because the temperature service in this example currently only returns a simple `String`. If the logic accessed a service that returns a more complicated dataset, then it would be advisable to take the extra step to build a special Java class to contain the return data. I would recommend using a Java XML document representation of the incoming data.

The actual code is relatively straightforward. First, several overloaded constructors were created to make initialization of the class easy. Then several properties to describe an error were added to the class.

The new property of most consequence is the `errorSeverity` property:

```
private int    errorSeverity = 0;
```

This property will be used to help the system determine how to handle the error. We will use two rules here. First, any error with a negative severity needs to be logged with the JSP container. Second, any error that has a positive severity needs to be sent to the user.

The other major change is to override the `toString` function to include the additional error information stored in our error class:

```
/* Override the toString function to include our extra data */
public String toString()
{ String ls_newMessage =  super.toString()    + "\n";
```

```
        ls_newMessage       += "Error Level:"      + getErrorSeverity();
        ls_newMessage       += "\n Received Data:" + getDataReceived();
        return(ls_newMessage);
    }
```

The advantage of building a customized exception class is that the service JavaBeans can easily pass additional information to our tag handler. With the extra information, the tag handler can react with more precision to problems with a service.

It's time to start the second step and build a JavaBean to access the Web service in question, as shown in Listing 8.2. The file to be created is `webapps/xmlbook/WEB-INF/classes/xmlbook/chapter8/TempService.java`.

LISTING 8.2 Encapsulating the Temperature Service Call in a JavaBean

```
package xmlbook.chapter8;

import java.net.*;
import java.util.*;
import org.apache.soap.*;
import org.apache.soap.rpc.*;

public class TempService extends Object
{
public TempService() {}

public String getTemperature(String as_zip) throws ServiceBookException
{   String ls_result  = "N/A";

    /* Step 1) Validate the zip code to use.
               If no zip code was provided then throw user error. */
    if (as_zip == null || as_zip.length() == 0 || as_zip.length() > 5)
    { throw new ServiceBookException("Require a valid Zip Code",as_zip,1);}

    try
    {
    /* Step 2) Create the Call object to access the service with. */
    Call call = new Call ();
    call.setTargetObjectURI("urn:xmethods-Temperature");
    call.setMethodName ("getTemp");
    call.setEncodingStyleURI(Constants.NS_URI_SOAP_ENC);

    /* Step 3) Create the parameters to pass to the Web service. */
```

LISTING 8.2 Continued

```
    Vector params = new Vector ();
    params.addElement (new Parameter("zipcode", String.class,as_zip, null));
    call.setParams (params);

    /*Step 4) Perform the call. */
    URL url =
    new URL ("http://services.xmethods.net:80/soap/servlet/rpcrouter");
    Response resp = call.invoke (url, "");

      /*Step 5) Determine what was returned, and sort out the data.*/
      if (resp.generatedFault())
      {Fault fault=resp.getFault();
       ls_result = " Fault code: " + fault.getFaultCode();
       ls_result = " Fault Description: " +fault.getFaultString();
       throw  new ServiceBookException(ls_result,"Service is Unavailable",-1);
      }
      else
      {Parameter result = resp.getReturnValue();
       ls_result  = result.getValue().toString();
      }
    }
    /* Step 6) Return any errors encountered along the way. */
    catch(ServiceBookException e)
    {/*If return had a service exception then throw it up the error chain.*/
       throw e;
    }
    catch(Exception e)
    {  //log any unknown error received.
       throw new ServiceBookException(e.toString(),ls_result,-1);
    }

    /* Step 7) Once we have real data, perform basic validation
               to check if it is reasonable. If not, return error. */
    float lf_validate;
    try
    { lf_validate = Float.parseFloat(ls_result.trim());}
    catch (NumberFormatException e)
    { throw  new ServiceBookException("Bad Data Returned","N/A",0);}

    if (lf_validate > 125 || lf_validate < -100)
    { throw  new ServiceBookException("Bad Data Returned","N/A",0);}
```

LISTING 8.2 Continued

```
    /* Step 8) Whew! Return successful service call results. */
    return ls_result;
}
}
```

After this is done, don't forget to compile the code.

The code is almost identical in logic (but not in appearance) to the code found in the AccessService.jsp example (Listing 3.7). The only difference is the addition of error handling to the logic. Because the service functionality is the same, we will only review the added error handling found here.

The first checking performed is to make sure the parameters being sent are valid. If a problem exists with the user-supplied data, the code creates an error. In this exception, a positive severity error will indicate that the user should be alerted about the current error:

```
if (as_zip == null || as_zip.length() == 0 || as_zip.length() > 5)
{ throw new ServiceBookException("Require a valid Zip Code",as_zip,1);}
```

The next error to look out for is when something goes wrong with the actual call to the service:

```
if (resp.generatedFault())
      {Fault fault=resp.getFault();
       ls_result = " Fault code: " + fault.getFaultCode();
       ls_result = " Fault Description: " +fault.getFaultString();
       throw  new ServiceBookException(ls_result,"Service is Unavailable",-1);
      }
```

If something goes wrong here, the code creates a new `ServiceBookException` object. This time the code will flag the error to be logged within the JSP server's log file. The code then throws an error to be dealt with by the tag library.

Finally, if nothing went wrong with the actual service call, then the code validates the data received from the service call:

```
try
    { li_validate = Integer.parseInt(ls_result.trim());}
    catch (NumberFormatException e)
    { throw  new ServiceBookException("Bad Data Returned","N/A",0);}

    if (li_validate > 125 || li_validate < -100)
    { throw  new ServiceBookException("Bad Data Returned","N/A",0);}
```

If the data is invalid, again the code reports the error. This time it indicates that it isn't sure what to do with the error, by logging the error with a severity of zero.

The JavaBean will never directly handle the error. All it should do is report any errors. The JavaBean makes suggestions on how to handle the error through the severity code within the `ServiceBookException` class. However, it's up to our application interface to actually take action upon an error. In this process, the interface to the application will be the tag handler being built in the next step. The tag handler will receive any error event data and then decide the appropriate actions to take when an error occurs. This makes the JavaBean purer, because it only has to handle its own business process of calling the Web service. It only knows how to deal with the Web service, pass data back to the application, and then pass back any errors that occurred.

When this JavaBean is used in production, the code should be re-factored down into several more functions. In this case, it's easier to teach the logic in a single function call. However, the logic can be broken down into several more generic service calls and groupings of logic. The goal should be to make the methods as atomic as possible. This makes maintenance simpler, and the code easier to reuse and document. The logic here has four actions: validate data coming in, set up the service call, perform the service call and validate the results. This functionality can be broken down into four smaller private functions to be accessed through a central public function.

It should be noted that the original JSP page did perform some error checking. All JSP pages have a `try-catch` block, but it's behind the scenes. When the JSP container builds a servlet, all code within a scriptlet is automatically placed within a `try-catch` block for us. The disadvantage of the JSP page creating the `try-catch` block for us is the lack of control once an error happens. In the code here, using our own `try-catch` blocks permits us to intercept and handle errors before the JSP page has a chance to report a generic error and confuse the users.

Now it's time to build the tag library to access the Web service JavaBean, as shown in Listing 8.3. The file should be saved as `webapps/xmlbook/WEB-INF/classes/xmlbook/chapter8/TempServiceTag.java`.

LISTING 8.3 Building the Temperature Service Tag Handler

```
package xmlbook.chapter8;

import javax.servlet.jsp.tagext.*;
import javax.servlet.jsp.*;
```

LISTING 8.3 Continued

```
public class TempServiceTag extends TagSupport
{   private String zipCode = null;

    public void setZipCode(String as_zip) { zipCode = as_zip; }

    public String getZipCode() { return zipCode; }

    public int doEndTag() throws JspException
    {   String ls_result  = "";

        /* Step 1) Create our service object. */
        TempService tempservice = new TempService();

        /* Step 2) Access our service. Take corrective action on an error. */
        try
        { ls_result = tempservice.getTemperature(getZipCode()); }
        catch(ServiceBookException sbe)
        {   int li_error_severity = sbe.getErrorSeverity();

            if (li_error_severity > 0)
            { ls_result = sbe.getMessage();}

            if (li_error_severity == 0)
            { ls_result = sbe.getDataReceived();}

            if (li_error_severity < 0)
            { pageContext.getServletContext().log("Service Access Error",sbe);
              ls_result = sbe.getDataReceived();
            }
        }

        /* Step 3) Display the results. */
        try
        {   pageContext.getOut().print(ls_result);  }
        catch(Exception e)
        {   throw new JspException(e.toString());   }

        return EVAL_PAGE;
    }
}
```

This tag handler has one attribute in which the JSP page will store the current zip code for us:

```
private String zipCode = null;

    public void setZipCode(String as_zip) { zipCode = as_zip; }

    public String getZipCode() { return zipCode; }
```

The tag handler will only begin processing when the end of the tag is encountered. This is because the code is placed within the `doEndTag` function that is triggered when the page reaches the end of our tag. Once called, the function will create a `TempService` object, pass in the zip code, and grab the result.

```
/* Step 2) Access our service. Take corrective action on an error. */
        try
        { ls_result = tempservice.getTemperature(getZipCode()); }
        catch(ServiceBookException sbe)
        {   int li_error_severity = sbe.getErrorSeverity();

            if (li_error_severity > 0)
            { ls_result = sbe.getMessage();}

            if (li_error_severity == 0)
            { ls_result = sbe.getDataReceived();}

            if (li_error_severity < 0)
            { pageContext.getServletContext().log("Service Access Error",sbe);
              ls_result = sbe.getDataReceived();
            }
        }
```

However, in running the service request, the tag handler is also looking to see whether anything went wrong. When something does go wrong, the code takes different actions, depending on the severity of the error reported from the service JavaBean. For extremely serious errors (indicated with a negative severity number), the code will first access the application's implicit object through the `pageContext.getServletContext()` call. Once the handle is found, the code then writes the error straight to the JSP container's log file. For user-based errors, the code will display the error message generated by the service JavaBean. For various generic errors, it merely shows whatever result the service JavaBean decides is appropriate to return. In a normal service call, the response should be a little more robust on various error conditions.

This example merely shows the potential of what a JSP programmer can set up. It is always recommended to log more severe errors, such as a service call failure. This is especially true any time a programmer might be using an outside Web service. Keeping a physical log of the errors will be an important communication tools with any service provider.

Once the code receives the data, the next step is to send the results back to the JSP page. This is done by using the `pageContext` object to communicate with the calling JSP page. With the `pageContext` object, the code is able to get a handle to the `out` implicit object. With the `out` object, it's then possible to push the result into the output stream of the JSP page.

Also, if an exception occurs while trying to deal with the JSP page, the code will pass the error back up to the servlet to handle automatically:

```
throw new JspException(e.toString());
```

At this point, it would be better to push `Exceptions` back up to the JSP container to handle. An error here would be rare, and it would be better to have the JSP container just log a JSP tag-related error. We will handle the Web service errors and let the system handle the higher-level JSP errors.

Now that the tag handler is finished, the next step is to build the tag library descriptor (TLD) file, shown in Listing 8.4. The file being created is `webapps/xmlbook/WEB-INF/services.tld`.

LISTING 8.4 Building the Services TLD File

```
<?xml version="1.0" encoding="UTF-8"?>

<!DOCTYPE taglib
        PUBLIC "-//Sun Microsystems, Inc.//DTD JSP Tag Library 1.2//EN"
               "http://java.sun.com/dtd/Web-jsptaglibrary_1_2.dtd">

<taglib>
    <tlib-version>1.0</tlib-version>
    <jsp-version>1.2</jsp-version>
    <short-name>services</short-name>
    <uri>xmlbook.services</uri>
    <tag>
        <name>gettemp</name>
        <tag-class>xmlbook.chapter8.TempServiceTag</tag-class>
        <body-content>empty</body-content>
        <description>Accessing the Xmethods temperature service</description>
        <attribute>
```

LISTING 8.4 Continued

```
            <name>zipCode</name>
            <required>true</required>
            <rtexprvalue>true</rtexprvalue>
            <description>check temp at this zipcode</description>
        </attribute>
    </tag>
</taglib>
```

The services.tld file is basic. Right now, only one tag reference exists for the current tag handler built for the temperature service call.

After the services.tld file is created, it is time to register the TLD in the web.xml file (`webapps/xmlbook/WEB-INF/web.xml`), as shown in Listing 8.5.

LISTING 8.5 Modify the web.xml File to Register the Tag Library

```
    <taglib>
      <taglib-uri>xmlbook.services</taglib-uri>
      <taglib-location>/WEB-INF/services.tld</taglib-location>
    </taglib>
```

Before running any code, stop and restart the Tomcat container; because web.xml was modified, Tomcat must register the new Java classes. Now it's time to use the Web service tag we just built. The JSP page in Listing 8.6 will be saved as `webapps/xmlbook/chapter8/DailyTemperature.jsp`.

LISTING 8.6 Building a JSP Page to Access the Temperature Service

```
<%@page contentType="text/html"
        import="xmlbook.chapter8.*"%>

<%@taglib uri="xmlbook.services" prefix="service" %>

<% String ls_zipcode = (String) request.getParameter("zip");
   if (ls_zipcode== null) ls_zipcode = "07931";
%>
<html>
<head><title>Using Services in JSP</title></head>
<body>
The result of the web service call is <br/>
The temperature at <%= ls_zipcode %>
```

LISTING 8.6 Continued

```
is currently: <service:gettemp zipCode="<%= ls_zipcode%>"/>

<form  method="post" action="DailyTemperature.jsp">
    <input type="text" name="zip" id="zip" value="<%= ls_zipcode %>" />
    <input type="submit" value="Enter New Zip Code" />
</form>
</body>
</html>
```

Note that when using NetBeans, you might need to manually launch the JSP page from the browser. Why? NetBeans version 3.2.1 has problems finding the tag handler because of path issues. All the code is correct; it's just that NetBeans is unable to make the translation.

This page is much simpler than our original AccessService.jsp example. Of course, all the work is now happening within the JavaBean, and the tag handler is doing all of the processing to access that JavaBean. The biggest advantage is that when the Web service fails, instead of the JSP page exploding in a stack trace, the user receives cleaner results, as shown in Figure 8.1.

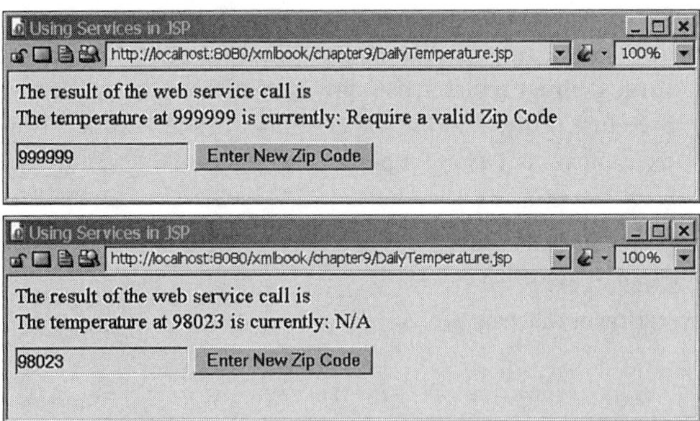

FIGURE 8.1 Two examples of calling a Web service with access errors.

It's clear from the clean presentation that having a failure reported in this fashion is the way to show problems to a user. More importantly, this code also tracks any serious errors in the Tomcat log file. When something goes wrong, the logs will give us a reliable record of what went wrong, as shown in Figure 8.2. Using log files to track problems will always be more reliable than relying on user feedback.

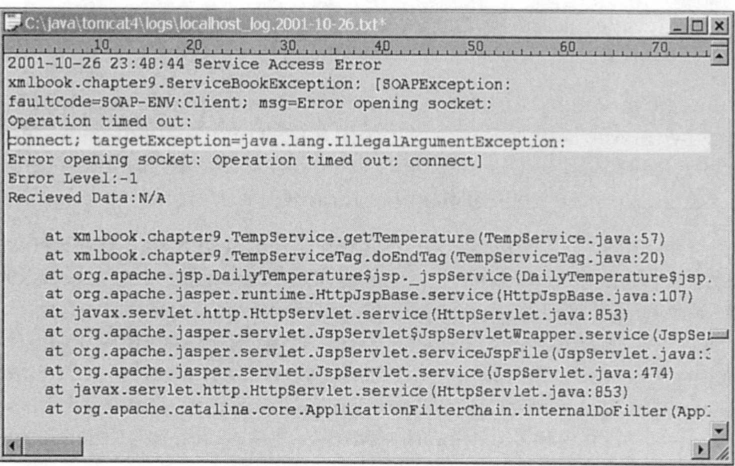

```
C:\java\tomcat4\logs\localhost_log.2001-10-26.txt*
2001-10-26 23:48:44 Service Access Error
xmlbook.chapter9.ServiceBookException: [SOAPException:
faultCode=SOAP-ENV:Client; msg=Error opening socket:
Operation timed out:
connect; targetException=java.lang.IllegalArgumentException:
Error opening socket: Operation timed out: connect]
Error Level:-1
Recieved Data:N/A

      at xmlbook.chapter9.TempService.getTemperature(TempService.java:57)
      at xmlbook.chapter9.TempServiceTag.doEndTag(TempServiceTag.java:20)
      at org.apache.jsp.DailyTemperature$jsp._jspService(DailyTemperature$jsp.
      at org.apache.jasper.runtime.HttpJspBase.service(HttpJspBase.java:107)
      at javax.servlet.http.HttpServlet.service(HttpServlet.java:853)
      at org.apache.jasper.servlet.JspServlet$JspServletWrapper.service(JspSe
      at org.apache.jasper.servlet.JspServlet.serviceJspFile(JspServlet.java:
      at org.apache.jasper.servlet.JspServlet.service(JspServlet.java:474)
      at javax.servlet.http.HttpServlet.service(HttpServlet.java:853)
      at org.apache.catalina.core.ApplicationFilterChain.internalDoFilter(App
```

FIGURE 8.2 Showing the log file of the error produced from Figure 8.1.

The log files for Tomcat are stored under the `tomcat/log` directory.

The other major advantage of accessing the service call in this manner is the decoupling of the service call and the actual JSP page. If the code accessed services directly from the JSP page, any change in the service would mean changing each JSP page using that service. By moving to a tag library/JavaBean combination, we only need to maintain one set of objects compared to countless JSP pages. As an example, to change the error handling, just change the way the tag library reports the errors. If you want to change the error message, then only change the one service JavaBean. Maintenance and expansion become easy with this model.

A Tag Library/Service Warning

Using a tag library creates an easy-to-maintain interface within your JSP page. As a design rule, tag libraries should be used as often as possible when building reusable logic within a JSP page. However, consider another rule that is equally important: The performance of a JSP page must be acceptable for the user.

Tag libraries come with performance issues. Properly designed and used correctly, the average tag library produces acceptable response times. The trouble comes from the fact that "acceptable response time" is a relative term. Every project has its own definition of what is acceptable. However, no matter how you define what is acceptable for your project, tag libraries introduce an additional layer of logic to achieve reusability. Any tag library you build should be tested and optimized for performance. If a tag library cannot be built to be responsive enough, skip the tag library step and use JavaBeans and servlets. Use tag libraries with the understanding that your service calls won't always need a tag library interface.

Unfortunately, too many variables exist to give an acceptable practice list for using a tag library with Web services. Your JSP container, complexity of code, server load, Web service load, Web service reliability, and your project's response time needs will all play a factor in how well this combination will perform.

The main reason this is being strongly emphasized here is that the Web service call itself is an unpredictable factor in performance. This makes sense, considering that the Web service call is also going through many layers to get data. Using tag libraries and services together makes a lot of sense in terms of reusability. It's in the area of performance that the programmer needs to exercise extra caution. The main lesson is that testing is critical to ensuring acceptable performance. Don't let this warning scare you away from using tag libraries with Web services; let it merely reinforce the idea that our job as programmers includes performance testing.

Fixing Some Network Issues

Proxy servers and Web services don't always get along. A proxy server's tendency to act as a middleman can confuse a Web service. When a Web application is making a Web service call behind a proxy server, it might be required to modify the execution of the call in Listing 8.2 slightly. Use code similar to this:

```
SOAPHTTPConnection conn = new SOAPHTTPConnection();
conn.setProxyHost("your Web proxy name");
conn.setProxyPort(Port # Web proxy is listening on);
Call call = new Call();
call.setSOAPTransport(conn);
```

This should permit the Apache SOAP server to navigate safely through a proxy server.

In addition, when the system has a firewall set up, other problems can be encountered by a Web service. In my setup, the code wouldn't work until the firewall's settings were modified as follows:

```
IPSec Pass through set to disabled.
```

IPSec (Internet Protocol Security) is a new security standard which happens to be secure enough to also block this Web service. The tale gets stranger: When the example code was executed, it would always work with the first request, but fail on the second request. Due to the success of the first, I initially assumed that the firewall wasn't the problem—an incorrect assumption that ended up costing a full day of tracking down ghosts. The other interesting fact is that this code wouldn't work through an AT&T or MSN dial-up connection. This indicates that the AT&T and MSN dial-up provider has filter features that blocked the Web service request. The lesson learned is that entering the world of Web services also means crossing over at times to the networking world. This is an area where not all JSP programmers will have expertise with troubleshooting problems. For programmers not familiar with their network setup, try to make sure you have access to the network administrator to help solve firewall and proxy server problems.

Web Service Reliability

This topic was mentioned earlier, but because of the nature of Web services, warrants some extra discussion. The example shown here is only the first step in the proper handling of a service, wrapping the service call around objects and error handling. This should always be done as a matter of good programming practice. The second issue is the need to pick services built by outside sources carefully. A Web service user needs to make sure that any production service is both available and has acceptable response time 99.999% of the time. A service with only 99% reliability is not good enough—99% means 1 out of 100 customers will be lost. Over time, you'll lose more customers than is reasonable even with a 99% success rate.

To be practical, a Web service should only have a failure once every 10,000 or more uses. Is this unreasonable to expect? No, especially not when your business is on the line. Web services promise to help lower production costs by farming out various services; however, the cost savings are meaningless when you're losing users because of a poorly performing service. Balance this hidden cost when deciding to use an inexpensive Web service over a custom-built solution.

Ironically, a Web service should tend towards being a more reliable solution than a custom-built solution. Why? The Web service has a larger audience, and thus more time for the testing and removal of serious bugs thanks to the larger audience. Don't be the first person on the block to use a Web service. Let the market temper and prove a Web service before buying into it. Also, don't get trapped by a badly performing Web service. Understand the alternatives, and have backup plans in place if a Web service provider doesn't provide the level of service you expect. From a business angle, using a Web service is similar to using a host provider. Use the same care as when picking a hosting solution for a Web application when shopping for Web services.

When Should You Build Your Own Web Service?

Organizations using Web services have several angles from which to approach Web services. Up to this point, this chapter has concentrated on using Web services over building a Web service. Now it's time to look more closely at building your own Web services.

Let's examine some cases where a project should build its own Web service:

- Your project wants to expose a method for other projects to use.

  With programming resources getting harder to maintain, being able to reuse your logic centrally has a high appeal for organizations that need to maintain many applications.

- Your company has several applications that need to share a process or data.

  Many companies tend to collect computer systems like dandruff. In the past, few effective options were available to integrate different systems. Usually the answer was to rebuild a new system and integrate all the functionality of the older systems. This approach tends to be very expensive to implement or fail. The second approach is to share data, but sharing data tends to be a logistical nightmare, where data wars erupt over data ownership.

  Web services are a perfect solution for companies in this position. Web services are application-neutral, and can be built to centralize key processes and data handling between your multiple applications. Since XML is used to represent data, XSL transformations or programming logic can be used to transform data in line with your various applications.

- To replace a poorly performing commercial service. Don't get stuck using a poorly performing Web service. The code is already set up to use a service, so it would be a simple (however, not necessarily cheap) solution to build a new module to replace a poor service provider. Services should be plug-and-play. By encapsulating them as shown earlier in this chapter, you can ensure that they truly are plug-and-play within all your JSP pages.

We will build two services in this book, the first of which will be in this chapter. It will take the banner text rotator from Chapter 7 and convert it to a Web service. This will be the fully integrated example, using XML, a database, and services promised earlier in the book. While very basic, the text rotator does have the practical use of being usable across multiple sites. As an example, if the JSP Insider Web site expanded to include various other Web sites, using a text banner service would make it easy to centralize the text messages for display at the top and bottom of each page across Web sites. As another use, this Web service can be modified to provide common HTML as output. This means that a Web service could replace include files or other static HTML sources. A large government or corporate Web site might find this to be an attractive way to provide static headers or footers. Since it's a Web service, any site using the service doesn't necessarily need to be on the same network. A Web service like this is a perfect method to promote centralized features, no matter where a Web site is located relative to the parent organization.

It's time to ponder these ideas a bit further. If a service similar to this one were to be built, it might seem to be a slow way to provide static content. The basic problem is bandwidth and round trips. Using a service to provide reusable static content would be an expensive solution in terms of service calls. It would be similar to the problem of using a JSP page to always re-parse static XML files. However, in this case, the solution is as simple as using smart caching techniques. To make the system faster with static content, the Web service calls could be cached to the application, session, or even static class variables within the initialization of the JSP page itself. Once cached, the data is then quickly resolved by a given JSP page.

JSP Pages Versus Web Service

One of the most interesting questions I have encountered to date is Why should a programmer use a Web service, when it's possible to build a JSP page to produce output for someone to use? In other words, a JSP page is doing the same thing as a Web service—returning character-based data. Why use a Web service?

This turns out to be a hard question to answer. In a sense, accessing a JSP page could be considered the same as accessing a Web service. If you think about it, calling a JSP page is a large method packaged in the form of a servlet, which sends back character output. The biggest difference is in the packaging.

A Web service defines an interface through which it's possible to define exactly the data being sent to and from the Web service. The JSP page, on the other hand, just hands back a large character text stream in the HTTP wrapper. This makes it hard to parse a JSP result for finer work. This makes a Web service easier to use programmatically over a straight JSP page. Whenever fine control of the data being sent over a HTTP request is required, it is time to use a Web service.

The next fact to consider is state. One thing JSP and servlets give the programmer is a concept of state: application, session, page, and so on. A service isn't as tied to the concept of state. In fact, keeping a Web service stateless has the advantage of making a Web service easier to scale and move around from project to project. However, a Web service doesn't necessarily have access to maintaining state in the same manner as a JSP page. State within a Web service will depend on the Web service server implementation being used by a project. Some Web service servers will not maintain state; others, such as Microsoft's .NET, will provide their Web services the exact same options of state that an ASP page enjoys (application, session, and so on). Apache SOAP does provide state management, and we will explore this idea further.

Building a Corporate Web Service

A corporate Web service's implementation is the same as any other Web service. The difference is merely in usage. Rather than broadcasting the service for outside projects to use, the Web service will only be used by internal corporate projects. It should be mentioned that a corporate Web service might not be intranet-based, but rather based over the Internet. This would make sense when a company has many sites across the Internet, but not necessarily on the same internal network. An internal service could still be exposed on the Internet in order to allow your various sites access to the Web service. When this is the case, some additional steps of security should be taken to prevent other entities from accessing your Web service. In Chapter 15, "Advanced Application Design," we will examine several methods, such as servlet filtering and Tomcat security realms, to achieve some protection for your Web services.

Chapter 7 built the text banner rotator to use an XML model. Now let's expand the example to produce an internal Web service. The bulk of the code is going to stay the same. The new code will create and access the service. As a warning, be extra careful where the code is saved. This example places code into two different Web applications. The majority of the code will be saved to the SOAP Web application, which was set up in Chapter 3.

Goal of This Web Service Example

This example has several goals. The first and most basic goal is to show an integrated example of building and using a full Web service. The second goal is to show several more advanced concepts, such as how to use application and session state within a Web service.

Realities of Building a Web Service

In building Web services, I have discovered one abundantly clear truth: The way to build a Web service is heavily dependent on a Web service server. This has several distinct effects.

The first is that code written for one server might not work within another Web service server. For example, the SOAP server is not part of the J2EE specification. Code written for the Apache SOAP server will not port over to a custom Java SOAP-based server that comes bundled with a J2EE server (unless that J2EE server uses Apache SOAP). Of course, you could always install and use Apache SOAP within any J2EE implementation. However, the code is specific to the Web service implementation. The Web service *calls* are, in theory, platform- and language-independent; the final Web service *code* is extremely platform- and language-dependent. For your project, this means choosing a Web service server that meets long-term plans and needs. We should also confine the occurrence of any business logic to outside the actual Web service objects. This is to permit easier movement to a different Web service server when required to change platforms.

The second effect is one of learning. Lessons learned from one Web service server won't necessarily transfer to another. Automatic features of one service server will not be present in another server solution. The code in our example is based on the Apache SOAP server, and lessons learned here wouldn't be the same with the Microsoft SOAP server.

The last effect comes from the fact that Web service servers are based upon an *implementation* of SOAP and other standards. An implementation of any specification is more of a programmer's opinion on what the specification means. In practice, the various Web service servers are usually different in the usage and implementation of a Web service. This ends up creating problems for us as end users. This means that Web services cannot necessarily be accessed on all platforms in the exact same manner. Not all SOAP servers and clients can just talk to each other automatically. It's very similar to the old Java saying "Write once, test everywhere." The biggest area of heartache is between the Apache SOAP and Microsoft SOAP servers. A Web service written in one won't necessarily be accessible by the other. Although over time this problem is being resolved, earlier SOAP server/clients can be a pain to use for this reason. When writing a Web service to be accessed by a Web service client other than the one you are using, it would be wise to set up test cases for the various potential clients.

Setting Up the Example

The first step to setting up the example is to copy the contents of `xmlbook/WEB-INF/classes/chapter7` over to `soap/WEB-INF/classes/chapter7`. We will be able to use this code directly from the Apache SOAP server.

The second step is to copy over the database initialization file. It is good practice to reuse as much code as possible. So, copy `xmlbook/WEB-INF/database.xml` over to `soap/WEB-INF/database.xml`.

Initializing Data

Following the pattern set up from earlier examples, this example will cache the static data someplace where the code can quickly access it. Normally, this would mean it's time to build a new listener file. Depending on the Web service server, this may or may not be an option. In our example, the Apache SOAP server runs within a servlet container to manage the Web service requests. It is still possible to build a listener object.

This time around, the banners will get stashed within an `Array` object stored in the application memory. The actual Web service will access this array of banners. Since the data doesn't change often, this example will only create it once upon starting up, and it will persist in memory.

NOTE

It's recommended to build an additional JSP page to perform the occasional update of the banner ad array as required by the system. This page is not built here, as it doesn't directly affect the overall Web service example for this chapter.

It's time to start coding. The first step is to initialize our banner data into the `ServletContext`. The code uses a `ServletContextListener`, so the data is created when the Apache Soap server begins running.

This listener file, as shown in Listing 8.7, will be saved to `soap/WEB-INF/classes/chapter8/BannerInitialization.java`.

LISTING 8.7 Initializing the Data for the Banner Service

```
package xmlbook.chapter8;

import javax.servlet.ServletContext;
import javax.servlet.ServletContextEvent;
import javax.servlet.ServletContextListener;
import xmlbook.chapter7.*;

public final class BannerInitialization implements ServletContextListener
{    public void contextInitialized(ServletContextEvent event)
     { ServletContext application = event.getServletContext();
       try
       {  String  ls_xml  = application.getRealPath("WEB-INF/database.xml");
          DatabaseParameter dbdata = new DatabaseParameter(ls_xml);

          BannerAdStore banners     = new BannerAdStore(dbdata);

          application.setAttribute("Banners",banners.bannerArray ());
       }
       catch (Exception e)
       { application.log("Problem encountered at startup:" + e.toString());}
     }

     public void contextDestroyed(ServletContextEvent event)
     {  }
}
```

The actual code here is nothing new. It uses our business objects from Chapter 7, and the logic for using the listener is almost identical to that shown in Chapter 7.

The next step is to register the listener file. This means updating the file `soap/WEB-INF/web.xml`, as shown in Listing 8.8. The additional lines of code are noted in bold.

LISTING 8.8 Updating the web.xml File for the Banner Service

```
<?xml version="1.0" encoding="ISO-8859-1"?>

<!DOCTYPE Web-app
    PUBLIC "-//Sun Microsystems, Inc.//DTD Web Application 2.3//EN"
    "http://java.sun.com/j2ee/dtds/Web-app_2_3.dtd">
<Web-app>
  <display-name>Apache-SOAP</display-name>
  <description>no description</description>

  <listener>
    <listener-class>
        xmlbook.chapter8.BannerInitialization
    </listener-class>
  </listener>

 etc., etc.,;file continues as normal.
```

In this example, please make sure to update web.xml to use 2.3 DTD.

Accessing Application Data

Everything looks as it should, but then when you start building a Web service, the realization strikes that you are building a Java class, not a JSP page or a tag handler. You might ask yourself: How do I access the `ServletContext` object?

This question will be complicated further when using a different SOAP server. Depending on how the class is created by the Web service server, the code might or might not have access to the `ServletContext` object. While it's reasonable to expect various Web service managers to give us access to this type of information, don't assume that that will always be the case. Two methods stand out in which to get the information from the Apache SOAP server.

The first method is a little strange. It's possible to use a combination of static variables and an implementation of the `HttpSessionBindingListener` class. By implementing `HttpSessionBindingListener`, our service class could be notified whenever the application variables are created or modified within the JSP container. By placing the data into static variables, the data is available for all instances of the service being called by users. I don't recommend using this method—it's pointed out as an interesting and extreme means of getting to the data.

The second method is specific to the Apache SOAP server. It is possible to write the service methods to request a `SOAPContext` object. The Apache SOAP server will automatically pass this object to the method. Once this object is received, it only takes a little work and code to dig your way back to the `ServletContext` object of the Web application. This object will also get us back to the session and request information relative to the service call. The problem of course is that this method is specific to the Apache SOAP server.

Building the Actual Web Service

The next step is to build the class file that will be our Web service. This means creating the file `soap/WEB-INF/classes/xmlbook/chapter8/ProduceBanner.java`, as shown in Listing 8.9.

LISTING 8.9 Creating a Banner Service

```
package xmlbook.chapter8;

import javax.servlet.http.HttpServlet;
import javax.servlet.http.HttpSession;
import javax.servlet.ServletContext;
import org.apache.soap.rpc.SOAPContext;
import org.apache.soap.Constants;

public class ProduceBanner implements java.io.Serializable
{   private String[] banners  = null;
    private int bannercount   = 0;

    public ProduceBanner() {}

    private void gatherBanners(SOAPContext a_soapcontext)
    {   if (banners == null)
        {   HttpServlet servlet = (HttpServlet)
                        a_soapcontext.getProperty(Constants.BAG_HTTPSERVLET );

            ServletContext application = servlet.getServletContext();

            banners     = (String[]) application.getAttribute("Banners");
            bannercount = banners.length;
        }
    }
```

LISTING 8.9 Continued

```
    private String randomChoice ()
    {   int li_row = (int) (Math.random() * bannercount);
        if (bannercount == 0)
            return "Banner Initialization Failed. No Banners Stored in System";
        return banners[li_row];
    }

    public String getBanner (SOAPContext a_soapcontext, boolean ab_order)
    {   gatherBanners(a_soapcontext);
        if (bannercount == 0)
            return "Banner Initialization Failed. No Banners Stored in System";

        if (ab_order)
        {   HttpSession session = (HttpSession)
                        a_soapcontext.getProperty(Constants.BAG_HTTPSESSION);

            Integer lastbanner = (Integer) session.getAttribute("LastBanner");
            int currentbanner  = 0;
            if (lastbanner != null)
            { currentbanner = lastbanner.intValue() + 1;}
            if ( currentbanner + 1 > bannercount) currentbanner = 0;

            String ls_return = "Banner Number: " + currentbanner + "<br>";
            session.setAttribute("LastBanner",new Integer(currentbanner));
            return (ls_return + banners[currentbanner]);
        }
        else
        { return randomChoice();}
    }

    public String randomBanner (SOAPContext a_soapcontext)
    {  String ls_return = "";
       gatherBanners(a_soapcontext);
       return randomChoice();
    }
}
```

Since this object will live as long as a user has a session, the code will stash the banners into its own array called banners to reduce the trips to the application object, as shown in the following code fragment. Although not technically necessary, it's done to illustrate that the Web service can keep data alive across several requests.

```
private String[] banners  = null;
private int bannercount   = 0;
```

The gatherBanners method is used to populate these variables. This method also illustrates how to mine the application context. The trick is to get the current SOAPContext of the Web service. Once we have this object, it's possible to get a handle to the HttpServlet object that the Web service is embedded within:

```
HttpServlet servlet = (HttpServlet)
                      a_soapcontext.getProperty(Constants.BAG_HTTPSERVLET );
```

Once we have the HttpServlet, it becomes a simple effort to call the getServletContext method that gives us access to the ServletContext, better known as the application object:

```
ServletContext application = servlet.getServletContext();
```

The whole trick is to get the SOAPContext object. To do this, define the Web service method with the extra argument of SOAPContext:

```
public String getBanner (SOAPContext a_soapcontext, boolean ab_order)
```

The Apache SOAP server will automatically pass this object to the method. Keep in mind that different SOAP servers most likely will take a different approach to this application context.

The other interesting fact within this code is that the getBanner method will track the user session by mining the SOAPContext object to get a handle to the session object:

```
HttpSession session = (HttpSession)
                      a_soapcontext.getProperty(Constants.BAG_HTTPSESSION);
```

Once the session object is in hand, it's used in the same way as the JSP session object. This particular code example will only stash the current banner number the user is viewing. The code will increment the banner by one each time the user calls the Web page. While the code is simple, it's a practical example of how to access the session object.

The rest of the code is standard Java code to access and return the results of an array. The amount of code specific to the Web service is minor. The code in this example, which is Web service–specific, is only code to access context information within which the Web service is running. Keeping this in mind, the majority of the code for most Web services will be business-specific, with only a few minor links back to the SOAP server. Most of the work to make the Web service happen occurs in the Web service server. It's the server's job to marshal data back and forth between the Web service and the client.

After compiling this Java class, the next step is to deploy it as a Web service on the server.

Deploying a Web Service

We have our service class, but the Web service server needs to be told how to access the class. This means the actual class in Listing 8.9 will be registered to the SOAP server. This registration will expose our service and its methods for access by a service call. In Chapter 3, Apache SOAP's graphical interface was introduced to show how to quickly register a service. This chapter will take a different approach. The problem with the graphical interface is re-entering everything to make a simple change (a reality when developing a Web service initially). Apache provides another method to use, create a deployment descriptor XML file, and then use the descriptor file to manually register the service with Apache SOAP. While this is a bit more up-front work for us, in the end it is easier than tweaking and experimenting with your Web service. Also, note that this method is specific to the Apache SOAP server. Different Web service servers will have other means of registering a Web service.

Let's first build the deployment descriptor XML file, as shown in Listing 8.10. The file to be created is `xmlbook/chapter8/ProduceBannerService.xml`.

LISTING 8.10 Creating a Deployment Descriptor XML File

```
<isd:service xmlns:isd="http://xml.apache.org/xml-soap/deployment"
             id="xmlbook.bannerservice">

  <isd:provider type="java"
                scope="Session"
                methods="getBanner randomBanner">
    <isd:java class="xmlbook.chapter8.ProduceBanner" static="false"/>
  </isd:provider>

<isd:faultListener>org.apache.soap.server.DOMFaultListener</isd:faultListener>

<isd:mappings>
  <isd:map
    encodingStyle="http://schemas.xmlsoap.org/soap/encoding/"
    xmlns:x=""
    qname="x:order"
    xml2JavaClassName="org.apache.soap.encoding.soapenc.BooleanDeserializer"/>
</isd:mappings>
</isd:service>
```

Notice that the file is being saved to the xmlbook application. It doesn't matter where we store this file. In fact, this example will create a simple JSP page to deploy the service from the xmlbook Web application.

Let's review the options and what they mean.

The `isd:service` element defines the actual reference identification for the Web service:

```
<isd:service xmlns:isd="http://xml.apache.org/xml-soap/deployment"
            id="xmlbook.bannerservice">
```

The most important data to notice here is the `id` attribute. The `id` is used to identify the actual service. When using a URI to reference the Web service in this example, it will be `xmlbook.bannerservice`.

The next element to examine is the provider element:

```
  <isd:provider type="java"
               scope="Session"
               methods="getBanner randomBanner">
    <isd:java class="xmlbook.chapter8.ProduceBanner" static="false"/>
  </isd:provider>
```

The provider defines the actual Web service, as described in Tables 8.1 and 8.2.

TABLE 8.1 Description of the `isd:provider` Element

Subelement	Description
`type`	The provider language type. This can be `java`, `script`, or user-defined. Since our code is written in Java, the type will be `java`. It's interesting to note that the possibility exists to write the service with JavaScript and embed the code within the deployment descriptor file.
`scope`	The life span of the Web service object. **Request**: The service lasts only for the length of the actual service call. **Session**: The object stays alive as long as the HTTP session is active for the service caller. **Application**: Once the Web service object is created, every user shares it across all calls to the Web service.
`methods`	A space-separated list of the methods the Web service exposes.

TABLE 8.2 Description of the `isd:java` Element

Subelement	Description
`class`	A fully qualified class name representing the actual Web service.
`static`	True if the Web service methods are static.

Then the system is told how to handle errors with the `isd:faultListener` element:

```
<isd:faultListener>org.apache.soap.server.DOMFaultListener</isd:faultListener>
```

Apache SOAP supports two different fault listeners: `org.apache.soap.server.DOMFaultListener` and `org.apache.soap.server.ExceptionFaultListener`. The more commonly used is the `DOMFaultListener`. This listener will add a DOM element representing the actual exception to the SOAP message being sent back to the client. The `ExceptionFaultListener` adds an additional parameter to the SOAP message. Any exception is then returned within this extra parameter. This doesn't mean much to us as users, but it is telling Apache SOAP how to package up the errors. In all the examples, we are capturing the errors as if they have been packaged with the `DOMFaultListener`.

Now that the Web service is defined, the next step is to indicate what arguments are used within the Web service. This step is accomplished with the `isd:mappings` element. Each `isd:map` subelement will define one of our arguments:

```
<isd:mappings>
  <isd:map
    encodingStyle="http://schemas.xmlsoap.org/soap/encoding/"
    xmlns:x=""
    qname="x:order"
    xml2JavaClassName="org.apache.soap.encoding.soapenc.BooleanDeserializer"/>
</isd:mappings>
```

Table 8.3 describes the element.

TABLE 8.3 Description of the `isd:map` Element

Subelement	Description
`encodingStyle`	The encoding style used within the SOAP message. In other words, this is the encoding rules used to define the data within the SOAP message. Usually this entry will be `http://schemas.xmlsoap.org/soap/encoding/`.
`xmlns:x`	All XML elements being used as parameters need to be namespace qualified. However, in practice this can be left blank.

TABLE 8.3 Continued

Subelement	Description
`qname`	The name of the actual parameter. Notice in our example the `xmlns:x` namespace is appended to the name for us here.
`xml2JavaClassName`	This is the class used to translate the received XML parameter into a Java parameter. Apache SOAP will take care of marshaling the data to and from the method. Apache SOAP provides many pre-built classes to handle this conversion. For example, the `BooleanDeserializer` is used to convert a parameter to the Boolean wrapper class. If the parameter is a primitive Boolean, Apache SOAP will automatically convert the data to the primitive type. The Apache SOAP JavaDocs have a complete list of all the classes available for de-serialization of XML data. Apache has classes for each of the Java primitive types, and standard objects such as `Vector`. For any custom class, a programmer will need to create his own conversion class.
`java2XMLClassName`	Similar to the `xml2JavaClassName` parameter, except it refers to the class being used to serialize a result being sent from the Web service. This means the Java parameter is translated into the XML being sent in the SOAP message. The Apache SOAP JavaDocs have a complete list of all the classes available for serialization of Java to XML.
`javaType`	Used to define your own custom JavaBean class for when a nonstandard class is being used as a parameter.

Where Is the WSDL?

With all this discussion about the deployment descriptor file, you might wonder why it isn't in the WSDL format? After all, WSDL is a specification used to define a Web service. WSDL is designed to provide a client with the information required to use a Web service. The Apache deployment descriptor is used to define a Web service for the server to register. These are two slightly different functions. The deployment descriptor contains some information not found in the WSDL format. Currently, there isn't any way to automatically convert from a WSDL file to a deployment descriptor or vice versa.

Because this example is only being used locally by us, we won't build a WSDL file. Chapter 14, " Building a Web Service," will get into building a WSDL file for the JSPBuzz Web service example.

Writing a JSP Page to Deploy the Descriptor File

All the examples that come with Apache SOAP use a .bat file to register the deployment descriptor file. Personally, as a JSP programmer, I prefer to build a JSP page to perform the functionality of the .bat file. So, we create a quick example page, as shown in Listing 8.11, named `xmlbook/chapter8/DeployService.jsp`.

LISTING 8.11 Creating a Batch JSP Deployment Page

```
<%@ page import="java.net.URL,
                 org.apache.soap.server.ServiceManagerClient" %>

<%
/* The location of our Apache SOAP Server */
URL url = new URL ("http://localhost:8080/soap/servlet/rpcrouter");

/* The location of our deployment file */
String  ls_xml  = application.getRealPath("chapter8/ProduceBannerService.xml");

/* Create a new service manager */
ServiceManagerClient service = new ServiceManagerClient(url);

/* arguments are 1) Location of soap server
                 2) The action to take
                 3) The XML descriptor file */
String input[] = { "http://localhost:8080/soap/servlet/rpcrouter",
                   "deploy",
                   ls_xml};

/* Deploy our service */
service.main(input);
%>

<html><head><title>Deploy Service</title></head><body>
<h1>Deploy a Service</h1>
    Finished Deploying The <%= ls_xml %> Service
</body>
</html>
```

Calling this page will deploy our service created in this example. Whenever you want to update the service, just update the XML descriptor file and resubmit this page. With this, I encourage you to change the parameters of the service around to see how doing so affects your results.

This page isn't fancy; it's just a simple page to deploy a Web service. However, in addition to being easier to use than a batch file, it also shows that the Web service can be managed remotely. If you haven't done so yet, execute this JSP page and move on to the next step of building the client side of accessing the Web service.

More on Security

Listing 8.11 wasn't programmed only to show how easy it is to manage Web services, but also to stress the importance of security. If your Web service server is available on the Internet, then extreme care should be taken to lock down unauthorized access. For example, it would be very simple to write a similar script to un-deploy a Web service on a Web service server. An outside programmer could even introduce undesired script-based Web services. A simple fix for Apache SOAP can be found at `http://soap.manilasites.com/stories/storyReader$13`. The point boils down to the fact that Web service servers are still new, and security holes are ever present. Extra time should be taken to evaluate the security of a Web service server. Chapter 15 will discuss this issue in greater detail.

Building a Page to Access the Service

The last step is to build a JSP page to access our new service. This part of the example will use the `ServiceBookException` class developed in the first half of the chapter to make life easier for us. Because we want to access the Web service from outside the Web service server, the code will be placed in the xmlbook Web application.

The first step is to create a generic JavaBean to access the Web service just deployed in the previous step. The JavaBean, shown in Listing 8.12, will be saved as `xmlbook/WEB-INF/classes/xmlbook/chapter8/BannerService.java`.

LISTING 8.12 Creating a JavaBean to Access the Web Service

```
package xmlbook.chapter8;

import java.net.URL;
import java.util.Vector;
import javax.servlet.http.HttpSession;
import org.apache.soap.*;
import org.apache.soap.rpc.*;

public class BannerService extends Object
{
public BannerService() {}
```

LISTING 8.12 Continued

```
private String performCall(Call call) throws ServiceBookException
    { String ls_result = "";

      try
      {  URL url = new URL ("http://localhost:8080/soap/servlet/rpcrouter");
         Response resp = call.invoke (url, "");

          if (resp.generatedFault())
          {Fault fault=resp.getFault();
           ls_result = " Fault code: " + fault.getFaultCode();
           ls_result = " Fault Description: " +fault.getFaultString();
           throw new ServiceBookException(ls_result,"Unavailable Service",-1);
          }
          else
          {Parameter result = resp.getReturnValue();
           ls_result  = result.getValue().toString();
          }
      }
      catch(Exception e)
      {throw new ServiceBookException(e.toString(),"Bad URL",0);}

      /*Determine what was returned, and sort out the data.*/

      return ls_result;
    }

public String getNextBanner(HttpSession session) throws ServiceBookException
{ String ls_result  = "";

  Call call = (Call)session.getAttribute("CallBanner");
  if (call == null)
  {   call = new Call();
      call.setTargetObjectURI("xmlbook.bannerservice");
      call.setMethodName ("getBanner");
      call.setEncodingStyleURI(Constants.NS_URI_SOAP_ENC);

      /* Create the parameters to pass to the Web service */
      Vector params = new Vector ();
      params.addElement (new Parameter("order", Boolean.class, "true", null));
```

LISTING 8.12 Continued

```
      call.setParams (params);
      session.setAttribute("CallBanner",call);
  }

    try{ ls_result = performCall(call);}
    catch(ServiceBookException sbe)
    {ls_result = sbe.toString();}

    return ls_result;
}

public String getRandomBanner() throws ServiceBookException
    {   String ls_result  = "";
        Call call = new Call();
        call.setTargetObjectURI("xmlbook.bannerservice");
        call.setMethodName ("randomBanner");
        call.setEncodingStyleURI(Constants.NS_URI_SOAP_ENC);

        try{ ls_result = performCall(call);}
        catch(ServiceBookException sbe)
        {ls_result = sbe.toString();}

        return ls_result;
    }
}
```

Let's examine what's happening in the JavaBean.

The method `performCall` is actually a repeat of previously used code to perform the service call. Because we have several methods that need to call the Web service, the code was re-factored out into a `private` reusable method.

The JavaBean then has two method calls. The simple `getRandomBanner` method is just a call to the Web service method named `randomBanner`. The actual call doesn't require any special processing.

The method that requires a bit more explanation is the `getNextBanner` method. The logic is very similar to previous methods we've built, except that the code needs to access the session object. In order for us to retain session state using the Apache SOAP server, *the same* `Call` *object must be used every time.*

The implications of this are twofold: Currently, to retain state using the Apache SOAP server means using the Apache SOAP client. Another SOAP client will not be able to retain session state across calls. The second implication is that to retain session within the Web service call, the `Call` object being used by the client must also be stashed away within the session object. The code checks to see if a `Call` object already exists. If the `Call` object exists, then it's retrieved and reused by the JavaBean. If it doesn't exist, a new `Call` object is created and stored away to the session object.

By default, the Apache SOAP server leaves session state on. To manually control the session state, it's possible to use the `SOAPHTTPConnection` object to control what is happening within the connection. The code will be similar to the following snippet:

```
/*  By default Apache Soap maintains state;
    to do it manually these are
    steps to turn it on or off.  */
        SOAPHTTPConnection shc = new SOAPHTTPConnection ();
        shc.setMaintainSession (true);
        call.setSOAPTransport(shc);
```

The balance of the logic used within the JavaBean is similar to code used earlier in the chapter.

In this example, we will use the JavaBean straight within the JSP page. Technically, at this point the JSP page should wrap up the service call within a tag library. However, doing so here wouldn't show anything new. In addition, the current code is so simple that the only true reason to use the tag library would be to create some nicer error handling, as shown in the earlier examples of this chapter. As a result, this example will just directly call the JavaBean.

Save the JSP page shown in Listing 8.13 as `xmlbook/xmlbook/chapter8/ShowBannerService.jsp`.

LISTING 8.13 Creating a JSP Page to Access the Web Service

```
<%@page contentType="text/html"
        import="xmlbook.chapter8.*"
%>


<%    BannerService banner = new BannerService();  %>
<html>
<head><title>Running a Local Web Service</title></head>
<body>
The result of the getRandomBanner Web service call is <br/>
<%= banner.getRandomBanner()%>
<br/><br/>
```

LISTING 8.13 Continued

```
The result of the getNextBanner Web service call is <br/>
<%= banner.getNextBanner(session) %>

</body>
</html>
```

When this page is executed, the output in Figure 8.3 is displayed.

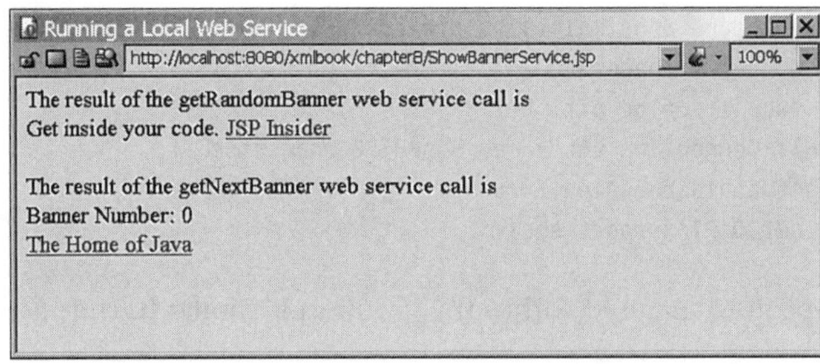

FIGURE 8.3 Showing the result of calling our Web services.

Refresh the page several times to see that the service call is indeed retaining session state, and that the `getNextBanner` method is showing the banners in correct incremental order, rather than randomly.

Apache SOAP Help

This chapter only touched the surface of using Web services. Because the chapter used Apache SOAP as the SOAP server, a good portion of questions will be geared towards problems encountered with this server. The best resource to use is the archive of the Apache SOAP user community. The archive can be found at `http://marc.theaimsgroup.com/?l=soap-user&r=1&w=2`.

Unfortunately, the Apache SOAP server version 2.2 documentation isn't very good yet. The good news is that the Apache SOAP server is very widely used, and the archives of Apache SOAP are very good. They should be the first place to visit whenever you have a question.

Summary

This chapter reviewed the basics of using Web services within a JSP application. Building the Web service isn't hard, and much of the work is just encapsulating the logic to make the code easier to implement. The most difficult work isn't the code, but actually learning how to use the SOAP Web server software. Unfortunately, each server implementation will have its own unique learning curve. Web services are new, and the tools to implement a Web service tend to reflect this state with less-than-complete documentation. Expect to spend extra time sorting out the tools as they settle down into mature versions of production software.

The next chapter will cover more advanced XML topics, including additional Web service topics.

9

Advanced JSP and XML Techniques

IN THIS CHAPTER

- Accessing Web Services from a Browser
- Handling Large XML Documents
- Handling Special Characters and Encoding
- Using XML Tag Libraries

Now that the previous chapters have gotten you started with Web services and XML, it is time to discuss some more advanced topics. This chapter begins by examining how to access a Web service from within an HTML page. This concept will open up new techniques of coding HTML pages and has profound implications for Web application design. Next, the chapter discusses encoding issues and ways of processing large XML documents. Following that, some useful aspects of the two XML-related tab libraries that can be found in the new Jakarta tag library will be highlighted.

Accessing Web Services from a Browser

One aspect of Web services that shows tremendous promise is the ability to access a Web service directly from an HTML page. A few lines of description cannot begin to convey the impact that this will have on Web applications. This ability will increase the flexibility of what is possible within a traditional HTML page. Instead of requesting an entirely new page from the server to perform an update, it's now possible to dynamically change elements on the HTML page with only a single Web service call. For example, a person could select one item in a drop-down box, and then have a Web service database call refresh the other elements on the page. It means validation of entries can be made directly against a database server rather than having to refresh the entire page. To newer programmers, this might not seem huge; however, this simple capability borders on revolutionary for Web application design.

NOTE

The technique shown in this chapter for accessing a Web service using a browser will involve an applet. To make the applet work, it currently requires a JAR file of about 800Kb in size to hold the required classes. As such, this technique is geared towards an intranet solution rather than an Internet solution. Over time this situation will improve, especially as some of the class files required migrate towards the standard Java distribution. In addition, applet caching can be used to reduce the long-term impact of downloading the midsize JAR file for Internet-based business systems. However, for a typical Internet page, this isn't a good solution yet. Microsoft has a similar solution, which will function in the same way as this example. The Microsoft solution uses a 60Kb file. However, the Microsoft version of this technique will only work in Internet Explorer. This technique is still young, but it will improve with time.

Let's begin by building a generic example to show how an HTML page can talk back to a Web service. The question becomes how to go about accessing a Web service. JavaScript seems to be the right tool as a scripting language to access a Web service, especially because JavaScript is the standard language used to modify and access the HTML page from within a browser. However, JavaScript cannot access a Web server directly. This means that a bridge between JavaScript and the Web service needs to be built.

It turns out that two methods exist to perform the magic we need. The first is to use an applet and the second is to use a Web service DHTML behavior. Currently, the DHTML behavior solution is a Microsoft-only solution within Internet Explorer 5 or better browsers. An applet solution will work in any browser that supports a Java JVM of version 1.3.1_01a or later. This makes the applet solution the more generic approach, so this chapter will focus on the applet solution.

Using an Applet

Applets are a well-known commodity within Java. However, applets have one quality that makes them very important to this example: They are able to communicate back to the server that hosted their page. We will use this quality to access a Web service.

The most important first step is to make sure that the browser used to run this example is using a current JVM. Make sure that your browser is using Java 1.3.1_01a. Many browsers will still be using an older version of the JVM, which will cause this example not to work. If this example doesn't work for you, this could be the problem.

If you are having problems getting your browser to work with the latest Java JVM plug-in, check out the Sun site for help. The current link to get the latest Java plug-in is `http://java.sun.com/getjava/installer.html`.

Don't get confused by the Java 1.3.1 plug-in, which comes with the Netscape 6.2 browser. At the time of writing, it's very important that, at a *minimum*, the Java 1.3.1_01a plug-in be installed for this example to work! In addition, Opera doesn't use a plug-in—rather, it works against your machine's local JVM. Therefore, you will need to make sure that Opera is using the correct JVM if you have multiple JVMs installed on your machine. Finally, two flavors of the plug-in exist: Consumer and IT Professional. At the time of this writing, the Consumer version is more up-to-date and is the one we want to use. Unfortunately, this means that searching for the 1.3.1_01a JRE might be a bit confusing. Hopefully, by the time you read this, a newer version will have been released and this point will be inconsequential.

Because we are using an applet, the code to access the Web service is still Java. This means that the code within the applet to access a Web service would be the same as it is within the JSP examples in the previous chapters. To illustrate this point and make the code easy to write, the example here reuses the banner Web service code that was written in Chapter 8, "Integrating JSP and Web Services."

Now it's time to get to the example, which means building an applet. This book doesn't cover the details of building an applet. For programmers who need a refresher course on the basics of applets, check out the Sun Java trail for applets, found at `http://java.sun.com/docs/books/tutorial/applet/`.

This applet class shown in Listing 9.1 should be saved as `webapps/xmlbook/chapter9/BannerApplet.java`.

LISTING 9.1 An Applet to Communicate with a Web Service

```
import java.applet.Applet;
import java.awt.*;
import java.awt.event.ActionListener;
import java.awt.event.ActionEvent;
import xmlbook.chapter8.BannerService;

public class BannerApplet extends Applet implements ActionListener {

    private List      bannerlist     = new List(5,true);
    private TextField currentbanner  = new TextField(50);
    private Button    clear          = new Button("Clear");
    private Button    newbanner      = new Button("New");

    private BannerService banner = new BannerService();

    public void init()
    {   GridBagLayout gridbag   = new GridBagLayout();
```

LISTING 9.1 Continued

```
setLayout(gridbag);
   GridBagConstraints gbc  = new GridBagConstraints();
   gbc.gridy = 0;

   gbc.gridx = 0;
   gridbag.setConstraints(newbanner, gbc);
   add(newbanner);

   gbc.gridx = 1;
   gridbag.setConstraints(clear, gbc);
   add(clear);

   gbc.gridx = 2;
   gbc.gridwidth  = GridBagConstraints.REMAINDER;
   gridbag.setConstraints(currentbanner, gbc);
   currentbanner.setEditable(false);
   add(currentbanner);

   gbc.gridy   = 1;
   gbc.gridx   = 0;
   gbc.fill    = GridBagConstraints.BOTH;
   gridbag.setConstraints(bannerlist, gbc);
   add(bannerlist);

   clear.addActionListener(this);
   newbanner.addActionListener(this);
}

public void actionPerformed(ActionEvent e)
{   String action = e.getActionCommand();

    if(action == "New")
    { updateCurrentBanner();}
    if(action == "Clear")
    { ClearAll(); }
}

public String getBanner()
{   try
    { return banner.getRandomBanner(); }
    catch (Exception e)
```

LISTING 9.1 Continued

```
        { return ("Error Retrieving Banner");}
    }

    public void updateCurrentBanner()
    {   String servicebanner = getBanner();
        currentbanner.setText(servicebanner);
        bannerlist.add(servicebanner);
    }

    public void inputNewBanner(String data)
    {   currentbanner.setText(data);
        bannerlist.add(data);
    }

    public void ClearAll()
    {     bannerlist.removeAll();
          currentbanner.setText("");
    }
}
```

Now, let's review the highlights of this applet class. The first point is the lack of a package. This particular class isn't going to be reused, so the goal is just to keep the code simple. The applet will be stored next to the calling Web page.

There isn't much to comment on within the code. The applet has several methods to modify the applet display. One method to consider is `ClearAll`, which clears the applet. Another method is `inputNewBanner`, which accepts a `String` to create a new banner to display within the applet. These methods were created to show that it's possible to invoke applet methods from the HTML page. The other method of interest is `getBanner`. This method will be used to call the Web service and return a new banner from the server. The example will show how to access this method from the HTML page and transfer the results to the HTML page.

In looking at the applet, we see that all the interesting Web service functionality has been encapsulated within the `BannerService` object. The point is to break the logic into reusable objects. Just as it's a bad design to call a service directly from a JSP, the same is true for an applet class.

Now, it's time to place `BannerApplet` within a page. This page, shown in Listing 9.2, should be saved as `webapps/xmlbook/chapter9/AppletTestBench.jsp`.

LISTING 9.2 AppletTestBench.jsp Test Page Calling a Web Service

```
<%@page contentType="text/html"%>
<html>
<head><title>Applet Test Bench Page</title></head>
<body>
<strong>The Applet Which Accesses the Web Service</strong><br/><br/>
<applet code="BannerApplet.class"
        id  ="BannerApplet"
        codebase = "."
        archive="jaxp.jar,crimson.jar,soap.jar,mail.jar,
                 activation.jar,xmlbook.jar"
        width  =500
        height =120>
</applet>

<br/><br/><strong>Html Form to Call The Applet</strong><br/><br/>
<form name="applet_test" id="applet_test">
        <input name="data"   id="data"   type="text" maxlenth="20"
              value="Data to send to applet" />
        <input name="update" id="update" type="button"
              onclick="f_tweakapplet(data.value);" value="Update Applet"/>
        <input name="clear" id="clear"   type="button"
              onclick="f_clearapplet();" value="Clear Applet"/>
        <input name="getdata" id="getdata"   type="button"
              onclick="f_getdata();"      value="Get Applet Data"/>
</form>

<br/><p><strong> Result Area to Show What Happens </strong></p><br/>
<div id="banner">Original Text. This will be where we display a Banner.</div>

<script language=Javascript>
function f_tweakapplet(data)
{  document.applets[0].inputNewBanner(data); }

function f_clearapplet()
{   /* For this method to work the id attribute of the
       applet element must be declared! */
    var applet = document.getElementById("BannerApplet");
    applet.ClearAll();
    // Note you can also use dot notation as follows
    // document.BannerApplet.ClearAll();
}
```

LISTING 9.2 Continued

```
function f_getdata()
{   /* For this method to work the id attribute of the
       applet element must be declared! */
    var applet  = document.getElementById("BannerApplet");
    var banner  = applet.getBanner();

    var display = document.getElementById("banner");
    display.innerHTML = "<p> Web Service Banner:</p> " + banner;
}
</script>

</body>
</html>
```

Although the page created is a JSP, it could be any HTML page. This particular page doesn't perform any server-side actions.

The most important point to notice is that the `BannerApplet` class reuses the `BannerService` object created back in Chapter 8. Accessing a Web service from an applet isn't different from the Chapter 8 examples. However, the location of the code is quite different. The examples from Chapter 8 all run from within the Tomcat container, whereas this applet will run from the browser. This means that the JVM browser needs access to all required classes to make the applet work as a SOAP client. The JVM browser won't have the Apache SOAP class files. The applet tag needs to tell the JVM where to find every required class file, which is achieved with the `archive` attribute:

```
archive="jaxp.jar,crimson.jar,soap.jar,mail.jar,
         activation.jar,xmlbook.jar"
```

This attribute tells the applet tag where to download the jar files listed. Although it's possible to use the `codebase` attribute to change the download location of the applet and jar files, this example uses a `codebase` attribute of `.`. This means that the jar files and applet classes are to be found in the same directory as the Web page itself.

So, to make this example work, place the following files within the `webapps/xmlbook/chapter9/` directory: jaxp.jar, crimson.jar, soap.jar, mail.jar, activation.jar, and xmlbook.jar. The xmlbook.jar is a new jar file, which you need to create now. Because this example uses `BannerService`, the new jar file is needed to hold the contents of the xmlbook.chapter8 package created in Chapter 8. Within the xmlbook.jar file, also place the `BannerApplet.class` file created in Listing 9.1.

The other applet tag attribute of interest is the id attribute. Because we will need to access the applet through JavaScript, it's required to assign a unique id to the applet to make access simpler:

```
id  ="BannerApplet"
```

For this example, the JavaScript will be able to access the applet using the BannerApplet id value:

```
function f_clearapplet()
{   /* For this method to work the id attribute of the
       applet element must be declared! */
    var applet = document.getElementById("BannerApplet");
    applet.ClearAll();
    // Note you can also use dot notation as follows
    // document.BannerApplet.ClearAll();
}
```

Looking at the JavaScript f_clearapplet function, you can see that the id applet is being accessed by the code. Because the browser is using a DOM Document to represent the HTML page, notice that it's possible to use the familiar DOM methods to work with the page. In this case, we can make the call document.getElementById to get the applet object. When we have the handle to the applet object, it's possible to invoke any public method. In this JavaScript function, the code invokes the ClearAll method.

Of more interest is the actual invoking of a Web service call and then gathering the results. The code is similar to the previous JavaScript function:

```
function f_getdata()
{   /* For this method to work the id attribute of the
       applet element must be declared! */
    var applet  = document.getElementById("BannerApplet");
    var banner  = applet.getBanner();

    var display = document.getElementById("banner");
    display.innerHTML = "<p> Web Service Banner:</p> " + banner;
}
```

The only difference is to create a JavaScript variable to store the result of the Web service call. This is very simple. After we have the data, it's only a matter of using standard JavaScript techniques to modify the HTML page. In this example, the code gets a handle of the banner div element. When this element is retrieved, the JavaScript uses the innerHTML method to replace the current contents of the banner `div` element with the newly retrieved banner link from the Web service call. When the `innerHTML` method is executed, the browser automatically repaints the HTML screen to reflect the new value. This method of applet and `innerHTML` modification opens up the possibility of dynamic client-side HTML pages.

Calling Listing 9.2 produces the results shown in Figure 9.1.

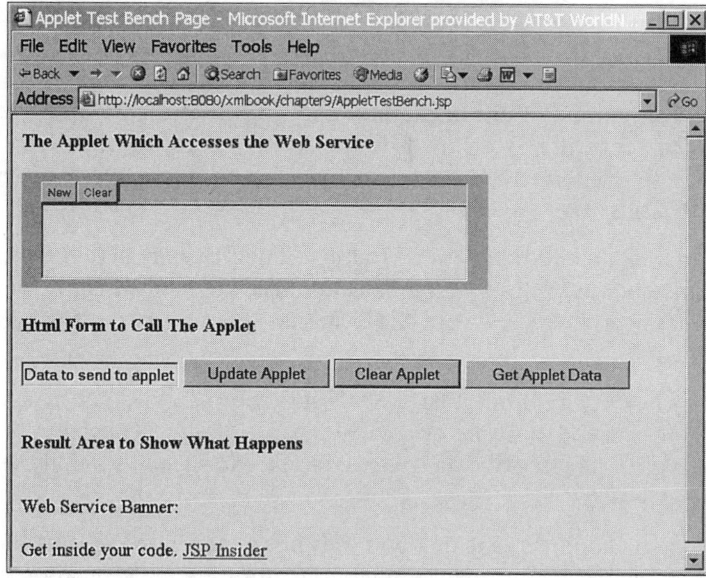

FIGURE 9.1 Viewing the Applet Test Bench Page.

On the page shown in Figure 9.1, I took the liberty of clicking the Get Applet Data button. To get a true appreciation of the page, you should play around with it and closely examine the code.

The basic techniques shown here will go quite a long way to opening up Web applications to new capabilities. However, if additional resources are required, investigate the `LiveConnect` JavaScript packages. The URL to reference is `http://developer.netscape.com/docs/manuals/js/client/jsguide/lc.htm`. This is the best place to start. Note that the use of LiveConnect started with Netscape. Internet Explorer also has some support for these packages.

Handling Large XML Documents

There isn't a single technique for handling large XML files. Rather, dealing with large XML files is as much a discipline of planning, as it's a collection of programming techniques. The other aspect to consider is that *large* is a relative term. A large XML file for one project might be considered small for another project. The term *large*, therefore, should usually be thought of in terms of acceptable processing time rather than file size. This means that a large file is any XML file that causes delays to your process because of its size in processing.

The other way to think about what constitutes large for an XML file is to consider the size of the final internal representation used to manipulate the XML data for DOM. This size can be quite different from the original document. The size of the actual representation will be proportional to the size and complexity of the original document. For example, a rule of thumb for DOM is that the DOM representation of an XML document will be roughly three times larger than the original file. For planning purposes, I conservatively use a 5 to 1 ratio to ensure that there is enough RAM to deal with XML files.

To summarize, a large XML file is one that has a negative impact on either performance or memory use within your application. Having defined large, the question now becomes how do we deal with XML datasets that impact our site because of data overload?

The trick is one of perception. A large XML file is fine as is; we just need to look at it differently. To this end, it means approaching large files as a collection of data instead of as a single piece of data. We need to be choosy and carefully select the data we need to use.

Now we have two options. The first option is not to generate the large file in the first place. When we are fortunate enough to control the file generation process, it's often best to limit the size of the file to be reasonable for our process. However, we won't examine this option. Oftentimes we don't control the final file size. In addition, that isn't an XML discussion but rather a file generation issue.

What is the best way to handle monster XML files when we have no choice in the matter? The first option to consider is the venerable SAX parser. To this end, SAX is the dominant way to process a large file. In this, a file can be handled sequentially. It's also possible to use SAX to run through a file and build a smaller document. After an XML document is parsed using SAX, our internal data representation would only contain the bare minimum required to use the dataset. It's also possible to use SAX to only partially read a file and exit when the process has enough data—yet another way to save time when every second counts. Chapter 10, "Using XSL/JSP in Web Site Design," is built around a SAX example, which illustrates both of these techniques.

This is fine for SAX, but how do we handle large XML files in the other parsers? After we break away from SAX, dealing with larger XML files gets more difficult.

JDOM

At the time of writing, JDOM doesn't have any special large file handling capacities. This means that the best way to handle a large file is to build a customized SAX handler to import only the data needed within your JDOM representation. However, the JDOM authors have been busy at work incorporating features for handling large XML files. This means that you should inspect the JDOM documentation for the latest methods to handle large XML files. Knowing the crew at JDOM, I have the greatest confidence they will implement some great solutions.

dom4j

Similar to JDOM, one solution to handling large files is to build our own customized SAX handler to import only the data needed within the JDOM representation. However, dom4j also supports creating an inline handler to perform this task.

The one advantage of using the inline handler is the ability to use path statements to indicate which elements should be processed by the handler.

Let's build an example. This example will use the JSPBuzz XML file from Listing 7.11, located in `webapps/xmlbook/chapter7/buzz_10_09_2001.xml`.

Although this example uses a smaller XML file, the principles would be the same if a larger XML file were to be accessed by the code.

The example itself will be a simple search engine to display only JSPBuzz links a user requests to see. This example will show how to construct a dom4j representation that is smaller than the original XML file. Of course, the dom4j representation will be smaller because it won't have all the data. However, we will have the data required to get the job done.

The first piece is a helper class to search through elements within the document. The file, shown in Listing 9.3, should be saved as `webapps/xmlbook/WEB-INF/classes/xmlbook/chapter9/QueryElement.java`.

LISTING 9.3 A Recursive Method to Search Through Elements

```
package xmlbook.chapter9;

import java.util.Iterator;
import org.dom4j.Element;

public class QueryElement
{   public QueryElement() {}

    public boolean findString(String as_search, Element   element)
```

LISTING 9.3 Continued

```
    {   as_search = as_search.toLowerCase();
        if (element.getText().toLowerCase().indexOf(as_search)> -1) return true;
        Iterator elementlist = element.elementIterator();

        while (elementlist.hasNext() )
        { Element child = (Element) elementlist.next();
          boolean lb_test = findString( as_search, child);
          if (lb_test) return lb_test;
        }
         return false;
    }
}
```

The actual code just recursively loops through an `Element` object and any sub-elements to search for a string. The `findString` method returns true if the search string was found; otherwise, it returns false.

The next piece required is the handler defining which document elements to keep within the `Document` representation. The file, shown in Listing 9.4, should be saved as `webapps/xmlbook/WEB-INF/classes/xmlbook/chapter9/SearchHandler.java`.

LISTING 9.4 A Handler to Sort Out and Keep Only Desired Elements

```
package xmlbook.chapter9;

import java.util.Iterator;
import org.dom4j.Element;
import org.dom4j.ElementHandler;
import org.dom4j.ElementPath;

public class SearchHandler implements ElementHandler
{
   private String search = "";
   public  void setSearch(String as_data){ search = as_data; }

   private QueryElement testelement = new QueryElement();

   public SearchHandler() {}
   public SearchHandler(String as_search) {setSearch(as_search);}

   public void onStart(ElementPath path) {}
```

LISTING 9.4 Continued

```
    public void onEnd(ElementPath path)
    {    Element row = path.getCurrent();
         /* Remove BuzzStories that don't match the search */
         if (testelement.findString(search,row) == false)
         row.detach();
    }
}
```

Listing 9.4 shows the customized `ElementHandler`, which is used to filter out unneeded elements. The search string is passed in to the handler upon creation. Two events exist. The first is `onStart`, which dom4j calls at the start of the processing of an `Element`. The second event, `onEnd`, is called after dom4j has finished processing the `Element`. The code will be in `onEnd` because this way we have all the data stored in dom4j objects. This means that it's slightly easier to perform our logic, such as using the `findString` method constructed in the Listing 9.3 `QueryElement` class. When an `Element` is determined not to be needed, the `detach` method is used to remove it from the `Document` object. In this manner, we can control the size of the final document and yet be able to process through an extremely large XML file.

The next step is the actual reading in of the XML file. The class to do this is shown in Listing 9.5 and should be saved as `webapps/xmlbook/WEB-INF/classes/xmlbook/chapter9/SearchBuzz.java`.

LISTING 9.5 The `SearchBuzz.java` Class Used to Read in an XML File

```
package xmlbook.chapter9;

import java.io.File;
import java.io.IOException;
import javax.servlet.jsp.JspWriter;
import org.dom4j.Document;
import org.dom4j.io.SAXReader;
import xmlbook.chapter7.*;

public class SearchBuzz
{   public SearchBuzz() {}

    public void findEntries( String     as_search,
                             String     as_xml,
                             String     as_xsl,
                             JspWriter out) throws  IOException
```

LISTING 9.5 Continued

```
    { try
      { SAXReader reader = new SAXReader();
        SearchHandler filter = new SearchHandler(as_search);
        reader.addHandler("/jspbuzz/buzzlink",filter);

        Document document = reader.read(new File(as_xml));

        ProcessDom4J transform = new ProcessDom4J();
        transform.applyXSL (out, document, as_xsl);
      }
      catch(Exception e)
      {   out.print(e.toString()); }
    }
}
```

Not very much is new in `SearchBuzz.java`; in fact, we reuse code from Chapter 7, "Successfully Using JSP and XML in an Application," in the form of the `ProcessDom4J` class to help speed up the coding. The only new line of code is the call to the `addHandler` method:

```
SearchHandler filter = new SearchHandler(as_search);
reader.addHandler("/jspbuzz/buzzlink",filter);
```

The `addHandler` method is how the code attaches the `SearchHandler` class from Listing 9.4 to work with the SAX reader.

To aid in the display of the data, the example creates a simple XSL file to create a simple presentation of the final XML file. The XSL page, shown in Listing 9.6, should be saved as `webapps/xmlbook/chapter9/BuzzLink.xsl`.

LISTING 9.6 The `BuzzLink.xsl` Stylesheet to Format the XML Document

```
<?xml version="1.0" encoding="UTF-8"?>
<!DOCTYPE xsl:stylesheet [<!ENTITY nbsp " ">]>
<xsl:stylesheet version="1.0" xmlns:xsl="http://www.w3.org/1999/XSL/Transform"
                              xmlns:fo="http://www.w3.org/1999/XSL/Format">
<xsl:output method="html"/>

<xsl:template match="/">
    <table border="0" width="90%">
        <xsl:apply-templates select="jspbuzz/buzzlink">
                <xsl:sort data-type="number" select="@type"/>
```

LISTING 9.6 Continued

```
        </xsl:apply-templates>
    </table>
</xsl:template>

<xsl:template match="jspbuzz/buzzlink">
    <tr><td width="100%">
    <a href="{link}"
       name="{@type}{@position}" target="_window" style="font-weight:bold;">
            <xsl:value-of select="title"/>
    </a>
    </td></tr>
    <xsl:if test="string-length(author)>0 or string-length(date)>0  ">
    <tr><td >
        <table><tr>
        <td nowrap="nowrap" width="400px">
             <xsl:value-of select="author"/> </td>
        <td> <xsl:value-of select="date"/>   </td>
        </tr></table>
    </td></tr>
    </xsl:if>
<xsl:apply-templates select="body" />
</xsl:template>

<xsl:template match="body" >
        <tr><td valign="top" ><xsl:value-of select="."/></td></tr>
</xsl:template>
</xsl:stylesheet>
```

The actual stylesheet is unremarkable. It's a vastly simplified version of the original stylesheet used to generate the production version of the JSPBuzz newsletter. The only interesting note is the ease of building this stylesheet. The stylesheet was coded in just a few moments because I worked from a master template. A nice feature of stylesheets is the ability to reuse and modify an existing stylesheet for different uses. It's always a good idea to keep an original master template stylesheet to work from to help create new stylesheets. This is especially true when you're expecting many variations of presentation output for an XML document.

The final piece of the example is the JSP to display the selected JSPBuzz links. The JSP, shown in Listing 9.7, should be saved as `webapps/xmlbook/chapter9/SearchResults.jsp`.

LISTING 9.7 The `SearchResults.jsp` Class Used to Read in an XML File

```
<%@page contentType="text/html"
        import="xmlbook.chapter9.SearchBuzz"%>
<html>
<head><title>Parsing Large XML files</title></head>
<body>
<% String ls_search = (String)request.getParameter("find"); %>
<form action="SearchResults.jsp"  method="post" name="frm_search">
  <table>
  <tr><td>Enter the exact search phrase:</td>
      <td><input type="text" name="find" value="<%=ls_search%>" size="15"/></td>
      <td><input type="submit" name="submit" id="submit" /></td>
  </tr>
  </table>
</form>

<div>
<%
  if (ls_search != null && ls_search.trim().length() > 0)
  {   String xmlpath  = application.getRealPath("chapter7/buzz_10_09_2001.xml");
      String xslpath  = application.getRealPath("chapter9/BuzzLink.xsl");
      SearchBuzz sb   = new SearchBuzz();
      sb.findEntries(ls_search,xmlpath,xslpath,out);
  }
  else
  {out.print("Type in a search phrase to list buzz links of interest.");}
%>
</div>
</body>
</html>
```

When Listing 9.7 is executed and a search on Jakarta is performed, we should see the results shown in Figure 9.2.

Keep in mind that this example shows how to work with and create a `Document` to represent only the data we need. The example could be modified to also use the data not included in the final representation to modify the final `Document` object during the creation process.

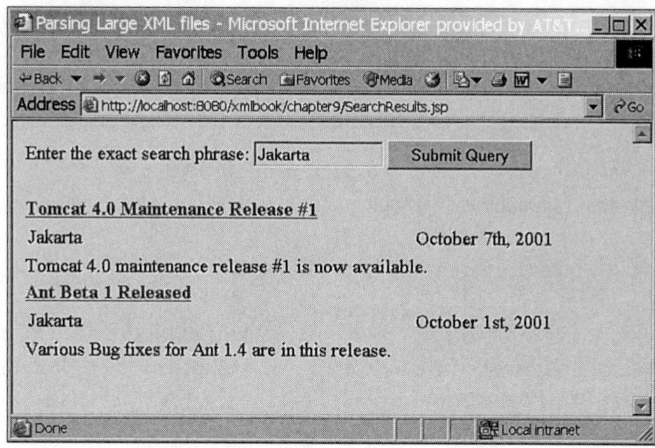

FIGURE 9.2 Viewing SearchResults.

Handling Special Characters and Encoding

A simple topic, but one that causes problems to many new programmers, is character encoding and parsing. The basic problem is embedded characters into the XML file not supported by the specified encoding standard. This situation will cause XML parsers to fail. This happens more than it should because programmers will default to using the UTF-8 character encoding scheme. Although using UTF-8 is a good choice, it won't always be the correct default encoding for an XML document.

One problem with UTF-8 is Latin1 incompatibility. What this means in practice is that ASCII symbols in the range 160-255 can cause problems. Let's create an example. The file, shown in Listing 9.8, should be saved as `webapps/xmlbook/chapter9/SpecialChars.xml`.

LISTING 9.8 Using the Wrong Encoding for © and ™

```
<?xml version="1.0" encoding="UTF-8"?>
<jspbuzz volumn="example" issue="100">
   <buzzlink type="link" numericdate="20010925" position="1">
        <reference>Special Characters</reference>
        <title>Playing With Special Characters</title>
        <body>A discussion on copyright © and
              Trademark ™ </body>
    </buzzlink>
</jspbuzz>
```

The trademark symbol's value is 153 and won't be a problem. However, the copyright symbol's value is 169, and it will cause some problems. Running this XML file through a SAX parser will give us an error. The exact error would depend on the SAX implementation used in the code. In dom4j the following error results:

```
org.dom4j.DocumentException: Error on line 6 of document
file:/C:/java/tomcat4/webapps/xmlbook/chapter9/SpecialChars2.xml
An invalid XML character (Unicode: 0xa9)
was found in the element content of the document.
```

To add to the confusion factor, not every parser will explode. For example, the preceding XML file will work fine when an XSL stylesheet is applied against it in Internet Explorer. Why? A different parser is at work. SAX parsers tend to be the most strict and unforgiving in this department.

Now, the best way to handle this error is to fix the encoding at the top of the file. In this example, everything will work fine if the following change is made:

```
<?xml version="1.0" encoding="ISO-8859-1"?>
```

ISO-8859-1 works for this example because it is built specifically for the Latin1 characters. Technically, we should use UTF-16 as the character encoding because it's the more complete encoding. However, UTF-16 isn't always accepted. For example, using the following XML header

```
<?xml version="1.0" encoding="UTF-16"?>
```

within dom4j will result in this error:

```
org.dom4j.DocumentException: Error on line 0 of document
: The encoding "UTF-16" is not supported.
Nested exception: The encoding "UTF-16" is not supported.
```

The other way to fix this problem is not to embed the character, but to represent the character with its raw decimal value. So if we were to revise the last example to read

```
<body>A discussion on copyright &#169; and
```

that would fix the problem and SAX would handle the translation correctly. That's a pain, but one we have to deal with in character encoding. Sadly, this can introduce another problem. Some tools have problems displaying these UTF-8 characters, and the result might look like Â©. Most newer browsers will correctly display the data.

Another fun fact is that changing the encoding from UTF-8 introduces new problems to our programming because many methods will use UTF-8 by default. For example, in the JAXB API, using the following method to write out XML could cause problems:

```
XMLWriter(java.io.OutputStream out)
```

By default, it will write out using the UTF-8 encoding. This means that if the actual output needed is UTF-16, it could cause problems in a manner that might not be caught for a while. (As an example, a test file was compatible with UTF-8, but the production version has the special characters specified in UTF-16.) To get around this problem, specify the output encoding in the following manner:

```
XMLWriter(java.io.OutputStream out, String encoding)
```

This means that, when creating new documents, you should programmatically check your settings to make sure that the encoding property is set correctly rather than have the code default to one for your document.

NOTE

To make matters more confusing, the default encoding might depend on the platform on which the code is being executed. Typically, this is UTF-8, but it is set by the JVM and can vary from platform to platform.

The problems with encoding come from the basic fact that 95% of the files being written are encoded using UTF-8. The reality is we need to be careful to use the actual encoding that is required in our XML files.

Why is it best to fix this manually rather than make the change programmatically? It depends on the API being used. The basic problem is that changing the encoding isn't always possible. For example, in DOM specification 1 or 2, it's impossible to change the XML declaration line. This was done because the XML declaration was thought to be an inherent property that should not be modified. The DOM level 3 specification will fix this. But, until DOM level 3 is more widely accepted, the initial encoding stated is the encoding that the file will use. In SAX, you can't modify the encoding because SAX is read-only. SAX relies on the encoding to be specified correctly within the XML file. It's very important to use the correct encoding in your XML files. Over time, expect to encounter many wrongly encoded XML files around the Internet. Don't get trapped by using the wrong encoding.

Using XML Tag Libraries

At the time of writing, the early-access release of the *Java Standard Tag Library (JSTL)* has just become available. This set of tag libraries for working with JSP encapsulates much of the functionality that is common to JSP Web applications. While this

Standard release has not been finalized yet, I expect the API of the two tag libraries demonstrated here to remain constant. As such, it's possible that these examples won't function correctly. If that occurs, use the documentation link found later to access current examples of the usage of these tag libraries.

The two tag libraries that are of specific use are the XSL and XTags libraries. Through the use of the XSL library, an XML document can be processed with an XSL stylesheet, and the results can be inserted in place. The XTags library is useful for working with XSLT and XPath. XTags allows you to navigate, process, and style XML documents directly in JSP.

XSL Tag Library

The XSL tag library consists of the following three custom tags:

- `apply`—Transforms the specified XML data source with the specified XSL stylesheet and outputs the results.
- `import`—Imports the contents of the specified page and assigns it as a `String` to the specified scripting variable.
- `include`—Captures the contents of the specified page as body content of the surrounding tag. This is similar to `<jsp:include>` except that it doesn't cause the resource to be output directly.

The following example demonstrates one use of the XSL tag library. This example will take the XML file BannerAds.xml from Listing 4.1 and apply the stylesheet of the same name from Listing 4.2.

To download and install the JSTL, go to `http://jakarta.apache.org/taglibs/doc/standard-doc/intro.html`. This page will also provide links to documentation and example pages. Note that this tag library requires the Xerces XML parser and the Xalan XSL parser. Installation instructions for those can be found in Chapter 4, "A Quick Start to JSP and XML Together."

The example JSP page, shown in Listing 9.9, should be saved as `/webapps/xmlbook/chapter9/XSLTagExample.jsp`.

LISTING 9.9 XSLTagExample.jsp

```
<%@taglib uri="http://jakarta.apache.org/taglibs/xsl-1.0" prefix="xsltag" %>

<html>
<head>
<title>XSL Tag Library Example</title>
</head>
```

LISTING 9.9 Continued

```
<body bgColor="lightblue" >

<table border="1" bgColor="white">
    <tr><td>This output was created reading both an external stylesheet
        and an external XML document using the 'xsl' and 'xml' attributes.
    </td></tr>
    <tr><td>
        <xsltag:apply xml="/chapter4/BannerAds.xml"
            xsl="/chapter4/BannerAds.xsl"/>
</td></tr>
</table><br />
<table border="1" bgColor="white">
    <tr><td>This output was created by loading nested content with
        the &lt;xsltag:include&gt; action, and using an external stylesheet
        like above. This technique could be used to acquire XML data
        resulting from another JSP.
    </td></tr>
    <tr><td>
        <xsltag:apply xsl="/chapter4/BannerAds.xsl">
            <xsltag:include page="/chapter4/BannerAds.xml"/>
        </xsltag:apply>
    </td></tr>
</table><br />
<table border="1" bgColor="white">
    <tr><td>This output was created by importing data into a page-scope
        attribute and then applying an external stylesheet to it.
    </td></tr>
    <tr><td>
        <xsltag:import id="data" page="/chapter4/BannerAds.xml"/>
        <xsltag:apply nameXml="data" xsl="/chapter4/BannerAds.xsl"/>
    </td></tr>
</table>
</body>
```

The majority of this file is HTML markup and text that, when output, will explain each usage of the `apply` custom tag. The first part of the example is transformation with the following line of code:

```
<xsltag:apply xml="/chapter4/BannerAds.xml" xsl="/chapter4/BannerAds.xsl"/>
```

The `xsl` and `xml` attributes of the `apply` tag specify the source documents of the XML document and the stylesheets. The results of the transformation are then output.

The next part of the example uses the `apply` tag in a similar way. The difference is that this time the body of the tag contains the XML document to transform. That document is obtained through the `include` tag as shown here:

```
<xsltag:apply xsl="/chapter4/BannerAds.xsl">
    <xsltag:include page="/chapter4/BannerAds.xml"/>
</xsltag:apply>
```

The last part of the example imports the XML document through the following `import` tag. As a `String`, the XML document is then assigned to the scripting variable `data`.

```
<xsltag:import id="data" page="/chapter4/BannerAds.xml"/>
<xsltag:apply nameXml="data" xsl="/chapter4/BannerAds.xsl"/>
```

Finally when the page is loaded in our browser, the output is as shown in Figure 9.3. (If you get an error, make sure that you have installed the tag library properly.)

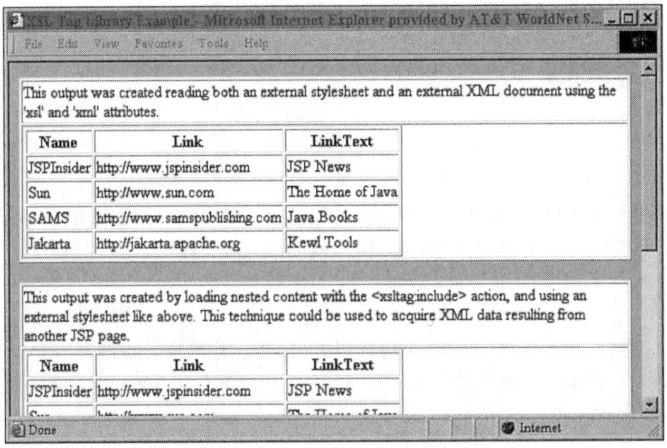

XSL Tag Library Example - Microsoft Internet Explorer provided by AT&T WorldNet S...

This output was created reading both an external stylesheet and an external XML document using the 'xsl' and 'xml' attributes.

Name	Link	LinkText
JSPInsider	http://www.jspinsider.com	JSP News
Sun	http://www.sun.com	The Home of Java
SAMS	http://www.samspublishing.com	Java Books
Jakarta	http://jakarta.apache.org	Kewl Tools

This output was created by loading nested content with the <xsltag:include> action, and using an external stylesheet like above. This technique could be used to acquire XML data resulting from another JSP page.

Name	Link	LinkText
JSPInsider	http://www.jspinsider.com	JSP News

FIGURE 9.3 Results of XSLTagExample.jsp.

The XSL Standard tag library provides a simple way to perform XML transformations. The XML data source can be the result of another JSP, it can be an external file, or it can be found in the body of this library's `apply` tag. This tool can be a timesaver in those Web applications that don't require a specific parser.

XTags Library for XML

The XTags library consists of some custom tags that behave similarly to those found in the XSL stylesheet language. In addition to those, there are others that add new functionality to XML transformations. As a result, these custom tags can be used inline in JSPs to output transformed XML. This makes it possible to style XML without the need for an external stylesheet.

The XTags library uses dom4j. As a result, if this .jar file has not been added to Tomcat yet, it is time to do so. Download dom4j from `http://www.dom4j.org/`. Place the dom4j.jar file in the `lib` directory found under the Tomcat installation. Stop and restart the server so that Tomcat registers the new classes.

The first example will begin by parsing an external XML source, namely the BannerAds.xml file from Listing 4.1. When this file has been parsed, inline custom tags will be used to output the transformed XML. Save the example shown in Listing 9.10 as `/webapps/xmlbook/chapter9/XTagsJSPStyle.jsp`.

LISTING 9.10 XTagsJSPStyle.jsp

```
<html>
<%@ taglib uri="http://jakarta.apache.org/taglibs/xtags-1.0" prefix="xtags" %>
<head>
<title>XTags Standard Library Example</title>
</head>
<body>

<xtags:parse uri="/chapter4/BannerAds.xml" />
<table border="1">
    <xtags:forEach select="//BANNERAD">
            <tr>
                <td><b><xtags:valueOf select="NAME"/></b></td>
                <td><a href=" <xtags:valueOf select="LINK" /> " />
                    <xtags:valueOf select="LINKTEXT"/>
                </td>
            </tr>
    </xtags:forEach>
</table>
</body>
</html>
```

This example should look very similar to the stylesheet from Listing 4.2. The JSP begins by parsing an XML document through the use of the following `parse` custom tag:

```
<xtags:parse uri="/chapter4/BannerAds.xml" />
```

Once parsed, this XML document is processed through the use of other XTag custom tags. The result is as shown in Figure 9.4.

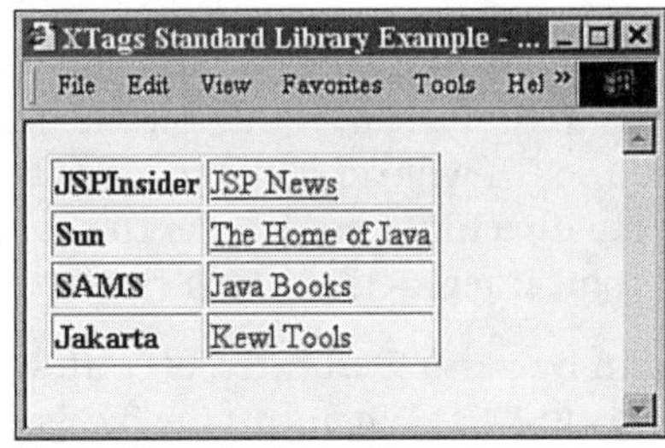

FIGURE 9.4 Results of XTagsJSPStyle.jsp.

This tag library is not limited to the transformation and output of XML. It also includes several custom tags for the manipulation of the parsed XML document.

In Listing 9.11, we will add an `Element` to our parsed XML document through a custom action named `add`. This new element will be added to the current node, and that node must be an `Element`. Once completed, the resulting XML document will be transformed using other XTags.

After outputting some HTML and parsing the XML document, we find the following tag. This context tag selects the currently selected node. In this case, we are selecting the root element `BANNERS`.

```
<xtags:context select="/BANNERS" >
```

Within the body of the preceding `context` custom tag, we find the `add` tag. This results in the addition of the XML fragment found in its body to the current node previously selected.

```
    <xtags:add>
```

The example shown in Listing 9.11 should be saved as `/webapps/xmlbook/chapter9/XTagsAdd.jsp`.

LISTING 9.11 XTagsAdd.jsp

```
<html>
<%@ taglib uri="http://jakarta.apache.org/taglibs/xtags-1.0" prefix="xtags" %>
<head>
```

LISTING 9.11 Continued

```
<title>XTags Standard Library Example</title>
</head>
<body>

<xtags:parse uri="/chapter4/BannerAds.xml" />
<xtags:context select="/BANNERS" >
    <xtags:add>
        <BANNERAD>
            <NAME>XML Spec</NAME>
            <LINK>http://www.w3.org</LINK>
            <LINKTEXT>W3C</LINKTEXT>
        </BANNERAD>
    </xtags:add>
</xtags:context>

<table border="1">
    <xtags:forEach select="//BANNERAD">
            <tr>
                <td><b><xtags:valueOf select="NAME"/></b></td>
                <td><a href=" <xtags:valueOf select="LINK" /> " />
                    <xtags:valueOf select="LINKTEXT"/>
                </td>
           </tr>
    </xtags:forEach>
</table>
</body>
</html>
```

The output is as shown in Figure 9.5. Notice that there is a new table row displaying the text data added through the body of the `add` custom tag.

In the same way that an element was added with the use of the `add` custom tag, elements can be removed or replaced using the `remove` and `replace` custom tags. The `remove` tag will delete all nodes that are matched through the XPath statement found in this tag's `select` attribute, whereas the `replace` tag will replace the current node, which must be an `Element`, with the XML fragment contents of its body.

Similar to the XSL tags of the previous section, the XTags library also provides a method for transforming an XML document with an external stylesheet. This can be useful when the page contents are made up of multiple XML documents, each of which must be transformed.

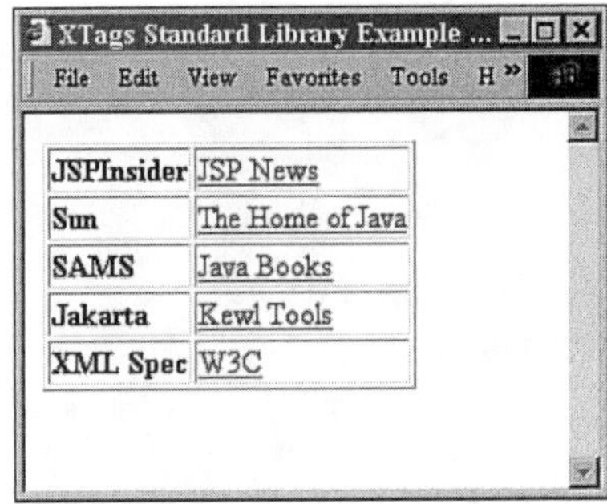

FIGURE 9.5 Results of XTagsAdd.jsp.

In Listing 9.12, we will transform an external XML document with an external stylesheet in only one line of code. Save the code in Listing 9.12 as `webapps/xmlbook/chapter9/XTagsStyle.jsp`.

LISTING 9.12 XTagsStyle.jsp

```
<html>
<%@ taglib uri="http://jakarta.apache.org/taglibs/xtags-1.0" prefix="xtags" %>
<head>
<title>XTags Standard Library Example</title>
</head>
<body>

<xtags:style xml="/chapter4/BannerAds.xml" xsl="/chapter4/BannerAds.xsl"/>

</body>
</html>
```

The output can be seen in Figure 9.6.

Besides the custom tags that replicate the functionality of XSL tags, there are also tags that perform new operations. One such custom tag is `break`. This tag allows a `forEach` custom tag, similar to the `for-each` of XSLT, to be exited before all nodes selected are processed. (This lack of a simple looping break mechanism has been one minor limiting factor of the XSL language.)

Similar to the previous examples, the `BANNERAD` elements will be selected and processed one by one. The difference this time is that when the `NAME` element—whose value is equal to `Sun`—is encountered, the `forEach` loop is exited. The `break` tag placed within the `if` tag enables this. Save the code in Listing 9.13 as `webapps/xmlbook/chapter9/XTagsBreak.jsp`.

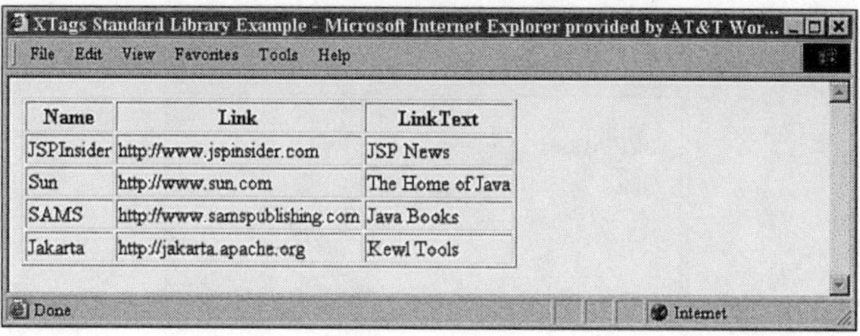

FIGURE 9.6 Results of XTagsStyle.jsp.

LISTING 9.13 XTagsBreak.jsp

```
<html>
<%@ taglib uri="http://jakarta.apache.org/taglibs/xtags-1.0" prefix="xtags" %>
<head>
<title>XTags Standard Library Example</title>
</head>
<body>

<xtags:parse uri="/chapter4/BannerAds.xml" />
<table border="1">
    <xtags:forEach select="//BANNERAD">
            <tr>
                <td><b><xtags:valueOf select="NAME"/></b></td>
                <td><a href=" <xtags:valueOf select="LINK" /> " />
                    <xtags:valueOf select="LINKTEXT"/>
                </td>
            </tr>
            <xtags:if test="NAME = 'Sun'">
                <xtags:break/>
            </xtags:if>
    </xtags:forEach>
</table>
</body>
</html>
```

The results of XTagsBreak.jsp are shown in Figure 9.7. Notice that the first two `BANNERAD` elements were processed within the `forEach` tag, and then the processing ended when the test condition was met.

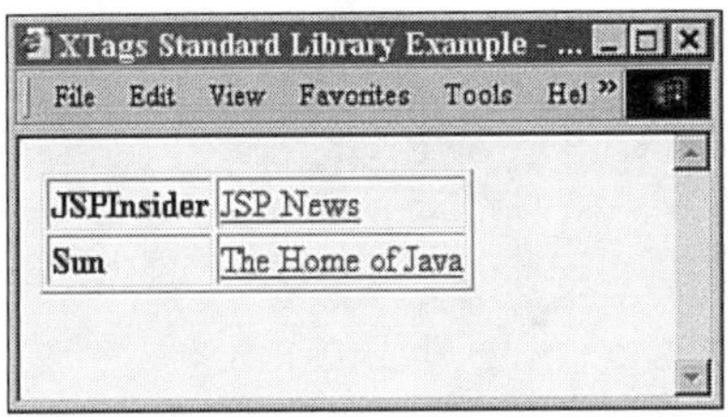

FIGURE 9.7 Results of XTagsBreak.jsp.

Another custom tag that performs new transformation functionality is the `context` tag. This tag is similar to the `forEach` custom tag in how it iterates over the list of nodes selected by the XPath statement found in the `select` attribute. However, unlike the `forEach` custom tag, the body of the `context` tag will always be processed at least once.

In Listing 9.14, we will add a `context` tag that selects a non-existing element. The output will demonstrate that the body of this loop was indeed processed. Save this file as `webapps/xmlbook/chapter9/XTagsContext.jsp`.

LISTING 9.14 XTagsContext.jsp

```
<html>
<%@ taglib uri="http://jakarta.apache.org/taglibs/xtags-1.0" prefix="xtags" %>
<head>
<title>XTags Standard Library Example</title>
</head>
<body>

<xtags:parse uri="/chapter4/BannerAds.xml" />
<table border="1">
    <xtags:forEach select="//BANNERAD">
            <tr>
                <td><b><xtags:valueOf select="NAME"/></b></td>
                <td><a href=" <xtags:valueOf select="LINK" /> " />
                <xtags:valueOf select="LINKTEXT"/>
            </td></tr>
    </xtags:forEach>
</table>
<br />
<xtags:context select="//TEST">
    Context body executes without any selected elements
</xtags:context>
```

LISTING 9.14 Continued

```
</body>
</html>
```

The results of the JSP are shown in Figure 9.8. Note that even though no `TEST` elements are in the XML document, the body of the `context` custom tag executed once. There will be a time in the creation of stylesheets that this functionality will be very useful.

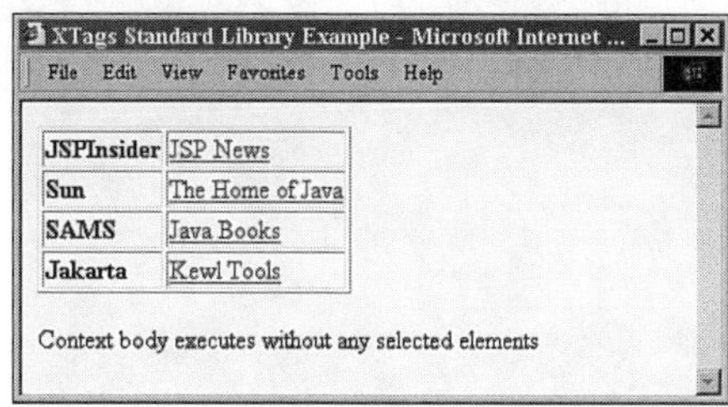

FIGURE 9.8 Results of XTagsContext.jsp.

Summary

This chapter introduced a few topics and tools that the advanced XML developer needs to be familiar with. Besides these topics, many more advanced topics are covered in Part III, "Building JSP Sites to Use XML." Chapter 10 introduces the concept of servlet mapping in order to automatically handle requests for XML resources. In Chapters 11, "Using XML in Reporting Systems," and 12, "Advanced XML in Reporting Systems," stylesheet and JSP techniques for the creation of useful reporting systems are demonstrated. Techniques for client-side processing and sorting of a few of those same reports are explained in Chapter 13, "Browser Considerations with XML." Chapter 14, "Building a Web Service," demonstrates how to set up a Web service server to provide data to others, and Chapter 15, "Advanced Application Design," discusses the ins and outs of the JSP 1.2 XML syntax, which will enable the self-modification of code.

PART III

Building JSP Sites to Use XML

IN THIS PART

10

Using XSL/JSP in Web Site Design

IN THIS CHAPTER

- Handling XML Files Directly
- Building an XML Servlet Handler

Up to this point, this book has been geared towards building your skill set and familiarizing you with using XML. The first two parts of the book covered the most important APIs required to craft and manage XML documents. Using APIs such as SAX, dom4j, and JDOM, you've learned to access and use XML within JSP. We've also discussed how to incorporate XML into the logic being accessed by a JSP page. However, over the next few chapters, we will switch focus slightly and examine JSP and XML usage from a site perspective rather than a JSP perspective.

JSP holds together many components. In this context, a good JSP page is one that minimizes the Java code in the JSP. This concept can be taken a step further. In a JSP application, not every page needs to be based on JSP. Many successful JSP applications merge several server-side technologies. This chapter will examine what is possible by going back to the roots of JSP—that is, by using servlets. The goal of the chapter will be to examine generic XML handling. This means that the initial processing of an XML document can happen at the application level rather than at the page level. This chapter will show how to capture and route the processing of an XML page directly to a servlet.

Handling XML Files Directly

We have built quite a few XML files in earlier chapters. However, one issue not touched on so far is how to properly handle direct access to an XML file.

The question to ponder is this: How should the XML files within a Web application be handled when the user directly requests them?

The first problem encountered is the browser. Figure 10.1 takes a quick look at the House.xml file created in Chapter 5, "Using DOM."

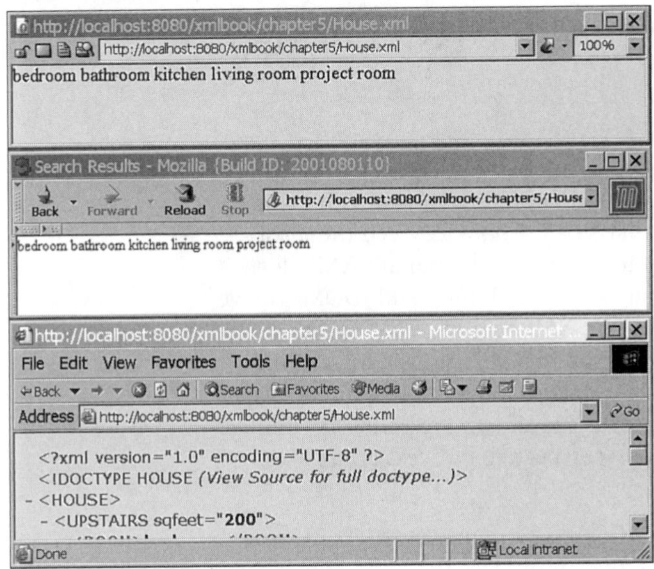

FIGURE 10.1 Using Opera, Netscape, and Explorer to view XML.

The first thing to notice is that each browser will view the raw XML differently. The second fact to consider is that the browsers view the raw XML in a format not easily used by most people. We could improve the display of the XML by using an XSL stylesheet. However, while this might solve the raw XML formatting problem, it won't always solve the presentation problem. Each browser implements a different XML processor, which means that browsers' XSLT processing capabilities vary widely.

The second issue to consider is security. Simply exposing every XML file on a site doesn't make sense. An XML file may contain information that only a particular user should see, or perhaps only portions of the XML file should be accessible. Generally, it doesn't make sense for user to see an XML file directly.

A simple solution to these problems is to create a servlet mapping. This enables a JSP application to intercept all file requests and perform special processing for any file. Using a servlet mapping will solve both the security and presentation problems with direct XML file access. It will permit us to block all unwanted access to an XML file. It also lets the Web site process any XML file to an acceptable format on the server before the file is sent to the user.

How Servlet Mappings Work

A servlet mapping is controlled within the web.xml file. Within this file, we must do two things: define the servlet and define the mapping.

The first step is to define the servlet itself for the container. This step only requires an entry defining a handle to the servlet and the location of the servlet class itself. The declaration would look like this:

```
<servlet>
    <servlet-name>
     ProcessXML
    </servlet-name>
    <servlet-class>ProcessXML</servlet-class>
</servlet>
```

Refer to Table 10.1 for the subelements that can be used to fully define a servlet.

TABLE 10.1 Servlet Definition

Element	Description
`servlet-name`	This element functions as the servlet's handle. Any references to the servlet within the web.xml file will be through this name.
`display-name`	This is a short name intended for display by GUI tools.
`description`	This element is a short description of the servlet.
`servlet-class` or `jsp-file`	This is the actual class file, which drives the servlet. This entry can be either `servlet-class` or `jsp-file`. The `servlet-class` element contains the fully qualified class name of the servlet. The element `jsp-file` is the full path to a JSP file.
`init-param`	`init-param` contains an initialization parameter to the servlet. This element uses subelements of `param-name`, `param-value` and `description` to define the overall parameter.
`load-on-startup`	If this element exists, it means the servlet should be loaded when the container starts. No value or a negative value means the container is free to determine the timing of servlet loading during the startup of the container. A positive integer will indicate the order of loading. Lower numbers are loaded before higher numbers.
`run-as`	A container needs a way to handle users that are not authenticated through the container. This element permits the assignment of a security identity to such users. This identity can then be passed to an EJB as the role defined within this element. This element isn't used very often. This element uses subelements of `description` and `role-name` to further define the overall parameter.

TABLE 10.1 Continued

Element	Description
security-role-ref	This element ties a servlet to a security role defined within a <security-role> element. This permits the container to apply basic access security to the servlet. This element uses subelements of description, role-name, and role-link to further define the overall parameter.

The second step in creating a servlet mapping is to define an actual mapping. A servlet mapping can look like this:

```
<servlet-mapping>
    <servlet-name>ProcessXML</servlet-name>
    <url-pattern>*.xml</url-pattern>
</servlet-mapping>
```

The servlet-mapping element only uses the servlet-name element to match the mapping to a servlet. The url-pattern element defines the actual mapping request, which will invoke the given servlet.

The rules defining a mapping are as follows:

- The container will first select against an exact match of the full path- and filename.
- The container will try to match a request to the longest path mapping that matches the file request.
- The container will attempt to match a file to a mapping with the correct general file prefix.

The rules for building a string contained within the url-pattern element are as follows:

- When defining the pattern, the path is case sensitive.
- A pattern that begins with / and ends with /* is used to map paths (for example, /chapter10/*).
- A pattern that begins with *. is used to map a file extension to a servlet (for example, *.shtml).
- A pattern that only has / indicates the servlet to be executed when no file is requested by the user.
- All other patterns must be an exact file match (for example, /chapter10/NoXSL.xml).

These rules *cannot* be mixed and matched. So, for instance, `*.xml` matches all `.xml` files, and `/chapter10/*` matches all files in the `chapter10` directory. However, `/chapter10/*.xml` won't work at all in Tomcat. Different JSP containers might allow a bit more flexibility in the interpretation of the specifications. However, you should generally avoid experimenting if you plan to deploy on multiple JSP container implementations.

File matching is a powerful tool, as it will permit a site to handle XML files in many different fashions. For example, it is possible to build custom servlets to handle different directories. A reporting directory could have one servlet to process files and another servlet for generic XML handling.

Building an XML Servlet Handler

In this chapter, we will build a generic servlet to intercept all XML requests within the xmlbook Web application.

The servlet will use the following business rules:

- It returns a file-not-found error when the requested XML file doesn't exist.
- The XML file is parsed to determine whether it declares a stylesheet. If a stylesheet has been declared, it's to be applied against the XML file. The results are sent back to the user instead of the original XML file.
- To speed access, the results of the parsing of the XML file will be cached to memory space. The cache will have one of three values: a filename when the stylesheet is found, `false` when no stylesheet has been found, or `null` if the parsing hasn't been performed. Memory caching will only be performed once during the application life cycle.
- If a stylesheet is not found, the servlet will search for a JSP page that matches the same name as the XML file. If such a JSP page exists, it will be launched to process the XML file.
- If neither stylesheet nor matching JSP is found, the system will return a file-not-found error. This step is to protect raw XML files from direct access.

It would be easy to modify this example to use other rules. For example, a more robust memory caching mechanism should be in place for a production system.

Constructing the actual example takes several steps:

1. Build a SAX reader.
2. Create a servlet to process the XML file.

3. Register the servlet.
4. Build the error page.
5. Create the various test XML files to show everything working.

Building a SAX Reader

One of the most exciting aspects of this example is building a customized SAX handler. The example will show how to use SAX to read only a partial file. In addition, the example will demonstrate how to customize a `DefaultHandler` to work directly with another XML API, in this example dom4j.

This example has one major problem to deal with: ascertaining whether a stylesheet declaration is embedded within an XML file. There are two ways to determine whether a stylesheet has been declared within the XML file.

The first option is to create a JDOM or dom4j object representation. Once the XML document is in memory, it is simple to use the appropriate stylesheet and perform an XSLT transformation. This solution is only good if the majority of XML files have a stylesheet defined and the XML files are generally small. For our example, this solution would be a poor option, because it cannot be assumed that these conditions will always be true for you. As a result, the example will use a more flexible two-pass approach to the problem.

The second option is to perform a two-pass process. The first pass will perform a quick scan of the XML file. This scan will only verify and gather information if a stylesheet processing instruction (PI) exists. If a stylesheet PI does exist, the process will save the data and stop reading the XML file. Because the stylesheet is typically one of the first processing commands embedded within an XML file, usually only a small portion of the XML file needs to be examined. If no PI is found, the SAX process is geared to be as efficient as possible in reading the file and processing the XML file quickly. No extra steps are wasted creating a full-blown XML representation. If a stylesheet is found, a full-blown XSLT transformation will be performed on the XML file.

While this is a two-pass system, in practice it would be extremely rare to have the system perform two complete passes. Why? If no stylesheet PI exists, only the fast and efficient SAX pass happens. If a stylesheet does exist, the stylesheet PI is usually in the first few lines, resulting in only a few extra lines being parsed rather than the whole XML file.

The interesting part of this is the ability to stop the SAX process in the middle of reading an XML file. However, the method to stop SAX is not immediately apparent. Currently, the only way to stop a SAX process is to throw a `SAXException`. While this may seem strange, it turns out to be efficient. Since the code will be throwing an exception, it makes sense to create a customized `SAXException` to make the overall logic simple.

The extended `SAXException` class, shown in Listing 10.1, should be saved as `webapps/xmlbook/WEB-INF/classes/xmlbook/chapter10/StopSaxParsing.java`.

LISTING 10.1 A Customized `SAXException` for Stopping SAX Processing

```
package xmlbook.chapter10;

import org.xml.sax.SAXException;

public class StopSaxParsing extends SAXException
{
    public StopSaxParsing(String text, boolean finished)
    {   super(text);
        dataretrieved = finished;};

    private boolean dataretrieved = false;
}
```

The `StopSaxParsing.java` class is simple and only adds one attribute. This attribute indicates whether an XSL stylesheet was found or not. The real advantage of the `StopSaxParsing.java` class is the actual class definition itself. When the SAX process throws a `StopSaxParsing` exception, the code knows that a stylesheet was found. So all the code needs to do is check for a `StopSaxParsing` exception to determine whether a stylesheet was obtained by SAX.

The next step is to build a SAX reader. The SAX reader, shown in Listing 10.2, will extend the SAX2 class `DefaultHandler`. The code should be saved as `webapps/xmlbook/WEB-INF/classes/xmlbook/chapter10/DetermineStyleSheet.java`.

LISTING 10.2 A Customized SAX Handler for Quick Scanning of XML Files

```
package xmlbook.chapter10;

import org.dom4j.Document;
import org.dom4j.DocumentFactory;
import org.xml.sax.*;
import org.xml.sax.helpers.DefaultHandler;
import org.xml.sax.SAXParseException;

public class DetermineStyleSheet extends DefaultHandler
```

LISTING 10.2 Continued

```
{
    private Document doc = DocumentFactory.getInstance().createDocument();

    public  Document getDocument() { return doc; }

    public DetermineStyleSheet(){}

    public void processingInstruction(String target, String data)
    throws SAXException
    {   doc.addProcessingInstruction(target, data);
        if(target.equals("xml-stylesheet"))
        { throw new StopSaxParsing ("Finished getting stylesheet.",true);}
    }
}
```

The code for the `DetermineStyleSheet` class is minimal. It should be, since the example only needs to determine the existence of a stylesheet processing instruction.

We covered how to stop processing, but how does the SAX handler return data? A SAX reader doesn't pass variables directly back to the process calling it. However, the reader can store data within itself that can be accessed by the calling process. In this case, the code will create a dom4j `Document` to store processing instructions. The reason for using the `Document` object is that it's already built to read and parse the XML data into its structure. This means that when the code finds a PI, it only needs to invoke the `addProcessingInstruction` method to add the PI to the `Document`.

Now the code will process all processing instructions. However, when an `xml-stylesheet` instruction has been found, the `StopSaxParsing` exception is thrown to stop the reading process.

As a side note, this process can be made more efficient so that it only reads in the data up to the point of the root element. We can do this because the stylesheet PI appears before the root element. If no stylesheet is found before the root element, it is easy to exit from the parsing.

Creating a Servlet to Process XML Files

The central part of this example is the actual servlet. The code shown in Listing 10.3 should be saved as `webapps/xmlbook/WEB-INF/classes/ProcessXML.java`.

LISTING 10.3 A Customized Servlet for Generically Processing XML Files

```
import java.io.*;
import javax.servlet.*;
import javax.servlet.http.*;
import javax.xml.parsers.*;
import javax.xml.transform.*;
import javax.xml.transform.stream.*;
import org.dom4j.Document;
import org.dom4j.ProcessingInstruction;
import org.xml.sax.helpers.*;
import org.xml.sax.*;
import xmlbook.chapter10.*;

public class ProcessXML extends HttpServlet {

public void doGet(HttpServletRequest request, HttpServletResponse response)
     throws IOException, ServletException
{
  // Step 1) Get a handle to system objects
  ServletContext application = this.getServletConfig().getServletContext();
  PrintWriter            out = response.getWriter();

  // Step 2) Determine file names and paths
  String spath    = request.getServletPath();
  String file     = spath.substring(spath.lastIndexOf("/") + 1,spath.length());
  String xmlpath  = application.getRealPath(spath);
  String path     = xmlpath.substring(0,xmlpath.indexOf(file));
  // See if we have the data stashed already in app space.
  String xslpath  = (String)application.getAttribute(xmlpath);
  String errorpage= "/chapter10/XMLError.jsp";

   /* The data stored in xslpath is null, equals "false" or equals a file
     name. If it equals a file name, then assign it to xslpath. If null, then
     the check never has happened yet. So check to see if a XSL file exists*/
    if (xslpath == null)
    {  try
       {String saxparser = "org.apache.xerces.parsers.SAXParser";
        XMLReader reader = XMLReaderFactory.createXMLReader(saxparser);
        reader.setFeature("http://xml.org/sax/features/validation", false);

        //create instance of special handler class for this process
        DetermineStyleSheet dss = new DetermineStyleSheet();
```

LISTING 10.3 Continued

```
        //register handler class
        reader.setContentHandler(dss);

        //set application variable to false as default value.
        application.setAttribute(xmlpath,"false");

        //parse the XML document
        try {reader.parse(xmlpath);}
        catch(StopSaxParsing ssp)
        {/*The XSL stylesheet is only found when we throw StopSaxParsing.
           When this is the case, get the filename and stash it to memory */
        Document doc = dss.getDocument();
        ProcessingInstruction pi = doc.processingInstruction("xml-stylesheet");
        xslpath = path + pi.getValue("href");
        application.setAttribute(xmlpath,xslpath);
        }
        }
        catch(Exception e)
        { application.log("Error Determining XSL file" + xmlpath,e); }
  }

 //Step 3) Determine which files exist
 File xmlfile = new File(xmlpath);
 File xslfile = null;
 if (xslpath != null && xslpath.equals("false") == false)
 {xslfile = new File(xslpath);}
 if (xmlfile.exists() == false)
 { // Requested XML file doesn't exist, so let user know.
   request.setAttribute("XMLPage",file);
   application.getRequestDispatcher(errorpage).forward(request, response);
   return;
 }

 if (xslfile == null || xslfile.exists() == false)
 { String jsppage  = spath.substring(0,spath.lastIndexOf(".xml")) + ".jsp";
   File jspfile    = new File(application.getRealPath(jsppage));
     if (jspfile.exists() == true)
     {application.getRequestDispatcher(jsppage).forward(request, response);
      return;
     }
     else
```

LISTING 10.3 Continued

```
        {request.setAttribute("XMLPage",file);
         application.getRequestDispatcher(errorpage).forward(request, response);
         return;
        }
    }
    else
    {   // Apply stylesheet if one exists
        response.setContentType("text/html");
        try
        {    StreamSource xml    = new StreamSource(xmlfile);
             StreamSource xsl    = new StreamSource(xslfile);
             StreamResult result = new StreamResult(out);

             TransformerFactory tFactory = TransformerFactory.newInstance();
             Transformer transformer     = tFactory.newTransformer(xsl);
             transformer.transform(xml, result);
        }
        catch(Exception e)
        {   application.log("Error Transforming XML file:" + xmlpath,e);
            out.print(" XML resource is unavailible ");
        }
        out.close();
    }
}

}
```

It's time to step through the servlet in Listing 10.3. The first thing to note is that the code is dealing with a servlet. Even if you are new to servlets, this example should be relatively easy to follow. However, if you have questions regarding servlets, please visit the Sun servlet tutorial at `http://java.sun.com/docs/books/tutorial/servlets/`.

The servlet class built here will extend the `HttpServlet` class. The `HttpServlet` class is geared towards building a servlet based on HTTP requests. The code for this example will be placed within the `doGet` method. This method is invoked upon receiving a `get` request for the XML file.

A servlet doesn't have direct access to an application implicit object. However, the servlet does have access to a configuration object. The configuration object makes it possible to get a handle to the application implicit object:

```
ServletContext application = this.getServletConfig().getServletContext();
```

The second part to consider is

```
String xslpath  = (String)application.getAttribute(xmlpath);
```

One of the business rules for this servlet states that it is to store information regarding the existence of a stylesheet for an XML file. This caching of information is important in that it reduces the need for parsing every XML file each time it's requested. Re-parsing a large XML file every time would be slow and an inefficient use of resources. This servlet will store the results found after parsing an XML file under an application attribute. This attribute's name will match the full pathname of the XML file, as shown here:

```
application.setAttribute(xmlpath,xslpath);
```

The caching here is simple and only happens once per file request. Once the results are cached, this servlet will not check again. A slightly more robust caching mechanism should be built for systems where the stylesheet declaration within the XML files changes frequently, something that usually isn't the case.

The next item to consider is the SAX reader. The steps here are similar to the previous SAX examples up to the point of the handler class:

```
DetermineStyleSheet dss = new DetermineStyleSheet();
reader.setContentHandler(dss);
```

This example creates and sets the `DetermineStyleSheet` class as the `ContentHandler` to use for the SAX reader. Next, the code uses SAX to parse the file. Because the `DetermineStyleSheet` class will throw an exception when it's done, the code needs to be placed in a `try-catch` block:

```
try {reader.parse(xmlpath);}
catch(StopSaxParsing ssp)
```

We know upon catching the `StopSaxParsing` exception that the stylesheet has been found. This is the *only* way this exception can be thrown. Therefore, once this exception is thrown, the code queries the `ContentHandler` to get the `Document` object created within the `DetermineStyleSheet` class:

```
Document doc = dss.getDocument();
```

Once this `Document` object is in hand, it's an easy step to query and get the stylesheet within the `Document`:

```
ProcessingInstruction pi = doc.processingInstruction("xml-stylesheet");
xslpath = path + pi.getValue("href");
```

Overall, this method of using SAX is very powerful and it's possible to modify or add more to this basic example depending on what the project needs to accomplish.

Once the data is in hand, the code stores the results to the application attribute:

```
application.setAttribute(xmlpath,xslpath);
```

This code is also using the `RequestDispatcher` object. This object is used within a servlet to access another resource, such as the page shown in Listing 10.5:

```
application.getRequestDispatcher(errorpage).forward(request, response);
```

In order to use a `RequestDispatcher`, the code used a `String` containing the URL of the resource to be accessed within the code. Once this is obtained, it's possible to forward the request and response to the destination page.

The rest of the logic within this page is similar to logic we've used in earlier chapters. For example, the servlet uses JAXP, as shown in Chapter 4, "A Quick Start to JSP and XML Together," to perform the XSLT transformation of the XML file. Also, if something goes wrong, the code logs the error to the log file in a way similar to that of the logic shown in previous chapters. It is easy to reuse code from process to process when handling XML files.

Register the Servlet

Once the servlet is finished, it's a quick task to modify the web.xml file stored in `webapps/xmlbook/WEB-INF/web.xml`, as shown in Listing 10.4. (Add the following code after any listener declarations.)

LISTING 10.4 Updating web.xml

```
<servlet>
    <servlet-name>
     ProcessXML
    </servlet-name>
    <servlet-class>ProcessXML</servlet-class>
</servlet>

<servlet-mapping>
    <servlet-name>ProcessXML</servlet-name>
    <url-pattern>*.xml</url-pattern>
</servlet-mapping>
```

For now, the example will intercept all XML file requests.

Building the Error Page

The servlet in Listing 10.3 refers to an error page. The error page is just a collector spot in case something goes wrong. The actual JSP page, shown in Listing 10.5, should be saved as `webapps/xmlbook/chapter10/XMLError.jsp`.

LISTING 10.5 JSP Error Display

```
<%@page contentType="text/html" %>

<% String xmlpage = (String) request.getAttribute("XMLPage");
   if (xmlpage == null) xmlpage = "";
%>
<html>
<head><title>No XML File Page</title></head>
<body>
    A simple error page to alert the user.
<br/><br/>
    The XML File: <%= xmlpage %> cannot be accessed.<br/>
</body>
</html>
```

The page currently only takes the data stored in the request attribute called `XMLPage`. In practice, this page could do a little more depending on your project needs.

Creating Some Test Files

Now everything is ready. Let's create a few test XML files for the `ProcessXML` servlet. The first test file is a copy of buzz_10_09_2001.xml from Chapter 7, "Successfully Using JSP and XML in an Application," with one slight modification—the addition of the `xml-stylesheet` processing instruction (see the line in boldface type in Listing 10.6). The new file should be saved as `webapps/xmlbook/chapter10/buzz_10_09_2001.xml`.

LISTING 10.6 buzz_10_09_2001.xml

```
<?xml version="1.0" encoding="UTF-8"?>
<?xml-stylesheet type="text/xsl" href="Buzz.xsl"?>
<jspbuzz volumn="II" issue="19">
```

The new XML file references the Buzz.xsl file, which is created in Listing 10.7. This stylesheet is based on the production JSPBuzz stylesheet. The file should be saved as `webapps/xmlbook/chapter10/Buzz.xsl`.

LISTING 10.7 Buzz.xsl

```
<?xml version="1.0" encoding="UTF-8"?>
<!DOCTYPE xsl:stylesheet [<!ENTITY nbsp " ">]>
<xsl:stylesheet version="1.0"
                xmlns:xsl="http://www.w3.org/1999/XSL/Transform"
                xmlns:fo="http://www.w3.org/1999/XSL/Format">
<xsl:output method="html"/>
<xsl:template match="/">
<html>
      <head><title>JSP Insider - XML to HTML - Test Page</title>
      <style>
      .10ptBold { font-size:10pt; font-weight:bold; font-family:arial;}
      .12ptBold { font-size:12pt; font-weight:bold; font-family:arial;}
       td {font-family: verdana, Arial; font-size: 10pt; border-style: groove;
           border-width:2px; border-color:#ffffff; padding:2px;}
      .Clear {background: #ffffff; border-width:0px; padding-left:0px;
                                                padding-right:0px;}
      .LightGreyBox {background: #eeeeee;}
      .LightGrey {background: #eeeeee; border-width:0px;}
      .OffWhite {background: #f5f5f5; border-width:0px;}
      .OffWhiteBox {background: #f5f5f5;}
      .GreenBox {background: #aabbbb;}
      </style></head>
      <body>
        <table cellspacing="0" width="100%">
            <tr><td class="OffWhite">
                <p class="12ptBold" align="center">
                JSP Buzz: Issue #<xsl:value-of select="jspbuzz/@issue"/>
                </p>
                <p align="center" class="12ptBold">
                        <xsl:value-of select="jspbuzz/title"/>
                </p>
                <p align="center"><xsl:value-of select="jspbuzz/buzzdate"/>
                </p>
            </td></tr>
            <tr><td class="GreenBox">
                <div class="12ptBold">Table of Contents</div>
            </td></tr>
```

LISTING 10.7 Continued

```
            <tr><td class="OffWhiteBox">
                <div class="10ptBold"><a href="#links">Links of Interest</a>
                </div>
                <ol>
                <xsl:apply-templates select="jspbuzz/buzzlink[@type='link']"
                                     mode="contents">
                        <xsl:sort data-type="number" select="@position"/>
                </xsl:apply-templates>
                </ol>
            </td></tr>
            <tr><td class="GreenBox">
                <div class="12ptBold"><a name="links"/>Links</div>
            </td></tr>
            <tr><td class="WhiteBox">
                <table border="0" width="90%">
                <xsl:apply-templates select="jspbuzz/buzzlink[@type='link']">
                        <xsl:sort data-type="number" select="@position"/>
                </xsl:apply-templates>
                </table>
            </td></tr>
        </table>
        </body>
</html>
</xsl:template>

<xsl:template match="jspbuzz/buzzlink" mode="contents">
     <li><a href="#{@type}{@position}"><xsl:value-of select="title"/></a></li>
</xsl:template>

<xsl:template match="jspbuzz/buzzlink">
        <tr><td class="LightGreyBox"  width="100%">
        <a href="{link}"
         name="{@type}{@position}" target="_window" style="font-weight:bold;">
                <xsl:value-of select="title"/>
        </a>
        </td></tr>
        <xsl:if test="string-length(author)>0 or string-length(date)>0  ">
        <tr><td  class="LightGreyBox">
                <table><tr>
                <td class="LightGrey" nowrap="nowrap" width="400px">
                        <xsl:value-of select="author"/> </td>
```

LISTING 10.7 Continued

```
                <td class="LightGrey">
                        <xsl:value-of select="date"/> </td>
                </tr></table>
        </td></tr>
        </xsl:if>
        <xsl:apply-templates select="body" />

</xsl:template>

<xsl:template match="body" >
      <tr><td class="Clear" valign="top" ><xsl:value-of select="."/></td></tr>
</xsl:template>

</xsl:stylesheet>
```

The stylesheet is unremarkable. However, one thing to note is the use of CSS style commands. Using CSS is recommended as a method to keep the XSLT code cleaner and make maintenance easier. Using CSS has many advantages, with one of the main strengths being the increased formatting capabilities it brings to HTML and XML. However, the real reason to use CSS within XSL is that CSS gives you the ability to create predefined formats. This in turn makes it simple to change and update styles within the page. CSS will also make the XSLT easier to maintain when using a readable naming convention. CSS styles *aren't* written as XML. This makes it easy to create class and style attributes within an XML/XSL file without interfering with the XML. Since HTML uses tag elements, using HTML within an XML data file can at times interfere with the XML file. However, it's simple to store CSS style attributes within the same XML file without markup conflicts.

You should also note the use of the `mode` attribute in Listing 10.7. At times, you will want to create multiple templates using the same XPath selection statement. This is done using the `mode` attribute:

```
<xsl:template match="jspbuzz/buzzlink" mode="contents">
   <li><a href="#{@type}{@position}"><xsl:value-of select="title"/></a></li>
</xsl:template>

<xsl:template match="jspbuzz/buzzlink">
        <tr><td class="LightGreyBox"  width="100%">
etc.
```

Using the `mode` attribute lets the XSLT define which template to call for a given selection. The `apply-templates` command

```
<xsl:apply-templates select="jspbuzz/buzzlink[@type='link']" mode="contents">
```

would call the following template:

```
<xsl:template match="jspbuzz/buzzlink" mode="contents">
```

Let's run Listing 10.6 to see what happens. As always, don't forget to compile everything, then stop and restart the Tomcat container. Figure 10.2 shows the result.

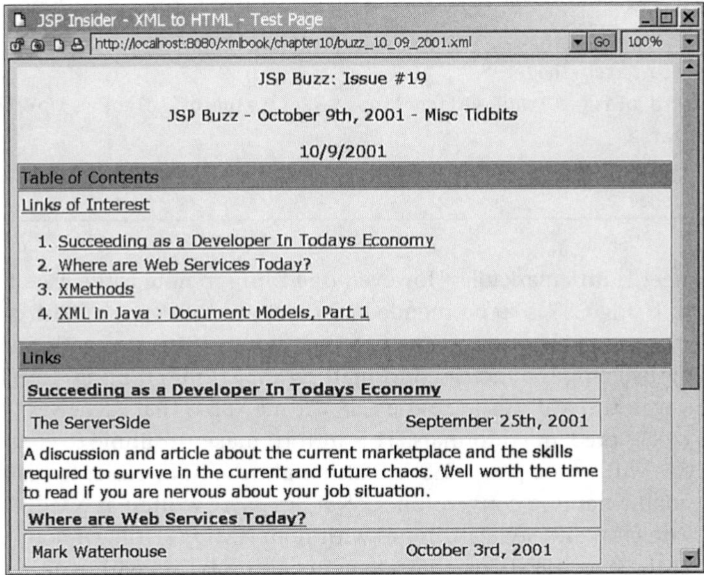

FIGURE 10.2 Results of running buzz_10_09_2001.xml.

Notice that even though this example requests the XML file, the server returns the HTML created by the XSL transformation against the XML file. Viewing the source code of this file would show the HTML from the transformation, not the XML file. This is due to the transformation occurring on the server rather than within the browser.

Now let's build another example. First, we'll create a test XML file. The example will again copy buzz_10_09_2001.xml from the `chapter7` directory to the `chapter10` directory of the xmlbook Web site. This time, create an exact copy of the buzz_10_09_2001.xml file from Chapter 7. The new file should be saved as `webapps/xmlbook/chapter10/NoXSL.xml`.

The goal of NoXSL.xml is to show how to build a JSP handler page that will be executed by the `ProcessXML` servlet (see Listing 10.8). Keep in mind that if `ProcessXML` doesn't find a stylesheet, it searches for a JSP with the same name as the XML file. Save the following file as `webapps/xmlbook/chapter10/NoXSL.jsp`.

LISTING 10.8 A Customized JSP to Handle an XML File

```
<%@page contentType="text/html"
        import="xmlbook.chapter7.*"%>
<html><head><title>Dedicated JSP Page To Process XML File</title>
<style>
    td { font-family: verdana, Arial, ; font-size: 10pt; border-style: groove;
         border-width:2px; border-color:#ffffff; padding:2px;}
.Clear{background:#ffffff;border-width:0px;padding-left:0px;padding-right:0px;}
.OffWhiteBox {background: #f5f5f5;}
.GreenBox {background: #aabbbb;}
</style>
</head>
<body>
<% ProduceListing listing = new ProduceListing();
   String spath  = request.getServletPath();
   String file   = spath.substring(spath.lastIndexOf("/") + 1,spath.length());
   String xmlpath= application.getRealPath(spath);
   String path   = xmlpath.substring(0,xmlpath.indexOf(file));

   listing.listContent("","NoXSL.xml", path, out);
%>

</body>
</html>
```

The code here is unremarkable. In fact, the code reuses `ProduceListing.java` from Chapter 7 in order to reduce the amount of coding needed. The purpose of this page is simply to show how to tie the XML file to a JSP file through the servlet.

When NoXSL.xml is accessed, the results shown in Figure 10.3 appear in the browser.

Finally, to show that everything is working, let's view an XML page that has no stylesheet or JSP page to process it. When `http://localhost:8080/xmlbook/chapter6/Books.xml` runs, the results shown in Figure 10.4 should appear.

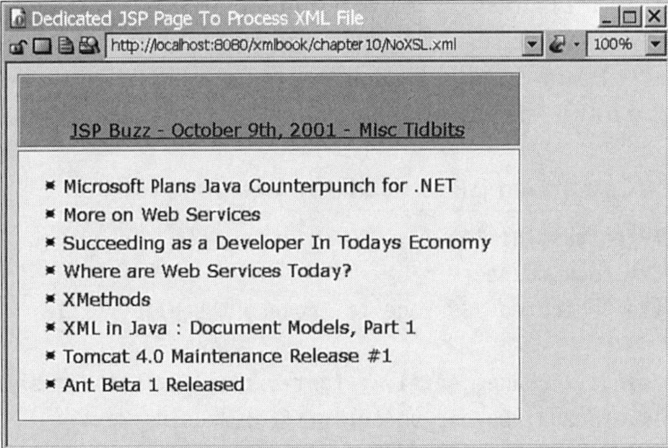

FIGURE 10.3 Accessing NoXSL.xml.

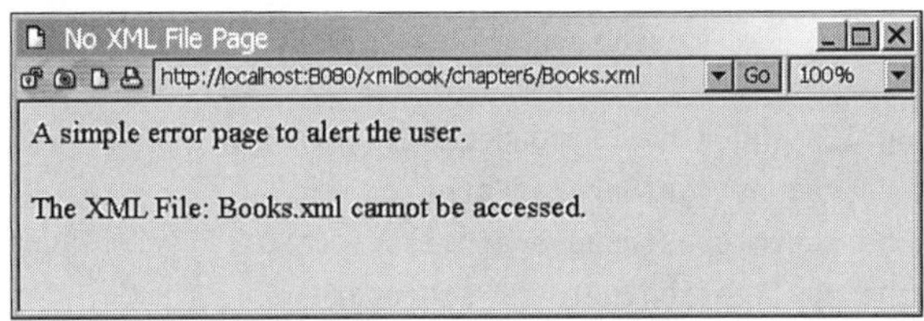

FIGURE 10.4 Accessing Books.xml.

The example receives the error page, as expected for an XML file not tied to a stylesheet or JSP.

Accessing XML Directly

This chapter shows how easy it is to build a servlet to intercept all XML file requests. Generally, this is a valid approach, and it will be a common practice across many JSP applications. Does this mean that you should take this approach every time? The answer is no.

While JSP sites generally offer data to users in a visual format, it isn't uncommon to provide direct data feeds to users. At these times, it's fine to access XML files directly. After all, XML is best used for data transfer.

Another point to keep in mind is that the various browsers are getting better at offering XSL support. At some point in the future, general XSL support will be solid enough that it will be an acceptable solution to use client-side processing of the XML files. In fact, browser considerations will be closely examined in Chapter 13,

"Browser Considerations with XML." Before working on the examples in Chapter 13, you will need to turn off the generic XML processing this chapter performs. To do so, just remove the `<servlet-mapping>` entry created in Listing 10.4 and restart Tomcat.

This shows the other drawback of the system created in this chapter. Using pattern matching is great when all the files need to be processed through a single servlet controller. However, in practice, the pattern strings allowed to create the actual mappings are not as flexible as they could be. It isn't possible to create a `/chapter10/*.xml` pattern to only affect XML files in the `chapter10` directory. Instead, some finesse is required in creating the required pattern matching. For example, one could possibly match to `/chapter10/*` or selectively match to individual files such as `/chapter10/NoXSL.xml`. This entails building a more complicated version of the example to implement a selective solution. Hopefully, future versions of Tomcat and the servlet specification will expand the pattern matching capabilities of the `<servlet-mapping>` entry. Ironically, a simple workaround exists. The pattern matching is case sensitive. This means that the `*.xml` pattern only matches lowercase `.xml`. Any XML file with the `.XML` (uppercase) extension would be ignored by this example's servlet mapping. Thus, an application could use `.xml` for secure XML files and `.XML` for XML files that the client will access directly. That's not the best solution, but it's easy to implement.

Summary

JSP is a wonderful tool that simplifies using servlets. However, at times, using specialized servlets can greatly enhance a JSP site. In the case of XML, building generic handlers for XML pages can be a great boon to a JSP application. It's possible to provide extra security by preventing unwanted access to XML pages. Using servlets can reduce the amount of work within the JSP site by creating reusable templates to process an XML file in different directories.

11

Using XML in Reporting Systems

IN THIS CHAPTER

- Architecture of Reporting Systems
- When to Use XML with Reports
- Data Source for Reports
- `ResultSet` to XML
- Bringing It All Together
- The Sorting Table Stylesheet
- The Cross Tab Stylesheet

No matter what the Web application, or where it's implemented, it's a safe bet to assume that there will be some reporting involved. Even applications that don't have databases are likely to have some aspect of reporting. However, non-database systems are more likely to be looking at reports regarding numbers of page usage and data exclusive to system usage. The development of either of these reporting systems can benefit from the appropriate placement and usage of XML.

After creating a JSP that will fill the database with as much data as needed, JDOM and XSL will be used to create two reports. Before explaining those report components, we will explain a Java class that builds a JDOM XML representation from a database `ResultSet`.

Architecture of Reporting Systems

The different types of reporting systems that exist have to do most notably with the types of reports to create, and the structure of the entire system. The main types of reports are tables, cross tabs, and aggregate. Our first stylesheet will create a very generic table-creating stylesheet with dynamic sorting label links, while the second stylesheet will create a cross tab report from the same data source.

This brings us into the overall reporting system structure. The ideal system would have database-stored procedures perform the initial filtering and sorting of data, and have stylesheets that would each produce several reports. One stylesheet can produce multiple reports by using stylesheet parameters and changing filtering or sorting methods.

Even more ideally, these stylesheets would be created generically enough to be usable on multiple datasets. In this way, a very robust reporting system can be created quickly, after which the more specific, data-dependent reports can be created.

Another thing to consider when creating reporting systems has to do with security and access rights. Different people will be permitted to see only some reports, and it is important to incorporate a simple model to maintain this security. A common design is to have a database table that contains a record for each report. Then another table will have a record for each report and login type that has access to it. In this way, it is simple to change access rights to reports without having to touch the reporting pages themselves.

The reporting examples throughout this chapter and the next will use a database from which to create the JDOM documents that will be transformed with a generic stylesheet into our resulting HTML output page. We will glue these pieces together using a JSP to do the transformation and finally output the results. It is relatively simple to change the backend and create the JDOM document from another source.

When to Use XML with Reports

XML is not always the proper choice in reporting systems. It must be understood that its use includes an extra layer of processing beyond just programmatically converting a database `ResultSet` into the output desired. The difference resides in the speed at which these systems can be built because, if carefully created, the stylesheets are reusable across datasets, and fewer stored procedures have to be created.

DOM document models consume memory proportional to the size and complexity of the datasets being modeled. Database data will maintain the same complexity across `ResultSets`, but can be extremely large. The size of the data sets being used to create JDOMs must be considered when creating these systems, or some troubles will result.

In the next chapter an example of a paging report will be demonstrated. This report will only display a set maximum number of records per page, but it will create links that enable the rest of the data to be seen on different "pages" of the same report. This is one method of handling potentially large data sets. Another method is writing JavaBeans that will iterate through the `ResultSet` to create the desired output. In this way, the memory limitations of DOM will be avoided.

While SAX can be very useful in some reporting situations where there is a large amount of similarly formatted data, we are not using it here. This is because we are using the XSL sorting capabilities instead of sorting the data at the database.

Data Source for Reports

The data source for the examples in this and the following chapters come from two tables in the `xmlbook` database created in Appendix A, "Setting Up." The data in these tables contains some very basic information about clinic patients and their health ailments. These tables are ReportClientData and ReportClientAilment and between them there is a one-to-many relationships. That is, for each patient in ReportClientData, there might be multiple ailment records in ReportClientAilment. This relationship was created, and will be used in the next two chapters, to aid in demonstrating stylesheet methods for dealing with these types of data relationships.

Creating Database Data

The first thing that must be done is to populate the two previously mentioned tables with data. A JSP has been created to create as many records as are necessary for this purpose, and its description follows. This JSP contains a simple form that allows the user to enter the number of client records to be created.

When the form is submitted, the same JSP will begin by creating the requested number of client records. As each client record is created, a random number of ailment records are created corresponding to that client record.

The JSP named CreateDBData.jsp found in Listing 11.1 begins with an import statement and the small HTML form that allows the user to enter the number of rows of data that are created. Next, the variables are set, and the parameter entered through the form is parsed through a `try-catch` block as follows:

```
try{
    client_rows = Integer.parseInt(request.getParameter("client_rows"));
}
//catch any and all errors with form data
catch(NumberFormatException e){
    client_rows = 0;
}
```

If any errors result from the parsing of the form variable, such as a nonexistent value or a non-integer value, the parameter is set to `0` in the preceding `catch` block. This will prevent the creation of any new records.

After creating our database `Connection` and `Statement` objects, the looping construct that will insert client records into the database begins:

```
for(int i = 0; i < client_rows; i++){
    db_statement.execute(createQueryClient());
    ResultSet rs = db_statement.executeQuery("select LAST_INSERT_ID()");
```

```
rs.last();
int last_insert_id = rs.getInt(1);
```

Each iteration of the preceding `for` loop will insert one record into the ReportClientData table. After which, a statement is executed, and the resulting `ResultSet` is traversed to find the identity value of the newly inserted record.

This identity value is used to key ailment records with a client record. The identity value of the corresponding client record will be contained in each ailment record. This will result a one-client-to-many-ailments relationship that will be used in the following reporting chapter.

Next, a random number is generated to determine how many ailment records will be created for the current client. This number is used to loop through the creation of each ailment record:

```
int client_ailment = (int) (Math.random() * 5);
for(int k = 0; k < client_ailment; k++){
    try{
        db_statement.execute(createQueryAilment(last_insert_id));
        out.print("<br />Ailment added for record index: " +
            last_insert_id + ". With " + (k+1) + " out of " +
            client_ailment + " Records.");
        ailment_rows++;
    }catch (SQLException e){
        out.print("<br />Ailment skipped for record index:" +
            last_insert_id + ". Due to duplicate." );
    }
}
```

The processing of these statements is wrapped in a `try-catch` block to enable the handling of `SQLExceptions`. All the data is created randomly, and this causes the occasional duplicate ailment record to be created. Duplicates are unacceptable in this table because each client can only have one record indicating an ailment. This duplication error is handled in the preceding `catch` block, and permits the rest of the processing to continue.

Next is the code that outputs status statements and `catch` blocks to catch the various exceptions that the previous statements can create. The page declaration follows the end of the scriptlet.

This is where the methods that create our dates, names, and other record data reside. Following these are the methods that bring it all together to create the complete insert statements executed against the database.

The complete JSP that will dynamically create and insert data can be found in Listing 11.1 and should be saved as `\webapps\xmlbook\chapter11\CreateDBData.jsp`.

LISTING 11.1 CreateDBData.jsp in Its Complete Form

```
<%@page import = "java.sql.*" %>

<html>
<head><title></title></head>
<body>
<form method="post">
<table>
    <tr>
        <td align="right">Number of rows to create:</td>
        <td><input type="text" name="client_rows" value="" size="5"/></td>
    </tr>
<tr>
    <td colspan="2" align="left">
        <br /><br /><input type="submit" value="Create Records" />
    </td>
</tr>
<table>

</form>

<%
    // 1. Initialize variables
    int client_rows;
    String final_status   = "There were 0 Client Data records added.";
    String db_query    = "";
    String db_location    = "jdbc:mysql://localhost/xmlbook";
    String db_driver = "org.gjt.mm.mysql.Driver";
    int ailment_rows = 0;

    try{
        client_rows = Integer.parseInt(request.getParameter("client_rows"));
    }
    //catch any and all errors with form data
    catch(NumberFormatException e){
        client_rows = 0;
    }

    // 2. Make a database connection
```

LISTING 11.1 Continued

```
Connection db_connection = null;
try{
    Class.forName(db_driver);
    db_connection = DriverManager.getConnection(db_location);
    Statement db_statement = db_connection.createStatement();

 // 3. Create records for ReportClientData table in xmlbook database
    for(int i = 0; i < client_rows; i++){
        db_statement.execute(createQueryClient());
        ResultSet rs = db_statement.executeQuery
            ("select LAST_INSERT_ID()");
        rs.last();
        int last_insert_id = rs.getInt(1);
        int client_ailment = (int) (Math.random() * 5);
        for(int k = 0; k < client_ailment; k++){
            try{
                db_statement.execute(createQueryAilment(last_insert_id));
                out.print("<br />Ailment added for record index: " +
                    last_insert_id + ". With " + (k+1) + " out of " +
                    client_ailment + " Records.");
                ailment_rows++;
            }catch (SQLException e){
                out.print("<br />Ailment skipped for record index:" +
                    last_insert_id + ". Due to duplicate." );
            }
        }
        if (client_rows -1 == i)
            final_status = "There were " + client_rows +
                    " Client Data records added.";
    }

}
catch (ClassNotFoundException e)
{   final_status  = " Error creating database drive class!";
    final_status += " <br />" +  e.toString();
}
catch (SQLException e)
{   final_status  = " Error processing the SQL!";
    final_status += " <br />" +  e.toString();
}
finally
```

LISTING 11.1 Continued

```
    {
        /* We must close the database connection now */
        try
        {   if (db_connection != null)
            { db_connection.close(); }
        }
        catch (SQLException e)
        {   final_status  = "Error in closing connection.";
            final_status += " <br />" +  e.toString();
        }
    }
%>

<br /><br />
<font color="blue"><%=final_status%>
    <br />And <%=ailment_rows%> Ailment Data records added.
</font>
<br /><br />
</body>
</html>

<%!
char letters[] = {'a', 'b', 'c', 'd', 'e', 'f',
    'g', 'h', 'i', 'j', 'k', 'l', 'm', 'n', 'o',
    'p', 'q', 'r', 's', 't', 'u', 'v', 'w', 'x', 'y', 'z'};

private String createString(int length){

    String result = "";

    for(int i = 0; i < length; i++){
        int temp = (int) (Math.random() * 26);
        //capitalize the first letter in this string
        if (i == 0)
            result += Character.toUpperCase(letters[temp]);
        else
            result += letters[temp];
    }

    return new String(result);
}
```

LISTING 11.1 Continued

```
//1 means birthdate (1930 - 1996)
//2 means ailment 10 years (1980 - 1997)
private String createDate(int year_range){

    String result = "19";

    if (year_range == 1)
        result += "" + (30 + (int) (Math.random() * 67));
    else
        result += "" + (80 + (int) (Math.random() * 18));
    result += "-" + (1 + (int) (Math.random() * 12));
    result += "-" + (1 + (int) (Math.random() * 28));

    return new String(result);
}

private String createColor(){

    String result = "";
    int pick_a_color = (int) (Math.random() * 6);

    switch (pick_a_color) {
        case 0: result = "red";
                break;
        case 1: result = "yellow";
                break;
        case 2: result = "blue";
                break;
        case 3: result = "green";
                break;
        case 4: result = "purple";
                break;
        case 5: result = "orange";
                break;
        default: result = "black";
    }
    return result;
}

private String createQueryClient(){
```

LISTING 11.1 Continued

```
    String db_query = " insert into ReportClientData ";
    db_query += "(RCD_lname,RCD_fname,RCD_clinic,RCD_dob,RCD_color)";
    db_query += " values (";
    db_query += "'" + createString( 7 ) + "' ,";
    db_query += "'" + createString( 5 ) + "' ,";
    db_query += "'" + (1 + (int) (Math.random() * 5)) + "' ,";
    db_query += "'" + createDate(1) + "' ,";
    db_query += "'" + createColor() + "')";

    return db_query;
}
private String createQueryAilment(int clientID){

    String db_query  = " insert into ReportClientAilments ";
    db_query += "(RCA_medicalailment,RCA_datefound,RCA_clientID)";
    db_query += " values (";
    db_query += "'" + createString( 1 ) + "' ,";
    db_query += "'" + createDate(2) + "' ,";
    db_query += "'" + clientID + "' )";

    return db_query;
}
%>
```

Now that some data exists, let's start creating some reports. The first step in this process is creating a class that will create a JDOM representation out of a `ResultSet`.

ResultSet to XML

`RStoXML` is a class that will return a JDOM representation of a database `ResultSet` upon the invocation of the `build()` method. Before this method is used, properties of the returned JDOM document can be specified. Some of the properties available include changing the default element names from the record column names and declaring columns to be created as attributes instead of elements. Another important property available is the maximum number of records that will be converted into the JDOM representation. The use of this property will be demonstrated in the next chapter when a paging report is created.

This class is a starting point for the creation of a more versatile production-oriented object. The capability to filter which columns of the `ResultSet` get included in the JDOM creation can easily be added with another `HashMap`, some more property setting methods, and some additional logic in the `build()` method.

What It Does

RStoXML.java at its simplest will create a JDOM document from a ResultSet object. At its default setting, RStoXML will create sibling Element nodes for each field of data found in a record. These nodes will be placed together as children of an Element node, each of which represents a record. This causes the record elements to be children of the root node, and all data containing elements to be grandchildren.

For example, the default XML structure returned from RStoXML is shown following Table 11.1, which contains two sample records.

TABLE 11.1 Two Records from the ReportClientData Table

RCD_index	RCD_lname	RCD_fname	RCD_dob	RCD_clinic	RCD_color
1	Nowitz	Kerry	1970-08-29	1	yellow
2	Muller	Todd	1981-02-08	2	green

Using all the defaults of RStoXML, the sample records found in Table 11.1 would result in a JDOM representation of the XML document shown in Listing 11.2.

LISTING 11.2 Default JDOM Document Returned from RStoXML

```
<ROOT>
  <RECORD>
    <RCD_index>1</RCD_index>
    <RCD_lname>Nowitz</RCD_lname>
    <RCD_fname>Kerry</RCD_fname>
    <RCD_dob>1970-08-29</RCD_dob>
    <RCD_clinic>1</RCD_clinic>
    <RCD_color>yellow</RCD_color>
  </RECORD>
  <RECORD>
    <RCD_index>2</RCD_index>
    <RCD_lname>Muller</RCD_lname>
    <RCD_fname>Todd</RCD_fname>
    <RCD_dob>1981-02-08</RCD_dob>
    <RCD_clinic>2</RCD_clinic>
    <RCD_color>green</RCD_color>
  </RECORD>
</ROOT>
```

RStoXML is not limited to outputting Elements to represent the structure of the ResultSet. Methods such as setAsAttribute() and setAllAttribute() exist to set one or all columns of data to attributes of the RECORD element. For example, if setAllAttribute() were invoked before the JDOM representation were built through the build() method, the JDOM structure as represented in Listing 11.3 would result.

LISTING 11.3 JDOM Document Returned from RStoXML

```
<ROOT>
  <RECORD RCD_index="1" RCD_lname="Nowitz" RCD_fname="Kerry"
          RCD_dob="1970-08-29" RCD_clinic="1" RCD_color="yellow" />
  <RECORD RCD_index="2" RCD_lname="Muller" RCD_fname="Todd"
          RCD_dob="1981-02-08" RCD_clinic="2" RCD_color="green" />
</ROOT>
```

Nor is RStoXML limited to the default column names that exist in the database table definition. Sometimes these names can be very long, depending upon the database schema. As a result, methods such as setName() permit the setting of the attribute or element name with which a ResultSet data column will be labeled.

The source code to this class follows in Listing 11.4. It will not be explained because it is straightforward Java. Save and compile this file as webapps\xmlbook\WEB-INF\classes\xmlbook\chapter11.

LISTING 11.4 RStoXML.java

```
package xmlbook.chapter11;

import java.io.*;
import java.sql.*;
import java.text.*;
import java.util.*;

import org.jdom.*;

public class RStoXML {

    private SQLException exception;

    private ResultSet rs;
    private int intColCount;
    private ResultSetMetaData rsmd;

    //key is original column name keyed to replacement name
    private Map newNames = new HashMap();
```

LISTING 11.4 Continued

```
//key is original db column, true or false
private Map attribs = new HashMap();
int maxRows = Integer.MAX_VALUE;        // default to all
private String rootName = "ROOT";
private String rowName = "RECORD";


 public RStoXML(ResultSet rs) {
 this.rs = rs;
 try {
    rsmd = rs.getMetaData();
    intColCount = rsmd.getColumnCount();

  }
  catch (SQLException e) {
    // Hold the exception until build() is called
    exception = e;
  }

 }
public RStoXML(ResultSet rs, String rootName, String rowName)  {
    this(rs);
    setRootName(rootName);
    setRowName(rowName);

}

public Document build() throws JDOMException {
  if (exception != null) {
    throw new JDOMException("Database problem", exception);
  }
  try {

    Element root = new Element(rootName);
    Document doc = new Document(root);

    int rowCount = 0;

    // get column names for the record set
    String[] columnName = new String[intColCount];
    for (int index = 0; index < intColCount; index++) {
```

LISTING 11.4 Continued

```
            columnName[index] = rsmd.getColumnName(index+1);
        }

        // build the org.jdom.Document out of the result set
        String name;
        String value;
        Element record;
        Element child;

        while (rs.next() && (rowCount++ < maxRows)) {
            record = new Element(rowName);
            for (int col = 1; col <= intColCount; col++) {
                if (newNames.isEmpty() ||
                    (newNames.get(columnName[col-1].toLowerCase()) == null))
                    name = columnName[col-1];
                else
                    name = lookupName(columnName[col-1]);
                value = rs.getString(col);
                if ( attribs.containsKey(columnName[col-1].toLowerCase())) {
                    //if the value of the column is in attribs
                    //and notnull create attribute
                    record.setAttribute(name, value);
                }
                else {
                    //other wise create child element
                    child = new Element(name);
                    if (!rs.wasNull())
                        child.setText(value);
                    record.addContent(child);
                }
            }
            root.addContent(record);
            }

            return doc;
            }
            catch (SQLException e) {
                throw new JDOMException("Database problem", e) ;
            }
        }
```

LISTING 11.4 Continued

```
    //origName is column name in db, if name exists in the newNames hashmap
    //return it, else returned passed in name.
   private String lookupName(String origName) {
                  String name = (String) newNames.get(origName.toLowerCase());
                  if (name != null) {
                    return name;
                  }
                  else {
                    return origName;
                  }
    }

    public void setRootName(String rootName) {
      this.rootName = rootName;
    }

    public void setRowName(String rowName) {
      this.rowName = rowName;
    }

    public void setMaxRows(int maxRows) {
      this.maxRows = maxRows;
    }

    public void setAsAttribute(String columnName, String attribName) {
      String name = columnName.toLowerCase();
      attribs.put(name, "t");
      newNames.put(name, attribName);
    }

    public void setAllAttribute() throws JDOMException{
        try{
            int intColCount = rsmd.getColumnCount();
            for (int index = 0; index < intColCount; index++) {
                attribs.put(rsmd.getColumnName(index+1).toLowerCase(), "t");
         }
        }catch (SQLException e) {
        throw new JDOMException("Database problem", e);
       }
    }
```

LISTING 11.4 Continued

```
    public void setName(String columnName, String name){
        newNames.put(columnName.toLowerCase(), name);
    }
   //set a database column name to a specific element name
   public void setAsName(String columnName, String elemName) {
      String name = columnName.toLowerCase();
      newNames.put(name, elemName);
    }

}
```

Bringing It All Together

Next is the JSP that will bring everything together. This JSP will connect to a database and execute a statement that will produce a `ResultSet`. After that, the `ResultSet` will be passed into the newly created `RStoXML` and used to obtain a JDOM representation. This will then be transformed with a stylesheet, and the results output.

The TableSort.xsl stylesheet will create an HTML table whose label cells are links. Each of these links will provide the column number in the query string, so that when the string is followed, the JSP will obtain this parameter from the URL. Once obtained, that value will be passed into the stylesheet to result in the appropriate sort.

After parsing the import statements, DBtoXML.jsp parses the query string to find the column number to sort on. If this parse results in an error, the default defined in the JSP will be used:

```
<%  // 1. get parameters from url
    int sort_by;
    try{
        sort_by = Integer.parseInt(request.getParameter("sort"));
    }catch(NumberFormatException e){
        //if invalid or nonexistent parameter, sort by RCD_lname
        sort_by = 1;
    }
```

The page then initializes the variables that will be used throughout the rest of the page. These variables include those for database processing, such as the query statement and the XSLT stylesheet filename.

After this, the page will connect to the database, execute the SQL statement, return a ResultSet, and release the resources used. These statements have been explained previously, and will not be re-explained here.

After the ResultSet has been obtained, the process of conversion to a JDOM representation is started through the creation of an RStoXML object:

```
// create a resultsetbuilder to transform resultset to XML
RStoXML rsb = new RStoXML(rs, "ROOT", "RECORD");
```

Two constructors exist for RStoXML. One uses all the defaults of the class, and therefore only requires the ResultSet parameter. The other, shown here, takes a ResultSet and two Strings as parameters. The first String parameter sets the root element name of the resulting JDOM representation, and the other sets the name of the elements that will each represent one record:

```
//create the XML from resultset
org.jdom.Document jdomdoc = rsb.build();
rs = null;
```

The build() method is then invoked upon the object that will cause the creation of the JDOM representation, and the resources used in the ResultSet are released.

If any properties are to be set, such as setAllAttribute(), the setter methods must be called before the build() method is invoked. Otherwise, all the class defaults are used.

Now that the JDOM representation is available, it's time to create the Transformer object to do the transformation. This Transformer is created with the stylesheet previously defined by the variable xsl:

```
//create transformer
Transformer transformer = TransformerFactory.newInstance()
        .newTransformer(new StreamSource(xsl));
```

With the help of the newly created Transformer, the two parameters that exist at the root level of the XSL stylesheet are set as shown below. The first is the column number that the resulting table will be sorted on, and the second is the name of the page that the linked table labels should be directed to. The presence of this parameter enables the stylesheet to be completely generic and not bound to any dataset, column names, or page names.

```
transformer.setParameter("Sort", new Integer(sort_by));
transformer.setParameter("Page", "DBtoXML.jsp");
```

With the parameters set, the stylesheet is ready to transform the JDOM representation. Before this occurs, a `JDOMResult` object is created to hold the results of the transformation. It is now time to `transform()` the JDOM representation of the `ResultSet` with the stylesheet using the `Transformer` object. Again, we release the resources used by the `jdomdoc` source object after it is no longer useful:

```
JDOMResult jdomresults = new JDOMResult();
transformer.transform(new JDOMSource(jdomdoc), jdomresults);
jdomdoc = null;
```

The results of the transformation are now in `jdomresults` and need to be output. An easy way of doing this is through the use of the `XMLOutputter` class found in the `org.jdom.output` package. This class will format the JDOM document into a stream through which it can be output to the user through the output of the JSP. The `Document` of the transformation results are obtained and output:

```
//create outputter to output results
        XMLOutputter output = new XMLOutputter("    ", true);
        //output the results
        Document docResults = jdomresults.getDocument();
        output.output(docResults, out);
```

Notice that the constructor used here for `XMLOutputter` takes two parameters. These parameters determine the indentation, and whether new lines will be included in the output. Through the use of these parameters, the tidiness of the output HTML can be altered. The settings chosen here will cause the output HTML to be formatted in a readable form.

After handling some possible exceptions that might occur, the page is complete. DBtoXML.jsp can be found in its entirety in Listing 11.5.

LISTING 11.5 Complete DBtoXML.jsp File

```
<%@page import = "java.sql.*,
        org.jdom.*,
        org.jdom.output.*,
        javax.xml.transform.*,
        javax.xml.transform.stream.*,
        org.jdom.transform.*,
        xmlbook.chapter11.*" %>
<html>
<head><title>DB to XML and XSL</title></head>
<body>
<div>
```

LISTING 11.5 Continued

```
<%  // 1. get parameters from url
    int sort_by;
    try{
        sort_by = Integer.parseInt(request.getParameter("sort"));
    }catch(NumberFormatException e){
    //if invalid or nonexistent parameter, sort by RCD_lname
        sort_by = 1;
    }

    // 2. Initialize other variables
    String final_status   = "";
    String db_query       = "select RCD_lname, RCD_fname, ";
           db_query       +="DATE_FORMAT(RCD_dob, '%Y-%m-%d') as RCD_dob , ";
           db_query       +="RCD_clinic, RCD_color from reportclientdata";
    String db_location    = "jdbc:mysql://localhost/xmlbook";
    String db_driver      = "org.gjt.mm.mysql.Driver";
    String stylesheet     = "TableSort.xsl";

    // 3. Make a database connection
    Connection db_connection = null;
    Statement db_statement = null;
    ResultSet rs = null;
    try{
        Class.forName(db_driver);
        db_connection = DriverManager.getConnection(db_location);
        db_statement = db_connection.createStatement();

        //get a resultset
        rs = db_statement.executeQuery(db_query);
    }
    catch (ClassNotFoundException e){
        final_status  = "Error: Unable to create database drive class.";
        final_status += " <br />" +  e.toString();
    }
    catch(SQLException e){
        final_status = "Error: Unable to make database connection";
        final_status += "or execute statement.";
        final_status += " <br />" +  e.toString();
    }
    finally
    {  /* We must close the database connection now */
```

LISTING 11.5 Continued

```
        try
        {   if (db_connection != null)
            { db_connection.close(); }
        }
        catch (SQLException e)
        {   final_status  = "Error: Unable to close database connection.";
            final_status += " <br />" +  e.toString();
        }
    }
    try{
        // create a resultsetbuilder to transform resultset to XML
        RStoXML rsxml = new RStoXML(rs, "ROOT", "RECORD");

        //create the XML from recordset
        org.jdom.Document jdomdoc = rsxml.build();
        rs = null;

        //get the stylesheet
        String path = request.getServletPath();
        path = path.substring(0,path.indexOf("DBtoXML.jsp")) ;
        String  xsl  = application.getRealPath(path + stylesheet);

        //create transformer
        Transformer transformer = TransformerFactory.newInstance()
                  .newTransformer(new StreamSource(xsl));
        transformer.setParameter("Sort", new Integer(sort_by));
        transformer.setParameter("Page", "DBtoXML.jsp");
        //transformer.setParameter("NFilter", new Integer(nFilter_by));
        //transformer.setParameter("CFilter", cFilter_by);

        JDOMResult jdomresults = new JDOMResult();
        transformer.transform(new JDOMSource(jdomdoc), jdomresults);
        jdomdoc = null;

        //create outputter to output results
        XMLOutputter output = new XMLOutputter("   ", true);
        //output the results
        Document docResults = jdomresults.getDocument();
        output.output(docResults, out);
    }
    catch (TransformerFactoryConfigurationError e) {
```

LISTING 11.5 Continued

```
        final_status = "Error: Unable to create factory to transform ";
        final_status = "XSL and XML.";
        final_status += "<br />" +  e.toString();
    }
    catch (TransformerException e) {
        final_status = "Error: Unable to transform XSL and XML.";
        final_status += "<br />" +  e.toString();
    }
    catch (JDOMException e)
    {   final_status  = "Error: Unable to create XML from database query.";
        final_status += "<br />" +  e.toString();
    }

    if(final_status != "")
        out.print("<br><font color=\"red\"><H2>" + final_status +
            "</H2></font>");
%>

</div>
</body>
</html>
```

The Sorting Table Stylesheet

Now that we have walked through the process of converting a `ResultSet` to a JDOM representation, it's time to take a look at the transforming stylesheet.

This XSL stylesheet is as generic as possible. In fact, it can be used to transform many different sets of data without altering anything. Any XML document that has grandchild elements with text data and child elements that group the grandchild elements can be output as a table with linked labels using this stylesheet.

The stylesheet has two root-level parameters. The first, `Sort`, is the column number by which to sort the resulting table. This parameter is used to enable the JSP to pass this sorting information through from the URL parameter. The value of the second parameter, `Page`, is used to create the links that will cause the re-sorting of the report.

The stylesheet is composed of three templates. The first template will match on the root element and begin the processing of the entire document. The next template will create all the table column labels, which are linked to cause the document to reload sorted on the chosen row. The last template will match each child of the root element in turn and output all element children as table cells.

The stylesheet begins with the XML document declaration, and root `xsl:stylesheet` element that describes the namespace of the XSL elements. The root level parameters are then declared void of default values, and the output method is set:

```
<?xml version="1.0" encoding="UTF-8"?>
<xsl:stylesheet version="1.0"
     xmlns:xsl="http://www.w3.org/1999/XSL/Transform">

<xsl:param name="Sort"/>
<xsl:param name="Page"/>
<xsl:output method="html" />
```

Next is the start of the first template. This template matches the root of the XML document with the match attribute value of `/`. This causes the entire XML document to pass into this template. The HTML `div` and `table` elements are output at this point, and the `header` template is called with an empty body through the `call-template` element. Then, the body of the header template is executed with the context node as the root of the document:

```
<xsl:template match="/">

<table border="1">
    <xsl:call-template name="header"/>
```

Next, an `apply-templates` is used to select each element that matches the XPath statement `*/*`. This statement will select each child element of the root in turn and match each to a template with a matching `select` attribute.

Notice that the body of this template tag is not empty. Inside, there is a sort element that selects which of a set of nodes to be sorted on. More specifically, this `sort` element selects the child whose position number is equal to the `$Sort` parameter by which to sort. This parameter-dependent statement enables us to dynamically sort the output. When these operations are completed, the end table HTML tag is output and the template is finished:

```
    <xsl:apply-templates select="*/*">
        <xsl:sort select="*[$Sort]" />
    </xsl:apply-templates>
</table>

</xsl:template>
```

Let's look at the next template that creates the linked table labels. This again starts out by defining the template tag with the `name` attribute value of the header:

```
<!-- creates the table headers from the tag names -->
<xsl:template name="header">
```

Next, a table row tag is output, followed by the beginning of a `for-each` loop. This loop selects each grandchild of the root element whose parent is first in the sibling position. This results in the exclusive selection in turn of each child that is descended from the first child of the root element. In other words, it selects each column of data one at a time from the first record of the `ResultSet` from which this XML descends:

```
<tr>
    <xsl:for-each select="*/*[1]/*">
```

This causes the stylesheet to properly handle any number of data columns from the original `ResultSet`.

Within this loop, each link is created through the use of the appropriate text and stylesheet parameters. In this case, `href` is equal to the `$Page` variable set previously through the JSP, and the number of the data column in terms of sibling position returned by the `position()` method:

```
        <th>
            <A href="{$Page}?sort={position()}">
```

In the preceding code snippet, the shorthand `value-of` notation is used—namely the curly brackets. This permits the inclusion of the results of XPath expressions within other output tags. If this feature were unavailable, the only way to access this information would be through the use of a `value-of` tag. This would make it impossible to dynamically create HTML element attribute values, because tags cannot contain other tags.

Now that the anchor element has been created with the proper `href` attribute value, the tag name of each element will be selected. This enables us to label the HTML table with each element's tag name regardless of the number of columns found in the original record set. This is achieved through the use of the `local-name()` method with the `.` parameter, which denotes `this`:

```
                <xsl:value-of select="local-name(.)" />
```

Next, the anchor and table head cell is closed, as is the `for-each` loop that iterated through each element. The table row is closed and the template is complete:

```
            </A>
        </th>
    </xsl:for-each>
```

```
</tr>
</xsl:template>
```

Last up is the template that will select each child element of the root, no matter how many, and output a table row formatted with cells for each text data containing child elements.

Like the previous template, this one iterates through each child of the root—except this one doesn't exclude all but the first child element. Once matched, a table row tag will be output, and a `for-each` element will iterate through each child element of the currently selected element through the `*`:

```
<!-- creates a row for each child of root, -->
<!-- and cell for each grandchild of root -->
<xsl:template match="*/*">
    <tr>
        <xsl:for-each select="*">
```

Next, the `.` notation is used to output the value of `this`, which will be each column of data found in one record. Finally, the table row is closed, and the template ended:

```
    <td><xsl:value-of select="." /></td>
        </xsl:for-each>
    </tr>
</xsl:template>
```

Finally, the stylesheet root element is closed, and the document is finished. The complete stylesheet follows in Listing 11.6, and should be saved as `\webapps\xmlbook\chapter11\TableSort.xsl`.

LISTING 11.6 TableSort.xsl

```
<?xml version="1.0" encoding="UTF-8"?>
<xsl:stylesheet version="1.0"
    xmlns:xsl="http://www.w3.org/1999/XSL/Transform">

<xsl:param name="Sort"/>
<xsl:param name="Page"/>
<xsl:output method="html" />

<xsl:template match="/">

<table border="1">
    <xsl:call-template name="header"/>
```

LISTING 11.6 Continued

```
    <xsl:apply-templates select="*/*">
        <xsl:sort select="*[$Sort]" />
    </xsl:apply-templates>
</table>

</xsl:template>

<!-- creates the table headers from the tag names -->
<xsl:template name="header">
<tr>
    <xsl:for-each select="*/*[1]/*">
        <th>
            <A href="{$Page}?sort={position()}">
                <xsl:value-of select="local-name(.)" />
           </A>
         </th>
    </xsl:for-each>
</tr>
</xsl:template>

<!-- creates a row for each child of root, -->
<!-- and cell for each grandchild of root -->
<xsl:template match="*/*">
    <tr>
        <xsl:for-each select="*">
            <td><xsl:value-of select="." /></td>
        </xsl:for-each>
    </tr>
</xsl:template>

</xsl:stylesheet>
```

The output of the previous Java class, JSP, and XSL stylesheet is as shown in Figure 11.1.

NOTE

If you encounter problems, verify that Xerces, Xalan, and JDOM have been installed. These examples depend on that software for successful execution.

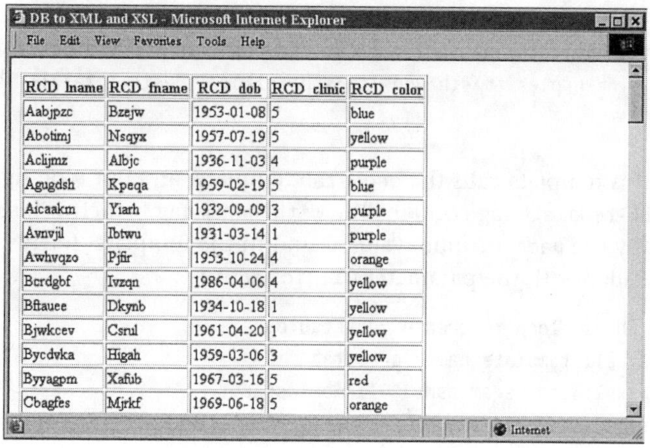

DB to XML and XSL - Microsoft Internet Explorer

File Edit View Favorites Tools Help

RCD lname	RCD fname	RCD dob	RCD clinic	RCD color
Aabjpzc	Bzejw	1953-01-08	5	blue
Abotimj	Nsqyx	1957-07-19	5	yellow
Aclijmz	Albjc	1936-11-03	4	purple
Agugdsh	Kpeqa	1959-02-19	5	blue
Aicaakm	Yiarh	1932-09-09	3	purple
Avnvjil	Ibtwu	1931-03-14	1	purple
Awhvqzo	Pjfir	1953-10-24	4	orange
Bcrdgbf	Ivzqn	1986-04-06	4	yellow
Bftauee	Dkynb	1934-10-18	1	yellow
Bjwkcev	Csrul	1961-04-20	1	yellow
Bycdvka	Higah	1959-03-06	3	yellow
Byyagpm	Xafub	1967-03-16	5	red
Cbagfes	Mjrkf	1969-06-18	5	orange

Internet

FIGURE 11.1 Results of DBtoXML.jsp, RStoXML.java, and TableSort.xsl.

Notice that the column heads are linked properly in order to cause the re-sorting of the document as shown, with the URL shown in the status bar. Also, the data is sorted on column number `1`, as was set in the `catch` loop of parsing the query parameter in the JSP. To change this default value, just alter the parameter in the JSP.

This has been an example to demonstrate how easy it is to create a large number of reports. Simply by changing the data set that the stylesheet transforms, a large number of custom-arrangeable table reports can be created.

The Cross Tab Stylesheet

In the next example, we'll change the stylesheet in order to create a cross tab report on the same dataset. Unlike the previous stylesheet, this one is not completely generic, but depends upon a particular dataset. However, with the addition of more parameters set within the JSP, this stylesheet can be converted into a more generic form.

The CrossTab.xsl stylesheet begins with a parameter called `NumClinics`, whose default value is `5`. This parameter will be used as the counter in the looping template used to iterate the rows of the resulting cross tab report:

```
<xsl:param name="NumClinics" select="5"/>
```

Next are two templates. The first begins by matching on the root of the XML document and creating the resulting table labels:

```
<xsl:template match="/">
    <table border="1">
```

```
        <!-- crosstab labels of first row-->
        <tr><th> </th><th>Blue</th><th>Green</th><th>Orange</th>
            <th>Purple</th><th>Red</th><th>Yellow</th><th>Totals:</th>
        </tr>
```

The rest of this template calls the `crosstab` template, and our looping begins. Notice that the `call-template` tag contains the `with-param` tag, which will set the parameter denoted by the `name` attribute value found in the template. In this case, the template is called with the parameter `Clinics` set to `1`:

```
        <!-- begin loop to create crosstab body -->
        <xsl:call-template name="crosstab" >
            <xsl:with-param name="Clinics" select="1"/>
        </xsl:call-template>
    </table>
</xsl:template>
```

Our looping template called `crosstab` then begins with the `Clinic` parameter creation and output via the `value-of` tag, surrounded by some HTML table-related tags:

```
<xsl:template name="crosstab">
    <xsl:param name="Clinics"/>
        <tr><th><xsl:value-of select="$Clinics" /></th>
```

Next is the output of the `count()` of the number of elements meeting the criteria as stated in the XPath statement. This particular statement counts the number of child elements (that is, records) that match the following criteria: The statement requires the `RCD_color` element to contain the text data `blue`, and the `RCD_clinic` element must contain the text data that `$Clinics` resolves to. In this case, the `$Clinics` parameter was set to `1` upon the start of this template. As a result, this `value-of` will return the number of records with data `blue`, and `1`:

```
            <td><xsl:value-of select="count(*/*[RCD_color='blue' and
                                        RCD_clinic=$Clinics])" /></td>
```

The following lines also follow the same format as the previous fragment, except with a different color value:

```
            <td><xsl:value-of select="count(*/*[RCD_color='green' and
                                            RCD_clinic=$Clinics])" /></td>
            <td><xsl:value-of select="count(*/*[RCD_color='orange' and
                                            RCD_clinic=$Clinics])" /></td>
```

```
        <td><xsl:value-of select="count(*/*[RCD_color='purple' and
                                          RCD_clinic=$Clinics])" /></td>
        <td><xsl:value-of select="count(*/*[RCD_color='red' and
                                          RCD_clinic=$Clinics])" /></td>
        <td><xsl:value-of select="count(*/*[RCD_color='yellow' and
                                          RCD_clinic=$Clinics])" /></td>
        <td><xsl:value-of select="count(*/*[RCD_clinic=$Clinics])" /></td>
    </tr>
```

This closes the creation of one row of the cross tab report being created. The only thing left is to iterate through the template the correct number of times to create the remaining rows.

This is done by using an `if` tag and making sure `$Clinics` is less than `$NumClinics`. If the condition is true, then the `crosstab` template is called again with the incremented value of `$Clinics`:

```
<!-- continue looping when condition met -->
<xsl:if test="$Clinics &lt; $NumClinics">
    <xsl:call-template name="crosstab">
        <xsl:with-param name="Clinics" select="$Clinics + 1"/>
    </xsl:call-template>
</xsl:if>
```

And thus the template is recursive, and any recursive template can be created using the same method.

Finally, the last row of the table is output when the two parameters are equal, and the recursion is complete:

```
<xsl:if test="$Clinics=$NumClinics">
    <tr><th>Totals:</th>
        <td><xsl:value-of select="count(*/*[RCD_color='blue'])" /></td>
        <td><xsl:value-of select="count(*/*[RCD_color='green'])" /></td>
        <td><xsl:value-of select="count(*/*[RCD_color='orange'])" /></td>
        <td><xsl:value-of select="count(*/*[RCD_color='purple'])" /></td>
        <td><xsl:value-of select="count(*/*[RCD_color='red'])" /></td>
        <td><xsl:value-of select="count(*/*[RCD_color='yellow'])" /></td>
        <td><xsl:value-of select="count(*/*)" /></td>
    </tr>
</xsl:if>
```

Besides some closing tags, this completes the cross tab stylesheet. The complete stylesheet can be seen in Listing 11.7 and should be saved as `\webapps\xmlbook\chapter11\CrossTab.xsl`.

LISTING 11.7 CrossTab.xsl

```
<?xml version="1.0" encoding="UTF-8"?>
<xsl:stylesheet version="1.0"
    xmlns:xsl="http://www.w3.org/1999/XSL/Transform">

<xsl:param name="NumClinics" select="5"/>
<xsl:output method="html" />

<xsl:template match="/">
    <table border="1">

        <!-- crosstab labels of first row-->
        <tr><th> </th><th>Blue</th><th>Green</th><th>Orange</th>
            <th>Purple</th><th>Red</th><th>Yellow</th><th>Totals:</th>
        </tr>

        <!-- begin loop to create crosstab body -->
        <xsl:call-template name="crosstab" >
            <xsl:with-param name="Clinics" select="1"/>
        </xsl:call-template>
    </table>
</xsl:template>

<xsl:template name="crosstab">
    <xsl:param name="Clinics"/>
        <tr><th><xsl:value-of select="$Clinics" /></th>
            <td><xsl:value-of select="count(*/*[RCD_color='blue' and
                                    RCD_clinic=$Clinics])" /></td>
            <td><xsl:value-of select="count(*/*[RCD_color='green' and
                                    RCD_clinic=$Clinics])" /></td>
            <td><xsl:value-of select="count(*/*[RCD_color='orange' and
                                    RCD_clinic=$Clinics])" /></td>
            <td><xsl:value-of select="count(*/*[RCD_color='purple' and
                                    RCD_clinic=$Clinics])" /></td>
            <td><xsl:value-of select="count(*/*[RCD_color='red' and
                                    RCD_clinic=$Clinics])" /></td>
            <td><xsl:value-of select="count(*/*[RCD_color='yellow' and
                                    RCD_clinic=$Clinics])" /></td>
            <td><xsl:value-of select="count(*/*[RCD_clinic=$Clinics])" /></td>
        </tr>

        <!-- continue looping when condition met -->
```

LISTING 11.7 Continued

```
        <xsl:if test="$Clinics &lt; $NumClinics">
            <xsl:call-template name="crosstab">
                <xsl:with-param name="Clinics" select="$Clinics + 1"/>
            </xsl:call-template>
        </xsl:if>

        <!-- table foot -->
        <xsl:if test="$Clinics=$NumClinics">
            <tr><th>Totals:</th>
             <td><xsl:value-of select="count(*/*[RCD_color='blue'])" /></td>
             <td><xsl:value-of select="count(*/*[RCD_color='green'])" /></td>
             <td><xsl:value-of select="count(*/*[RCD_color='orange'])" /></td>
             <td><xsl:value-of select="count(*/*[RCD_color='purple'])" /></td>
             <td><xsl:value-of select="count(*/*[RCD_color='red'])" /></td>
             <td><xsl:value-of select="count(*/*[RCD_color='yellow'])" /></td>
             <td><xsl:value-of select="count(*/*)" /></td>
            </tr>
        </xsl:if>
</xsl:template>

</xsl:stylesheet>
```

The last thing that we need to do is to change the stylesheet being used in DBtoXML.jsp in Listing 11.5 to CrossTab.xsl. This can be achieved by changing the value of the variable `stylesheet` from

```
String stylesheet     = "TableSort.xsl"
```

to

```
String stylesheet     = "CrossTab.xsl"
```

After this has been done, the results will look like those in Figure 11.2. Note that the actual counts will vary depending on the data in your database.

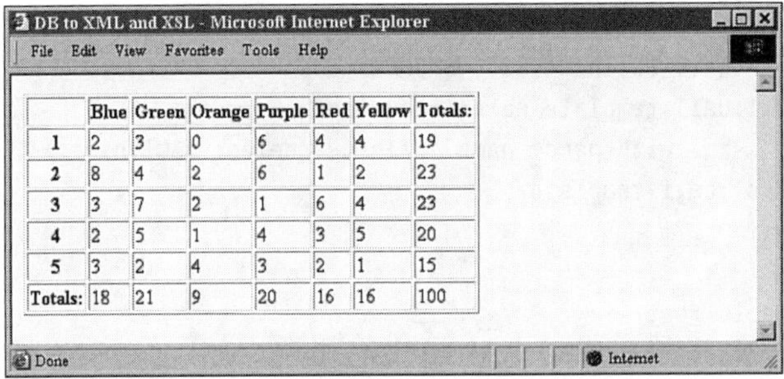

	Blue	Green	Orange	Purple	Red	Yellow	Totals:
1	2	3	0	6	4	4	19
2	8	4	2	6	1	2	23
3	3	7	2	1	6	4	23
4	2	5	1	4	3	5	20
5	3	2	4	3	2	1	15
Totals:	18	21	9	20	16	16	100

FIGURE 11.2 Results of DBtoXML.jsp, RStoXML.java, and CrossTab.xsl.

Summary

Depending upon the data and reports needed, XML can be a very powerful tool. It can enable the quick creation of many different reports. This can be done through the use of the same stylesheets for multiple sets of data. XML also aids development by enabling the database to perform the initial data filtering, and then using stylesheets to add an additional layer of filtering. As demonstrated through the stylesheets of this chapter, the usefulness of generic stylesheets in terms of reporting systems becomes clear.

Combined with HTML forms, stored procedures, and JSPs, XML and XSL assist in the speedy creation of extremely robust reporting systems with many filter and sorting options. More of these capabilities will be demonstrated in the next chapter, where a "paging" report will be created to handle large sets of data, and other stylesheet techniques will be used.

12

Advanced XML in Reporting Systems

IN THIS CHAPTER

- Multiple-Page Reports
- Reports on Data with One-to-Many Relationships
- Real-World Reporting Systems
- Well-Formed Documents Revisited

In the previous chapter, all the necessary components to output HTML from database records using XML were created. Some components will be reused in this chapter. However, other components, such as RStoXML.java from Listing 11.4, will not. Others, such as DBtoXML.jsp from Listing 11.5, will be modified to better suit the specific report being created. This chapter's examples depend on the examples from Chapter 11, "Using XML in Reporting Systems." As a result, reused portions of these components will not be explained here. However, explanations of changes and additions will be included, as well as references to the original examples of the component.

This chapter builds on the examples from the previous chapter. The first example report will build on the table sort report from the previous chapter to add the functionality of paging. This causes the report of a very large set of data to be broken down into viewable pages, which enables the timely display and processing of large data sets and makes viewing the data more manageable.

Next, a report will be created that shows a one-to-many relationship. In this example, each ailment that a specific client has will be displayed beneath the information about the client. Any number of ailments can exist per client, and this report will handle all these cases. This example illustrates how to create reports that show a one-to-many relationship in the database.

Multiple-Page Reports

The final goal of most reporting systems is the presentation of data in a useful way. One aspect to this goal is how to handle reports containing so much data that they are no longer useful. This could be because of the slow speed of report creation or the large output. Both of these factors reduce the usefulness of a report and might frustrate the end user.

One way to handle this problem is through the use of a report that pages through the data. Such a report displays a subset of the entire report at any time. Each page can be sorted by any of the columns on the report. This results in the report being generated more quickly and presenting a more manageable set of data to view.

The output of the paging report is an HTML table with headers and labels. Some of these labels include linked numbers that go to each of the possible report pages and navigation links that will flip the report forward or back a page. Also, linked column labels will redisplay the report sorted on the appropriate column.

The JSP for the Multiple-Page Report

The report is built on the JSP named DBtoXML.jsp found in Listing 11.5. The modifications to the JSP include the following:

- The addition of a query string parameter containing the page number requested of the report
- The modification of the SQL statement executed against the database to return only a select subset of the report data
- The addition of a second SQL `select` statement to query the total number of records that exist in the report, which enables the dynamic creation of the correct number of report pages

The JSP begins by parsing the requesting query string to obtain the information necessary for the creation of the proper report page. Next, a statement is executed against the database to obtain the data from the `ReportClientData` table found in the `xmlbook` database for the appropriate page of the output report. At this point, another database statement is executed to obtain the total number of records for this report. This number is necessary to calculate the total number of possible report pages.

The database `ResultSet` is then converted into a JDOM representation using the class `RStoXML.java` found in Listing 11.4. Finally, the JDOM structure is transformed using the TblPageSort.xsl stylesheet, and the report page is output.

The JSP code begins with some HTML output. Following this, the query string is parsed within a `try` block for the value of the `pagenum` parameter, as shown in the following code. If the parameter is not found, the `catch` block will set the Java variable `rpt_page` to the default value of `1`. This indicates that the default first page of the report will be displayed.

```
int rpt_page;
try{
    rpt_page = Integer.parseInt(request.getParameter("pagenum"));
}catch(NumberFormatException e){

    rpt_page = 1;
}
```

After some other processing, the SQL statement to select the client records will be created as shown in the following code. This statement must only select those records that should be displayed on the requested report page. This is done with the use of the `LIMIT` keyword.

```
String db_query      = "select RCD_lname, RCD_fname, ";
       db_query      +="DATE_FORMAT(RCD_dob, '%Y-%m-%d') as RCD_dob , ";
       db_query      +="RCD_clinic, RCD_color from reportclientdata ";
       db_query      +="order by RCD_lname LIMIT ";
       db_query      += (rpt_page - 1) * recPerPage + ", " + recPerPage;
```

The `LIMIT` keyword selects a specific subset of the records returned by the statement. The two numbers separated by a comma following the `LIMIT` keyword determine this subset. The first of these numbers indicates the record number from which to start the selection—in this case, that depends on the report page being requested—whereas the second number indicates the number of records to select, starting from that point.

When the preceding statement is executed, the selected records are first sorted according to the `RCD_lname` field. Once completed, the appropriate subset is selected using the `LIMIT` keyword and some calculations.

NOTE

It is important to note that the `LIMIT` keyword is database implementation specific. You can obtain the same information from the database using a stored procedure.

The `recPerPage` variable contains the number of records to be displayed per page. This variable and the calculations depending on it allow the number of records output per page to be easily altered without any other stylesheet or JSP required alterations.

Now that the appropriate SQL statement has been created for the report page being displayed, the `stylesheet` variable is set to the stylesheet for this report.

After the creation of the database connection, the SQL statement is executed, and the ResultSet is placed in the rs object as shown in the following code. Notice that another ResultSet is created and placed into the rsCnt object. This second ResultSet contains the total number of records in all pages of this report. This information is obtained and placed in the recordCnt variable:

```
//get a resultset or two
rs = db_statement.executeQuery(db_query);
rsCnt = db_statementCnt.executeQuery
    ("select count(*) from reportclientdata");
rsCnt.first();
int recordCnt = rsCnt.getInt(1);
```

After the total number of records has been obtained, this information will be used to calculate the total number of pages that this report will have. The result of this calculation is placed into the rpt_pages variable as shown in the following:

```
rpt_pages = (int) java.lang.Math.ceil((float) recordCnt / recPerPage);
```

After the various error handling and database related statements, the ResultSet is transformed into a JDOM representation using the RStoXML class as shown in the following code. This class was created and demonstrated in Listings 11.4 and 11.5, respectively.

```
// create a resultsetbuilder to transform resultset to XML
RStoXML rsxml = new RStoXML(rs, "ROOT", "RECORD");

//create the XML from recordset
org.jdom.Document jdomdoc = rsxml.build();
```

Next, the stylesheet is obtained and loaded into a Transformation object. Once completed, four stylesheet parameters are set. The two new parameters are the currently displayed page number found in PageNum and the total number of possible report pages found in Total as follows:

```
transformer.setParameter("PageNum", new Integer(rpt_page));
transformer.setParameter("Total", new Integer(rpt_pages));
```

The stylesheet uses these parameters to create the appropriate links for the resulting report page.

The rest of the JSP transforms the JDOM representation with the stylesheet, performs various error handling, and outputs the results like the original JSP.

This JSP depends on the existence of the `RStoXML.java` class found in Listing 11.4 and saved in the `webapps\xmlbook\WEB-INF\classes\xmlbook\chapter11` directory.

The complete JSP can be seen in Listing 12.1 and should be saved as `webapps\xmlbook\chapter12\PagingRpt.jsp`. The additions and changes from DBtoXML.jsp found in Listing 11.5 appear in boldface type.

LISTING 12.1 PagingRpt.jsp

```
<%@page import = "java.sql.*,
        org.jdom.*,
        org.jdom.output.*,
        javax.xml.transform.*,
        javax.xml.transform.stream.*,
        org.jdom.transform.*,
        xmlbook.chapter11.*" %>
<html>
<head><title>Paging Report</title></head>
<body>
<div>
<%  // 1. get parameters from url
    int sort_by;
    int rpt_page;
    try{
        rpt_page = Integer.parseInt(request.getParameter("pagenum"));
    }catch(NumberFormatException e){
        rpt_page = 1;
    }
    try{
        sort_by = Integer.parseInt(request.getParameter("sort"));
    }catch(NumberFormatException e){
        //if invalid or nonexistent parameter, sort by RCD_lname
        sort_by = 1;
    }

    // 2. Initialize other variables
    int recPerPage          = 20;
    String final_status     = "";
    String db_query         = "select RCD_lname, RCD_fname, ";
           db_query         +="DATE_FORMAT(RCD_dob, '%Y-%m-%d') as RCD_dob , ";
           db_query         +="RCD_clinic, RCD_color from reportclientdata ";
           db_query         +="order by RCD_lname LIMIT ";
           db_query         += (rpt_page - 1) * recPerPage + ", " + recPerPage;
```

LISTING 12.1 Continued

```
String db_location    = "jdbc:mysql://localhost/xmlbook";
String db_driver      = "org.gjt.mm.mysql.Driver";
String stylesheet     = "TblPageSort.xsl";
int rpt_pages          = 0;

// 3. Make a database connection
Connection db_connection = null;
Statement db_statement = null;
Statement db_statementCnt = null;
ResultSet rs = null;
ResultSet rsCnt =  null;
try{
    Class.forName(db_driver);
    db_connection = DriverManager.getConnection(db_location);
    db_statement = db_connection.createStatement();
    db_statementCnt = db_connection.createStatement();

    //get a resultset or two
    rs = db_statement.executeQuery(db_query);
    rsCnt = db_statementCnt.executeQuery
        ("select count(*) from reportclientdata");
    rsCnt.first();
    int recordCnt = rsCnt.getInt(1);
    rpt_pages = (int) java.lang.Math.ceil((float) recordCnt / recPerPage) ;

}
catch (ClassNotFoundException e){
    final_status  = "Error: Unable to create database drive class.";
    final_status += " <br />" +  e.toString();
}
catch(SQLException e){
    final_status = "Error: Unable to make database connection";
    final_status += "or execute statement.";
    final_status += " <br />" +  e.toString();
}
finally
{  /* We must close the database connection now */
    try
    {   if (db_connection != null)
        { db_connection.close(); }
    }
```

LISTING 12.1 Continued

```
        catch (SQLException e)
        {   final_status  = "Error: Unable to close database connection.";
            final_status += " <br />" +  e.toString();
        }
    }
    try{
        // create a resultsetbuilder to transform resultset to XML
        RStoXML rsxml = new RStoXML(rs, "ROOT", "RECORD");

        //create the XML from recordset
        org.jdom.Document jdomdoc = rsxml.build();
        rs = null;

        //get the stylesheet
        String path = request.getServletPath();
        path = path.substring(0,path.indexOf("PagingRpt.jsp")) ;
        String  xsl  = application.getRealPath(path + stylesheet);

        //create transformer
        Transformer transformer = TransformerFactory.newInstance()
                 .newTransformer(new StreamSource(xsl));
        transformer.setParameter("Sort", new Integer(sort_by));
        transformer.setParameter("Page", "PagingRpt.jsp");
        transformer.setParameter("PageNum", new Integer(rpt_page));
        transformer.setParameter("Total", new Integer(rpt_pages));

        JDOMResult jdomresults = new JDOMResult();
        transformer.transform(new JDOMSource(jdomdoc), jdomresults);
        jdomdoc = null;

        //create outputter to output results
        XMLOutputter output = new XMLOutputter("    ", true);
        //output the results
        Document docResults = jdomresults.getDocument();
        output.output(docResults, out);
    }
    catch (TransformerFactoryConfigurationError e) {
        final_status = "Error: Unable to create factory to transform ";
        final_status = "XSL and XML.";
        final_status += "<br />" +  e.toString();
    }
```

LISTING 12.1 Continued

```
    catch (TransformerException e) {
        final_status = "Error: Unable to transform XSL and XML.";
        final_status += "<br />" +  e.toString();
    }
    catch (JDOMException e)
    {   final_status  = "Error: Unable to create XML from database query.";
        final_status += "<br />" +  e.toString();
    }

    if(final_status != "")
        out.print("<br><font color=\"red\"><H2>" + final_status +
            "</H2></font>");
%>

</div>
</body>
</html>
```

Now that the JSP has been completed, it's time to look over the stylesheet necessary for the paging report. Built on the TableSort.xsl stylesheet found in Listing 11.6, this stylesheet contains four templates.

The Stylesheet for the Multiple-Page Report

The first template matches the root of the JDOM representation. As a result of this matching, the processing of the XML document begins through the various calls to other templates. This template hasn't changed from its use in Listing 11.6.

The second template, named `header`, creates the first five rows of the output HTML table. These rows contain the various links that allow the navigation through the report pages and the sorting on each column.

Next, the recursive `PageLinks` template outputs one linked number for each page of the complete report. When followed, these links will call the JSP and, as a result, the appropriate report page will be displayed.

The last template outputs a table row for each record of the JDOM document. This template is the same as it was in TableSort.xsl found in Listing 11.6.

The stylesheet code begins with the addition of two new parameters as shown in the following code. The stylesheet obtains the number of pages that make up the entire report and the page number of this page through these parameters. These numbers are necessary for the output of the correct links and labels.

```
<xsl:param name="PageNum"/>
<xsl:param name="Total" />
```

Next comes the template that matches the root; it hasn't changed from Listing 11.6. This template calls the `header` template and applies the other templates within an HTML table element.

The `header` template is next and starts with the beginning of a table row as shown here:

```
<!-- creates all of the table header, 5 rows -->
<xsl:template name="header">
    <!-- prev and next page links created here -->
    <tr bgColor="#fffeee">
```

Within the table row is an `xsl:choose` tag that allows the creation of a Java-like `select` switching structure. That is, it allows one of a number of choices to be selected based on some test condition. The `xsl:choose` element can contain any number of `xsl:when` elements, only one of which will be selected. The following code only shows one `xsl:when` child element, but there are more to come:

```
    <xsl:choose>
        <!-- if first page, don't show 'prev page' link -->
        <xsl:when test="$PageNum = 1">
            <th colspan="2">First Page</th>
            <th> Page <xsl:value-of select="$PageNum" /></th>
            <th colspan="2"><a href="{$Page}?pagenum={$PageNum + number(1)}">
                Next Page</a></th>
        </xsl:when>
```

The `xsl:when` structure selected is the one whose `test` expression is the first to resolve to `true`. If there are no `xsl:when test` attributes that resolve to true, the `xsl:otherwise` element is selected, if it is present.

The preceding `xsl:choose` element is used to pick one of three possible outputs for the Previous Page and Next Page links. The expression found in the `test` attribute of the first `xsl:when` element tests whether the `PageNum` parameter is equal to `1`. If it is, text will read First Page instead of a Previous Page link being added.

The following `xsl:when` element tests to see whether `PageNum` is equal to `Total`. If they are equal, this is the last page of the report pages. As a result, the Next Page link will instead read Last Page.

```
        <!-- if last page, don't show 'next page' link -->
        <xsl:when test="$PageNum = $Total">
```

```
        <th colspan="2"><a href="{$Page}?pagenum={$PageNum - number(1)}">
                Previous Page</a></th>
        <th> Page <xsl:value-of select="$PageNum" /></th>
        <th colspan="2">Last Page</th>
    </xsl:when>
```

Finally, the `xsl:otherwise` element will match all other cases, as seen in the following code. When selected, this element will output both Previous Page and Next Page links. If the `PageNum` doesn't equal `1` or the `Total` number of pages, this `xsl:otherwise` element will be selected.

```
    <!-- in all cases, show both links -->
    <xsl:otherwise>
        <th colspan="2"><a href="{$Page}?pagenum={$PageNum - number(1)}">
                Previous Page</a></th>
        <th> Page <xsl:value-of select="$PageNum" /></th>
        <th colspan="2"><a href="{$Page}?pagenum={$PageNum + number(1)}">
                Next Page</a></th>
    </xsl:otherwise>
```

Last, the `xsl:choose` element is closed, and the first row of the resulting report table has been created.

Next, the stylesheet outputs the start of the next table row. Contained in this row are linked numbers for each possible page of the report. This will permit the user to click a number and be taken to the appropriate page.

The following XSL begins the recursion of the `PageLinks` template that will result in the creation of those linked page numbers. Notice that contained in the body of this `xsl:call-template` element is an `xsl:with-param` element. This causes the template `PageLinks` to be called with the `Cnt` parameter set to `1`.

```
<!-- create linked page number for each possible report page -->
<tr bgColor="#fffeee">
    <td align="left" colspan="5">
        <xsl:call-template name="PageLinks">
            <xsl:with-param name="Cnt" select="1"/>
        </xsl:call-template>
    </td>
</tr>
```

Some HTML table tags are output, and the final table header row is created in the following code. This row becomes the linked column headers that will cause the newly sorted report page to display. When these links are followed, they place parameters on the query string that the JSP will parse for and process.

```
<!-- create each linked column label -->
    <tr bgColor="#fffeee">
        <xsl:for-each select="*/*[1]/*">
            <td>
                <A href="{$Page}?pagenum={$PageNum}&amp;sort={position()}">
                      
                    <xsl:value-of select="local-name(.)" />
                      
                </A>
            </td>
        </xsl:for-each>
    </tr>
```

With the addition of the closing `xsl:template` tag, the `header` template is complete. Next on the stylesheet is the `PageLinks` template. This template was called from the `header` template and results in the creation of the linked page numbers.

As in the following code, this template begins by declaring the `Cnt` parameter using an `xsl:param` tag. Next, an `xsl:if` element tests to see whether the current value of the `Cnt` parameter is the same as the `PageNum` parameter. If they are equal, the value of `Cnt` is output without a link because a link to the same page of the report is useless.

```
<!-- recursive linked page number creation -->
<xsl:template name="PageLinks">
    <xsl:param name="Cnt"/>
    <xsl:if test="$Cnt = $PageNum" >
        <xsl:value-of select="$Cnt" />  
    </xsl:if>
```

The next `xsl:if` element of this template, shown as follows, tests to make sure that `Cnt` and `PageNum` are not equal to each other. When this condition is true, the body of the `xsl:if` element is selected, and the value of the `Cnt` parameter is output linked to the appropriate report page.

```
    <xsl:if test="$Cnt != $PageNum" >
        <a href="{$Page}?pagenum={$Cnt}">
            <xsl:value-of select="$Cnt" />
        </a>  
    </xsl:if>
```

The last part of the `PageLinks` template is the final `xsl:if` element, as shown in the following. When matched, this element causes the recursion by recalling this template when the value of `Cnt` is less than `Total`.

```
<xsl:if test="$Cnt &lt; $Total">
    <xsl:call-template name="PageLinks">
        <xsl:with-param name="Cnt" select="$Cnt + 1"/>
    </xsl:call-template>
</xsl:if>
```

The last template is the same as that of TableSort.xsl found in Listing 11.6. This template creates a table row for each child of the root. Within that row, each table cell contains the text data of that selected element's children.

Besides the closing `template` and `stylesheet` tags, this completes the stylesheet. TblPageSort.xsl is shown in its entirety in Listing 12.2 and should be saved as `webapps\xmlbook\chapter12\TblPageSort.xsl`. All additions and changes to TableSort.xsl, found in Listing 11.6, appear in boldface type except for changes to HTML markup.

LISTING 12.2 TblPageSort.xsl

```
<?xml version="1.0" encoding="UTF-8"?>
<xsl:stylesheet version="1.0" xmlns:xsl="http://www.w3.org/1999/XSL/Transform">

<xsl:param name="Sort"/>
<xsl:param name="Page"/>
<xsl:param name="PageNum"/>
<xsl:param name="Total" />
<xsl:output method="html" />

<xsl:template match="/">
    <table border="1">

        <xsl:call-template name="header"/>

        <!-- select and format each record -->
        <xsl:apply-templates select="*/*">
            <xsl:sort select="*[$Sort]" />
        </xsl:apply-templates>
    </table>
</xsl:template>

<!-- creates all of the table header, 5 rows -->
<xsl:template name="header">
    <!-- prev and next page links created here -->
    <tr bgColor="#fffeee">
```

LISTING 12.2 Continued

```
        <xsl:choose>
            <!-- if first page, don't show 'prev page' link -->
            <xsl:when test="$PageNum = 1">
            <th colspan="2">First Page</th>
            <th> Page <xsl:value-of select="$PageNum" /></th>
            <th colspan="2"><a href="{$Page}?pagenum={$PageNum + number(1)}">
                    Next Page</a></th>
            </xsl:when>
            <!-- if last page, don't show 'next page' link -->
            <xsl:when test="$PageNum = $Total">
            <th colspan="2"><a href="{$Page}?pagenum={$PageNum - number(1)}">
                    Previous Page</a></th>
            <th> Page <xsl:value-of select="$PageNum" /></th>
            <th colspan="2">Last Page</th>
            </xsl:when>
            <!-- in all cases, show both links -->
            <xsl:otherwise>
            <th colspan="2"><a href="{$Page}?pagenum={$PageNum - number(1)}">
                    Previous Page</a></th>
            <th> Page <xsl:value-of select="$PageNum" /></th>
            <th colspan="2"><a href="{$Page}?pagenum={$PageNum + number(1)}">
                    Next Page</a></th>
            </xsl:otherwise>
        </xsl:choose>
    </tr>
    <tr bgColor="#eeefff"><td colspan="5"> </td></tr>

    <!-- create linked page number for each possible report page -->
    <tr bgColor="#fffeee">
        <td align="left" colspan="5">
            <xsl:call-template name="PageLinks">
                <xsl:with-param name="Cnt" select="1"/>
            </xsl:call-template>
        </td>
    </tr>
    <tr bgColor="#eeefff"><td colspan="5"> </td></tr>

    <!-- create each linked column label -->
    <tr bgColor="#fffeee">
        <xsl:for-each select="*/*[1]/*">
            <td>
```

LISTING 12.2 Continued

```
                <A href="{$Page}?pagenum={$PageNum}&amp;sort={position()}">
                      
                    <xsl:value-of select="local-name(.)" />
                      
                </A>
            </td>
        </xsl:for-each>
    </tr>
</xsl:template>

<!-- recursive linked page number creation -->
<xsl:template name="PageLinks">
    <xsl:param name="Cnt"/>
    <xsl:if test="$Cnt = $PageNum" >
        <xsl:value-of select="$Cnt" />  
    </xsl:if>
    <xsl:if test="$Cnt != $PageNum" >
        <a href="{$Page}?pagenum={$Cnt}">
            <xsl:value-of select="$Cnt" />
        </a>  
    </xsl:if>

    <xsl:if test="$Cnt &lt; $Total">
        <xsl:call-template name="PageLinks">
            <xsl:with-param name="Cnt" select="$Cnt + 1"/>
        </xsl:call-template>
    </xsl:if>
</xsl:template>

<!-- creates a table row for each record, and cell for each column -->
<xsl:template match="*/*">
    <tr bgColor="#eeefff">
        <xsl:for-each select="*">
            <td><xsl:value-of select="." /></td>
        </xsl:for-each>
    </tr>
</xsl:template>

</xsl:stylesheet>
```

The first page of the report is shown in Figure 12.1, and the fourth page is shown in Figure 12.2. The actual results will vary depending on how much data is contained in your database table. To add more data, use the JSP named CreateDBData.jsp, which was created in Listing 11.1.

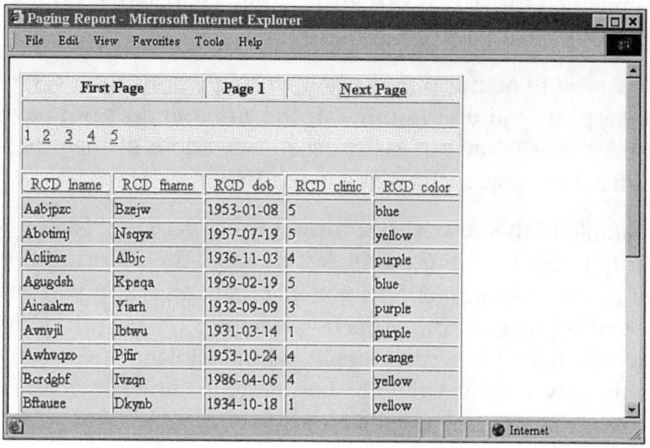
Paging Report - Microsoft Internet Explorer
File Edit View Favorites Tools Help
First Page
Page 1
Next Page
1 2 3 4 5
RCD lname
RCD fname
RCD dob
RCD clinic
RCD color
Aabjpzc Bzejw 1953-01-08 5 blue
Abotimj Nsqyx 1957-07-19 5 yellow
Aclijmz Albjc 1936-11-03 4 purple
Agugdsh Kpeqa 1959-02-19 5 blue
Aicaakm Yiarh 1932-09-09 3 purple
Avnvjil Ibtwu 1931-03-14 1 purple
Awhvqzo Pjfir 1953-10-24 4 orange
Bcrdgbf Ivzqn 1986-04-06 4 yellow
Bftauee Dkynb 1934-10-18 1 yellow
Internet

FIGURE 12.1 The first page of PagingRpt.jsp and TblPageSort.xsl.

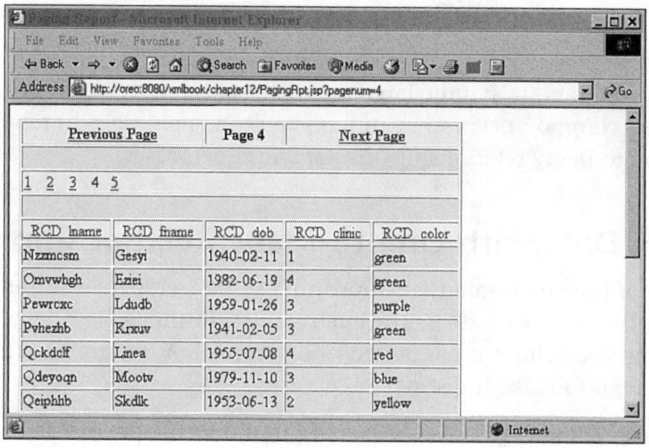
File Edit View Favorites Tools Help
Back Search Favorites Media
Address http://oreo:8080/xmlbook/chapter12/PagingRpt.jsp?pagenum=4
Go
Previous Page
Page 4
Next Page
1 2 3 4 5
RCD lname
RCD fname
RCD dob
RCD clinic
RCD color
Nzzmcsm Gesyi 1940-02-11 1 green
Omvwhgh Eziei 1982-06-19 4 green
Pewrcxc Ldudb 1959-01-26 3 purple
Pvhezhb Krxuv 1941-02-05 3 green
Qckdclf Linea 1955-07-08 4 red
Qdeyoqn Mootv 1979-11-10 3 blue
Qeiphhb Skdlk 1953-06-13 2 yellow
Internet

FIGURE 12.2 The fourth page of PagingRpt.jsp and TblPageSort.xsl.

Notice that the table headers include the appropriate links to flip to the next and previous pages. Also, links to each page except the current page of the report have been created. They are dynamically created, and thus will function no matter how large the dataset becomes or how many records are displayed per page. Finally, a table row with linked column labels has been created to allow every report page to be sorted by any column.

The database records displayed on each page will always be the same, regardless of the column on which the data is sorted. The only change that occurs is the order in which the records of that page are displayed.

At this point, I need to mention that when writing reports for a system, it is very important to keep the end user in mind. If the end user does not have input on the reports that are created, they can easily become creations of the programmer instead of being beneficial to people who actually use them.

A possible example of this relates to sorting. In the preceding paging report, the data is separated into pages according to the last name of the clients. Although this might appear useful to the programmer, it is possible that this report will be viewed most frequently sorted by date of birth. This might appear to be a minor distinction, but the difference can make a report useless. It is impossible for the creator of this report to know exactly how a report would be best designed unless he has access to the people using it or has amazing specifications to work from.

On that note, it would be a relatively simple addition to this stylesheet and JSP to allow the user to select which column the report data is sorted to before being broken into pages. This could be done with a radio button or some other HTML form element, which would allow the user to access the exact report format he needs.

Now that one method to handle large reports has been covered, it's time to demonstrate another common occurrence in reporting—namely ways to report on the common one-to-many relationships contained in databases.

Reports on Data with One-to-Many Relationships

An example of the one-to-many relationship can be seen between the ReportClientData and ReportClientAilment tables. In the ReportClientData table, all the data about each client is contained in one record. A unique integer is associated with each record to make it distinct.

Each ailment is contained in its own record found in the ReportClientAilment table. That record contains the unique client index of the related client who has the ailment described in the record. This causes the possibility of multiple ailments to be associated with one client, and thus we have a one-to-many relationship.

With the following one-to-many report, we will create a stylesheet that displays this relationship. The default page of this report can be seen in Figure 12.3. When this report is initially loaded, it looks a lot like the report shown in Figure 11.1, except for some HTML markup differences.

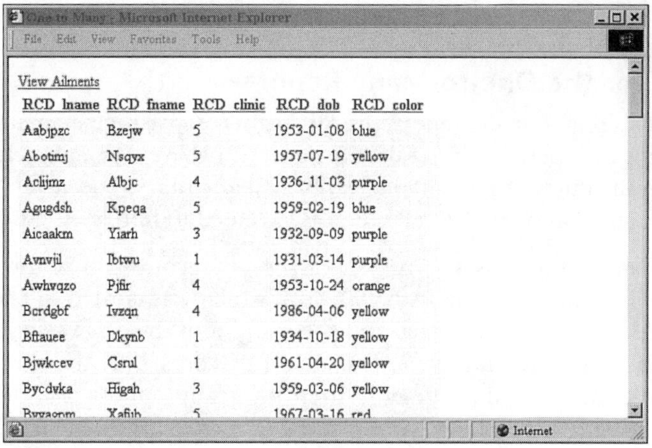

FIGURE 12.3 The default page of OneMany.jsp and OneMany.xsl.

However, once the View Ailments link is selected, the report is reloaded with the ailments for each client listed as shown in Figure 12.4. The ailment records can be hidden again by using the Hide Ailments link.

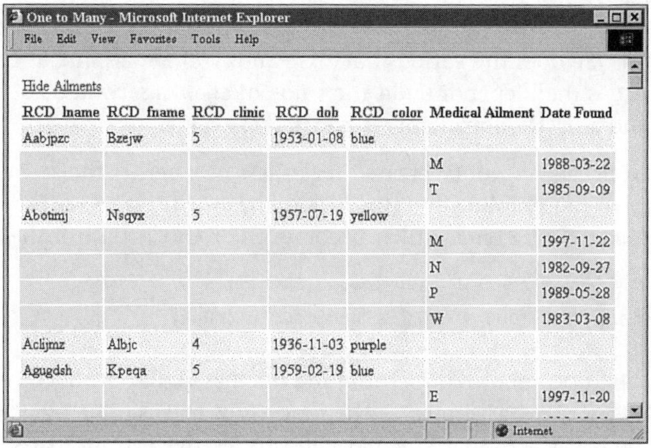

FIGURE 12.4 View Ailments displayed in OneMany.jsp.

Similar to the paging report we looked at earlier in this chapter, this report will sort the data by the column selected when the column label links are followed. When the report is redisplayed, the ailment records will remain in their current state (viewable or hidden).

The JSP for the One-to-Many Report

To create this one-to-many report, the JSP begins by parsing parameters from the query string and then obtaining data from the database. The data selected will depend on the query string parameters. If the ailments will be visible on the resulting report, an additional SQL statement is executed to retrieve these records.

When the ailment records are visible, both sets of records will be used to each create a JDOM representation using RStoXML.java, which was created in Listing 11.4. Next, a new JDOM document is created and the content of the other two JDOMs is added. On the other hand, when there are no ailment records, only the client records are added to the third JDOM document. After the creation of the resulting JDOM, it is transformed with a stylesheet.

The JSP code begins with the parsing of the URL to find the value of the `show` parameter, as shown in the following. When this parameter is unavailable, the JSP variable is set to `0`; otherwise, it is set to `1`. The ailment records are only fetched from the database and added to the resulting JDOM document when the value of `show` is `1`. In all other cases, the ailment records are not retrieved.

```
String show = request.getParameter("show");
show = (show) != null ? "1" : "0";
```

The rest of this JSP does the various database and XML processing as before. The only difference is that depending on the value of `show`, a second database query, `ResultSet`, and a JDOM document will be processed.

A third JDOM `Document` will be created regardless of whether the second `ResultSet` exists. As shown in the following, this is done by creating an `Element` and using it to create a `Document`. This `Element` then becomes the root `Element` of the `Document`.

```
Element rootElement = new Element("ROOT");
Document resultdoc = new Document(rootElement);
```

Next, the JDOM document representing the first `ResultSet` is added to this newly created JDOM `Document` as shown in the following. This is done by getting the root `Element` of the JDOM and invoking `detach()` to remove it from its parent `Document`. After this has been done, it can be added to the resulting JDOM `Document` using the `addContent()` method, as can the second JDOM.

```
rootElement.addContent(jdomdoc.getRootElement().detach());
```

The rest of the JSP is the same as PagingRpt.jsp found in Listing 12.1. The final JDOM document is transformed using the OneMany.xsl stylesheet and then output. Then there is some error handling and the page is finished.

The complete JSP is shown in Listing 12.3 and should be saved as `webapps\xmlbook\chapter12\OneMany.jsp`. The differences between OneMany.jsp and DBtoXML.jsp from Listing 11.5 appear in boldface type.

LISTING 12.3 OneMany.jsp

```
<%@page import = "java.sql.*,
        org.jdom.*,
        org.jdom.output.*,
        org.jdom.input.*,
        java.io.*,
        javax.xml.transform.*,
        javax.xml.transform.stream.*,
        org.jdom.transform.*,
        xmlbook.chapter11.*" %>
<html>
<head><title>One to Many</title></head>
<body>
<div>
<%  // 1. get parameters from url

    String show = request.getParameter("show");
    show = (show) != null ? "1" : "0";
    int sort_by;
    try{

        sort_by = Integer.parseInt(request.getParameter("sort"));
    }catch(NumberFormatException e){
        //if invalid or nonexistent parameter, sort by RCD_lname
        sort_by = 2;
    }

    // 2. Initialize other variables
    String final_status    = "";
    String db_query        = "select * from reportclientdata ";
    String db_query2       = "select * from reportclientailments";
    String db_location     = "jdbc:mysql://localhost/xmlbook";
    String db_driver       = "org.gjt.mm.mysql.Driver";
    String stylesheet      = "OneMany.xsl";
```

LISTING 12.3 Continued

```
// 3. Make a database connection
Connection db_connection = null;
Statement db_statement = null;
ResultSet rs = null;
Statement db_statement2 =  null;
ResultSet rs2 = null;

try{
    Class.forName(db_driver);
    db_connection = DriverManager.getConnection(db_location);
    db_statement = db_connection.createStatement();
    rs = db_statement.executeQuery(db_query);
    if (show != "0"){
        db_statement2 = db_connection.createStatement();
        rs2 = db_statement2.executeQuery(db_query2);
    }
}
catch (ClassNotFoundException e){
    final_status  = "Error: Unable to create database drive class.";
    final_status += " <br />" +  e.toString();
}
catch(SQLException e){
    final_status = "Error: Unable to make database connection";
    final_status += "or execute statement.";
    final_status += " <br />" +  e.toString();
}
finally
{  /* We must close the database connection now */
    try
    {   if (db_connection != null)
        { db_connection.close(); }
    }
    catch (SQLException e)
    {   final_status  = "Error: Unable to close database connection." ;
        final_status += " <br />" +  e.toString();
    }
}
try{
    // create a resultsetbuilder to transform resultset to XML
    RStoXML rsxml = new RStoXML(rs, "RS1", "REC1");
    Document jdomdoc = rsxml.build();
```

LISTING 12.3 Continued

```
        Document jdomdoc2 = null;
        if (show != "0"){
            RStoXML rsxml2 = new RStoXML(rs2, "RS2", "REC2");
            jdomdoc2 = rsxml2.build();
            rs2 = null;
            rsxml2 = null;
        }
        rs = null;
        rsxml = null;

       //get the stylesheet
        String path = request.getServletPath();
        path = path.substring(0,path.indexOf("OneMany.jsp")) ;
        String  xsl  = application.getRealPath(path + stylesheet);

        Element rootElement = new Element("ROOT");
        Document resultdoc = new Document(rootElement);
        rootElement.addContent(jdomdoc.getRootElement().detach());
        if (show != "0")
            rootElement.addContent(jdomdoc2.getRootElement().detach());

        jdomdoc2 = null;
        jdomdoc = null;

        //create transformer
        Transformer transformer = TransformerFactory.newInstance()
                 .newTransformer(new StreamSource(xsl));
        transformer.setParameter("Sort", new Integer(sort_by));
        transformer.setParameter("Page", "OneMany.jsp");
        transformer.setParameter("Show", show);

        JDOMResult jdomresults = new JDOMResult();
        transformer.transform(new JDOMSource(resultdoc), jdomresults);
        resultdoc = null;
        //create outputter to output results
        XMLOutputter output = new XMLOutputter("    ", true);
        //output the results
        Document docResults = jdomresults.getDocument();
        output.output(docResults, out);
    }
    catch (TransformerFactoryConfigurationError e) {
```

LISTING 12.3 Continued

```
        final_status = "Error: Unable to create factory to transform ";
        final_status = "XSL and XML.";
        final_status += "<br />" +  e.toString();
    }
    catch (TransformerException e) {
        final_status = "Error: Unable to transform XSL and XML.";
        final_status += "<br />" +  e.toString();
   }
   catch (JDOMException e)
    {   final_status  = "Error: Unable to create XML from database query." ;
        final_status += "<br />" +  e.toString();
    }

    if(final_status != "")
        out.print("<br><font color=\"red\"><H2>" + final_status +
            "</H2></font>");
%>

</div>
</body>
</html>
```

Now that the JSP has been completed, it's time to look at the stylesheet. This stylesheet produces the table either with or without ailment records displayed and is named OneMany.xsl.

The Stylesheet for the One-to-Many Report

The stylesheet contains three templates. The first template matches on the root and does almost all the processing of the page. The other two templates are both for the creation of the table column labels. One is used to create the header when the ailment records are present, whereas the other is used in their absence.

The stylesheet begins with the template that matches the document root. This template starts out by using the following two `xsl:if` elements to choose which headers should be displayed. It does this by counting the number of children of the root. If more than one child exists, the ailment records are present, and the `headershow` template is selected. Otherwise, the `headerhide` template is selected.

```
<!-- create the proper link and headers according to content -->
<xsl:if test="count(/*/*) &gt; 1">
    <tr><td colspan="100%"><a href="{$Page}">Hide Ailments</a></td></tr>
```

```
        <xsl:call-template name="headershow"/>
    </xsl:if>
    <xsl:if test="count(/*/*) = 1">
        <a href="{$Page}?show=1">View Ailments</a>
        <xsl:call-template name="headerhide"/>
    </xsl:if>
```

Next, an xsl:for-each element is encountered as shown in the following. This structure iterates through each element that is both a grandchild of the root and descends from the first child of the root. In this case, each record of the client ResultSet is in turn matched within this element. Notice that the first element within the iterating structure is an xsl:sort element. This causes the sorting on the numbered column before the iteration begins.

```
    <!-- iterate through each client record found in the first child of root -->
    <xsl:for-each select="*/*[1]/*" >
        <xsl:sort select="*[$Sort]" />
```

As each client record is iterated, a variable is created to hold the text data of the child RCD_index element. This is done so that this value can be used to select the corresponding ailment records.

```
        <!-- hold index of current client record -->
        <xsl:variable name="index" select="RCD_index" />
```

Next, some HTML markup is output. Then, the text data of each child of the currently selected client record is iterated through and output as shown here:

```
              <!-- select all client data except index to show -->
             <xsl:for-each select = "*[position() &gt; 1]" >
                 <td><xsl:value-of select = "." /></td>
             </xsl:for-each>
```

All the client data has been neatly wrapped in a table row. At this point, if there are any ailment records related to this client, they need to be output. This is done by using an xsl:for-each element to iterate through the set of Elements that match the select expression of /*/*[2]/*[RCA_clientID = $index] as shown here:

```
             <!-- select all ailment records whose client ID -->
             <!-- is the same as the current client -->
             <xsl:for-each select="/*/*[2]/*[RCA_clientID = $index]">
```

Notice the leading forward slash in the preceding select statement. This forward slash causes the selection to begin at the root of the JDOM representation. This statement selects all grandchild elements that descend from the second child of the root.

Each of these grandchildren must have text data in their RCA_clientID elements that is equal to the value of the $index variable.

This causes the selection of each ailment record that corresponds to the client record currently being processed. If no ailment records are present, nothing gets selected for output.

After the records have been selected, they are output within a table row as shown in the following. The text data of RCA_medicalailment and RCA_datefound are output in table cells with the use of xsl:value-of tags.

```
<xsl:sort select="RCA_medicalailment" />
<tr bgcolor="#eeefff"><td /><td /><td /><td /><td />
     <td ><xsl:value-of select = "RCA_medicalailment" /></td>
     <td ><xsl:value-of select = "RCA_datefound" /></td>
 </tr>
```

That concludes the first template. The next two templates output the table head depending on the presence of the second ResultSet. Each is similar to the header template found in TableSort.xsl from Listing 11.6. The techniques are used throughout each stylesheet in this and previous chapters.

Listing 12.4 shows the complete stylesheet. This file should be saved as webapps\xmlbook\chapter12\OneMany.xsl.

LISTING 12.4 OneMany.xsl

```
<?xml version="1.0" encoding="UTF-8"?>
<xsl:stylesheet version="1.0" xmlns:xsl="http://www.w3.org/1999/XSL/Transform">

<xsl:param name="Sort" />
<xsl:param name="Page" />
<xsl:output method="html" />

<xsl:template match="/">

    <table border="0" cellpadding="3">

    <!-- create the proper link and headers according to content-->
    <xsl:if test="count(/*/*) &gt; 1">
        <tr><td colspan="100%"><a href="{$Page}">Hide Ailments</a></td></tr>
        <xsl:call-template name="headershow"/>
    </xsl:if>
    <xsl:if test="count(/*/*) = 1">
        <a href="{$Page}?show=1">View Ailments</a>
```

LISTING 12.4 Continued

```
        <xsl:call-template name="headerhide"/>
    </xsl:if>

    <!-- iterate through each client record found in the first child of root -->
    <xsl:for-each select="*/*[1]/*" >
        <xsl:sort select="*[$Sort]" />

        <!-- hold index of current client record -->
        <xsl:variable name="index" select="RCD_index" />
        <tr bgcolor="#fffeee">

            <!-- select all client data except index to show -->
            <xsl:for-each select = "*[position() &gt; 1]" >
                <td><xsl:value-of select = "." /></td>
            </xsl:for-each>
            <td /><td />
        </tr>

            <!-- select all ailment records whose client ID -->
            <!-- is the same as the current client -->
            <xsl:for-each select="/*/*[2]/*[RCA_clientID = $index]">
               <xsl:sort select="RCA_medicalailment" />
               <tr bgcolor="#eeefff"><td /><td /><td /><td /><td />
                    <td ><xsl:value-of select = "RCA_medicalailment" /></td>
                    <td ><xsl:value-of select = "RCA_datefound" /></td>
                </tr>
            </xsl:for-each>
        </xsl:for-each>
    </table>

</xsl:template>

<!-- creates the table headers from the tag names -->
<xsl:template name="headershow">
<tr>
    <xsl:for-each select="*/*[1]/*[1]/*[position() &gt; 1]">
        <th>
            <A href="{$Page}?sort={position() + 1}&amp;show=1">
                <xsl:value-of select="local-name(.)" />
          </A>
        </th>
```

LISTING 12.4 Continued

```
    </xsl:for-each>
    <th>Medical Ailment</th>
    <th>Date Found</th>
</tr>
</xsl:template>

<xsl:template name="headerhide">
<tr>
    <xsl:for-each select="*/*[1]/*[1]/*[position() &gt; 1]">
        <th>
            <A href="{$Page}?sort={position() + 1}">
                <xsl:value-of select="local-name(.)" />
            </A>
        </th>
    </xsl:for-each>
</tr>
</xsl:template>

</xsl:stylesheet>
```

The output of OneMany.jsp and OneMany.xsl can be seen in Figures 12.3 and 12.4, found earlier in this chapter.

Real-World Reporting Systems

The examples found in this and the previous chapter are not adequate for production reporting systems. Why do I say this? The reason has to do with the lack of scalability contained in these JSPs. They were designed to be to the point to exemplify the stylesheet concepts that are important for reporting.

A production reporting system would have several differences. The most obvious is database connection pooling that would most likely be accessed through a JavaBean. Another difference would be the lack of SQL statements. Instead, precompiled stored procedures would be used for faster results. Also, the RStoXML.java class used to convert `ResultSets` to JDOM representations would be utilized through either a JavaBean or a tag library. Finally, the error handling would be better than displaying large red non-user-friendly text on the screen.

Well-Formed Documents Revisited

One more thing that requires comment is the structure of the output from these reporting examples. When a stylesheet and JDOM are transformed, the results are stored in another JDOM document and then output. This means that the results of the transformation must be well-formed; otherwise, an error will occur, and potentially unpredictable results will follow.

In all of our examples, the output was an HTML table. This table element forms the root of the resulting JDOM document. However, if an element is added before or after the table element, the resulting JDOM document no longer has a root element. Go ahead and add an HTML font element with some text before the start of the table to one of the stylesheets. When the results are loaded, is it there? No, it has been dropped from the resulting JDOM document. Go ahead and add it after the close of the table. Again, unpredictable results will occur. This time the entire body of the report disappears.

The point I'm trying to make is to be sure your resulting HTML will be well-formed XML, or parts of the report might disappear and other difficult problems might crop up that will need to be traced. Along the same lines, if mysterious problems occur, think about the output in terms of XML instead of HTML.

Summary

XML can be a useful reporting tool that enables the creation of many different kinds of reports with sorting capabilities. Some of those reports include the paging report and the one-to-many report found in this chapter. The previous chapter demonstrated a generic sorting table report and a cross tab report.

A good reporting system combines the capabilities of the database and stored procedures with the filtering and formatting capabilities of XSL. Throw in some well-written JSPs, and you can quickly develop a highly useful reporting system.

The majority of this book focuses on server-side XML. However, XML can be successfully used on the client-side to various advantages. These uses will be introduced and examined in the next chapter.

13

Browser Considerations with XML

IN THIS CHAPTER

- Client-Side XML and Browser Support
- Client-Side JavaScript and XML
- Client-Side Transformations and XML

The majority of XML processing in a Web application occurs on the server. One reason for this has to do with the fact that all developers know exactly what tools and configurations are available on the server. This permits greater control over the presentation of the content. They also know that those tools aren't going to change. As a result, server-side XML processing only has to be written in one way, for one configuration. This is unlike client-side XML processing, which includes code to verify access to the appropriate browser tools, and then XML processing code.

As a result, the option of client-side XML processing is often overlooked. The most common reason for this has to do with the wide variety of tools and implementations that exist across browsers and versions. Although this can be a strong factor in avoiding client-side processing, there are situations when these obstacles should be overcome and the client browser should be used to process XML.

This chapter will begin with a short discussion of the XML support in the two primary browsers, namely Microsoft Internet Explorer (IE) and Netscape. Next, we will walk through two options for client-side XML processing on both Netscape and IE. The first example uses DHTML and JavaScript to create an HTML table that displays the data contained within an XML document. The second example will also rely on JavaScript to demonstrate the repeated transformation of an XML document with different stylesheets completely on the client-side. The resulting reports provide various views of the same data that can be sorted.

Client-Side XML and Browser Support

The time has arrived when XML can be used successfully and predictably in Internet Explorer and Netscape. Although IE has provided XML support for some time now, Netscape has just recently been able to offer client-side XML and XSL support.

Netscape Gecko and Netscape 6 now include the open source Expat parser written by James Clark. He was the technical lead of the World Wide Web Consortium's (W3C) XML activity that developed the XML 1.0 recommendation. The result is that XML in Netscape is reliably parsed according to specification.

Although XML support is here, separate code must be written to take advantage of the client-side XML capabilities of both browsers due to differences in the API. In a perfect world, all browsers would have the same API, which would allow the same code to execute predictably and bug-free on all browsers.

With this in mind, there are times when client-side tools should be used. One such occasion is with systems where users typically look at many different reports generated on the same data. With many reporting systems, each time a report is sorted by the user, the server has to query the database for the same data and reconstruct the report. As a result, client-side XML processing can relieve the load on the database and Web server by reducing the number of requests, thus lowering the queries against the database.

A system that uses client-side XML processing must have the capability to control which browser versions are used. Although it is no longer necessary to only support IE, it is still necessary to require the more recent versions of Netscape.

The examples in this chapter depend upon the use of Netscape version 6.2 and Internet Explorer version 6.0. IE must also have MSXML2 4.0 installed.

Both examples also use the `RStoXML.java` class shown in Listing 11.4 of Chapter 11, "Using XML in Reporting Systems." This Java class converts a database `ResultSet` into a JDOM XML representation.

I chose not to demonstrate the use of client-side techniques that are dependent on a particular browser. One such technique is through the use of data islands, or IE-specific `<XML>` HTML elements.

Client-Side JavaScript and XML

The first example will use JavaScript on the client side to create an HTML table from an XML DOM. The DOM will also be created on the client from XML found inside an HTML `DIV` element.

The JSP begins with the output of HTML markup and JavaScript sent directly to the browser. Following that, the JSP queries the database for data. The results of the database query will then be processed into a JDOM representation and serialized to the client placed within a hidden HTML division. At this point, the client browser creates a DOM representation of the XML document found in the hidden `DIV`. JavaScript, combined with the data and structure of the XML, will be used to create the resulting HTML table.

The client browser will receive an HTML page that contains two divisions. The first division starts out empty and will be used to contain the resulting HTML table after it has been created. The second division is hidden, and contains the XML document resulting from the database query. The data and structure of the XML will be used to create the HTML table.

After the page is loaded, the JavaScript begins by creating a DOM representation of the XML document found in the second division. After the DOM is available, the script uses it to create the resulting HTML table. When this table has been completely built, it is displayed by appending it to the empty division.

Although this example processes the XML only once, it will demonstrate how to load an XML document in both Netscape and IE on the client side. Also, it shows the power and potential of scripting and client-side XML.

The JSP

The JSP code begins by importing the necessary packages and outputting some HTML. Contained in this HTML is the JavaScript that will perform the client-side processing.

The script begins with the `sniff()` function, which will set a variable indicating which browser it is executing in, as shown in the following example. The two variables are `ie` for Internet Explorer and `ns` for Netscape. The appropriate variable is set to `true` and is used to determine what code gets executed throughout the rest of the script:

```
function sniff() {
    if(window.ActiveXObject){
        ie = true;
    }
    else if (document.implementation
        && document.implementation.createDocument){
        ns = true;
    }
```

Notice that both `implementation` and `createDocument` are detected for Netscape. The reason for this is that, at the time of writing, Netscape for the Mac contained the `implementation` object but did not support the `createDocument()` function.

Finally, the function invokes the `loadXML()` function only if one of the browsers has been detected successfully:

```
    if(ns || ie)
        loadXML();
}
```

It is important to note that if the XML processing depends upon a particular version of the parser, that version should be detected to avoid client-side breakage. This can be done by creating the object in a `try` block and catching errors in the creation of the specific object in the `catch` block. In this way, you can determine whether or not the client has the necessary version installed. In this example for IE, we are not detecting the presence of a particular parser, but just that the browser is `ActiveXObject`-enabled.

Next, the function `loadXML()` begins by creating the DOM object for Netscape, as in the following code fragment. A new document element called `xmlDoc` is created through the use of the `createDocument()` function of the DOM level 2 specification. The three parameters of this function are the namespace URI, the qualified name of the root element, and the document type. These are left to empty strings and `null` because an XML document will be parsed into this object.

```
function loadXML(){
    if (ns){
        xmlDoc = document.implementation.createDocument("","",null);
```

Following this, a new `DOMParser`, which will be used to parse the XML string, is created:

```
        var domParser = new DOMParser();
```

Next, the XML string is obtained through the `innerHTML` property of the `xmlData` division in the following fragment. The string is then parsed into the `xmlDoc` by invoking the `parseFromString()` method of the `domParser` object. The `status()` function is then invoked to continue the processing:

```
var strXML = document.getElementById('xmlData').innerHTML;
            xmlDoc = domParser.parseFromString(strXML, 'text/xml');
        status();
    }
```

That concludes the creation of the XML representation for Netscape. Next, the DOM is created for IE. This processing begins with the creation of a new `MSXML2.DOMDocument` object, as seen in the following fragment. Once created, the status function is set to handle the onreadystatechange events. These events will indicate when the parsing has completed and processing should continue.

```
else if (ie){
xmlDoc = new ActiveXObject('MSXML2.DOMDocument.4.0');
xmlDoc.onreadystatechange = status;
```

Next, the xmlData division object is obtained, and its innerHTML used to load the xmlDoc as in the following fragment. When completed, xmlDoc will contain a DOM representation of the XML found within the xmlData division.

```
var xmlData = document.getElementById('xmlData');
xmlDoc.loadXML(xmlData.innerHTML);
```

The following status() function is used primarily to handle IE timing and loading issues. If the DOM is used before it has completed loading, errors will ensue. One way around this problem is to associate a function to handle the onreadystatechange events, as was done in the previous example. In this way, DOM usage can be stopped until it has completed loading and its readyState is equal to 4, as shown here:

```
function status(){
    if (ns){
        createTable();
    }
    else if (ie){
        if (xmlDoc.readyState == 4){
```

Following this is the createTable() function, which invokes HTML DOM functions that are documented in the W3C DOM level 1 specification. The only part of this function that changes according to the browser is the case of the element name as shown here:

```
       if (ns)
        tblRows = xmlDoc.getElementsByTagName('rec');
    else if (ie){
        tblRows = xmlDoc.getElementsByTagName('REC');
    }
```

Browser Buffering

When a browser receives an HTML document, it is processed and buffered. Slight processing differences exist between IE and Netscape. This is because both browsers process the division contents as HTML. IE will capitalize all tag names, while Netscape will convert all tag names to lowercase. (It is interesting to note that the

XHTML specification from the W3C states that tag names should be completely in lowercase.) This inconsistency can be very difficult to track down, especially considering the source for both browsers doesn't display what is found in the buffer.

The `createTable()` function then creates the table column labels and iterates through the `tblRows` collection creating a new table row for each. Table cells are then added to each row containing the text node values. After the iteration is complete, the entire table is appended to the empty `divResults`.

The rest of the JSP consists of the code necessary to use the database and create an XML string from the results. The complete file is shown in Listing 13.1 and should be saved as `webapps\xmlbook\chapter13\ClientScript.jsp`. This JSP and the others in this chapter require the class RStoXML from Listing 11.4, and the presence of data in the database. Data was added to the database through the JSP in Listing 11.1.

LISTING 13.1 ClientScript.jsp

```
<%@page import = "java.sql.*,
        org.jdom.*,
        org.jdom.output.*,
        javax.xml.transform.*,
        xmlbook.chapter11.*" %>


<html>
<head><title>Client Side XML Scripting</title>
<script language="JavaScript">
var xmlDoc;
var ns = false;
var ie = false;

function sniff() {
    if(window.ActiveXObject){
        ie = true;
    }
    else if (document.implementation
        && document.implementation.createDocument){
        ns = true;
    }
    if(ns || ie)
        loadXML();
}

function loadXML(){
    if (ns){
```

LISTING 13.1 Continued

```
        xmlDoc = document.implementation.createDocument("","",null);
        var domParser = new DOMParser();
        var strXML = document.getElementById('xmlData').innerHTML;
        xmlDoc = domParser.parseFromString(strXML, 'text/xml');
        status();
    }
    else if (ie){
        xmlDoc = new ActiveXObject('MSXML2.DOMDocument.4.0');
        xmlDoc.onreadystatechange = status;
        var xmlData = document.getElementById('xmlData');
        xmlDoc.loadXML(xmlData.innerHTML);

        if (xmlDoc.parseError.errorCode != 0)
            alert("Parse Error!");
    }
}

function status(){
    if (ns){
        createTable();
    }
    else if (ie){
        if (xmlDoc.readyState == 4) {
            createTable();
        }
    }
}

function createTable(){
    var tblRows;
    if (ns)
        tblRows = xmlDoc.getElementsByTagName('rec');
    else if (ie){
        tblRows = xmlDoc.getElementsByTagName('REC');
    }
    var tblResult = document.createElement('TABLE');
    tblResult.setAttribute('cellPadding',5);
    tblResult.setAttribute('border', 1);
    var tblTbody = document.createElement('TBODY');
    tblResult.appendChild(tblTbody);
    var row = document.createElement('TR');
```

LISTING 13.1 Continued

```
    for (j=0;j<tblRows[0].childNodes.length;j++){
        if (tblRows[0].childNodes[j].nodeType != 1)
            continue;
        var container = document.createElement('TH');
        var theData = document.createTextNode
           (tblRows[0].childNodes[j].nodeName);
        container.appendChild(theData);
        row.appendChild(container);
    }
    tblTbody.appendChild(row);
    for (i=0;i<tblRows.length;i++){
        var row = document.createElement('TR');
        for (j=0;j<tblRows[i].childNodes.length;j++){
            if (tblRows[i].childNodes[j].nodeType != 1)
                continue;
            var container = document.createElement('TD');
            var theData = document.createTextNode
                (tblRows[i].childNodes[j].firstChild.nodeValue);
            container.appendChild(theData);
            row.appendChild(container);
        }
        tblTbody.appendChild(row);
    }
    document.getElementById('divResults').appendChild(tblResult);
}
</script>
</head>
<body onload="javascript:sniff();">

<div id="divResults" ></div>
<div id="xmlData" style="visibility:hidden;" >
<%
    String final_status   = "";
    String db_query       = "select RCD_lname, RCD_fname, ";
           db_query       +="DATE_FORMAT(RCD_dob, '%Y-%m-%d') as RCD_dob , ";
           db_query       +="RCD_clinic, RCD_color from reportclientdata";

    String db_location    = "jdbc:mysql://localhost/xmlbook";
    String db_driver      = "org.gjt.mm.mysql.Driver";
```

LISTING 13.1 Continued

```
Connection db_connection = null;
Statement db_statement = null;
ResultSet rs = null;

try{
    Class.forName(db_driver);
    db_connection = DriverManager.getConnection(db_location);
    db_statement = db_connection.createStatement();
    rs = db_statement.executeQuery(db_query);

}
catch (ClassNotFoundException e){
    final_status  = "Error: Unable to create database drive class.";
    final_status += " <br />" +  e.toString();
}
catch(SQLException e){
    final_status = "Error: Unable to make database connection";
    final_status += "or execute statement.";
    final_status += " <br />" +  e.toString();
}
finally
{  /* We must close the database connection now */
    try
    {   if (db_connection != null)
        { db_connection.close(); }
    }
    catch (SQLException e)
    {   final_status  = "Error: Unable to close database connection.";
        final_status += " <br />" +  e.toString();
    }
}
try{
    // create a resultsetbuilder to transform resultset to XML
    RStoXML rsxml = new RStoXML(rs, "ROOT", "REC");
    org.jdom.Document jdomdoc = rsxml.build();

    rs = null;
    rsxml = null;

    //create outputter to output results
    XMLOutputter output = new XMLOutputter("   ", true);
```

LISTING 13.1 Continued

```
        output.output(jdomdoc, out);
        output = null;
    }
    catch (TransformerFactoryConfigurationError e) {
        final_status = "Error: Unable to create factory to transform ";
        final_status = "XSL and XML.";
        final_status += "<br />" +  e.toString();
    }

   catch (JDOMException e) {
        final_status  = "Error: Unable to create XML from database query.";
        final_status += "<br />" +  e.toString();
    }

    if(final_status != "")
        out.print("<br><font color=\"red\"><H2>" + final_status +
            "</H2></font>");
%>

</div>
</body>
</html>
```

The results of the client-side processing can be seen in Figures 13.1 and 13.2. Note that the table labels aren't consistent across the two browsers. This is a result of the browsers processing the HTML before placing it in their buffers. It is this buffered content that was parsed into the XML DOM representation.

With the use of DHTML and JavaScript, it is very simple to change the content of a Web page. It is also relatively simple to process XML in both IE and Netscape. Although the previous example only showed the XML being processed into a table once, it would be simple to repeatedly process the XML into different outputs using similar scripting techniques.

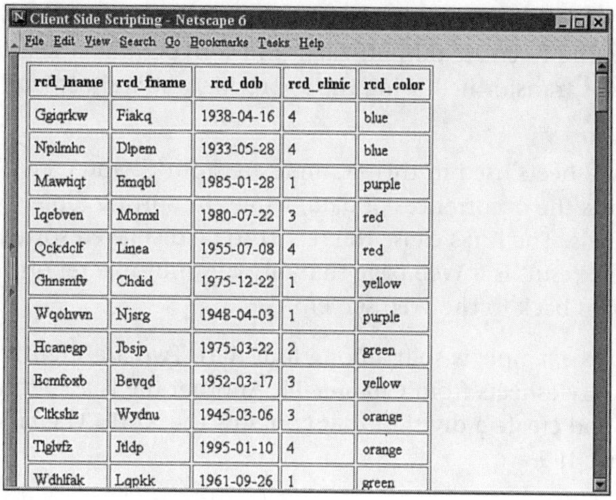

Client Side Scripting - Netscape 6

File Edit View Search Go Bookmarks Tasks Help

rcd_lname	rcd_fname	rcd_dob	rcd_clinic	rcd_color
Ggiqrkw	Fiakq	1938-04-16	4	blue
Npilmhc	Dlpem	1933-05-28	4	blue
Mawtiqt	Emqbl	1985-01-28	1	purple
Iqebven	Mbmxl	1980-07-22	3	red
Qckdclf	Linea	1955-07-08	4	red
Ghnsmfv	Chdid	1975-12-22	1	yellow
Wqohvvn	Njsrg	1948-04-03	1	purple
Hcanegp	Jbsjp	1975-03-22	2	green
Ecmfoxb	Bevqd	1952-03-17	3	yellow
Cltkshz	Wydnu	1945-03-06	3	orange
Tlglvfz	Jtldp	1995-01-10	4	orange
Wdhlfak	Lqpkk	1961-09-26	1	green

FIGURE 13.1 ClientScript.jsp in Netscape.

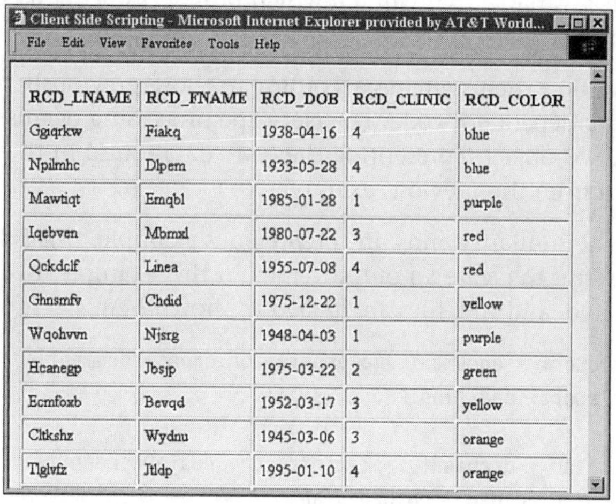

Client Side Scripting - Microsoft Internet Explorer provided by AT&T World...

File Edit View Favorites Tools Help

RCD_LNAME	RCD_FNAME	RCD_DOB	RCD_CLINIC	RCD_COLOR
Ggiqrkw	Fiakq	1938-04-16	4	blue
Npilmhc	Dlpem	1933-05-28	4	blue
Mawtiqt	Emqbl	1985-01-28	1	purple
Iqebven	Mbmxl	1980-07-22	3	red
Qckdclf	Linea	1955-07-08	4	red
Ghnsmfv	Chdid	1975-12-22	1	yellow
Wqohvvn	Njsrg	1948-04-03	1	purple
Hcanegp	Jbsjp	1975-03-22	2	green
Ecmfoxb	Bevqd	1952-03-17	3	yellow
Cltkshz	Wydnu	1945-03-06	3	orange
Tlglvfz	Jtldp	1995-01-10	4	orange

FIGURE 13.2 ClientScript.jsp in Internet Explorer.

Client-Side Transformations and XML

Another way to create different outputs of XML data without leaving the client side is through the use of stylesheets. In this way, the viewable content can change in response to user interaction by applying an XSL stylesheet to the XML DOM representation.

The next example will build upon the previous example by using XSL stylesheets instead of scripting to create output. Each time a hyperlink is selected by the user, the XML DOM is transformed using the appropriate stylesheet, and the results are displayed.

Both of the stylesheets used in this example are from Chapter 11. The cross tab stylesheet counts the occurrences of data, while the sorting table stylesheet creates linked table labels. The links cause the report to be displayed sorted on the appropriate column. The result is a Web page that displays multiple reports on a data set without any trips back to the Web server.

The code for this example is split among four files. Two are slightly modified versions of the stylesheets from Chapter 11. Another file is a JSP that will link to a JavaScript file and create a division that contains the XML. The last file is the JavaScript source file.

The Cross-Browser JavaScript Source File

The JavaScript source file begins with the `sniff()` function from the previous example. It sets a variable that will tell which browser is being used, then invoke the `load()` function.

The `load()` function then switches according to those previously set variables and executes browser-dependent code. The Netscape processing begins through the creation of a DOM object representing the XML data found in the HTML division. This is repeated from the previous example.

Here is where the similarity ends. In the previous example, this DOM object was used through script to create an output table. In this example, two more DOM objects are created, and XSL files are loaded as shown here:

```
objTableSort = document.implementation.createDocument("","",null);
objTableSort.load("TableSort.xsl");

objCrossTab = document.implementation.createDocument("","",null);
objCrossTab.onload = rptCrossTab;
objCrossTab.load("CrossTab.xsl");
```

Notice that the `rptCrossTab` function has been passed to the `objCrossTab` DOM object for its `onload` event handler. This will result in the invocation of the `rptCrossTab` function when the document has finished loading in Netscape.

Another DOM document is then created to hold the transformation results:

```
objOut = document.implementation.createDocument("","",null);
```

Finally, the `xsltProcessor()` method is used to construct the object that will perform all the transformations:

```
xsltProcessor = new XSLTProcessor();
```

Next in the `load()` function you find the IE-specific code. As in the previous example, the XML is obtained from the division and loaded into a DOM representation. Then the two stylesheets are also loaded into DOM objects using the MSXML2 parser as shown here:

```
objTableSort = new ActiveXObject('MSXML2.FreeThreadedDOMDocument.4.0');
objTableSort.load ("TableSort.xsl");

objCrossTab = new ActiveXObject('MSXML2.FreeThreadedDOMDocument.4.0');
objCrossTab.async = false;
objCrossTab.load ("CrossTab.xsl");
```

Note that in the previous code, the `async` property of `objCrossTab` is set to `false`. This causes the stylesheet download to complete before the next line of code is executed. Otherwise, the code would continue executing, and `objCrossTab` could possibly be used before it has completed loading.

After the stylesheets have been loaded, an `XSLTemplate` object is created to perform each of the possible transformations for IE:

```
objTrans = new ActiveXObject('MSXML2.XSLTemplate.4.0');
```

At this point, the `rptCrossTab()` function is invoked, which results in the display of the cross tab report. This simple function, shown in the following example, invokes the `transform()` function with the report name as a parameter. At this point, if the browser is IE, `transform()` is invoked on `xslProc`, causing the actual stylesheet and XML transformation. In Netscape, the actual transformation occurs in the JavaScript `transform()` function. Finally, `output()` is invoked to display the report:

```
function rptCrossTab(){
    transform( "CrossTab");
    if (ie){
        //perform transformation for Internet Explorer
        xslProc.transform();
    }
    output();
}
```

The `rptTableSort()` function is next, and will result in the display of the table sort report. This function is similar to the `rptCrossTab()` function, except that it includes code to handle stylesheet parameters.

As shown in the following example, the `rptTableSort()` code for Netscape begins by getting the `param` element from the stylesheet DOM object using `getElementsByTagName()`. Note that the local element name was used, not `xsl:param`. Using the first element of that list, the attribute named `select` is obtained. The `sort` parameter value is then assigned as the value of the `select` attribute of the stylesheet parameter. After this has been completed, the stylesheet parameter has been set and `transform()` is invoked:

```
function rptTableSort(sort){
    if (ns){
        var nodelist = objTableSort.getElementsByTagName("param");
        var nodeSort = nodelist[0].getAttributeNode('select');
        nodeSort.nodeValue = sort;
        transform( "TableSort" );
```

The block of code that executes for IE is shown in the following example. It is similar, but looks like it's in a different order. The `transform()` method is called first, which results in `xslProc` using the correct stylesheet. After that is completed, the stylesheet parameter is set using `addParameter()` with the parameter name and value. The last parameter to this function is for a namespace URI that isn't used in this example. Now that the stylesheet parameter has been set, the transformation is performed through the use of the `transform()` function invoked on `xslProc`:

```
    }else if (ie){
        transform("TableSort");
        xslProc.addParameter("Sort", sort, "");
        xslProc.transform();
    }
```

Finally, the `rptTableSort()` function ends with the invocation of `output()`, which results in the display of the report.

The next function is `transform()`, shown in the following code fragment. This function has the `stylesheet` parameter and uses that string to process the correct report. With Netscape, the `transformDocument()` function is invoked with the appropriate parameters. One of those parameters is the `objOut` DOM document, created in the `load()` function. This is where the results will be placed.

```
//transform the requested xml and stylesheet
function transform(stylesheet){
    if (ns){
```

```
        // perform transformation for Netscape
        if (stylesheet == "TableSort")
            xsltProcessor.transformDocument
                ( objData, objTableSort, objOut, null);
        else
            xsltProcessor.transformDocument
                ( objData, objCrossTab, objOut, null);
```

With IE the stylesheet property of `objTrans` is set to the `documentElement` of the XSL DOM object, as shown in the following example. A new processor is then created with the invocation of `createProcessor()`. Once completed, the XML DOM is assigned as the `input` for the new processor. Note that for IE the actual transformation doesn't occur in this function. Rather, it occurs in the report-specific functions described earlier.

```
    }else if (ie){
        //set up transformation in Internet Explorer
        if (stylesheet == "TableSort")
            objTrans.stylesheet = objTableSort.documentElement;
        else
            objTrans.stylesheet = objCrossTab.documentElement;
        xslProc = objTrans.createProcessor();
        xslProc.input = objData;
    }
```

The last function in the JavaScript file is `output()`. In short, this function takes the result of the transformation and places it into `divDisplay`. With IE, the output of `xslProc` is added to the `innerHTML` of `divDisplay` as shown here:

```
            document.getElementById("divDisplay").innerHTML += xslProc.output;
```

With Netscape, two steps are required to display the results. The first step is to use `getElementsByTagName()` to obtain a list that references each table element of the transformation results. Next, the first table element found is appended to `divDisplay`:

```
        }else if(netscape){
            var x = objOut.getElementsByTagName('table');
            document.getElementById("divDisplay").appendChild( x[0]);
```

With that, all the JavaScript code that powers this on-demand client-side transformation is complete. The JavaScript file is shown in its entirety in Listing 13.2 and should be saved as `webapps\xmlbook\chapter13\ClientTrans.js`.

LISTING 13.2 ClientTrans.js

```
var objData;
var objTableSort;
var objCrossTab;
var objTrans;   //ie only
var objOut; //netscape only
var xsltProcessor; //netscape only
var xmlData;
var divDisplay;
var xslProc;
var ns = false;
var ie = false;

function sniff() {
    if(window.ActiveXObject){
        ie = true;
    }
    else if (document.implementation
        && document.implementation.createDocument){
        ns = true;
    }
    if(ns || ie)
        load();
}

function load(){
    //sets up all the objects etc.
    divDisplay = document.getElementById('divDisplay');

    if (ns){
        objData = document.implementation.createDocument("","",null);
        var domParser = new DOMParser();
        var strSome = document.getElementById('xmlData').innerHTML;
        objData = domParser.parseFromString(strSome, 'text/xml');

        objTableSort = document.implementation.createDocument("","",null);
        objTableSort.load("TableSort.xsl");

        objCrossTab = document.implementation.createDocument("","",null);
        objCrossTab.onload = rptCrossTab;
        objCrossTab.load("CrossTab.xsl");
```

LISTING 13.2 Continued

```
        objOut = document.implementation.createDocument("","",null);
        xsltProcessor = new XSLTProcessor();

    } else if (ie){
        objData = new ActiveXObject('MSXML2.DOMDocument.4.0');
        xmlData = document.getElementById('xmlData');
        objData.loadXML(xmlData.innerHTML);

        objTableSort = new ActiveXObject
            ('MSXML2.FreeThreadedDOMDocument.4.0');
        objTableSort.load ("TableSort.xsl");

        objCrossTab = new ActiveXObject
            ('MSXML2.FreeThreadedDOMDocument.4.0');
        objCrossTab.async = false;
        objCrossTab.load ("CrossTab.xsl");

        objTrans = new ActiveXObject('MSXML2.XSLTemplate.4.0');
        rptCrossTab();
    }
}

function rptCrossTab(){
    transform( "CrossTab");
    if (ie){
        //perform transformation for Internet Explorer
        xslProc.transform();
    }
    output();
}

function rptTableSort(sort){
    if (ns){
        var nodelist = objTableSort.getElementsByTagName("param");
        var nodeSort = nodelist[0].getAttributeNode('select');
        nodeSort.nodeValue = sort;
        transform( "TableSort" );
    }else if (ie){
        transform("TableSort");
        xslProc.addParameter("Sort", sort, "");
        xslProc.transform();
```

LISTING 13.2 Continued

```
    }
    output();
}

//transform the requested xml and stylesheet
function transform(stylesheet){
    if (ns){
        // perform transformation for Netscape
        if (stylesheet == "TableSort")
            xsltProcessor.transformDocument
                ( objData, objTableSort, objOut, null);
        else
            xsltProcessor.transformDocument
                ( objData, objCrossTab, objOut, null);
    }else if (ie){
        //set up transformation in Internet Explorer
        if (stylesheet == "TableSort")
            objTrans.stylesheet = objTableSort.documentElement;
        else
            objTrans.stylesheet = objCrossTab.documentElement;
        xslProc = objTrans.createProcessor();
        xslProc.input = objData;
    }
}

//displays the transformation result
function output(){
    var strResult;

    strResult = "<a href='javascript:rptTableSort(1);' >TableSort</a><br/>"
        + "<a href='javascript:rptCrossTab();' >CrossTab</a><br/><br/><br/>"
    divDisplay.innerHTML = strResult;
    try{
        if(ie){
            document.getElementById("divDisplay").innerHTML += xslProc.output;
        }else if(netscape){
            var x = objOut.getElementsByTagName('table');
            document.getElementById("divDisplay").appendChild( x[0]);
        }
    }catch (e){
        alert("Error caught in output() : "
```

LISTING 13.2 Continued

```
            + e.description + "    " + e.number );
    }
}
```

The JSP

Listing 13.3 is the JSP, which holds everything together. It is very similar to the JSP found in the previous example, so it will not be explained. The changes from Listing 13.1 are noted in boldface type. Save the JSP as `webapps\xmlbook\chapter13\ClientTrans.jsp`.

LISTING 13.3 ClientTrans.jsp

```
<%@page import = "java.sql.*,
        org.jdom.*,
        org.jdom.output.*,
        javax.xml.transform.*,
        xmlbook.chapter11.*" %>

<html>
<head>
<script src="ClientTrans.js" ></script>

<title>Client-Side Stylesheet Transformations</title>
</head>
<body onload="sniff();">

<div style="position:absolute; left:0; top:75;" id="divDisplay">
</div>

<div id="xmlData" style="visibility:hidden;" >
<%
    String final_status     = "";
    String db_query         = "select RCD_lname, RCD_fname, ";
           db_query         +="DATE_FORMAT(RCD_dob, '%Y-%m-%d') as RCD_dob , ";
           db_query         +="RCD_clinic, RCD_color from reportclientdata";

    String db_location      = "jdbc:mysql://localhost/xmlbook";
    String db_driver        = "org.gjt.mm.mysql.Driver";
```

LISTING 13.3 Continued

```
Connection db_connection = null;
Statement db_statement = null;
ResultSet rs = null;

try{
    Class.forName(db_driver);
    db_connection = DriverManager.getConnection(db_location);
    db_statement = db_connection.createStatement();
    rs = db_statement.executeQuery(db_query);

}
catch (ClassNotFoundException e){
    final_status  = "Error: Unable to create database drive class.";
    final_status += " <br />" +  e.toString();
}
catch(SQLException e){
    final_status = "Error: Unable to make database connection";
    final_status += "or execute statement.";
    final_status += " <br />" +  e.toString();
}
finally
{  /* We must close the database connection now */
    try
    {   if (db_connection != null)
        { db_connection.close(); }
    }
    catch (SQLException e)
    {   final_status  = "Error: Unable to close database connection." ;
        final_status += " <br />" +  e.toString();
    }
}
try{
    // create a resultsetbuilder to transform resultset to XML
    RStoXML rsxml = new RStoXML(rs, "ROOT", "REC");
    org.jdom.Document jdomdoc = rsxml.build();

    rs = null;
    rsxml = null;

    //create outputter to output results
    XMLOutputter output = new XMLOutputter("    ", true);
```

LISTING 13.3 Continued

```
        output.output(jdomdoc, out);
        output = null;
    }
    catch (TransformerFactoryConfigurationError e) {
        final_status = "Error: Unable to create factory to transform ";
        final_status = "XSL and XML.";
        final_status += "<br />" +  e.toString();
    }

   catch (JDOMException e)
    {   final_status  = "Error: Unable to create XML from database query.";
        final_status += "<br />" +  e.toString();
    }

    if(final_status != "")
        out.print("<br><font color=\"red\"><H2>" + final_status +
            "</H2></font>");
%>

</div>
</body>
</html>
```

The Two XSL Stylesheets

Next, we find the two stylesheets. The first, shown in Listing 13.4, is for the sorting table report and should be saved as `webapps\xmlbook\chapter13\TableSort.xsl`. Two differences exist between this code and the original stylesheet in Listing 11.6. First, the `Page` stylesheet parameter element has been removed. Second, the `href` attribute value of the anchor element has changed.

LISTING 13.4 TableSort.xsl

```
<?xml version="1.0" encoding="UTF-8"?>
<xsl:stylesheet version="1.0" xmlns:xsl="http://www.w3.org/1999/XSL/Transform">

<xsl:param name="Sort" select="1" />

<xsl:output method="html" />
```

LISTING 13.4 Continued

```
<xsl:template match="/">
<table border="1" cellpadding="5">
    <thead>
    <xsl:call-template name="header"/>
    </thead><tbody>
    <xsl:apply-templates select="*/*">
        <xsl:sort select="*[$Sort]" />
    </xsl:apply-templates>
    </tbody><tfoot />
</table>
</xsl:template>

<!-- creates the table headers from the tag names -->
<xsl:template name="header">
<tr>
    <xsl:for-each select="*/*[1]/*">
        <th>
            <A href="javascript:rptTableSort({position()});">
                <xsl:value-of select="local-name(.)" />
            </A>
        </th>
    </xsl:for-each>
</tr>
</xsl:template>

<!-- creates a row for each child of root, and cell for -->
<!-- each grandchild of root -->
<xsl:template match="*/*">
    <tr>
        <xsl:for-each select="*">
            <td><xsl:value-of select="." /></td>
        </xsl:for-each>
    </tr>
</xsl:template>

</xsl:stylesheet>
```

The next stylesheet, shown in Listing 13.5, is for the cross tab report. This stylesheet has also changed only minimally from its original use in Listing 11.7. The only change is the addition of logic to handle the XML tags' change of case; this change is noted in boldface type in the following code. The change of case has to do with the browsers processing the XML as HTML before it is parsed into a DOM representation. IE capitalizes element names, while Netscape makes all letters lowercase. Save this file as `webapps\xmlbook\chapter13\CrossTab.xsl`.

LISTING 13.5 CrossTab.xsl

```
<?xml version="1.0" encoding="UTF-8"?>
<xsl:stylesheet version="1.0" xmlns:xsl="http://www.w3.org/1999/XSL/Transform">

<xsl:param name="NumClinics" select="5"/>
<xsl:output method="html" />

<xsl:template match="/">
    <table border="1">
        <!-- crosstab labels of first row-->
        <thead>
        <tr><th> </th><th>Blue</th><th>Green</th><th>Orange</th>
            <th>Purple</th><th>Red</th><th>Yellow</th><th>Totals:</th>
        </tr>
        </thead>
        <!-- begin loop to create crosstab body -->
        <tbody>
        <xsl:call-template name="crosstab" >
            <xsl:with-param name="Clinics" select="1"/>
        </xsl:call-template>
        </tbody>
        <tfoot></tfoot>
    </table>
</xsl:template>

<xsl:template name="crosstab">
    <xsl:param name="Clinics"/>
        <tr><th><xsl:value-of select="$Clinics" /></th>
            <td><xsl:value-of select="count(*/*[(rcd_color='blue'
                    and rcd_clinic=$Clinics) or (RCD_COLOR='blue'
                    and RCD_CLINIC=$Clinics)])" /></td>
            <td><xsl:value-of select="count(*/*[(rcd_color='green'
                    and rcd_clinic=$Clinics) or (RCD_COLOR='green'
                    and RCD_CLINIC=$Clinics)])" /></td>
            <td><xsl:value-of select="count(*/*[(rcd_color='orange'
                    and rcd_clinic=$Clinics) or (RCD_COLOR='orange'
                    and RCD_CLINIC=$Clinics)])" /></td>
```

LISTING 13.5 Continued

```
        <td><xsl:value-of select="count(*/*[(rcd_color='purple'
                and rcd_clinic=$Clinics) or (RCD_COLOR='purple'
                and RCD_CLINIC=$Clinics)])" /></td>
        <td><xsl:value-of select="count(*/*[(rcd_color='red'
                and rcd_clinic=$Clinics) or (RCD_COLOR='red'
                and RCD_CLINIC=$Clinics)])" /></td>
        <td><xsl:value-of select="count(*/*[(rcd_color='yellow'
                and rcd_clinic=$Clinics) or (RCD_COLOR='yellow'
                and RCD_CLINIC=$Clinics)])" /></td>
        <td><xsl:value-of select="count(*/*[rcd_clinic=$Clinics
            or RCD_CLINIC=$Clinics])" /></td>
    </tr>

    <!-- continue looping when condition met -->
    <xsl:if test="$Clinics &lt; $NumClinics">
        <xsl:call-template name="crosstab">
            <xsl:with-param name="Clinics" select="$Clinics + 1"/>
        </xsl:call-template>
    </xsl:if>

    <!-- table foot -->

    <xsl:if test="$Clinics=$NumClinics">

        <tr><th>Totals:</th>
            <td><xsl:value-of select="count(*/*[rcd_color='blue'
                 or RCD_COLOR='blue'])" /></td>
            <td><xsl:value-of select="count(*/*[rcd_color='green'
                 or RCD_COLOR='green'])" /></td>
            <td><xsl:value-of select="count(*/*[rcd_color='orange'
                 or RCD_COLOR='orange'])" /></td>
            <td><xsl:value-of select="count(*/*[rcd_color='purple'
                 or RCD_COLOR='purple'])" /></td>
            <td><xsl:value-of select="count(*/*[rcd_color='red'
                 or RCD_COLOR='red'])" /></td>
            <td><xsl:value-of select="count(*/*[rcd_color='yellow'
                 or RCD_COLOR='yellow'])" /></td>
            <td><xsl:value-of select="count(*/*)" /></td>
        </tr>
    </xsl:if>
```

LISTING 13.5 Continued

```
</xsl:template>

</xsl:stylesheet>
```

Combine them all together, and the cross tab report is displayed as shown in Figures 13.3 and 13.4.

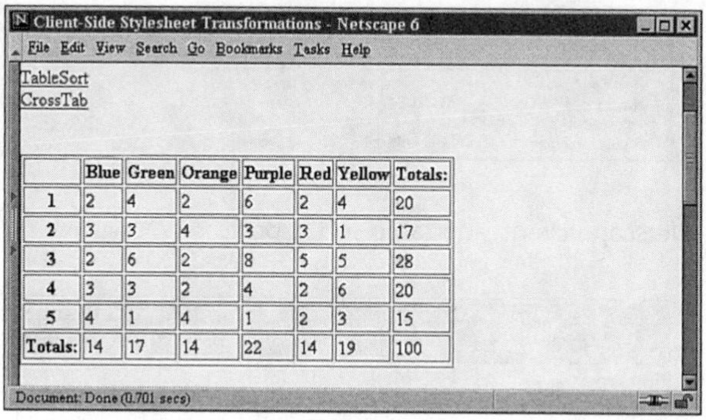

Client-Side Stylesheet Transformations - Netscape 6

TableSort
CrossTab

	Blue	Green	Orange	Purple	Red	Yellow	Totals:
1	2	4	2	6	2	4	20
2	3	3	4	3	3	1	17
3	2	6	2	8	5	5	28
4	3	3	2	4	2	6	20
5	4	1	4	1	2	3	15
Totals:	14	17	14	22	14	19	100

Document: Done (0.701 secs)

FIGURE 13.3 Netscape client-side cross tab report.

Client-Side Stylesheet Transformations - Microsoft Internet Explorer pro...

TableSort
CrossTab

	Blue	Green	Orange	Purple	Red	Yellow	Totals:
1	2	4	2	6	2	4	20
2	3	3	4	3	3	1	17
3	2	6	2	8	5	5	28
4	3	3	2	4	2	6	20
5	4	1	4	1	2	3	15
Totals:	14	17	14	22	14	19	100

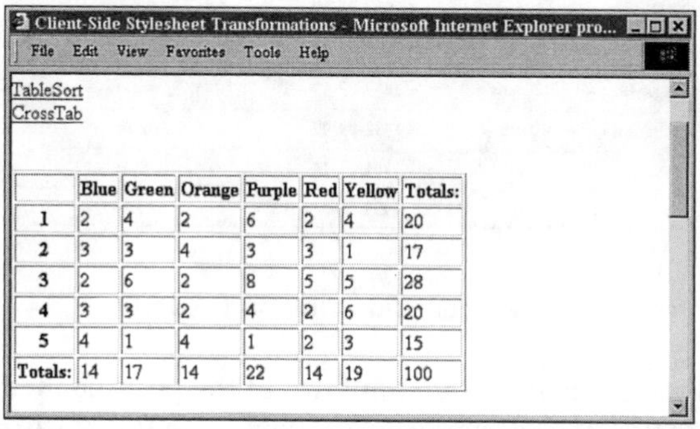

FIGURE 13.4 Internet Explorer client-side cross tab report.

Figures 13.5 and 13.6 show the table sort report part of this Web page. Note the linked table labels that provide a mechanism for re-sorting the data on the client side. Those links are capitalized differently in Netscape and IE because of the processing of the XML as HTML when it was stored inside the hidden division element.

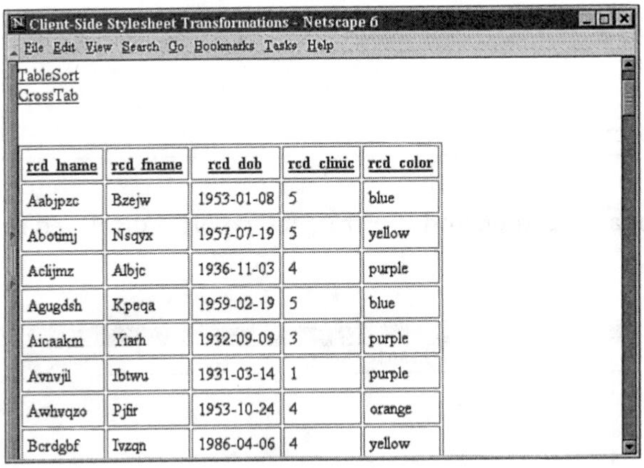

Client-Side Stylesheet Transformations - Netscape 6

File Edit View Search Go Bookmarks Tasks Help

TableSort
CrossTab

rcd lname	rcd fname	rcd dob	rcd clinic	rcd color
Aabjpzc	Bzejw	1953-01-08	5	blue
Abotimj	Nsqyx	1957-07-19	5	yellow
Aclijmz	Albjc	1936-11-03	4	purple
Agugdsh	Kpeqa	1959-02-19	5	blue
Aicaakm	Yiarh	1932-09-09	3	purple
Avnvjil	Ibtwu	1931-03-14	1	purple
Awhvqzo	Pjfir	1953-10-24	4	orange
Bcrdgbf	Ivzqn	1986-04-06	4	yellow

FIGURE 13.5 Netscape client-side table sort report.

Client-Side Stylesheet Transformations - Microsoft Internet Explorer pro...

File Edit View Favorites Tools Help

TableSort
CrossTab

RCD LNAME	RCD FNAME	RCD DOB	RCD CLINIC	RCD COLOR
Aabjpzc	Bzejw	1953-01-08	5	blue
Abotimj	Nsqyx	1957-07-19	5	yellow
Aclijmz	Albjc	1936-11-03	4	purple
Agugdsh	Kpeqa	1959-02-19	5	blue
Aicaakm	Yiarh	1932-09-09	3	purple
Avnvjil	Ibtwu	1931-03-14	1	purple
Awhvqzo	Pjfir	1953-10-24	4	orange

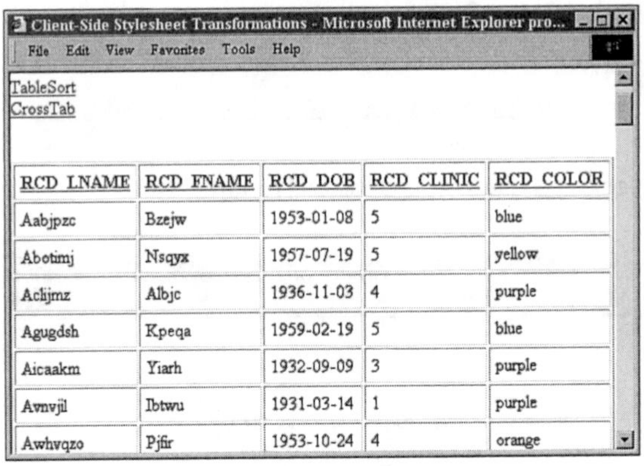

FIGURE 13.6 Internet Explorer client-side table sort report.

Using script and transformations are only two of the possible methods for displaying and formatting XML data. Another way is through the use of *cascading style sheets (CSS)*. Using CSS, XML data can be formatted across platforms and devices for both display and printing. Although both browsers support CSS, Netscape has been more thorough in implementing the W3C's CSS specification.

Summary

Three main choices exist for the client-side manipulation of data. One is through the use of JavaScript. Another is through the use of the XML DOM. The last is by using the DOM Level 2 CSS Interface from the W3C. Each of these choices provide the means for manipulating data, allowing it to be dynamically reformatted, hidden, and shown.

14 Building a Web Service

IN THIS CHAPTER

- Designing a Web Service
- Building the Web Service
- Creating a WSDL File
- Registering Within UDDI
- Using Java to Access a WSDL Document

This chapter will show you how to build a Web service system for news delivery. Using the JSPBuzz as an example, you will build a system for delivering news stories.

The Web services built so far in this book have been simple. Up to this point, we didn't worry about registering the Web services, because the service calls were hard-coded to work between the examples. Because the examples were not in a registry, there wasn't any need to create a WSDL description file. This chapter will take things one step further and walk through the creation of a simple WSDL file. With WSDL, it's possible to define a Web service that others can easily use. The other major new step shows how to register a service within a UDDI registry.

Web services are simple—it's the framework around the Web services that's complicated. A framework tends to be large, and building one consists of many tedious steps. Web service frameworks usually have five elements:

- The actual Web service business logic.
- A server. This is usually a SOAP server, and this server mediates traffic between a user and the Web service.
- A WSDL file to describe the Web service.
- A Web service registry. Typically, a framework provides direct access to one of the public registries, rather than a private registry.
- Automated code generation for most of the installation and usage of the Web service.

Although the Web service might be a simple class, building the overall framework is a larger and more complicated task. Manually creating every piece of a Web service framework is both time-consuming and prone to errors because of human mistakes. Fortunately, with frameworks most of the work can be automated by software. Using an automated tool is much advised for creating a Web service and the supporting framework. The time savings in using such a tool will be huge from both a development and maintenance perspective, and will more than make up for the cost of using such a tool.

NOTE

Because a framework automates part of the process of building a Web service, using one would actually be a hindrance in teaching you the basics behind building a Web service. Thus, this book doesn't use a framework.

The good news is that many commercial products are being created to fill the need for creating and supporting Web services. In fact, so many tools are popping up, that it's impossible to give a recommendation to any single product. Generally, this book has recommended using open source products because of the low cost and great support. Currently, no satisfactory open source products exist that we can recommend to fill this need. Although several options exist, none are up to the level of quality or completeness that would earn a solid recommendation. Eventually, a solid open source tool will appear; until then, don't hesitate to evaluate various commercial products and choose the solution that fits your needs.

Designing a Web Service

The first step in this chapter will be to build the actual Web service. Designing a Web service is no different than designing any other process—establishing a solid goal and defining service requirements are very important parts of the actual building of the service.

Because this chapter represents a small project in itself, the goals and requirements of the example will be outlined for the reader's benefit.

What Is the Goal?

Each Web service should have one goal and only one goal. If you have several goals, then chances are you have several Web services that need to be built. Unlike a general application, which can fulfill many needs, Web services are smaller packages of work for a single task. Keep each Web service as small and atomic as possible.

The goal of the JSPBuzz Web service is to produce a list of links to populate a newsfeed. Each link will take the reader back to the original JSPBuzz document, to the exact location of the news story.

What Are the Requirements?

The requirements should always be written down in a concise and understandable manner. Fortunately, we have a simple set of requirements for the JSPBuzz Web service:

1. Each link in the newsfeed needs to take the user back to the original page displaying the news story.
2. The Web service will permit the reader to type in a search string to narrow what stories are shown in the newsfeed.
3. The code in this version gets its data from a single JSPBuzz issue. However, the code needs to be set up so that in the future it will be easy for the process to work against multiple JSPBuzz documents at the same time.

One advantage to building Web services is that a Web service by itself is just a very small and controllable project. This makes building requirements for the Web service a relatively simple matter.

What Data Does the Service Need?

It's time to talk about data. A Web service server doesn't need to be located with your Web server, which means that a Web service server doesn't necessarily have access to the same resources as your Web server. In our example, the SOAP Web server can conveniently pull the XML files out of the xmlbook Web site. Remember to make sure your Web service has convenient, quick and reliable access to any data source it will require.

Building the Web Service

Much of the code in this example will be familiar, as it will reuse and expand much of what has already been shown in previous chapters. A new change is the directory. Because this code will be used at the JSP Insider site, the code has been placed within the `com.jspinsider.jspbuzz` package. For this example, the code will be installed on the local Apache SOAP server. This will make it possible to run and test the Web service locally. The example will use dom4j as the API to handle the XML documents.

Building a File Handler

The first class we'll build is a simple file handler. This class will determine where all the various files are located within the system. Because the files will be spread around, it makes sense to have one central class to find the files. Save the code in Listing 14.1 as `webapps/soap/WEB-INF/classes/com/jspinsider/jspbuzz/BuzzIssues.java`.

LISTING 14.1 A Java Class to Define the Location of XML Files

```
package com.jspinsider.jspbuzz;

import java.io.File;
import org.dom4j.Document;
import org.dom4j.io.SAXReader;

public class BuzzIssues
{   public BuzzIssues() {}

    public static String ls_tomcat_path = "c:/java/tomcat4/";
    public static String buzzurl  = "http://www.jspinsider.com/jspbuzz/2001/";
    public static String site_path      = "webapps/xmlbook/chapter7/";
    public static String service_path   = "webapps/xmlbook/chapter14/";

    public static String currentbuzzXML =
                        ls_tomcat_path + site_path + "buzz_10_09_2001.xml";

    public static String currentbuzzJSP = buzzurl + "buzz_10_09_2001.jsp";

    public static String currentbuzzXSL =
                        ls_tomcat_path + service_path + "BuzzList.xsl";

    public String getcurrentxml(){return currentbuzzXML;};
    public String getcurrentjsp(){return currentbuzzJSP;};
    public String getlistingxsl(){return currentbuzzXSL;};
}
```

Because the code from the overall example will be used in several places, it isn't a good idea to hard-code the files in the main classes. Instead, this one class will track all the files and provide helper functions to access the information. This particular version is hard-coded to make the example easy. The final production version will be driven by an XML file. This way, new files can be added without recompiling the actual class. Also, additional helper methods can be built to query directories for the various JSPBuzz issues. This would increase the usefulness of this class. Again, the code is not included here, as it's not required for the local example to run.

You will have to update the following line:

```
public static String ls_tomcat_path = "c:/java/tomcat4/";
```

The first thing to note is that this code was written for a Windows-based machine. You can use the `File.separator` string to create a platform-independent file path system instead of employing the hard-coded Windows-based separator (/). If you are using Unix or Linux, you will have to make the appropriate changes for your file path.

It's required to change the value to match your own local Tomcat directory. Also notice this code assumes the xmlbook directory is installed within the same Web context as the SOAP server. While this is the case for this example, in the future remember that your SOAP server could be located elsewhere, including on a different machine.

Building a Search Utility

To make the Web service useful, we want the user to be able to retrieve stories that match a search string. We will expand the `QueryElement` class found in Chapter 9, "Advanced JSP and XML Techniques," to perform this task.

Save the class in Listing 14.2 as `webapps/soap/WEB-INF/classes/com/jspinsider/jspbuzz/QueryElement.java`.

LISTING 14.2 Searching for String Matches in an XML Element

```
package com.jspinsider.jspbuzz;

import java.util.Iterator;
import java.util.StringTokenizer;
import org.dom4j.Element;

public class QueryElement
{   public QueryElement() {}

    public String[] buildSearchArray(String as_search)
    { StringTokenizer st = new StringTokenizer(as_search);
      int count     = st.countTokens();
      int index     = 0;
      if (count > 0)
      {String[] tokens = new String[count];
       while (st.hasMoreTokens())
       { tokens[index] = st.nextToken();
         index++;
       }
       return tokens;
      }
      return null;
    }
```

LISTING 14.2 Continued

```
    public boolean findString(String search, Element element)
    {   String[] searchlist = buildSearchArray(search);
        return findString(searchlist,element);
    }

    public boolean findString(String[] searchlist, Element element)
    {   if (searchlist == null) return false;
        for (int i = 0; i < searchlist.length; i++)
        { if (findExactString(searchlist[i],element)== false) return false;
        }
        return true;
    }

    public boolean findExactString(String as_search, Element   element)
    {  as_search = as_search.toLowerCase();
       if (element.getText().toLowerCase().indexOf(as_search)> -1) return true;
       Iterator elementlist = element.elementIterator();

       while (elementlist.hasNext() )
       { Element child = (Element) elementlist.next();
         boolean lb_test = findString( as_search, child);
         if (lb_test) return lb_test;
       }
       return false;
    }
}
```

This class has all the functionality of the original class. It has merely been expanded to perform an and-based search on a string array. The new class also contains a helper method `buildSearchArray`, which can be used to tokenize a string into an array.

Creating an `ElementHandler`

The Web service will be able to perform a search to select only the articles a user asks to read. This means that it makes sense to build the XML document representation to include only the links the user wants to see. Using a SAX handler, or more specifically a dom4j `ElementHandler`, lets you also work towards the other long-term goal of being able to search through multiple issues of the JSPBuzz and condense the results to a single dom4j `Document`. Although this example won't currently merge the files, the overall code structure has been built in modules to support this future enhancement. We will expand the `SearchHandler` class found in Chapter 9 to perform this task. The class shown in Listing 14.3 should be saved as `webapps/soap/WEB-INF/classes/com/jspinsider/jspbuzz/SearchHandler.java`.

LISTING 14.3 A Handler to Optimize Building a dom4j `Document` Object

```
package com.jspinsider.jspbuzz;

import java.util.Iterator;
import org.dom4j.Attribute;
import org.dom4j.Element;
import org.dom4j.ElementHandler;
import org.dom4j.ElementPath;

public class SearchHandler implements ElementHandler
{
   private String    search     = "";
   private String[]  searchlist = null;
   private String    linksource = "";

   public  void setSearch(String as_search)
   { search     = as_search;
     searchlist = testelement.buildSearchArray(as_search);
   }

   public  void setLinkSource(String as_source) { linksource = as_source;}

   private QueryElement testelement = new QueryElement();

   public SearchHandler() {}
   public SearchHandler(String as_search) {setSearch(as_search);}
   public SearchHandler(String as_search, String as_source)
   { setSearch(as_search);
     setLinkSource(as_source);
   }

   public void onStart(ElementPath path) {}

   public void onEnd(ElementPath path)
   {    Element row = path.getCurrent();
        /* Remove BuzzStories that don't match the search */
        if (search.length()> 0)
```

LISTING 14.3 Continued

```
        { if (testelement.findString(searchlist,row) == false)
          row.detach();
          else
          {attachSource(row);}
        }
        else
        {attachSource(row);}
   }

   public void attachSource(Element row)
   { if (linksource.length() > 0)
             {   Attribute link = row.attribute("linksource");
                 if (link == null)
                 {row.addAttribute("linksource",linksource); }
                 else
                 {link.setValue(linksource);}
             }
   }
}
```

Keep in mind that the dom4j `ElementHandler` we are creating here is applied during the SAX process, so this will be a fast and efficient way to build the `Document` object.

Now let's examine the new sections. The first builds a search array. It wouldn't make sense to build a search array every time an element is processed by this class. Instead, when the search string is initialized, the code also creates the search array:

```
public  void setSearch(String as_search)
{ search     = as_search;
  searchlist = testelement.buildSearchArray(as_search);
}
```

The other new piece of code is the `attachSource` method:

```
public void attachSource(Element row)
{ if (linksource.length() > 0)
          {   Attribute link = row.attribute("linksource");
              if (link == null)
              {row.addAttribute("linksource",linksource);}
              else
              {link.setValue(linksource);}
          }
}
```

This method attaches a new `Attribute` called `linksource` to each row `Element`. The business rule being enforced is that each link being displayed needs to be able to link back to the original story within a JSPBuzz page. The `linksource` attribute is used to store the parent page containing the story. It should be mentioned that the XML file containing the original JSPBuzz data does not contain this data—and shouldn't by design. An XML document should only know about itself and its dataset. Putting information about files using the XML dataset would result in rotten data, because this sort of data is likely to become out of date. What would happen if the destination file were to change, or the page locations were to move? The XML file would be left with bad data embedded within it.

The other problem arises from the requirement that this process will later merge together dozens of JSPBuzz newsletters. We need a way to embed reliable information for each link displayed to the user.

The best solution is to pass in the parent page reference for each individual link as the XML document is parsed. Then, when we do merge multiple documents, each link will safely have a reference to its parent page, or the `linksource` attribute in this case. This attribute is not used by the original document. Instead, it's used by the temporary dom4j `Document` to inform a stylesheet how to build a reference link. This way, each kept link will always have a correct and up-to-date reference to the JSP page displaying the original story.

The page being set within the `linksource` attribute is passed in just before the document is parsed with the `setLinkSource` method:

```
public  void setLinkSource(String as_source) { linksource = as_source;}
```

The next step is to build the actual `Document` object containing the data.

Building a `Document` Object

The code in this step follows previous examples closely, and nothing new has been done. The code, shown in Listing 14.4, should be saved as `webapps/soap/WEB-INF/classes/com/jspinsider/jspbuzz/CreateBuzzDocument.java`.

LISTING 14.4 Building a dom4j `Document` Object

```
package com.jspinsider.jspbuzz;

import java.io.File;
import org.dom4j.Document;
import org.dom4j.io.SAXReader;
```

LISTING 14.4 Continued

```
public class CreateBuzzDocument
{   public CreateBuzzDocument() {}

  public Document allEntries(String as_xml, String as_link) throws Exception
  {   try{ return findEntries(as_xml,as_link,"");}
      catch (Exception e) {throw e;}
  }

  public Document findEntries(String as_xml, String as_link, String as_search)
        throws Exception
  { try
    { SAXReader reader = new SAXReader();
      SearchHandler filter = new SearchHandler(as_search,as_link);
      reader.addHandler("/jspbuzz/buzzlink",filter);
      reader.addHandler("/jspbuzz/ramble"  ,filter);
      reader.addHandler("/jspbuzz/topic"  ,filter);

      Document document = reader.read(new File(as_xml));
     return document;
    }
    catch(Exception e) { throw e; }
  }
}
```

Notice that the code adds multiple handlers with the `addHandler` method. It would be possible to build various custom event handlers to gain extremely fine control of the final document being created in this process.

Applying a Stylesheet

In Chapter 7, "Successfully Using JSP and XML in an Application," we built the `ProcessDom4J` object. This chapter's example needs something similar. However, we won't have access to the `JspWriter` object; this will be a Web service. The output will be passed to the user as a `String`. This means we need to expand the `ProcessDom4J` class to do a little more for us in this example.

The code in Listing 14.5 should be saved as `webapps/soap/WEB-INF/classes/com/jspinsider/jspbuzz/ProcessDom4J.java`.

LISTING 14.5 Creating a New ProcessDom4J Object

```
package  com.jspinsider.jspbuzz;

import org.dom4j.Document;
import org.dom4j.io.DocumentResult;
import org.dom4j.io.DocumentSource;
import org.dom4j.io.*;

import java.io.*;
import javax.servlet.jsp.JspWriter;
import javax.xml.transform.Transformer;
import javax.xml.transform.TransformerFactory;
import javax.xml.transform.stream.*;

public class ProcessDom4J
{
public ProcessDom4J() {}

public void applyXSL (JspWriter out, Document a_xmlresult, String as_xsl)
       throws Exception
{       StreamSource xsl    = new StreamSource(new File(as_xsl));
        StreamResult result = new StreamResult(out);

        Transformer transformer;
        TransformerFactory factory = TransformerFactory.newInstance();
        transformer = factory.newTransformer( xsl );
        DocumentSource source = new DocumentSource( a_xmlresult );
        transformer.transform(source, result);
}

public String applyXSL (Document a_doc, String  as_xsl) throws Exception
{      try
       {StreamSource xsl    = new StreamSource(new File(as_xsl));
        StringWriter writer = new StringWriter();
        StreamResult result = new StreamResult(writer);

        Transformer transformer;
        TransformerFactory factory = TransformerFactory.newInstance();
        transformer = factory.newTransformer( xsl );

        DocumentSource source = new DocumentSource( a_doc );
        transformer.transform(source, result);
```

LISTING 14.5 Continued

```
        return( writer.toString());
       }
       catch (Exception e) {throw e;}
}
}
```

The new twist to this code is the writing to a `String` rather than the `JspWriter`:

```
StringWriter writer = new StringWriter();
StreamResult result = new StreamResult(writer);
```

This is accomplished by creating a `StringWriter` to direct the transformation stream:

```
return( writer.toString());
```

The last step is just to take the writer and convert it to a `String`.

Creating a Stylesheet

We will reuse the buzz_10_09_2001.xml file from Chapter 7. However, we do need to build a new stylesheet to get the results desired for the Web service.

The code in Listing 14.6 should be saved as `webapps/xmlbook/chapter14/BuzzList.xsl`.

LISTING 14.6 Stylesheet to Create Web Service Results

```
<?xml version="1.0" encoding="UTF-8"?>

<xsl:stylesheet version="1.0" xmlns:xsl="http://www.w3.org/1999/XSL/Transform">
<xsl:output method="html"/>

<xsl:template match="/">
<div>
<p align="center" class="12ptBold"><xsl:value-of select="jspbuzz/title"/></p>

    <xsl:if test="count(jspbuzz/buzzlink[@type='news']) > 0">
           <div class="10ptBold">News</div>
           <ol><xsl:apply-templates select="jspbuzz/buzzlink[@type='news']">
                          <xsl:sort data-type="number" select="@position"/>
               </xsl:apply-templates></ol>
    </xsl:if>
```

LISTING 14.6 Continued

```
    <xsl:if test="count(jspbuzz/ramble) >0">
           <div class="10ptBold">Rambles</div>
           <ol>
           <xsl:apply-templates select="jspbuzz/ramble">
                   <xsl:sort data-type="number" select="@position"/>
           </xsl:apply-templates></ol>
    </xsl:if>

    <div class="10ptBold">Links of Interest</div>
    <ol><xsl:apply-templates select="jspbuzz/buzzlink[@type='link']">
                    <xsl:sort data-type="number" select="@position"/>
        </xsl:apply-templates></ol>

    <xsl:if test="count(jspbuzz/buzzlink[@type='product']) >0">
           <div class="10ptBold">Products</div>
           <ol><xsl:apply-templates select="jspbuzz/buzzlink[@type='product']">
                           <xsl:sort data-type="number" select="@position"/>
               </xsl:apply-templates></ol>
    </xsl:if>

    <xsl:if test="count(jspbuzz/buzzlink[@type='review']) >0">
           <div class="10ptBold">Reviews</div>
           <ol><xsl:apply-templates select="jspbuzz/buzzlink[@type='review']">
                           <xsl:sort data-type="number" select="@position"/>
                   </xsl:apply-templates></ol>
    </xsl:if>

    <xsl:if test="count(jspbuzz/topic) >0">
            <div class="10ptBold">Main Topic</div>
            <p> <a href="#topic" ><xsl:value-of select="jspbuzz/topic/title"/>
                </a></p><br/>
    </xsl:if>
</div>
</xsl:template>

<xsl:template match="jspbuzz/buzzlink">
        <li><a href="{@linksource}#{@type}{@position}">
                      <xsl:value-of select="title"/>
            </a></li>
</xsl:template>
```

LISTING 14.6 Continued

```
<xsl:template match="jspbuzz/ramble">
        <li><a href="{@linksource}#ramble{@position}">
                        <xsl:value-of select="title"/>
            </a></li>
</xsl:template>

</xsl:stylesheet>
```

The stylesheet is not very exciting, but it's easier to build the stylesheet than to build the logic within a programming loop. In addition, this will give us the flexibility to swap stylesheets when we want to change the format of the output.

Building the Web Service at Last

We finally have all the pieces to build our Web service. The last step is to build the Java class representing the Web service. The code in Listing 14.7 should be saved as `webapps/soap/WEB-INF/classes/com/jspinsider/jspbuzz/BuzzWebServices.java`.

LISTING 14.7 The Web Service Class

```
package com.jspinsider.jspbuzz;

import org.dom4j.Document;

public class BuzzWebServices
{public BuzzWebServices() {}

 public String  currentList()
 { return currentListSearch("");}

 public String  currentListSearch(String as_find)
 { try
   { BuzzIssues issues  = new BuzzIssues();
     ProcessDom4J doxml = new ProcessDom4J();
     CreateBuzzDocument buzzdoc = new CreateBuzzDocument();

     String ls_jsp = issues.getcurrentjsp();
     String ls_xsl = issues.getlistingxsl();
     String ls_xml = issues.getcurrentxml();
     return doxml.applyXSL (buzzdoc.findEntries(ls_xml,ls_jsp,as_find),ls_xsl);
   }
```

LISTING 14.7 Continued

```
    catch(Exception e) { return e.toString();}
  }
}
```

Notice the brevity of the code. We want to keep this object as clean as possible. The real purpose of this class is to act as a front end for the Web service. All the actual code to make the magic happen should be placed into the various business objects.

Registering the Web Service with Apache SOAP

The last step to perform in building the Web service is to register it with the Apache SOAP server. Before you register the service, don't forget to compile everything and restart Tomcat! If you try to register a Web service when the class file doesn't exist, it will leave a dead entry within the Apache SOAP server registry.

While we didn't use a deployment file, an Apache SOAP deployment file would be similar to what is shown in Listing 14.8.

LISTING 14.8 Apache Soap Deployment File

```
<isd:service xmlns:isd="http://xml.apache.org/xml-soap/deployment"
             id="urn:jspbuzz.services">

<isd:provider type="java"
              scope="Request"
              methods="currentList currentListSearch">
  <isd:java class="com.jspinsider.jspbuzz.BuzzWebServices" static="false"/>
</isd:provider>

<isd:faultListener>org.apache.soap.server.DOMFaultListener</isd:faultListener>

</isd:service>
```

However, it's easy to manually enter the following data using the Apache SOAP Deployment screen:

- ID: `urn:jspbuzz.services`
- Scope: `Request`
- Methods: `currentList currentListSearch`
- Provider: Java
- Provider Class: `com.jspinsider.jspbuzz.BuzzWebServices`

We are done building the Web service. The same Web service has been deployed to the JSP Insider Web site. You will be able to access the service locally from your machine, or remotely from the JSP Insider site.

The next step will be to build a WSDL file to describe this Web service. We are not going to build a test page right away; instead, we will later build a generic class to read the WSDL file to create the actual Web service call. If you want to test this Web service, you can use a simple variation of Listing 3.7 from Chapter 3, "Understanding Web Services."

Creating a WSDL File

Because other programmers might be using the JSPBuzz Web service, it would be a good idea to create a WSDL document to describe the service. As a result, we will publish a WSDL document to enable others easy access to the JSPBuzz Web service. After this document is published, other users can download the WSDL file and determine how to use the Web service. Before creating a WSDL document for this chapter, let's examine WSDL in greater detail.

WSDL is an interesting beast. WSDL is not part of the SOAP specification. Instead, WSDL is all about defining a Web service, more specifically a network service. Because many Web services use SOAP, people automatically connect WSDL to SOAP. This is not right. A Web service can use any manner of standards to define the actual Web service content and then transmit the message. Currently, WSDL defines bindings that permit the use of SOAP 1.1, HTTP Get/Post, and MIME to define the actual Web service messages.

Many tools will generate a WSDL document. However, the tools that generate WSDL all tend to be within integrated Web service packages. These tools usually provide a whole range of capabilities to support a Web service. Apache SOAP is *not* a Web service tool; it's a SOAP server, which we happen to be using in this book to transmit the Web services. Because Apache SOAP doesn't directly use WSDL, it won't generate a WSDL document. This means we have to either generate a WSDL manually, or find another tool for the generation of the WSDL. For learning purposes this is a good thing, so let's dive in and create ours manually.

WSDL Namespaces

Now, the first thing to consider is namespaces. Technically, all references should be fully qualified with the proper namespaces. Some WSDL documents do not use namespaces properly. This may or may not cause a problem, depending on the Web service tools you are using. If you are having a problem with a WSDL file, the first thing you should double-check is that the namespaces are correct within the document.

By default, any WSDL element will use the `wsdl` namespace defined with the URI `http://schemas.xmlsoap.org/wsdl/`.

Typically, at least the `tns`, `xsd`, `soap`, and `wsdl` namespaces must be declared for a WSDL file.

Let's examine the `tns` namespace for a second. `tns` stands for "this namespace" and refers to the current document. A `tns` declaration would look something like this:

```
xmlns:tns="http://www.jspinsider.com/jspbuzz/services/JspBuzz.wsdl"
```

Usually, this namespace will just use the URL to the WSDL file itself as the definition. Here's an example:

```
<binding name="BuzzList_Binding" type="tns:BuzzWebServices_Port ">
```

The `type` attribute in this example says the `binding` element matches an element defined within the same document with the `id` of `BuzzWebServices_Port`. In this case, it refers back to the `portType` element with the name `BuzzWebServices_Port`:

```
<portType name="BuzzWebServices_Port">
```

Within a WSDL document, there will be quite a bit of cross-referencing between the elements.

The `xsd` namespace is used to define the data types used within the actual messages, while the `soap` namespace defines the SOAP elements used within the WSDL document. Typically, these namespaces are set as follows:

```
xmlns:xsd="http://www.w3.org/2001/XMLSchema"
xmlns:soap="http://schemas.xmlsoap.org/wsdl/soap/"
```

WSDL soaks itself in namespaces, so it wouldn't hurt to brush up on namespaces if you are going to hand-generate many of these files. Personally, I would prefer to use automated tools to create WSDL files. However, to date I haven't found an open source tool that adequately meets my needs, so I still manually create the files.

Creating the JSPBuzz WSDL File

The JSPBuzz WSDL file, shown in Listing 14.9, should be saved to `webapps/xmlbook/chapter14/JspBuzz.wsdl`. The file is also available directly at the JSP Insider Web site at `http://www.jspinsider.com/jspbuzz/services/JspBuzz.wsdl`.

One line of the file on the JSP Insider site is different, as it points back to the JSP Insider SOAP server. The WSDL file in Listing 14.9 points back to the local Apache SOAP server installed on your machine.

LISTING 14.9 A WSDL File to Define the JSPBuzz Web Service

```
<?xml version="1.0"?>
<definitions name="BuzzWebServices"
xmlns:tns="http://www.jspinsider.com/jspbuzz/services/JspBuzz.wsdl"
xmlns:xsd="http://www.w3.org/2001/XMLSchema"
xmlns:soap="http://schemas.xmlsoap.org/wsdl/soap/"
xmlns="http://schemas.xmlsoap.org/wsdl/">

<message name="currentList_Response">
    <part name="response" type="xsd:string"/>
</message>
<message name="currentList_Request"/>

<message name="currentListSearch_Response">
    <part name="response" type="xsd:string"/>
</message>
<message name="currentListSearch_Request">
    <part name="as_find" type="xsd:string"/>
</message>

<portType name="BuzzWebServices_Port">
  <operation name="currentList">
     <input name="currentList" message="tns:currentList_Request"/>
     <output name="currentList" message="tns:currentList_Response"/>
  </operation>
  <operation name="currentListSearch" parameterOrder="as_find">
   <input name="currentListSearch" message="tns:currentListSearch_Request"/>
   <output name="currentListSearch" message="tns:currentListSearch_Response"/>
  </operation>
</portType>

<binding name="BuzzList_Binding" type="tns:BuzzWebServices_Port">
 <soap:binding style="rpc" transport="http://schemas.xmlsoap.org/soap/http" />

  <operation name="currentList">
     <soap:operation soapAction="urn:jspbuzz.services" />
     <input>
          <soap:body use="encoded" namespace="urn:jspbuzz.services"
                  encodingStyle="http://schemas.xmlsoap.org/soap/encoding/" />
     </input>
     <output>
```

LISTING 14.9 Continued

```
          <soap:body use="encoded" namespace="urn:jspbuzz.services"
                  encodingStyle="http://schemas.xmlsoap.org/soap/encoding/" />
     </output>
  </operation>

  <operation name="currentListSearch">
     <soap:operation soapAction="urn:jspbuzz.services" />
     <input>
          <soap:body use="encoded" namespace="urn:jspbuzz.services"
                  encodingStyle="http://schemas.xmlsoap.org/soap/encoding/" />
     </input>
     <output>
          <soap:body use="encoded" namespace="urn:jspbuzz.services"
                  encodingStyle="http://schemas.xmlsoap.org/soap/encoding/" />
     </output>
  </operation>
</binding>

<service name="BuzzWebServices">
     <port name="BuzzWebPort" binding="tns:BuzzList_Binding">
          <soap:address
           location="http://localhost:8080/soap/servlet/rpcrouter" />
     </port>
</service>
</definitions>
```

The WSDL file takes a little bit of time to digest. At first glance, it isn't very friendly. On second and third glances, it's still not fun to look at. The only way to make sense of a WSDL file is to just walk through it with some friendly explanation of what is happening. This means that the best approach is to dive in and examine each section in turn.

The `definitions` Element

The `definitions` element is the root element of the WSDL document.

```
<definitions name="BuzzWebServices"
xmlns:tns="http://www.jspinsider.com/jspbuzz/services/JspBuzz.wsdl"
xmlns:xsd="http://www.w3.org/2001/XMLSchema"
xmlns:soap="http://schemas.xmlsoap.org/wsdl/soap/"
xmlns="http://schemas.xmlsoap.org/wsdl/">
```

All namespace declarations occur within the definition statement.

The `message` Element

Messages define the information packets being sent to and from each service method. As programmers, this translates to the method arguments and return values. The `message` element is merely a description for a packet of information that will be required to use the Web service.

For instance, the following statement defines a string packet (data stored in XML format used to represent a string) that will be used within the service:

```
<message name="currentListSearch_Response">
    <part name="response" type="xsd:string"/>
</message>
```

This describes a packet of data in the format of a string, according to the `xsd` namespace schema.

This `message` in itself doesn't tell us how the packet will be used by the service. The naming convention only gives us an indication as to the use of the `message`. The name in the `message` is arbitrary, and is merely a naming convention to make this element easier to read. If we were to skip ahead to the `operation` element within the `portType` element, we would see the actual binding of the message to the Web service method:

```
<operation name="currentListSearch" parameterOrder="as_find">
    <output name="currentListSearch" message="tns:currentListSearch_Response"/>
```

Notice that `tns:currentListSearch_Response` refers back to the `<message name="currentListSearch_Response">` statement. Within WSDL, this pattern of definition and then binding to the actual use within another element is repeated for most of the elements.

Another example is the message used to create the search parameter:

```
<message name="currentListSearch_Request">
    <part name="as_find" type="xsd:string"/>
</message>
```

Notice the `part` element. A `message` element can have multiple parts, which enables a message to have complicated parameters that need to be sent within the Web service.

The `portType` Element

A `portType` element defines the overall service in terms of the methods the service contains.

```
<portType name="BuzzWebServices_Port">
  <operation name="currentList">
     <input name="currentList" message="tns:currentList_Request"/>
     <output name="currentList" message="tns:currentList_Response"/>
  </operation>
  <operation name="currentListSearch" parameterOrder="as_find">
    <input name="currentListSearch" message="tns:currentListSearch_Request"/>
    <output name="currentListSearch" message="tns:currentListSearch_Response"/>
  </operation>
</portType>
```

The `portType` element must have a unique name. Within the `portType`, all methods available within the service are defined using the `operation` element.

The `operation` Element

Each method within a Web service is considered an operation within a WSDL file. Each `operation` element within a `portType` is given a unique name. An `operation` has an `input` element defining a message being sent to the operation:

```
  <operation name="currentListSearch" parameterOrder="as_find">
     <input name="currentListSearch" message="tns:currentListSearch_Request"/>
```

An `operation` also has an `output` element to define which message is being sent to the client:

```
     <output name="currentListSearch" message="tns:currentListSearch_Response"/>
  </operation>
```

Notice that for both the `input` and `output`, the `message` attribute ties back to a message element defined earlier in the WSDL file.

In relation to SOAP, all operations have an input and output message that needs to be defined for use.

The `binding` Element

Using a service is more than just calling a method. In order to call the method, a framework must exist to convey the messages. The `binding` element is the way in which the WSDL document describes this framework within which the Web service resides. Now, to refresh your memory, here is the `binding` element:

```
<binding name="BuzzList_Binding" type="tns:BuzzWebServices_Port">
  <soap:binding style="rpc" transport="http://schemas.xmlsoap.org/soap/http" />
```

```
<operation name="currentList">
   <soap:operation soapAction="urn:jspbuzz.services" />
   <input>
        <soap:body use="encoded" namespace="urn:jspbuzz.services"
                 encodingStyle="http://schemas.xmlsoap.org/soap/encoding/" />
   </input>
   <output>
        <soap:body use="encoded" namespace="urn:jspbuzz.services"
                 encodingStyle="http://schemas.xmlsoap.org/soap/encoding/" />
   </output>
</operation>
```

Let's examine the binding from another angle: The binding element takes the abstract messaging information required for the Web service and produces a real physical transport model to handle the Web service messages.

Typically, SOAP is used as the framework within which to transport a Web service method.

The first step is to create the binding and attach a `portType` to the binding:

```
<binding name="BuzzList_Binding" type="tns:BuzzWebServices_Port">
```

By attaching a `portType` to the binding, the WSDL document defines the messages the service will place within the message transport framework.

The next step is attaching SOAP as the means of message transport. Because we are using SOAP, the `soap:binding` element is a required element:

```
<soap:binding style="rpc" transport="http://schemas.xmlsoap.org/soap/http" />
```

The `transport` attribute indicates the protocol to use, in this case HTTP.

The next step is to define the layout of the SOAP message:

```
<operation name="currentList">
   <soap:operation soapAction="urn:jspbuzz.services" />
   <input>
        <soap:body use="encoded" namespace="urn:jspbuzz.services"
                 encodingStyle="http://schemas.xmlsoap.org/soap/encoding/" />
   </input>
```

We will create an entry to match each Web service message that has to be embedded within the SOAP message. Each operation defined within the WSDL file has a matching `soap:operation` element. For the `soap:operation` element, the `soapAction` attribute is the HTTP header the client sends when invoking the service. In our example, we have defined our service to have the action of `urn:jspbuzz.services`.

The message the Web service expects to receive to initiate this method is defined by the `input` block. The message the Web service sends is defined by the `output` element.

The `service` Element

The last piece of the puzzle is the `service` element. This element is used to define the Web service at a high level. Briefly, it contains the data informing the world of the location of the Web service server.

In this example, the whole `service` element appears as follows:

```
<service name="BuzzWebServices">
     <port name="BuzzWebPort" binding="tns:BuzzList_Binding">
          <soap:address
           location="http:/localhost:8080/soap/servlet/rpcrouter" />
     </port>
</service>
```

The first step is to create the `service` element:

```
<service name="BuzzWebServices">
```

The service name should match to the name defined in the definitions element. The purpose of the `service` element is to group related ports together. Each port will be mapped to a defined binding within the WSDL document. For our example, we have only one port, with a location of `http:/localhost:8080/soap/servlet/rpcrouter`. In addition, this port maps to the binding element with the `id` of `BuzzList_Binding`:

```
     <port name="BuzzWebPort" binding="tns:BuzzList_Binding">
          <soap:address
           location="http:/localhost:8080/soap/servlet/rpcrouter" />
```

For clarification purposes, WSDL defines a port to be a network endpoint—in other words, a Web service server. A port can only have one address, and a port only really defines the address information.

WSDL Implementation File

It is possible to split a WSDL file into two separate files—an interface file and an implementation file. The interface file would contain the binding information, while the implementation file would refer back to an appropriate implementation file and define the service information. The purpose of using two files is to permit some separation of logical definitions.

What we created in Listing 14.9 is a combination of both; the majority of examples you will see on the Web currently merge both files into a single implementation file. Some automatic tools will probably generate both files as a standard method of file creation. It doesn't make much difference for our purposes whether to use one or two files. In fact, it's a little simpler to manually create both as a single file.

For me, building a WSDL file is a pain, and I would rather just build it all in one shot. However, when using an automated tool, I would prefer to have the tool generate both WSDL files if that's an option.

WSDL Documentation

The specifications for the WSDL files can be found at `http://www.w3.org/TR/wsdl`. This particular set of documentation is confusing, as it's 100% technical, very concise, and doesn't explain in detail what is happening within the WSDL document. Be warned—go in fully awake along with several extra cups of coffee when tackling this documentation. Another good resource on WSDL is the IBM site at `http://www-106.ibm.com/developerworks/webservices/`. When at the IBM site, just search on the term WSDL and quite a few documents will turn up to help explain the mysteries of WSDL.

Registering Within UDDI

UDDI is a directory that enables businesses to list themselves on the Internet. More importantly, it is possible to register our WSDL file within a UDDI registry. This permits other programmers and projects to find our code.

Several UDDI registries exist on the Internet. The two biggest registries are supported by IBM and Microsoft. IBM's registry is located at `http://www-3.ibm.com/services/uddi/`. The Microsoft version of the registry is found at `http://uddi.microsoft.com/default.aspx`. It doesn't make a difference which UDDI registry you use. They both replicate data between each other. However, an account on one registry won't let you edit data entered from the other system. Therefore, in practice you should only use one of the two registries.

The UDDI registries are still relatively new. As a result, they are awkward to use. These registries are improving with time, but they have a long way to go before they're polished enough to be really user-friendly.

It should be noted that it is possible to create your own private UDDI registry. We will only examine the public UDDI registries.

Registering a Service

In order to register the service, the first step is to create an account. Creating an account is straightforward and a simple matter of following the provided instructions on the Web site. You won't create an account in this chapter, as we aren't registering any services. I have already registered the JSPBuzz service within the UDDI registry, and will show the highlights of registering the actual service. If you are interested in testing and have a service, then you can visit the test registry, located at `https://www-3.ibm.com/services/uddi/testregistry/protect/registry.html`. Keep in mind that to register a service, your Web service must be available over the Internet and not a Web service running off of your localhost server, as in this example.

Note that once a Web service is registered, it takes a few hours before it will be accessible through an automated search. When the JSPBuzz service was registered, I could see and view the entry right away. However, it took a day before the entry became viewable through third-party query tools.

I personally found the Microsoft setup screens to be less confusing than the IBM UDDI screens. Both systems pretty much do the same thing; it's more a question of layout. Because it's possible to show the same information with fewer screenshots, the Microsoft system is used here to demonstrate the creation of a UDDI registry.

NOTE

These systems are changing constantly, so some of these steps might have changed since this book was written.

To use either the Microsoft or the IBM system, the first step is to create an account.

For the Microsoft system, create a Passport account. If you already have a Passport account, the system will log you in automatically. If you have access to more than one account (as is the case for some developers), be careful that you are using the proper one. Once you have created your Passport account, you will need to accept the terms of the agreement. Then you will have to register your company within the UDDI system. Once all of these steps are done, you can register the Web service. To do so, find the Administer option. The Administer screens are the section where Web service registration occurs. In the Administer screen you will select the Add a New tModel option. *tModel* is the term used to describe the UDDI entry that represents the Web service.

The next step is to create the actual Web service and indicate the location of the WSDL document (see Figure 14.1).

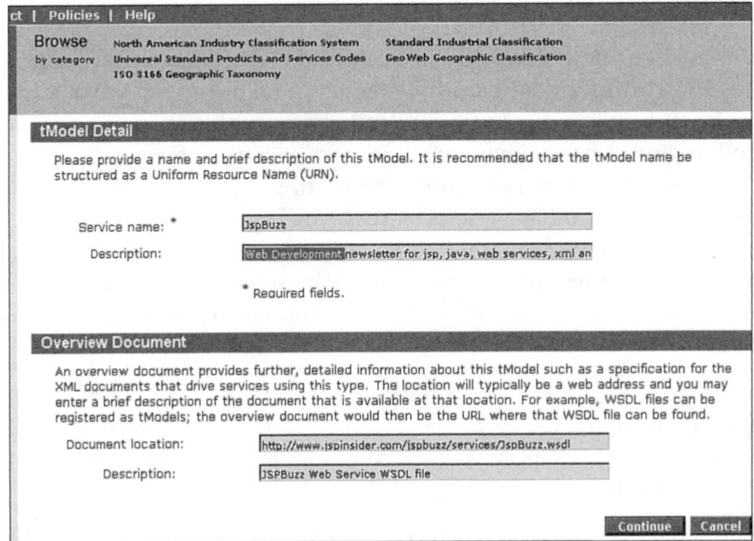

FIGURE 14.1 Registering a Web service tModel within Microsoft UDDI.

The data entered is very straightforward. We enter the service name, the location of the WSDL file, and two descriptions.

The next step is to identify some additional reference data to describe the service (see Figure 14.2).

These entries will permit you to enter various standard codes that match to your Web service. The goal is to help search engines querying the UDDI locate your Web service easily. The problem comes from the fact that finding a code that maps closely to your service can be a chore.

In the case of the JSPBuzz Web service, a single location code to indicate Washington state and three computer codes were selected as the closest match to the JSPBuzz (see Figure 14.3).

There isn't very much to do in registering the Web service. Overall, registering with the UDDI directory is a simple process. After the UDDI server validates your entry, it will become available to grab electronically. We are not going to build a Web page to query the UDDI registries, but it's possible. Many commercial software packages offer this capability.

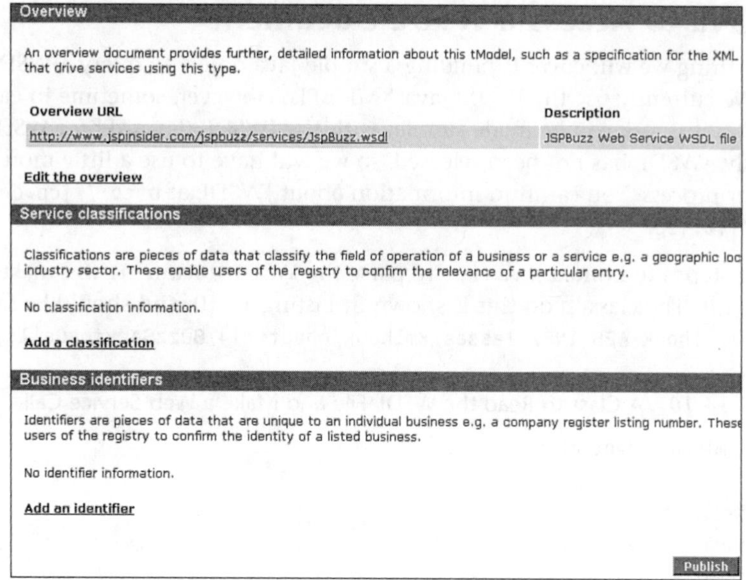

FIGURE 14.2 Adding information for your Web service within Microsoft UDDI.

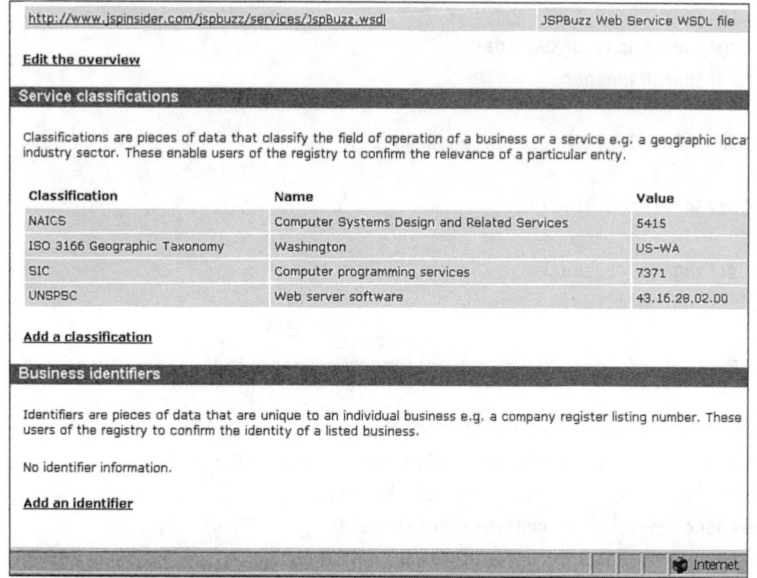

FIGURE 14.3 Codes used to describe the JSPBuzz Web service.

Using Java to Access a WSDL Document

The last thing we will cover is building a simple Java object to query a WSDL document. We currently use the JDOM Java XML APIs. However, sometime in early- to mid-2002, this task will be made simpler with the JWSDL (Java API for WSDL) API. Currently, JWSDL has not been released, so we will have to use a little more sweat to build our process. You can find information about JWSDL at `http://jcp.org/jsr/detail/110.jsp`.

The first step is to build a Java class to parse the WSDL document and make the Web service calls. The class to do this is shown in Listing 14.10, and should be saved as `webapps/xmlbook/WEB-INF/classes/xmlbook/chapter14/BuzzServiceCall.java`.

LISTING 14.10 A Class to Read the WSDL File and Make a Web Service Call

```
package xmlbook.chapter14;

import java.net.URL;
import java.util.Vector;
import javax.servlet.http.HttpSession;
import org.apache.soap.*;
import org.apache.soap.rpc.*;
import org.jdom.Document;
import org.jdom.Element;
import org.jdom.input.SAXBuilder;
import org.jdom.Namespace;

public class BuzzServiceCall extends Object
{
public BuzzServiceCall() {}

private String serviceserver = "";
private String objecturi     = "";

public  BuzzServiceCall(String as_url) throws Exception
{ try
  { SAXBuilder builder = new SAXBuilder();
    Document   doc     = builder.build(new URL(as_url));
    Element    root    = doc.getRootElement();
    Namespace  nsr     = root.getNamespace();
    Namespace  ns_soap = root.getNamespace("soap");
```

LISTING 14.10 Continued

```
    serviceserver = root.getChild("service",nsr)
                        .getChild("port",nsr)
                        .getChild("address",ns_soap)
                        .getAttribute("location").getValue();

    objecturi =  root.getChild("binding",nsr)
                      .getChild("operation",nsr)
                      .getChild("operation",ns_soap)
                      .getAttribute("soapAction").getValue();
  }
  catch(Exception e){throw e;};
}

private String performCall(Call call) throws Exception
    {   String ls_result = "";
        try
        {   Response resp = call.invoke (new URL (serviceserver), "");
            if (resp.generatedFault())
            {Fault fault=resp.getFault();
             ls_result = " Fault code: " + fault.getFaultCode();
             ls_result = " Fault Description: " +fault.getFaultString();
             throw new Exception(ls_result);
            }
            else
            {Parameter result = resp.getReturnValue();
             ls_result  = result.getValue().toString();
            }
        }
        catch(Exception e){throw e;}

        return ls_result;
    }

public String getBuzz()
    {   String ls_result  = "";
        Call call = new Call();
        call.setTargetObjectURI(objecturi);
        call.setMethodName ("currentList");
        call.setEncodingStyleURI(Constants.NS_URI_SOAP_ENC);
        try{ ls_result = performCall(call);}
        catch(Exception e)
```

LISTING 14.10 Continued

```
        {ls_result = e.toString();}
        return ls_result;
    }
}
```

The Web service code is recycled from previous examples. However, the JDOM code has some new tricks to discuss.

The WSDL file uses namespaces heavily. This means the code must use namespaces when accessing the elements within the XML file representation.

We must first obtain references to the namespaces we will be accessing:

```
Namespace nsr     = root.getNamespace();
```

The method call `root.getNamespace()` will obtain for the code the default namespace. The code will also need to get a handle to the `soap` namespace:

```
Namespace ns_soap = root.getNamespace("soap");
```

After the namespace handles are obtained, we must reference all elements and attributes, using both the name and the namespace:

```
serviceserver = root.getChild("service",nsr)
                    .getChild("port",nsr)
                    .getChild("address",ns_soap)
                    .getAttribute("location").getValue();
```

One fact to remember with namespaces is that if a namespace is not declared, an element inherits the namespace of the parent element.

The JDOM method calls will take this basic format:

```
getChild(element name, namespace)
```

It isn't very hard, but the first few attempts to use namespaces can be a bit confusing, especially because a programmer will forget to reference a namespace and then receive a null, rather than the data. This usually happens when referencing child elements. As stated earlier, a child element inherits a namespace. Newer XML programmers often forget this fact.

Now, let's build a JSP to run the `BuzzServiceCall` class within. Shown in Listing 14.11, the page should be saved as `webapps/xmlbook/chapter14/ValidateService.jsp`.

LISTING 14.11 ValidateService.jsp Used to Validate Web Service

```
<%@ page import="xmlbook.chapter14.*" %>
<html><head><title>Validate Service</title></head><body>
<p> Testing service calls </p>
<% String ls_wsdl = (String)request.getParameter("URL");
   if (ls_wsdl == null)   ls_wsdl = "";
%>
<form action="ValidateService.jsp"  method="post" name="frm_search">
  <table>
  <tr>
      <td>WSDL URL</td>
      <td><input type="text" name="URL" value="<%=ls_wsdl%>" size="75"/></td>
  </tr>
  <tr>
      <td></td>
      <td><input type="submit" name="submit" id="submit"  /></td>
  </tr>
  </table>
</form>
<p> Service Call for currentList method </p>
<%  if (ls_wsdl.length() > 0)
    { BuzzServiceCall bsc = new BuzzServiceCall(ls_wsdl);
      out.print( bsc.getBuzz());
    }
    else {out.print("Enter Buzz WSDL URL");;}
%>
</body>
</html>
```

This page is basic, simply showing that everything is running, so there is nothing worth commenting on. When the code is executed, you'll see the result shown in Figure 14.4.

Again, there's noting exciting, but the page shows the Web service is up and running. It's also a good demonstration of parsing an XML file with namespaces.

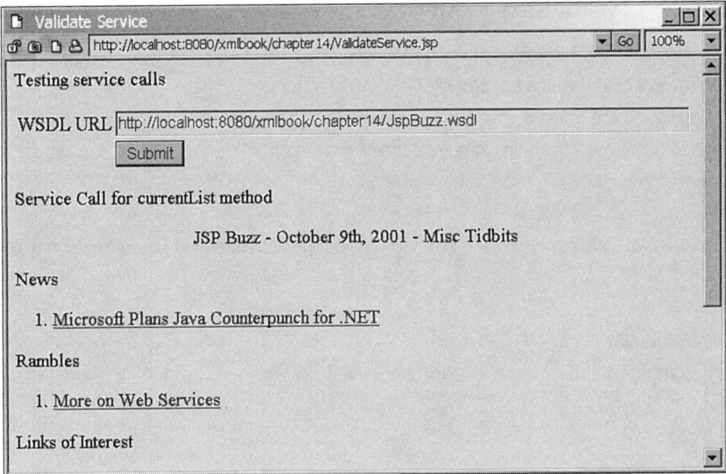

FIGURE 14.4 Running ValidateService.jsp.

Summary

Building a Web service is easy. The complications arise in integrating your Web service with the world. In this respect, Web services are still very new. The tools are still immature, and finding the knowledge can be tricky. All new technologies have this problem, and Web services are still in the early stages. The infrastructure to support Web services is still growing. The good news is that much of the integration will be automated in the future, and tools are now being developed to perform this integration.

15 Advanced Application Design

IN THIS CHAPTER

- Dynamic JSP
- SOAP Server Security Concerns
- Quick Takes

This final chapter will cover two main topics.

The first topic to consider is expanding the traditional boundaries of JSP. The chapter examines Dynamic JSP. In JSP 1.2, XML syntax is introduced to make JSP a 100% XML document. Because JSP is an interpreted language, this means that it's possible to write self-modifying code with the various XML techniques discussed in this book. This section builds an example page that will be dynamically modified depending on changing conditions.

The second application topic is the one of security. This is an extremely important topic at a time when anyone can access and probe our Web applications. As JSP developers, this is something that is a basic part of the construction of a Web application. However, we also need to think about security for our Web services because our Web services are usually hosted on exposed Web servers. For this reason, it makes sense to discuss some basic security techniques. Although these techniques will not be the final word in implementing security, they will form a starting point to begin understanding some security techniques.

Dynamic JSP

Dynamic JSP is a new term. It's so new that there really isn't a generic term for this type of process. The term that best describes this process is "automatic code generation." Personally, I coined the term Dynamic JSP in my previous writings because it's easier to write and makes more sense. Dynamic JSP refers to the ability to change the JSP page programmatically. Because JSP can be interpreted at runtime, any changes made will be compiled and a revised JSP page can then run automatically.

Although it was always possible to create Dynamic JSP pages, in the past it wasn't very practical because the string parsing would be difficult. In practice, this meant only complicated code engines would dynamically modify JSP pages. However, JSP XML syntax changes everything. Using the techniques described earlier in this book makes it easy to work with and change a JSP page programmatically.

Dynamic JSP is not a solution that should be done without thought. Recompiling a JSP page at runtime has a significant overhead in both time and processing requirements. Dynamic JSP has several important areas in which it can be very helpful:

- Building JSP pages, which are only updated occasionally against an XML file or a Web service
- IDE-based automatic code generators for JSP
- Building a site that can literally change itself depending on external conditions

This chapter only covers the first possible use of Dynamic JSP. The other two topics take Dynamic JSP too far away from the book's XML and Web service theme. However, Dynamic JSP does offer us some dramatic improvements for our XML and Web service handling.

In building a JSP page, constantly accessing an XML file or Web service can be very costly in terms of performance. This is especially true when the XML file or the Web service results don't change very often. A better solution is to build an automatic process that accesses your data (XML file or Web service) on a need-to-know basis. This automatic process will rebuild the JSP page to reflect the changed data. Using a solution such as this is incredible. It removes the need of a slow file or Web service access, and the recompilation of the JSP page only happens occasionally.

Now let's run through a simple example. It's possible to build a JSP page to detect when an XML file is placed into a directory. Once this file is detected, the JSP page can read the data from the file and incorporate the data straight into the JSP page. After the JSP page is rebuilt, the XML file is deleted because it's no longer needed by the process. The advantage of this system is the file is only read once. In addition, whereas the page does need recompilation, the recompilation only happens once per XML file reading. This is just one example of how to approach Dynamic JSP: Many other methods exist.

The last example brings up the topic of a trigger. We don't want a JSP page to rebuild itself every time it's called by a user. Instead, we need a *trigger*—something that will cause the Dynamic JSP process to only happen occasionally.

It's possible to build many different kinds of triggers to cause a JSP page to be rewritten. The five most common triggers that will be programmed are

- A scheduled system based on a time increment.
- A file-based system. The trigger is the actual creation of a file.
- An external process. A JSP page or servlet is called manually or automatically, which triggers the actual rebuild process.
- When the application starts, it rebuilds the various JSP pages to be current.
- A data field. Usually this field can be stored within a database, the application data space, or even the JSP page itself.

All these systems are valid as triggers, and the ones to use depend on your project needs. It's possible to combine several triggers together. For example, within this chapter's example, we will combine the first, third, and fifth trigger options.

It should be noted that using application and session starting events is not recommended for Dynamic JSP triggers. Application start events would generally be too infrequent. The goal is to avoid having to restart an application often. When building a trigger on application start, it would be a good idea at the very least to build an external process to supplement the application start event. Using a session start as a trigger tends to be a bit heavy because it means that quite a bit of recompilation will happen—far more than is required in most cases—causing unnecessary extra server load.

When Not to Use Dynamic JSP

Although Dynamic JSP is very powerful, it should be used sparingly for conditions that cannot be solved with traditional approaches. The two conditions in which Dynamic JSP should be *avoided* by a programmer are

- When every call would cause the JSP page to be recreated. This solution will result in very slow Web sites. In addition, other design options are usually better choices in this case.
- When building personalized pages or user-specific pages. Personal pages should be driven by using a database, other external data sources, or simply multiple pages.

Building a Dynamic JSP Example

This example shows you how to build a scheduled system. The goal is to build a page that on a timed basis goes out and calls a Web service to get some data. In this example, we will use the JSP Buzz newsletter service developed in Chapter 14, "Building a Web Service." The example will be a simple application. The page will just display the list results of the JSPBuzz news service, which is nothing special in itself. However, the JSPBuzz only changes once in awhile. It doesn't make sense to call the Web service every time a user requests the page. Instead, we will call the Web service once a day and rebuild our JSP page to contain the data directly. The advantage of this is that we only need to make one Web service call in the morning. In addition, we will set it up so that the page will call automatically.

Our example will use a combination of a scheduled system and an external process for maximum flexibility. This way, the system will automatically refresh itself on a timed basis, but as an administrator, we can run also run another JSP page to manually update the Dynamic JSP page.

The first step is to build our JSP display page. This JSP page must use the new JSP 1.2 XML syntax. This file, shown in Listing 15.1, should be saved as `webapps/xmlbook/chapter15/JSPBuzz.jsp`.

LISTING 15.1 JSPBuzz.jsp

```
<?xml version="1.0" encoding="UTF-8"?>
<jsp:root xmlns:jsp="http://java.sun.com/jsp_1_2" xmlns="">

<jsp:directive.page import="java.util.Calendar" />

<html>
<head><title>Current JSPBuzz</title>

<PageStats LastUpdate="" NextUpdate="" UpdateCycle="1">
    <jsp:scriptlet>Long date = new Long("0");</jsp:scriptlet>
</PageStats>

<jsp:scriptlet>
  <![CDATA[
      long startProcess    = date.longValue();
      Calendar currentDate = Calendar.getInstance();
      long time_accessed = currentDate.getTime().getTime();
      if (startProcess < time_accessed)
      { out.clear();
        RequestDispatcher rd = null;
        rd = application.getRequestDispatcher("/chapter15/RegenerateBuzz.jsp");
        rd.forward(request,response);
      }
  ]]>
</jsp:scriptlet>
```

LISTING 15.1 Continued

```
</head>
<body>
    <div></div>
</body>
</html>
</jsp:root>
```

Let's review the code. The first thing to point out is the fact we do have an XML document, which means that the JSP page in XML syntax must follow the same rules as an XML document. For programmers used to the original JSP syntax, this isn't as easy as it sounds. The original JSP syntax is not well formed, so it takes awhile to get used to the new format.

If you are new to JSP XML syntax, a handy reference is the JSP 1.2 Syntax Card, which can be downloaded at `http://java.sun.com/products/jsp/pdf/card12.pdf`.

The second point to note is that the code listing uses new elements:

```
<PageStats LastUpdate="" NextUpdate="" UpdateCycle="1">
    <jsp:scriptlet>Long date = new Long("0");</jsp:scriptlet>
</PageStats>
```

The `PageStats` element is an arbitrary element, which was created purely for this example. This element serves several important functions within this example.

This first function is that data can be stored within an element. The stored data can be used to communicate back to the Dynamic JSP process or to us as comments. The `LastUpdate` and `NextUpdate` attributes were created to permit the Dynamic JSP process to leave some data starting at when the last update happened and when the next update is scheduled to occur. These two attributes serve no logical coding purpose; they are comments to let the administrator know when the process ran and will run. The other attribute, `UpdateCycle`, will be used to tell the Dynamic JSP process when to set the next update to occur. The logic will be to run the next update *x* number of days after the current run time. This means that in this example the code is set up to run the process once a day.

The other purpose of the `PageStats` element is to act as a bookmark. Our Dynamic JSP process will rebuild the scriptlet within the `PageStats` element. The purpose will be to store a `Long` value indicating when the next update needs to be executed. Now the problem is that several `jsp:scriptlet` blocks are on this page. We need a way to tell our Dynamic JSP process which scriptlet block we want to process. The `PageStats` element serves as a useful reference point for our XML parsing code to find our scriptlet.

The ability to create elements to store data within and to mark code is extremely powerful. In fact, this is one of the reasons Dynamic JSP is very practical and easy to code.

Now let's examine the next scriptlet block:

```
<jsp:scriptlet>
  <![CDATA[
```

Notice that we have the scriptlet code embedded within a `<![CDATA[` block. This is required because our scriptlet code has the < sign. We have to embed the code within the `CDATA` block so Tomcat can successfully parse this JSP XML file. Without the `CDATA` block, the parser would try to interpret the `< time_accessed)` statement as an element.

The overall scriptlet code is simple for our page:

```
long startProcess    = date.longValue();
      Calendar currentDate = Calendar.getInstance();
      long time_accessed = currentDate.getTime().getTime();
```

The code first gets the next update time stored in the previous scriptlet block, and then gets the current time the JSP page is running:

```
if (startProcess < time_accessed)
      { out.clear();
        RequestDispatcher rd = null;
        rd = application.getRequestDispatcher("/chapter15/RegenerateBuzz.jsp");
        rd.forward(request,response);
      }
```

A check is done to see whether it's past the update time. If so, the code clears the buffer and forwards the user to the RegenerateBuzz.jsp page.

When the RegenerateBuzz.jsp page runs, it will store the data of the Web service request between the `<div>` block:

```
<body>
    <div></div>
</body>
```

On a more complicated page, we would assign an `id` attribute to the `<div>` blocks so the Dynamic JSP process could insert the data at the proper place with this page.

The basic logic flow of this page is simple: Check the update time, verify whether it's time to update, and, if so, call the update process.

The next step is to build a separate JSP page that will modify the JSPBuzz.jsp page. This file, shown in Listing 15.2, should be saved as `webapps/xmlbook/chapter15/RegenerateBuzz.jsp`.

LISTING 15.2 RegenerateBuzz.jsp

```
<%@ page import="java.util.Calendar,
                 xmlbook.chapter14.*,
                 java.io.*,
                 java.text.DateFormat,
                 java.util.*,
                 org.jdom.Document,
                 org.jdom.Element,
                 org.jdom.input.SAXBuilder,
                 org.jdom.Namespace,
                 org.jdom.output.XMLOutputter" %>

<%  /* Initialize our information */
    Calendar currentDate = Calendar.getInstance();
    String jsppath       = application.getRealPath("chapter15/JSPBuzz.jsp");

    SAXBuilder builder = new SAXBuilder();
    Document   doc     = builder.build(new File(jsppath));
    Element    root    = doc.getRootElement();
    Namespace  ns_jsp  = root.getNamespace();

    /* update statistics*/
    Element pagestats  = root.getChild("html")
                             .getChild("head")
                             .getChild("PageStats");

    String date = DateFormat.getDateInstance().format(currentDate.getTime());
    pagestats.getAttribute("LastUpdate").setValue(date);

    /* Determine and save next update time*/
    String updateCycle = pagestats.getAttribute("UpdateCycle").getValue();
    if (updateCycle == null) updateCycle = "1";
    int adddays = Integer.parseInt(updateCycle);
    currentDate.add(Calendar.DATE, adddays);
    date = DateFormat.getDateInstance().format(currentDate.getTime());
    pagestats.getAttribute("NextUpdate").setValue(date);
```

LISTING 15.2 Continued

```
    Element timescript = root.getChild("html")
                             .getChild("head")
                             .getChild("PageStats")
                             .getChild("scriptlet",ns_jsp);
    long nexttime = currentDate.getTime().getTime();
    timescript.setText("Long date = new Long(\"" + nexttime + "\");");

    /* Get the current JSPBuzz data and build listing section*/
    String ls_wsdl = "http://localhost:8080/xmlbook/chapter14/JspBuzz.wsdl";
    BuzzServiceCall bsc = new BuzzServiceCall(ls_wsdl);

    Element div = root.getChild("html")
                      .getChild("body")
                      .getChild("div");
    /* remove all old data within the element */
    String      buzz = "<div>" + bsc.getBuzz() + "</div>";
    Document buzzdoc = builder.build(new StringReader(buzz));
    Element buzzroot = buzzdoc.getRootElement();
    div.setText(null);

    List  divcontents = div.getChildren();
    divcontents.addAll(buzzroot.getChildren()) ;

    /* Re write out the JSPBuzz.jsp page*/
    FileOutputStream writejsp = new FileOutputStream(jsppath);
    XMLOutputter    formatxml = new XMLOutputter();
    formatxml.output(doc, writejsp);

    /* reforward the page to display the JSPBuzz.jsp results. */
    out.clear();
    RequestDispatcher rd = null;
    rd = application.getRequestDispatcher("/chapter15/JSPBuzz.jsp");
    rd.forward(request,response);
%>
```

Although this page will be called automatically, it can also be called manually. The example will use JDOM as the XML Java API.

The first step is to initialize our data:

```
Calendar currentDate = Calendar.getInstance();
String jsppath       = application.getRealPath("chapter15/JSPBuzz.jsp");
```

```
    SAXBuilder builder = new SAXBuilder();
    Document   doc     = builder.build(new File(jsppath));
    Element    root    = doc.getRootElement();
    Namespace  ns_jsp  = root.getNamespace();
```

We get the current time and then find our JSP page and read it in as a JDOM `Document` object. Because this JSP page will be using the JSP namespace, we also need to get a handle to the JSP namespace.

The next step is to update our user statistics:

```
Element pagestats  = root.getChild("html")
                         .getChild("head")
                         .getChild("PageStats");

    String date = DateFormat.getDateInstance().format(currentDate.getTime());
    pagestats.getAttribute("LastUpdate").setValue(date);
```

We get a handle to our `PageStats` element and then stash the date of the update within the `LastUpdate` attribute.

The next step determines when the next update is to occur and saves the results back to the `NextUpdate` attribute and the JSP scriptlet:

```
    String updateCycle = pagestats.getAttribute("UpdateCycle").getValue();
    if (updateCycle == null) updateCycle = "1";
    int adddays = Integer.parseInt(updateCycle);
    currentDate.add(Calendar.DATE, adddays);
    date = DateFormat.getDateInstance().format(currentDate.getTime());
    pagestats.getAttribute("NextUpdate").setValue(date);

    Element timescript = root.getChild("html")
                             .getChild("head")
                             .getChild("PageStats")
                             .getChild("scriptlet",ns_jsp);
    long nexttime = currentDate.getTime().getTime();
    timescript.setText("Long date = new Long(\"" + nexttime + "\");");
```

Notice that we are changing the JSP code within the JSPBuzz.jsp page. This opens up all sorts of powerful techniques. In this case, we are easily storing the next update time as a `Long`. After this value is stored in the scriptlet, we can have another scriptlet logically check the time and react accordingly. In the JSPBuzz.jsp pages case, it calls this process.

The next step is to call our actual Web service:

```
/* Get the current JSPBuzz data and build listing section*/
String ls_wsdl = "http://localhost:8080/xmlbook/chapter14/JspBuzz.wsdl";
BuzzServiceCall bsc = new BuzzServiceCall(ls_wsdl);
```

The code then gets a handle to the <div> block:

```
Element div = root.getChild("html")
                 .getChild("body")
                 .getChild("div");
```

Then the code takes the Web service results and translates the data into another JDOM Document object:

```
String      buzz = "<div>" + bsc.getBuzz() + "</div>";
Document buzzdoc = builder.build(new StringReader(buzz));
Element buzzroot = buzzdoc.getRootElement();
```

In creating the Document object, we perform a little prep work. In this case, the code properly enclosed the Web service call results within a <div> block. This was done because the Web service call returned an HTML rather than an XML statement. By adding the <div> blocks, we created a root element for the data so that it was a true XML fragment.

The code then empties out the current JSPBuzz.jsp <div> element with a setText call:

```
div.setText(null);
```

By using setText(null), the entire contents of the <div> block are wiped and emptied of data.

Then we take the data from the Web service call and append it to the JSPBuzz Document object:

```
List  divcontents = div.getChildren();
divcontents.addAll(buzzroot.getChildren()) ;
```

This is accomplished by using the List functions that JDOM exposes.

The last step is to write the data back out. More specifically, the code overwrites the old JSPBuzz.jsp file with the modified one we created in the JSPBuzz Document object:

```
FileOutputStream writejsp = new FileOutputStream(jsppath);
XMLOutputter    formatxml = new XMLOutputter();
formatxml.output(doc, writejsp);
```

```
/* reforward the page to display the JSPBuzz.jsp results. */
out.clear();
RequestDispatcher rd = null;
rd = application.getRequestDispatcher("/chapter15/JSPBuzz.jsp");
rd.forward(request,response);
```

When finished, we forward the request to the JSPBuzz.jsp page. This request will cause the page to be accessed, and the JSP container will recompile the page and show the user the new results.

Using JDOM `setText`

Now what would happen if the code tried to place the result of the JSPBuzz feed directly into the JDOM document using `setText`? The code would look like this:

```
div.setText(bsc.getBuzz());
```

This seems simple enough. If we were to run the page, the result in the JSPBuzz.jsp page would appear as follows:

```
<div>&lt;div&gt;
&lt;p class="12ptBold" align="center"&gt;
JSP Buzz - October 9th, 2001 - Misc Tidbits&lt;/p&gt;
&lt;div class="10ptBold"&gt;News&lt;/div&gt;
&lt;ol&gt;
&lt;li&gt;
etc etc more string data
```

JDOM will treat the string as text data, not as XML elements. This means that all the data is properly encoded to be a text result. This includes converting < to `<` and > to `>`, not a result we desire. When dealing with XML data, we need to be careful. In Java APIs such as JDOM and dom4j, XML fragments are text. We need to convert all XML fragments to `Document` objects and then merge the results.

Running the Example

When this runs, you will see the results shown in Figure 15.1.

Of more interest is how the actual JSP page has changed after the process. Don't forget; we rebuilt the JSP page dynamically. When viewed on the server, the page appears as shown in Listing 15.3.

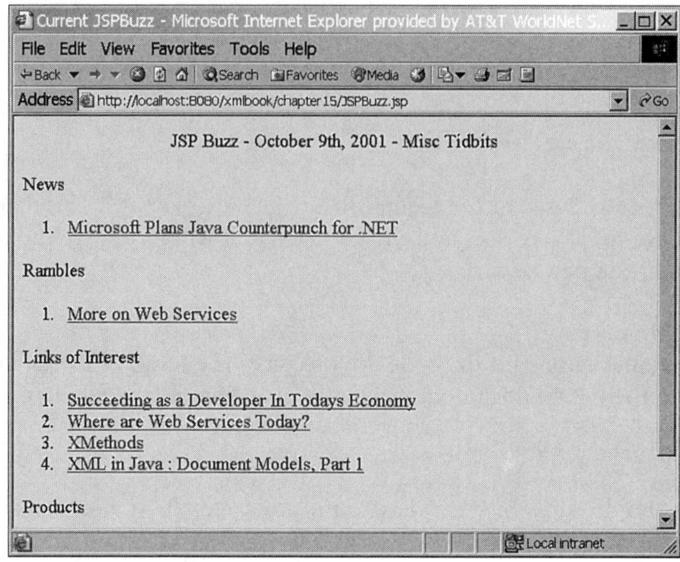

FIGURE 15.1 Running JSPBuzz.jsp.

LISTING 15.3 JSPBuzz.jsp After Being Rebuilt by RegenerateBuzz.jsp

```
<?xml version="1.0" encoding="UTF-8"?>
<jsp:root xmlns:jsp="http://java.sun.com/jsp_1_2" xmlns="">
<jsp:directive.page import="java.util.Calendar" />
<html>
<head><title>Current JSPBuzz</title>

<PageStats LastUpdate="Dec 18, 2001" NextUpdate="Dec 19, 2001" UpdateCycle="1">
    <jsp:scriptlet>Long date = new Long("1008812169641");</jsp:scriptlet>
</PageStats>

<jsp:scriptlet>
  <![CDATA[
      long startProcess    = date.longValue();
      Calendar currentDate = Calendar.getInstance();
      long time_accessed = currentDate.getTime().getTime();
      if (startProcess < time_accessed)
      { out.clear();
        RequestDispatcher rd = null;
        rd = application.getRequestDispatcher("/chapter15/RegenerateBuzz.jsp");
        rd.forward(request,response);
```

LISTING 15.3 Continued

```
      }
  ]]>
</jsp:scriptlet>

</head>
<body>
<div>
<div><p class="12ptBold" align="center">
JSP Buzz - October 9th, 2001 - Misc Tidbits</p>
<div class="10ptBold">News</div>
<ol>
<li><a href="http://www.jspinsider.com/jspbuzz/2001/buzz_10_09_2001.jsp#news1">
Microsoft Plans Java Counterpunch for .NET</a></li></ol>
<div class="10ptBold">Rambles</div>
<ol><li>
<a href="http://www.jspinsider.com/jspbuzz/2001/buzz_10_09_2001.jsp#ramble1">
More on Web Services</a></li></ol>
... more of the same ...
</div>
</div></body></html>
</jsp:root>
```

The sections of code that have changed are marked in bold.

Notice the `PageStats` element. The element shows that the page was last updated on December 18 and will be updated next on December 19.

```
<PageStats LastUpdate="Dec 18, 2001" NextUpdate="Dec 19, 2001" UpdateCycle="1">
    <jsp:scriptlet>Long date = new Long("1008812169641");</jsp:scriptlet>
</PageStats>
```

Also notice that the exact next time the page will be updated is 1008812169641. This `Long` value represents the number of milliseconds after Jan 1, 1970 00:00:00 GMT. Although a bit strange, it's the easiest way to store the time value for checking purposes.

Also notice that the JSPBuzz listing is now part of the JSP page. This is very efficient. Instead of calling a Web service to rebuild this page every time, we now have an optimized JSP page, which just performs one small time check to determine when to create a new page.

This technique can be used in many fashions. For instance, if you had a huge XML file to run, it's now possible to create a JSP batch process to read the data into the JSP page at a low load time. Later in the day, users could see the compiled version during high load times. Or, instead of performing expensive and complicated XML/XSL transforms every single time, we could again run the process once and then show the optimized results. The limits are only based on our imagination in how we can apply this technique to improve a JSP site.

SOAP Server Security Concerns

Setting up a SOAP server also includes setting up security. The SOAP server setup in this book is running as a Web application under Tomcat. As a Web application, our SOAP server will inherit all the potential security risks of a Web site. Unfortunately, the typical default installation of a SOAP server will not be secure, so several levels of security should be added to protect the SOAP server to prevent outside programmers from adding or changing the services on our machine. In these examples, the localhost is being used, which means that security isn't a high risk. However, as a topic, security is glossed over too often. Instead, we will take the time to set up some examples to show how you can add security to the basic SOAP setup. This chapter will set up two forms of security. The first will be to use the security realms. Using realms will permit Tomcat to validate security access relative to a user. The second level of security will be to use servlet filtering to only allow certain IP addresses to access the Apache SOAP administration pages. The other consideration is that the techniques shown here are generic; although being applied to Apache SOAP, they will be easily transferable to Apache Axis, other Java-based SOAP servers, or even a normal JSP site.

Before we go any further, remember that there is no such thing as perfect security. The steps shown here are only the most basic steps to take in securing a SOAP server.

Also remember that this example will be working against the SOAP Web application, not the xmlbook Web application.

Let's start with the easiest security step to take. Because the SOAP server is running through Tomcat in this example, we can use Tomcat to set up a security realm.

Using Tomcat Security Zones

The first step is to update the Tomcat user XML file.

This file, shown in Listing 15.4, should be saved in the `Tomcat` directory as `conf/tomcat-users.xml`.

LISTING 15.4 Updating the tomcat-users.xml File

```
<tomcat-users>
  <user name="soapadministrator" password="mypassword" roles="SoapAdmin" />
</tomcat-users>
```

This step defines the users who exist, the expected password for each user, and the roles each user will be assigned to within the security realm. Keep in mind that usernames and passwords will be case sensitive when trying to log on to the administrative screens.

The next step is to create the actual security zones. These settings are set up in each individual Web application. This is just a matter of modifying the web.xml file stored in `webapps/soap/WEB-INF/web.xml`, as shown in Listing 15.5. (Add the following code after the servlet-mapping.)

LISTING 15.5 Updating the web.xml File

```
<security-constraint>
    <web-resource-collection>
        <web-resource-name>SoapAdmin</web-resource-name>
        <url-pattern>/admin/*</url-pattern>
    </web-resource-collection>
    <auth-constraint>
        <role-name>SoapAdmin</role-name>
    </auth-constraint>
</security-constraint>
<login-config>
    <auth-method>BASIC</auth-method>
    <realm-name> SoapAdmin </realm-name>
</login-config>
```

Restart your server, and some basic security will now be in place.

If we were to access a page in the administrative directory, we would be stopped and prompted for a username and password, as shown in Figure 15.2.

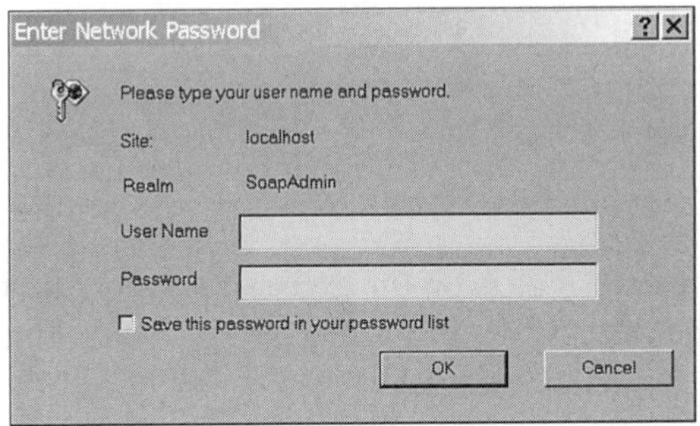

FIGURE 15.2 Basic login.

Servlet Filtering

The chances are that your Web service server will only be administered from a few IP addresses. This fact will permit us to block out any unwanted machine from accessing the SOAP administration tools. This is a perfect use for a servlet filter.

Filters were introduced with the Servlet 2.3 specifications. A filter permits the servlet container to intercept a request for a file or a directory. Here's a brief overview of what is possible with a filter:

- A filter can transform the content of HTTP requests and responses. Whereas a servlet is used to create a new HTTP response, a filter is designed to modify an existing request or response.
- It's possible to create a chain of filters that perform separate steps of pre- or post-processing to a file within a servlet container.
- Upon receiving a request, a filter can examine and modify any part of the request.
- A filter is able to block a request to a file, call the originally requested resource, or throw an exception to indicate there was a problem.

As a brief note, a filter is not a servlet. If you are new to filters and desire to learn more, check out the following filter overview at `http://java.sun.com/products/servlet/Filters.html`.

This example will only build a very simple filter. The filter will intercept any request for files in the admin directory of the Apache SOAP application. When the request comes from an approved IP address, the filter will allow the original page to be served to the administrator. If the request comes from any other IP address, the filter will block the request and transfer control to a Page Not Found error.

Declaring a Filter

A filter is declared and defined within the web.xml file.

Refer to Table 15.1 for the subelements that can be used to fully define a filter.

TABLE 15.1 Servlet Definition

Element	Description
`icon`	Represents a filename used to represent the filter for use within GUI development tools. This element is not required for a filter.
`filter-name`	This is the filter handle. Any references to the filter servlet within the web.xml file will be through this name.
`display-name`	This is a short name intended for display by GUI tools.
`description`	A short description of the servlet.
`filter-class`	The class file representing the filter action.
`init-param`	Contains an initialization parameter to the filter. This element uses subelements of `param-name`, `param-value`, and `description` to define the overall parameter. These parameters are retrieved by the filter with use of the `FilterConfig` interface.

In addition to a filter declaration, the system will need a `filter-mapping` element. This element is used to indicate what resources map to which filter:

```
<filter-mapping>
    <filter-name>a filter</filter-name>
    <url-pattern>a file or path</url-pattern>
</filter-mapping>
```

The `filter-mapping` element only uses the `filter-name` element to match the mapping to a servlet. The `url-pattern` element defines the actual mapping request, which will invoke the given filter. This element represents a directory or a file being matched to the `filter-name` filter. The rules for the `url-pattern` attribute are the same as for servlet mappings. A complete explanation can be found in the "How Servlet Mappings Work" section in Chapter 10, "Using XSL/JSP in Web Site Design." One other element exists within the `filter-mapping` element. Instead of defining a `url-pattern`, it's permissible to use the `servlet-name` element to map the filter to a specific servlet.

Now it's time to create a registration for our filtering example. This is just a matter of modifying the web.xml file stored in `webapps/soap/WEB-INF/web.xml`, as shown in Listing 15.6. (Add the following code before any listener declarations.)

LISTING 15.6 Updating web.xml

```
<filter>
  <filter-name>IPFilter</filter-name>
  <display-name>IPFilter</display-name>
  <description>This Filter will only permit a single
             IP address to maintain the Web services</description>
  <filter-class>xmlbook.chapter15.FilterIP</filter-class>
  <init-param>
        <param-name>IP</param-name>
        <param-value>192.168.1.30</param-value>
  </init-param>
  <init-param>
        <param-name>IP2</param-name>
        <param-value>127.0.0.1</param-value>
  </init-param>
</filter>

<filter-mapping>
   <filter-name>IPFilter</filter-name>
   <url-pattern>/admin/*</url-pattern>
</filter-mapping>
```

The first point to note is that the filter elements must be defined within Tomcat before the listener elements. Tomcat enforces the order of the elements to match the element order defined within the web-app_2_3.dtd specification. This brings up the second point. Apache SOAP was written under the Servlet 2.2 specification. We are coding to Servlets 2.3. Thus, you must make sure to update the web.xml file to use the Servlet 2.3 specification DTD as follows:

```
<!DOCTYPE web-app
  PUBLIC "-//Sun Microsystems, Inc.//DTD Web Application 2.3//EN"
  "http://java.sun.com/j2ee/dtds/web-app_2_3.dtd">
```

You will also have to modify Listing 15.6 for your own use. The following entry needs to be modified:

```
<param-value>192.168.1.30</param-value>
```

You will need to change this entry to match the IP of the machine from which you want to administer the SOAP server.

Creating a Filter

The first programming fact to know about filters is that they must implement the `javax.servlet.Filter` interface.

Creating the filter is an interesting process. The actual filter is only a single step of a larger process. From a design viewpoint, a filter should only perform a single action. When multiple actions are required, build multiple filters. Our process is a single step of blocking unwanted IP addresses, so there will only be one filter. However, as a programmer you might see the need for additional security steps. If this is the case, expand the process by adding filters rather than extending the one filter presented here for the IP blocking.

The file in Listing 15.7 should be saved to `webapps/soap/WEB-INF/classes/xmlbook/chapter15/FilterIP.java`.

LISTING 15.7 A Security Filter

```
package xmlbook.chapter15;

import java.io.PrintWriter;
import java.util.Enumeration;
import javax.servlet.*;
import javax.servlet.http.*;
import javax.servlet.http.HttpServletResponse;

public class FilterIP implements Filter {

private FilterConfig config  = null;

public void init(FilterConfig fc) throws ServletException
{ config = fc;}

public void doFilter(ServletRequest request, ServletResponse response,
                     FilterChain chain)
                     throws java.io.IOException, javax.servlet.ServletException
{       Enumeration IPlist  = config.getInitParameterNames();
        String incomingIP   = request.getRemoteAddr().trim();
        boolean processpage = false;

        while (IPlist.hasMoreElements())
        { String IP = config.getInitParameter((String) IPlist.nextElement());
          if (IP.equals(incomingIP))
          { processpage = true;
            break;
```

LISTING 15.7 Continued

```
          }
        }

        if (processpage)
        {   chain.doFilter(request,response);}
        else
        {   ServletContext application = config.getServletContext();
            application.log("Unauthorize access attempt from:" + incomingIP);
            if (response instanceof HttpServletResponse)
            { int notfound = HttpServletResponse.SC_NOT_FOUND;
              ((HttpServletResponse)response).sendError(notfound);
            }
            else
            {PrintWriter out = response.getWriter();
             out.print("No Page To Access");
            }
        }
}

public void destroy() { config = null;}
}
```

A review of the filter shows us some interesting features. The first is that all filters must implement the `Filter` interface. Then notice that the initialization parameters and the `ServletContext` are received from the `FilterConfig` object obtained in the `init` method. To make access easy, the data will be stored in a private `FilterConfig` object for access within the main `doFilter` method.

Now all the magic happens within the `doFilter` method. The first thing to notice is this method is not passed the more familiar `HttpServletRequest` and `HttpServletResponse` objects. This means that when we need to perform some special HTTP processing, some extra casting of the variables will be required by our code. For example, if we block a user in this filter, we want the server to return a Page Not Found error. This would entail using the `sendError` method of the `HttpServletResponse` object. However, to do so, the code needs to be written as follows:

```
if (response instanceof HttpServletResponse)
            { int notfound = HttpServletResponse.SC_NOT_FOUND;
              ((HttpServletResponse)response).sendError(notfound);
            }
```

In case we can't perform the casting of the `HttpServletResponse`, we perform a more traditional error message:

```
else
            {PrintWriter out = response.getWriter();
             out.print("No Page To Access");
            }
```

Why return a 404 error (Page Not Found)? The reason is simple. When dealing with *unauthorized* access, the error should give as little information as possible to the trespasser. If we were to return an unauthorized-access error, the error would be telling a trespasser that the page exists. However, if we return a 404 error, it helps to obscure the server setup to a larger degree. Security by obscurity isn't security in itself; however, obscurity when tied to actual security measures does strengthen the existing security measures.

The actual security check within the filter logic is simple:

```
boolean processpage = false;

while (IPlist.hasMoreElements())
{ String IP = config.getInitParameter((String) IPlist.nextElement());
  if (IP.equals(incomingIP))
  { processpage = true;
    break;
  }
}
```

The code loops through all the IP addresses sent in as parameters to the filter from the web.xml file. If any of these parameters matches the requesting IP address, the page is permitted to run as normal:

```
if (processpage)
{   chain.doFilter(request,response);}
```

The `chain.doFilter()` call merely tells the system to process all other filters and the requested resource. To not process the page, all we need to do is not call the `doFilter()` method.

Running this code isn't very exciting. When your IP address is allowed access, the pages will show up as normal. When an IP is blocked, the user will only see a 404 error.

Other Apache SOAP–Specific Security Steps

In using Apache SOAP, you should take additional security measures. One easy measure is to remove or rebuild the index.html page at the root. This page isn't needed by the SOAP server, and it exposes too much information about your SOAP server.

The next step is to plug the remote deployment security hole discussed in Chapter 8, "Integrating JSP and Web Services." We don't want outside users to be able to deploy services remotely through the `ServiceManagerClient` class. To plug this security hole, a special SOAP server configuration file needs to be created in the system.

> **NOTE**
>
> This fix is not implemented in the May 30, 2001, release of version 2.2. This means that to implement this version of the security patch, you will have to upgrade to version 2.3 if it has been released by the time you read this. Otherwise, you will have to download and install one of the newer nightly builds of 2.2, which have been updated to solve this security problem.

The first step is to modify the web.xml file stored in `webapps/soap/WEB-INF/web.xml` as shown in Listing 15.8.

LISTING 15.8 Updating web.xml to Turn Off Remote Service Deployment

```
<servlet>
  <servlet-name>rpcrouter</servlet-name>
  <display-name>Apache-SOAP RPC Router</display-name>
  <description>no description</description>
  <servlet-class>org.apache.soap.server.http.RPCRouterServlet</servlet-class>
  <init-param>
    <param-name>faultListener</param-name>
    <param-value>org.apache.soap.server.DOMFaultListener</param-value>
  </init-param>
  <init-param>
        <param-name>ConfigFile</param-name>
        <param-value>soap.xml</param-value>
  </init-param>
</servlet>
```

This step adds a new `<init-param>` entry to the `rpcrouter` servlet declaration within the web.xml file. This entry will have a `ConfigFile` parameter. The parameter itself will point to the soap.xml file. This means that we need to create the soap.xml file. Place the soap.xml file shown in Listing 15.9 into the same directory as web.xml.

LISTING 15.9 Creating the soap.xml Initialization File

```
<soapServer>
        <serviceManager>
          <option name="SOAPInterfaceEnabled" value="false" />
        </serviceManager>
        <configManager value="org.apache.soap.server.DefaultConfigManager" >
        </configManager>
</soapServer>
```

The entry of interest is the `SOAPInterfaceEnabled` entry:

```
<option name="SOAPInterfaceEnabled" value="false" />
```

The `value` attribute is a `boolean` to indicate whether remote deployment is on or off. For security reasons, we want it to be off, so we set it to false.

Once you've finished, stop and restart Tomcat.

Note that it's also possible to rebuild the `DefaultConfigManager` so that the code blocks all deploy or undeploy requests. The one advantage is we have a Java open source project in which it's possible to modify the code to our particular needs.

Quick Takes

Before concluding this book, two other topics need to be covered very briefly. We have reviewed and discussed many subjects within this book, but we have still only scratched the surface of the possibilities of using JSP and XML together. This section is geared to help point the reader to other topics of interest in using XML and Web services. This section lists a few resources that will aid you in exploring these new topics.

Web Services—SSL and Data Encryption

The topic of implementing SSL and data encryption within a Web service is beyond the scope of this book. Each of these topics properly done would consist of several healthy-sized chapters.

However, several resources on the Internet exist to help users. For using SSL and Apache SOAP together, two resources that could be of help exist. The first one is a nice beginning article found on the Apache SOAP site at `http://xml.apache.org/soap/docs/install/FAQ_Tomcat_SOAP_SSL.html`. This article will walk a user through setting up Tomcat and Apache SOAP to work together with SSL. The second resource is the soap-user list. Many other programmers are using SSL and SOAP, and unfortunately the combination isn't always a smooth path. For solving problems with SOAP and SSL, visit the soap-user list archive at `http://marc.theaimsgroup.com/?l=soap-user&w=2&r=1&s=SSL&q=b`. In the archive, just type **SSL** as the search parameter. The resulting information will give you a good idea of the problems other users are encountering when setting up and using SSL.

In terms of encryption, the Microsoft MSDN site has an interesting article on the subject. The link can be found at `http://msdn.microsoft.com/library/default.asp?url=/library/en-us/dnaspnet/html/asp09272001.asp`. This article is currently one of the few references to this particular subject. Although it is a good starting point, it has drawbacks. The first one is that the article isn't complete and is merely a starting point for the subject. The second drawback is that the example is written toward .NET and C#. However, it's still a good place to start reading on the subject.

Using Cocoon

The second topic is the concept of expanding JSP in yet another way, using Cocoon. Cocoon is a topic that deserves its own book. From this book's perspective, Cocoon offers a unique way to expand JSP. A Web application serves up data. This data can be in many formats. However, in addition to different destination formats, we have to consider the fact that different servers exist to generate the results. As an example, Cocoon is a Java publishing framework optimized for handling XML files for publication. It's possible for us to integrate Cocoon into our JSP applications.

NOTE

Cocoon can be found at `http://xml.apache.org/cocoon/`.

For questions about using Cocoon, the best place to go is the Cocoon user list. This list can be found at `http://marc.theaimsgroup.com/?l=xml-cocoon-users&r=1&w=2`.

Overall, Cocoon is a very robust project that will not go away. For programmers interested in using XML and XSL to aid in Web publishing, Cocoon is worth examining. Because Cocoon is a servlet-based application, it's possible to get Cocoon and JSP to work together. In setting up, you can get the two tools to work side by side or in conjunction with each other, depending on your needs.

The point is that Cocoon is built specifically for dealing with large sites of XML files. As a result, it has plenty of optimized XML handling for our Web applications to take advantage of. Cocoon ends up being another large tool set to expand our JSP applications into new territories.

Summary

This chapter serves as a source of some old and new ideas. Dynamic JSP introduces a method to automate handling XML and Web services. This automation can be used to great effectiveness in optimizing JSP pages to perform quickly when accessing data that doesn't change often. In some respects, this chapter applies the concept in a manner similar to old batch processes of the mainframe days. However, the idea is far more powerful. Using it as a batch process is only one of many ways that it can be applied effectively in a Web application. Dynamic JSP is a method to create code that can grow with changing conditions.

Next, the chapter covered a basic topic of security. You saw how to implement some security features to help protect a Web service server. Interestingly enough in the discussion, we also talked about servlet filters. Although servlet filters are used for security in this chapter, filters can have other uses with XML.

We hope that you have found this book both useful and informative. Writing a book such as this is an intense process. Many months of sweat, tears, and plain hard work went into this tome. We found for every topic written, there were two other topics we wanted to explore. However, only so much time can be allocated to write a book, so this is the final result. Thank you for reading our book. May your time using XML and Web services in your JSP projects be enjoyable.

PART IV
Appendixes

IN THIS PART

A
Setting Up

IN THIS APPENDIX

- Installing the JSP Environment
- NetBeans
- The MySQL Database Server

In order to run the examples in this book, the environment running on your machine must meet some minimum requirements. You can create such an environment for both Linux and Windows machines. This appendix will explain what needs to be installed and configured for the examples. We will first run through the installation of Apache Tomcat, the JSP container on which all of the examples were tested. Next, we will install NetBeans, an integrated development environment that is useful for the creation of JSPs, Java classes, and other JSP components. Finally, we will install the MySQL database, and create all the tables used in the book examples.

If you already have a JSP container and editor with which to work, we suggest you skip ahead to the database section.

Installing the JSP Environment

Most readers probably have a Java SDK installed on their machines already. This section is for those who still need to install it or who are relatively new to Java.

The Java Software Development Kit (SDK)

The Java SDK is a development kit necessary for writing any Java programs. Made by Sun's JavaSoft division, it contains everything a Java developer needs. This includes software and tools for compiling, debugging, and running applications written using the Java programming language. More specifically, it includes the most common class files, a compiler, a debugger, and a Java Virtual Machine (JVM). If your machine doesn't already have the Java SDK, you can download it along with the documentation from `http://java.sun.com/j2se/`. The site offers versions for Windows, Linux, and Solaris.

All the examples throughout this book use the Java SDK version 1.3.1 build 01.

If you have minimal experience with the Java programming language we recommend that you work through some Java tutorials to gain a better understanding of the language behind JSPs. Sun has a complete set of tutorials at `http://java.sun.com/docs/books/tutorial/`.

If you just need a review of JSPs, check out Appendix B, "Introduction to JSP and How Things Work," after finishing the installations described here.

If you need help compiling a Java program, visit `http://java.sun.com/docs/books/tutorial/getStarted/cupojava/`.

Finally, you might occasionally have more complicated Java questions. The Sun Java forum and the JavaRanch site are two good places to visit and ask a few questions. They are located at `http://forum.java.sun.com/` and `http://www.javaranch.com/`, respectively.

The Tomcat Server

Now that we've gotten what we need for the Java language, it's time to install the JSP container. The Tomcat server is a Web container that controls the execution of JSPs and servlets. Tomcat is the result of one subproject of the larger open source project called Jakarta. Jakarta organizes many different projects that fulfill the goal of providing production-quality server applications developed cooperatively based on the Java platform.

Tomcat is the standard reference JSP and Java servlet container. This means that any JSP code developed in Tomcat should work in any other container that follows the JSP specifications. Usually this is true, but sometimes you will have to modify code from one JSP container to another. This is not a problem with Tomcat, but some other servers don't implement the exact specification.

Tomcat 4.0 supports the Servlet 2.3 and JSP 1.2 specifications. As a pure Java server, it requires a Java runtime environment that was included in the Java SDK that we installed previously.

To install Tomcat, go to `http://jakarta.apache.org/tomcat/`. Under the download menu on the left side, choose binaries. Choose the latest release build of Tomcat. (We are using version 4.0.) Then download and install the appropriate file for your platform.

For more information on how to set up Tomcat, go to the Web site and look at the documentation. `http://jakarta.apache.org/tomcat/tomcat-4.0-doc/RUNNING.txt` describes platform-specific installation issues for all platforms and explains how to start and stop the server.

It is important to review the documentation on how to start up and shut down the Tomcat server for your operating system because there will be times when this is necessary. One of those times is when a new .war file is added to the webapps directory under the Tomcat installation directory.

A .war file is a compressed package of files in some ways similar to a .zip file. When the Tomcat server is stopped and restarted after a new .war file is placed in the webapps directory, Tomcat will automatically expand the file with the directory structure in the file maintained. This is very helpful when installing an entire Web application, and many tools used throughout this book will supply example Web applications in a .war file.

Once you have the Tomcat server installed, make sure it's working as expected. Open a Web browser and type `http://localhost:8080/`. If you don't see a Web page similar to the one in Figure A.1, use the link given for installation issues earlier in this section to fix the problem. While earlier versions of Tomcat required quite a bit of hand-tweaking to install correctly, Tomcat version 4.0 self-installs extremely well. Most users will not have to do anything special on the Tomcat installation.

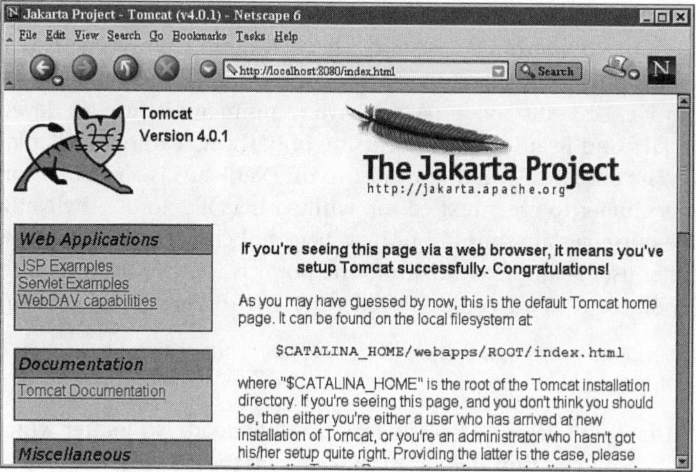

FIGURE A.1 Tomcat server welcome Web page.

Creating a Web Site for the Book

The next step is creating a Web application for the book. In Tomcat 4.0, this will initially be as easy as adding a few directories to the webapps directory found in your Tomcat installation. We named the Web application xmlbook, so we need to create an xmlbook directory under the webapps directory. Then we need to create WEB-INF and META-INF under the xmlbook directory Web application structure as shown in Listing A.1.

LISTING A.1 Directory Structure of xmlbook Web Site

```
webapps
   xmlbook
      chapter1
      META-INF
      WEB-INF
```

Be warned that Tomcat and JSP are case sensitive when referring to filenames. Make sure you have the case correct when referring to and saving files and directories. For users of Unix this won't be a problem, because Unix uses case-sensitive filenames. However, if an example doesn't work because a file isn't found, always check to make sure that you have the case correct in the file- and pathnames.

NetBeans

NetBeans is a free open source integrated development environment (IDE) that is used for developing Java programs. Among other things, this tool can be used to debug, compile, and edit Java programs. We recommend its use for developing and debugging JSPs and Beans. We will be using only those features available in the core download. The choice of whether or not to use NetBeans is a personal one. Some programmers prefer to use a text editor, while others like to use the NetBeans IDE. As authors, we ourselves are split in our own personal choices. One of us uses NetBeans and the other uses a simple text editor. The point is that NetBeans is intended to be a helpful tool. However, if you don't like it, stay with your favorite editing tool.

To install NetBeans, download it from http://www.netbeans.org/downloads.html#builds.

Make sure that you select the latest release to download. No matter which platform you are using, you can find help at http://www.netbeans.org/articles/faqs/installation.html.

The NetBeans interface is shown in Figure A.2.

Notice that on the left-hand side is the NetBeans Explorer. This is where directories will be mounted and used in JSP development. When a directory is mounted, its contents are available to NetBeans for use in executing code. Along the same lines, when the contents of a .jar file are used to execute a JSP, the .jar file must be mounted so that the class files are available. The webapps directory of the Tomcat installation should always be mounted. Through this directory, any JSP in Tomcat can be executed.

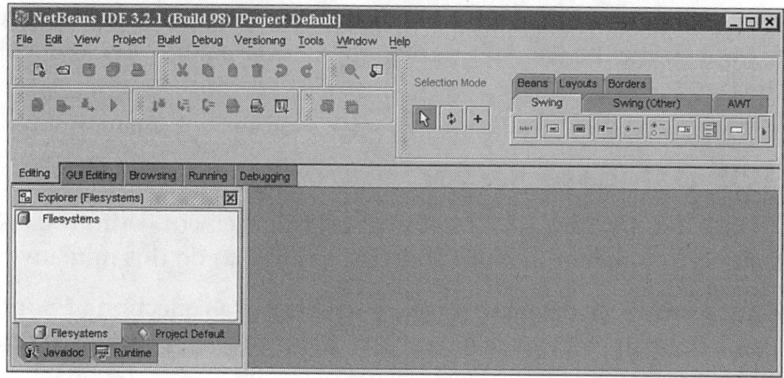

FIGURE A.2 View of NetBeans IDE.

Also notice that there are several tabs located near the top on the left-hand side. These are useful for flipping between different views, such as Running and Editing.

NetBeans has a lot to offer the Java programmer and may take some time to get used to. Many options and properties are available through the mouse menus. Keep exploring and use the very helpful documentation and FAQ found on the NetBeans Web site.

We need to change some configuration options in NetBeans. Go to the Tools menu and select Options. Then click the JSP option and note the properties that are available (see Figure A.3).

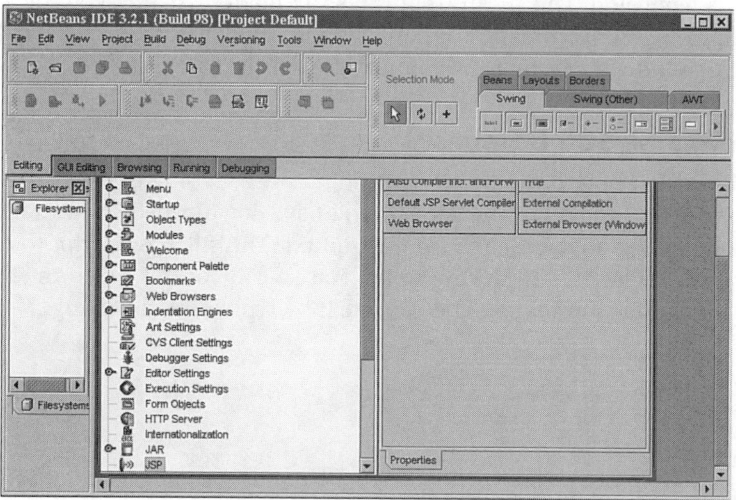

FIGURE A.3 JSP Web browser options in NetBeans IDE.

Change the Web Browser option to the External Browser for the platform you are using. This will enable the JSP output to go to the external browser and will make it easier to use.

The MySQL Database Server

The key to building any Web site is information management. Using a database to store and access information is a fast and efficient way to do this in many cases.

MySQL is an open source database server. A database is a collection of information that is organized in an efficient manner such that data can be quickly returned in response to requests.

To install MySQL, visit `http://www.mysql.com/products/`. Choose the link for the latest stable release of MySQL. This book uses MySQL version 3.23.41.

Scroll down to your platform and download the file. Upon the completion of your download, extract the files and install.

To make sure that the database server is running, go to the `bin` folder of the installation directory using a command prompt. To start the MySQL server, type `mysql` and press Enter.

You should then see some text about accessing help, and the `mysql` command prompt will appear. If you don't see this, use the installation documentation help at `http://mysql.com/doc/I/n/Installing.html`.

It is important to point out that at the end of each command given to the database server is a semicolon. This means that it doesn't matter whether you use a single line or multiple lines for commands. What is important is that the semicolon is used at the end to tell the server that the command is finished.

Creating a MySQL Database

Now that we have our database server running, we are going to create the database and tables used throughout the book. If you have downloaded and extracted our examples, you will find a file named dbscript.txt. This file has a script to create the database and tables used in the examples. Place a copy of this file in the `bin` directory of the MySQL installation and execute it by typing the following:

```
mysql> source dbscript.txt;
```

This script will create three tables within a newly created database named xmlbook. The three tables are as follows:

- BannerAds—Used to hold information for each banner ad used in our examples.
- ReportClientData—Used in Chapters 11–13, this table contains data about each client at our fictitious medical clinic.
- ReportClientAilment—Also used in Chapters 11–13, this table contains data about all the ailments that each client has.

If you don't have the script, use the following directions to create these tables.

To start out, we must create the database to hold the three tables. Type the following at the command prompt to do this:

```
mysql> create database xmlbook;
```

Now that we've created the database, we need to add tables within it to hold data. To do this, use the following command to choose the database that we are using:

```
mysql> use xmlbook;
```

This tells the MySQL server which database the commands that follow refer to. This command will be used each time a command should only be applied to a specific database.

Next, we will create the BannerAds table. Type the following command to create the new table structure:

```
create table BannerAds
(
name varchar(50) not null,
link varchar(255) not null,
linktext varchar(255) not null,
starttext varchar(255) null,
endtext varchar(255) null
);
```

It is not important to have this or any command span multiple lines. If you want another line, press Enter and the continue character sequence (->) will appear.

Next, we will add a primary key to the newly created BannerAds table with the following command:

```
mysql> alter table BannerAds
-> add primary key (name),
-> type=MyISAM;
```

The next table to create is ReportClientData. Create this using the following command:

```
mysql> create table ReportClientData
-> ( RCD_index bigint not null auto_increment,
-> RCD_lname varchar(100) not null,
-> RCD_fname varchar(100) null,
-> RCD_clinic tinyint not null,
-> RCD_dob date not null,
-> RCD_color varchar(8) not null,
-> primary key (RCD_index) );
```

Finally, we will create the ReportClientAilments table. This is done with the following command:

```
mysql> create table ReportClientAilments
-> ( RCA_medicalailment varchar(50) not null,
-> RCA_datefound date not null,
-> RCA_clientID bigint not null,
-> primary key (RCA_clientID, RCA_medicalailment) );
```

At this point, the database is almost ready for the examples in Chapter 1, "Integrating JSP and Data." We've created the database and a table to be used in it, but we haven't installed the JDBC yet. This is the component that will allow our JSPs to issue commands to the MySQL database server, and thus to our xmlbook database.

Now we have to close the MySQL database. This can be done by typing `quit` or `exit` at the command line. Whenever you run an example that requires the database, make sure that MySQL is up and running.

NOTE

You can find GUI interfaces to use with MySQL. About a half dozen exist within the marketplace last time we checked the Internet. You can find one of my favorites for Windows at `http://www.scibit.com/Products/Software/Utils/Mascon.htm`. In this book, this isn't important, as we perform most of our database connectivity through the code.

Installing a JDBC Driver

For MySQL, there is a decent database driver to be found at `http://mmmysql.sourceforge.net/`. Once there, scroll to the bottom of the page and pick the latest driver released that is not in beta. We use the 2.0.6 version here. This file is distributed as a self-extracting .jar file. After you extract the file, make sure to place the file `mm.mysql-2.0.6.jar` (or your version) into the `lib` directory of the Tomcat server installation. Then stop and restart the Tomcat server.

Summary

Now that we've installed the major components necessary to re-create the examples throughout this book, it's time to begin reading. If you are familiar with JSP, we suggest you start at Chapter 2, "Introduction to XML/XSL." Otherwise, begin with the first chapter.

B

Introduction to JSP and How Things Work

IN THIS APPENDIX

- JSP Basics
- JSP Actions, Directives, and Implicit Objects
- A More Robust JSP Example
- Additional Information About JSP

The goal of this appendix is to introduce JSP. Through examples, we will cover the basics of JSP. The goal is not to cover everything about JSP, but rather to give a new programmer enough knowledge to begin using JSP productively. We expect that you already have some basic Java and HTML knowledge.

JSP Basics

JSP is a simple Java-based specification for building dynamic Web sites. As an extension of Java servlets, JSP was designed to simplify the use of servlets. As a result, JSP is optimized to produce character-based output to a client, typically a person using a Web browser.

A new JSP developer needs to know six facts about servlets.

1. JSP is only designed to perform character-based output. When a JSP page becomes a servlet, that servlet is also built to send character-based output. Since XML is 100% character based, we have no need to do binary operations for this book.

2. All JSP pages are automatically compiled into a servlet by the JSP container. As a JSP programmer, the only required knowledge is the JSP code, because the container will take care of the rest.

3. Since JSP is built on top of servlets, the documentation for some of the JSP objects can be found within the servlet documentation. We will indicate when this is the case.

4. One reason JSP programmers eventually write servlets as they get more experienced is that servlets provide the ability to perform filtering on a request and response. Filtering is the ability to add a processing step either before or after the requested resource. For example, we could have our JSP pages output XML only, and have a filter that would apply an XSL stylesheet to that generated XML. The results would then be sent to the requesting client. Filters are part of the Servlet 2.3 specification.

5. Another reason JSP programmers will want to write servlets comes from the use of listeners. A listener is a way to add JSP events to your Java objects. This means that the JSP container can notify your object of events such as when the application starts or ends, or when a user logs on, or one of a few other predefined JSP events. As an example, it is possible to build a listener that is triggered when a JSP application first starts up. Upon startup, an object could create and read initialization XML files for the application. Listeners are part of the Servlet 2.3 specification.

6. Advanced JSP programmers tend to use servlets for nonvisual processing. An example of this would be a controller page. These pages never display a result, but rather redirect traffic to other JSP pages. JSP pages can still be used to perform nonvisual processing; servlets are just a little more robust for this task.

Several chapters of this book explore servlets. In Chapter 7, "Successfully Using JSP and XML in an Application," we build a listener to import an XML initialization file when the application starts. In Chapter 10, "Using XSL/JSP in Web Site Design," we write a servlet to process XML files generically. Finally, in Chapter 15, "Advanced Application Design," we show how to build a security filter. Keep in mind, it is possible that a JSP programmer will never need to directly program a servlet. However, more commonly, as JSP developers get more experienced in JSP, they will learn a few basic tricks with servlets to expand their JSP applications.

Let's look at how JSP works. The best way to do this is by building an example.

JSP Banner Example

JSP lets us use server-side processing to create client-side output. Typically, the output is an HTML page mixed with some client-side JavaScript. You can use and implement JSP pages in many different ways.

As an example, we build a simple text banner rotator (see Listing B.1). This text banner example is modified throughout the book as follows:

- This first example is built purely as a JSP page.
- We make the code reusable by implementing an include file and a JavaBean.

- In Chapter 1, "Integrating JSP and Data," we introduce databases and then show how to access banner information stored in a database.
- In Chapter 5, "Using DOM," we revise the example to work from an XML file.
- In Chapter 7, "Successfully Using JSP and XML in an Application," we create a fully integrated example using XML and a database to store and access the banner data.
- In Chapter 8, "Integrating JSP and Web Services," we make the example into a Web service.
- Finally, in Appendix C, "Tag Library," we show how to build the text banner as a tag library.

Save the file into Tomcat as `webapps/xmlbook/jspappendix/SimpleBanner.jsp`.

LISTING B.1 SimpleBanner.jsp; Inline Java Code Logic

```
<%@page contentType="text/html" %>
<html>
<head><title>Simple Text Banner Example One</title></head>
<body>
A very basic JSP page
<div align="center">
<%@page import = "java.util.Random" %>
<%
String ls_Banners[] = {"Mars","Neptune","Saturn","Jupiter"};
Random l_choose     = new Random();
out.print(" Visit " + ls_Banners[l_choose.nextInt(4)] );
%>
</div>
</body>
</html>
```

When we run this page, we will see something similar to Figure B.1. (The planet name may be different due to the randomizing that occurs in the code.)

Let's begin by going over what is happening to the JSP page. Remember that a JSP page is just server-side code. This code produces the output that is seen by the client. The JSP page appears to be an HTML page with Java code embedded within the page. The JSP page in Listing B.1 is merely a template. Remember, the JSP template is used by the JSP container to build a servlet, and a servlet is a Java class file.

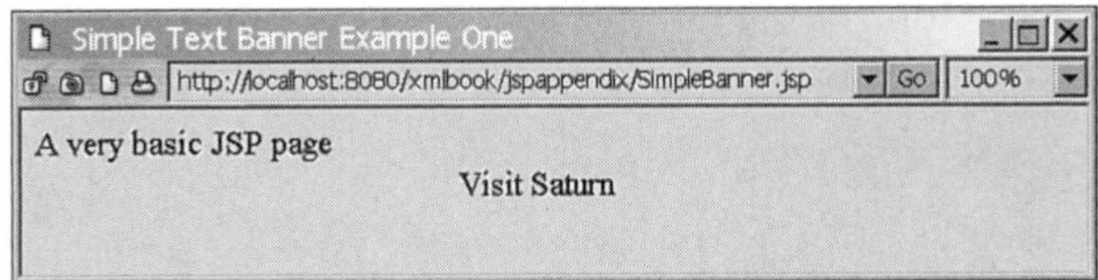

FIGURE B.1 Running SimpleBanner.jsp.

From this perspective, JSP can be considered an easy way to program servlets. Why not use servlets directly? The reason is that JSP is much easier to use and JSP templates retain the majority of the power of servlets. JSP offers a tremendous gain in productivity by offering an easy programming interface to servlets.

Think of a JSP page as a process. The first step in that process is telling the JSP container how we want our page to be set up. This is done through the JSP *directives*. The JSP directives are a way in which the JSP programmer sends messages to the JSP container about the page in which the directive resides. Directives use the format

```
<%@directive name %>
```

The text `directive name` is replaced with information. A directive produces no output, but rather passes information to the JSP container about how the servlet should be built. In our example page we have only one directive, the `page` directive, which looks like this:

```
<%@page contentType="text/html" %>
```

In this case, the page directive is informing the JSP container that this page will be of output type `text/html`. A few of the more common activities the page directive performs are

- declaring the Java import statements (for example, `<%@page import = "java.util.Random" %>`)
- setting up page buffering of the output (for example, `<%@page buffer = "16kb" %>`)
- setting up error handling (for example, `<%@page errorPage="SiteErrorPage.jsp" %>`)

The next part of the process to think about is the HTML tags found in the JSP page. What happens to those tags and text? Looking at our sample page, we can't help but notice that the page looks more like an HTML page than a Java class. (Remember that servlets are Java classes.) The JSP container takes all the HTML and text statements and writes them into the output buffer for us. In Listing B.1 we have the following statement:

```
<html>
```

But the actual code generated looks like this:

```
out.write("<html>\r\n");
```

All text-based code is generated into write statements. How do we tell the JSP container what is Java code and what is text? This is done by using scriptlets to indicate where our Java code resides. A scriptlet looks like this:

```
<% Your code %>
```

Any code contained within the delimiters `<% %>` is sent straight into the servlet to be executed as Java code.

Let's look at another part of Listing B.1:

```
<%
String ls_Banners[] = {"Mars","Neptune","Saturn","Jupiter"};
Random l_choose     = new Random();
out.print(" Visit " + ls_Banners[l_choose.nextInt(4)] );
%>
```

These lines are executed as Java code. In this case, the code just randomly chooses a `String` to display. At this point, you might stop and wonder about `out`. If this is Java, where is the `out` class defined? JSP provides several objects for us to use. These objects are called the *implicit objects* and are always available to use in any JSP page. The `out` implicit object lets us write data to the output stream that goes to the client. In this case, we are printing out the result of the banner string.

Clearly, there is a lot of processing involved in turning the JSP page into a servlet. The nice thing about JSP is that it permits us to use the familiar HTML-style format and mix in our Java code to suit our needs.

Actions

Our earlier simple example covered quite a few JSP basics, but we missed one that needs mentioning at this point: JSP *actions*. In the last example, we showed how to use scriptlets to indicate where the Java code resides. It turns out that JSP prepackages some ready-to-use Java code for us. These prepackaged code elements are called actions. Actions are always written as XML tags and have the following format:

```
<jsp:actionname> </jsp:actionname>
```

An example of an action is `<jsp:useBean>`. This particular action lets us call and create a JavaBean to use on a JSP page. JSP has a few prebuilt actions that will be covered in the next section. The neat thing about actions is that JSP enables us to build our own.

A custom action is also officially known as a JSP tag library. The fact is, by letting us build our own actions, JSP permits us an avenue of unlimited expansion to make efficiently programmed Web applications.

JSP Actions, Directives, and Implicit Objects

This section will cover a few of the common elements and objects used within JSP. Table B.1 shows the standard JSP and JSP XML tag formats of these elements. Table B.2 describes the elements. You might call these pieces the heart of JSP (with design concepts being the soul).

TABLE B.1 Format of JSP Elements

JSP Element	Standard JSP Format	JSP XML Tag Format
JSP comment	`<%-- Your Comment --%>`	N/A
Declaration	`<%! Code %>`	`<jsp:declaration>`
Expression	`<%= a Java expression %>`	`<jsp:expression>`
Forward	`<%jsp:forward page="relative URL" />`	same as standard JSP
Include action	`<jsp:include page="relative URL" flush="boolean"/>`	same as standard JSP
Include directive	`<%@include file="RelativeURL"%>`	`<jsp:directive.include file=""/>`
Page directive	`<%@page %>`	`<jsp:directive.page />`
PlugIn action	`<jsp:plugin><jsp:plugin>`	same as standard JSP
Tag library directive	`<%@taglib uri="" prefix="" %>`	N/A; called in root
UseBean action	`<jsp:useBean />`	same as standard JSP

TABLE B.2 JSP Element Descriptions

JSP Element	Description
JSP comment	Anything within a JSP comment only resides within the JSP page. Everything within the JSP comment is stripped out before the JSP page is created.

TABLE B.2 Continued

JSP Element	Description
Declaration	Declarations are the source of more problems than almost anything in JSP. A declaration may be used to define methods and variables. However, declarations are created within the JSP servlets class body. This means that for all practical purposes a declaration creates a class variable or method that is available across all active instances of a JSP page. If misused, this may in turn create threading and timing problems. We rarely use declarations in this book. This "bad boy" element is mentioned here as a warning to newer JSP developers. Until you understand all the implications of a declaration, do not use it.
Expression	An expression is effectively a shortcut for the `out.print` function. Note that a semicolon (`;`) is not used at the end of the expression. In addition, a JSP expression will automatically convert data results to a `String`. This means that any result of the expression that cannot be formatted as a `String` will cause an error to occur.
Forward	The `forward` command transfers the request of the current JSP page to a new JSP page.
Include action	This action imports a file into a JSP page. The action is processed while the page is executed after a user request of the page. Since this is processed during the request, JSP statements within the include action are evaluated at runtime rather than at compile time. The disadvantage is that the include action is much slower than the `include` directive because all the processing happens every time the page is requested by a user.
Include directive	This directive imports a file into the JSP page at the location of the directive. The include file is placed inline before the page is compiled into the servlet. Since this file is processed before the JSP page's servlet is created, it isn't possible to dynamically modify the `include` directive.
Page directive	This directive defines attributes that affect the processing of the JSP page. These attributes define properties of the JSP page itself.
PlugIn action	This action executes an applet or JavaBean within the JSP page.
Tag library directive	This directive creates a tag library definition for a JSP page to use. It also tells the JSP container which tag library mapping to use relative to the tag library instance called by the JSP page.
UseBean action	This action creates an instance of a JavaBean to be used within a JSP page.

The next important pieces within JSP are the implicit objects (listed and described in Table B.3). These objects are always available to any JSP page. They provide access to the entire JSP application environment and are critical in the day-to-day operations of any JSP page.

TABLE B.3 JSP Implicit Objects

Implicit Object	Description
application	The application implicit object gives access to data and objects, which are stored at a global level of your Web site. A JSP page can also use this object to communicate back to the JSP container. Each Web application within a JSP container has its own application object. This object is based on the javax.servlet.ServletContext class. This class is part of the Servlet specification.
config	This object is used by the servlet container to send information to a servlet during the servlet's initialization. This object isn't used very often by JSP developers. This object is based on the javax.servlet.ServletConfig class. This class is part of the Servlet specification.
exception	This object is used to transfer error messages to a JSP error page. JSP permits us to build specialized error pages to catch errors from any JSP page. The exception object contains the error from a JSP page that has JSP error handling turned on. This object is based on the javax.Lang.Throwable class.
out	This object is used to access the JSP output stream. This typically means using the print function to write data and text to the client. This object is based on the javax.servlet.jsp.JspWriter class.
page	This object is the instance of the current JSP page class. From a Java point of view, page translates into this. This object is based on the javax.lang.Object class.
pageContext	This is a very important object used for JSP pages. It is not commonly used by new JSP programmers, but is used often when building tag libraries. This object contains a reference to all the implicit objects that are listed. It is through this object that tag libraries have access to the JSP page that uses them. Tag libraries can only access the implicit objects using this object. This object is based on the javax.servlet.jsp.PageContext class.
request	The request object is used to gather information about the client request for the JSP page. This object is used to query the post and get values sent within the HTTP request. This object is based on the javax.servlet.ServletRequest class. This class is part of the Servlet specification.
response	This object has methods to aid in sending output to the client. It is not used very often by JSP programmers, as out is the object to use for directly communicating with the client. This object is based on the javax.servlet.ServletResponse class. This class is part of the Servlet specification.

TABLE B.3 Continued

Implicit Object	Description
session	The session object is extremely important within JSP. It provides a way to track information for the duration of a visitor's stay at a JSP application. The session permits us to track users as they use a JSP application. This object is based on the javax.servlet.http.HttpSession class. This class is part of the Servlet specification.

The implicit objects you will get to know extremely well over time are application, out, session, request, and pageContext.

Now that we have quickly reviewed the objects and elements of JSP, let's jump to our next example.

A More Robust JSP Example

The first example was limited, as it only ran on a single page. Let's expand the example a bit and make the code slightly more robust. To do so, we will add the following features to our example:

- Instead of using an array to store the data, we will build a special Java class to store it.
- We will store banner information in the application object, so any page can access the same data.
- We will build an include file that any page can use to display the banner.

Once all of these features are created, we will combine and use them in a separate page to show how it all comes together. Let's start off by building a JavaBean that is a class with the sole purpose of storing banner ad data, as shown in Listing B.2. Save this example as webapps/xmlbook/WEB-INF/classes/xmlbook/jspappendix/BannerAd.java.

LISTING B.2 BannerAd.java; Using a Bean for Logic

```
package xmlbook.jspappendix;
import java.beans.*;

public class BannerAd extends Object implements java.io.Serializable {

    private String name     = "undefined";
    private String link     = "undefined";
```

LISTING B.2 Continued

```
    private String linkText = "undefined";

    public BannerAd() {}

    public BannerAd(String as_name, String as_link, String as_text)
    {setName (as_name) ;
     setLink (as_link) ;
     setLinkText (as_text) ;
    }

    public String getName ()
    {   return name;   }

    public String getLink ()
    {   return link;   }

    public String getLinkText ()
    {   return linkText;   }

    public void setName (String as_data)
    {   name = as_data;    }

    public void setLink (String as_data)
    {   link = as_data;    }

    public void setLinkText (String as_data)
    {   linkText = as_data;    }
}
```

The whole purpose of the code just built is to take in the banner data and store it within the object. The data is stored within the private variables:

```
private String name     = "undefined";
```

The actual data is set and accessed through public methods:

```
    public String getName ()
    {   return name;   }
    public void setName (String as_data)
    {   name = as_data;    }
```

The object also has a convenience constructor method, which will set all the properties at once:

```
public BannerAd(String as_name, String as_link, String as_text)
```

Once we create a `BannerAd` object, we can save the object and retrieve the data easily with the methods within the class.

Once you've written this code, compile it. Also, don't forget to stop and restart Tomcat. This is to permit Tomcat to find and register the newly created class file. In this example, notice that we are saving the Java and class files in the `WEB-INF/classes` directory. By placing our files in this directory, we enable Tomcat to find and use the class files automatically for this particular Web application. While we could store the files anywhere, doing so would necessitate manually modifying the classpath that Tomcat uses to include our classes. Quite honestly, it's simpler to place them in the `WEB-INF/classes` directory and let Tomcat deal with the classpath.

Keep in mind, sometimes Java classes will be built that may be used in more than one Web application. When this is the case, it is better to package your classes into a JAR file (a compressed file that Java can extract automatically). Once you have a JAR file, it becomes easy to deploy it to the `WEB-INF/lib` directory of any Web application. When all the Web applications need to see some classes, move the JAR files to the root Tomcat `lib` directory so that all the Web applications executing on that server will have access to them.

This object happens to also be a simple JavaBean. A JavaBean is a Java object that implements the `Serializable` class and follows a few rules:

1. The object must have a constructor with no arguments.
2. Any property is exposed with a setter and getter method.
3. Getter methods are in the form *`getXYX`*, where *`XYX`* is the first-letter capitalized name of the variable. In our example, the `linkText` property has a getter method of `getLinkText`. The setter methods follow the same rules as the getter methods.

Generally, within a JSP project it's a good idea to place any reusable logic into a JavaBean. The fact that the code is within a reusable package makes Web applications easier to maintain, expand, and document. You might be wondering about JSP tag libraries at this point. Shouldn't we put reusable code in a tag library? The answer is yes, but with the understanding that the tag library built should also use JavaBeans for any of its reusable logic. The only code placed within the actual tag library will be JSP-specific interfacing code. All reusable business logic should still be in a JavaBean.

Let's briefly mention one advantage of using JavaBeans: documentation. Most experienced programmers agree that documenting a JSP project is a hassle. For example, the Java JavaDoc methodology *cannot* be used to document a JSP page. The good news is that JavaDoc *can* be used to document your JavaBeans. If you are using NetBeans, check out the JavaDoc support that is built into the editor. It is a nice feature worth using.

Next, let's build a JSP page to store the banner values in the BannerAd JavaBean built in Listing B.2. Once data is place within the JavaBean, the code will push the JavaBean into memory so that any of our JSP pages can access the data.

This next example, shown in Listing B.3, will be saved as `webapps/xmlbook/jspappendix/BannerStore.jsp`.

LISTING B.3 BannerStore.jsp; JSP Page Using Bean

```
<%@page contentType="text/html"
        import="xmlbook.jspappendix.*"%>
<%
BannerAd banners[] = new BannerAd[4];

banners[0] = new BannerAd("Sun","http://www.sun.com","The Home of Java");
banners[1] = new BannerAd("JSPInsider","http://www.JSPInsider.com","JSP News");
banners[2] = new BannerAd("SAMS","http://www.samspublishing.com","Java books");
banners[3] = new BannerAd("Jakarta","http://jakarta.apache.org/","Kewl Tools");

application.setAttribute("sitebanners",banners);
%>

<html>
<head><title>JSP Page</title></head>
<body>

Validating the data stored in the application object.<br/>
Banners placed in the application space were:<br/><br/>

<%
BannerAd[] testvalues =(BannerAd[]) application.getAttribute("sitebanners");
    for (int i = 0; i < testvalues.length ; i ++)
    {  out.print("<br/>" + testvalues[i].getName()); }
%>

</body>
</html>
```

The code is brief. It creates an array of BannerAd objects and initializes each element of the array with the data to represent a banner:

```
BannerAd banners[] = new BannerAd[4];

banners[0] = new BannerAd("Sun","http://www.sun.com","The Home of Java");
banners[1] = new BannerAd("JSPInsider","http://www.JSPInsider.com","JSP News");
banners[2] = new BannerAd("SAMS","http://www.samspublishing.com","Java books");
banners[3] = new BannerAd("Jakarta","http://jakarta.apache.org/","Kewl Tools");
```

Once the banners are created, the JSP page takes the array of BannerAd objects and stores it in the JSP application object:

```
application.setAttribute("sitebanners",banners);
```

In this case, the code creates an application attribute called sitebanners that contains an array of BannerAd.

Once in the application object, any other JSP page within the same Web application can access this data.

As a quick example, this page pulls the data back out of the application space to show that it is indeed stored properly:

```
<%
BannerAd[] testvalues =(BannerAd[]) application.getAttribute("sitebanners");
    for (int i = 0; i < testvalues.length ; i ++)
    {  out.print("<br/>" + testvalues[i].getName()); }
%>
```

Notice that when an attribute or object is stored in the application object, it's stored as a Java Object. This means that when the code retrieves the object, the object must be "typed" so that it can be returned to its original form:

```
BannerAd[] testvalues =(BannerAd[]) application.getAttribute("sitebanners");
```

Running the page created in Listing B.3 will produce the result shown in Figure B.2. (If NetBeans is the IDE you've chosen to use, make sure to mount the class directory above which the Bean is located. This will clear up any errors that may have occurred in compiling the class within NetBeans.)

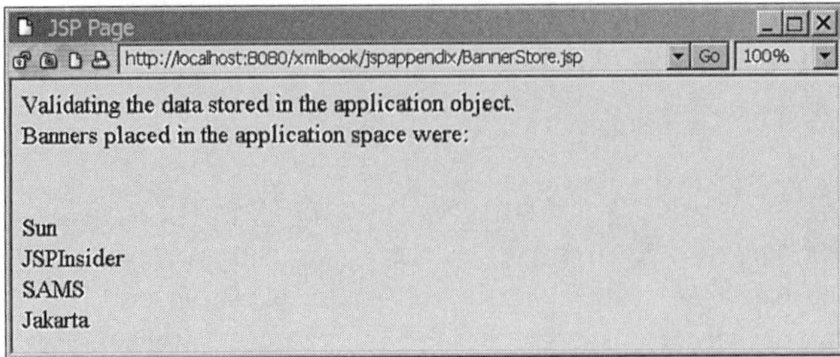

FIGURE B.2 Running BannerStore.jsp from Listing B.3.

The next step is to build an include file. This file will re-access the data that is stored in the application space.

An *include file* is a file that can be reused from JSP page to JSP page. The actual file to be included is inserted at the spot of the include request within the JSP page asking for the file.

We will choose the include directive because it is faster and we don't need the extra flexibility of the include action.

Save Listing B.4 as `webapps/xmlbook/jspappendix/inc_banner1.jsp`.

LISTING B.4 inc_banner1.jsp; Logic in Include File

```
<div align="center">

<%@page import = "java.util.Random,
                  xmlbook.jspappendix.*"%>
<%
BannerAd[] testvalues =(BannerAd[]) application.getAttribute("sitebanners");
    if (testvalues != null)
    {
        Random l_choose = new Random();
        int li_selection = l_choose.nextInt(testvalues.length);

        out.print("<a href=\"" + testvalues[li_selection].getLink());
        out.print("\">" + testvalues[li_selection].getLinkText() + "</a>");
    }
    else
    {
       out.print("<br/> No Banners are Stored in the Application. <br/>");
       out.print("<br/> Execute BannerStore Page to Initialize the System. <br/>");
```

LISTING B.4 Continued

```
    }
%>

</div>
```

Notice that this include file isn't a complete HTML document. Rather, it's a complete standalone piece of an HTML document. It begins and ends with a `div` tag so that it can stand alone as well-formed HTML. In reality, an include file can be any part of a legitimate XML, HTML, or JSP document. Likewise, the code within the file should have no dependencies on code within the host page it's included within. It's a good idea to keep include files as atomic (simple and performing only a single function) as possible. This makes them easier to reuse from page to page. In addition, it makes them easier to maintain.

Imagine the maintenance nightmare that would result if the include file depended on logic or tags being present in each file that included it. Let's say the include file is part of an HTML table, and the file that includes it will build the remainder of the table. A bad include file might look like the following:

```
<td> Mydata 1 is <%= myvalue1 %> </td>
<td> Mydata 2 is <%= myvalue2 %> </td>
<td> Mydata 3 is <%= myvalue3 %> </td>
```

This is a terrible design because it depends on the file using the include file to create the table correctly. In addition, if we need to make any changes to the include file, each file that uses this include file might also have to be changed. This defeats the purpose and usefulness of an include file. Try to keep include files self-sufficient. While a JSP page can depend on an include file, the include file should never depend on the host page.

Generally, reusable code should be placed within tag libraries or JavaBeans. Tag libraries and JavaBeans have three advantages over include files:

1. They are easier to move between projects.
2. They are easier to document.
3. They are easier to maintain.

However, include files are a venerable and accepted way to create reusable code. Most often they are used for building reusable header and footer blocks in a JSP project. With the inclusion of filters in JSP 1.2, we will probably see programmers replace include files with filters. However, old habits are hard to break, so include files will be around for a long time. Just keep in mind that more times than not, they aren't the best option. So now you may be asking, Why use an include file? They are easier to build and faster to implement. So an include file might be great to use in building a quick prototype system. Keep in mind that there are usually several different ways to do almost anything within JSP, but the final choice comes down to what tradeoffs you are willing to make for your implementation choice.

With all this in mind, let's build a page that uses our include file. Listing B.5 shows the code to enter. This page should be saved as `webapps/xmlbook/jspappendix/BannerPageInclude.jsp`.

LISTING B.5 BannerPageInclude.jsp; JSP Using an Include File

```
<%@page contentType="text/html" %>
<html>
<head><title>Using an Include File</title></head>
<body>
A little more complicated JSP Page.

<%@ include file="inc_banner1.jsp" %>


<%--
    <p><b> This line wont show in the final HTML </b></p>
    <!-- HTML comment -->
    <%
    /*just a brief mention on commenting */
    out.print(" this wont show due to the JSP comments!");
    %>
--%>
</body>
</html>
```

Running this page produces the output shown in Figure B.3.

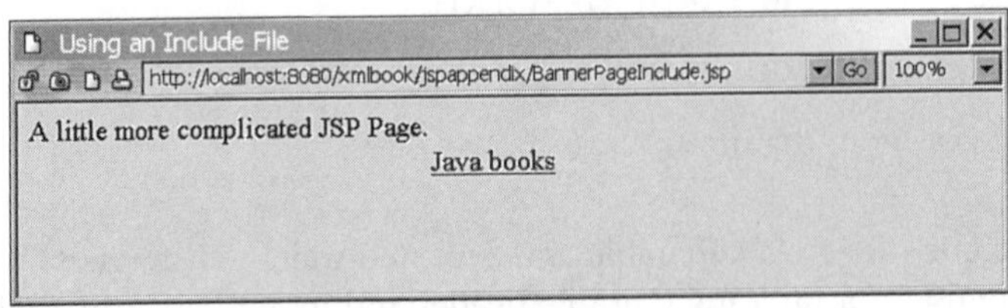

FIGURE B.3 Using an include file.

This example shows that the included file was indeed incorporated into the final page, generating a banner for us. Since the final page was so simple, we added an extra bit about using comments within a JSP page.

JSP allows comments to be expressed in the primary language of the page. Since most people use Java, you can use the standard Java coding comments that look like this:

```
<%
// your comment
/* your comment */
%>
```

Notice that the Java comments happen within the scriptlet. To comment HTML or XML, use the standard HTML comment:

```
<!-- comment here -->
```

However, JSP also adds a special comment known as the JSP comment to the mix. A JSP comment takes the following form:

```
<%--  your comment --%>
```

JSP comments are special. Anything within the JSP comment is excluded from the final servlet that gets generated by the JSP container. This means that not only are code and statements within a JSP comment not executed, they also are never sent down to the client. Java comments also aren't sent to the client, but do exist in the servlet created for the JSP page. JSP comments provide a great way to comment out testing code and code you are trying to debug.

As an example, say you want to test to see whether a problem exists in the include file or the JSP page; we could quickly modify Listing B.5 by just commenting out the include file statement like this:

```
<%-- <%@ include file="inc_banner1.jsp" %> --%>
```

This will let the JSP page run without the include file. Try it and see what happens. The include file step will never happen at all! JSP comments provide a great way to strip out sections of code without actually removing the code.

Additional Information About JSP

This appendix has shown the basics of JSP. Now let's examine a few more JSP-related topics.

What Is JSP and How Does It Work?

JSP provides a layer of abstraction from servlets. JSP is built on servlets and is designed to make it easy for less experienced programmers to create efficient servlet design and composition.

When any client first requests a specific JSP page, it is compiled into a servlet. At this point, the servlet is compiled and executed. The results are then sent back to the client. Once a JSP page has been compiled, any further requests will use the precompiled version. It is also possible to precompile all JSP pages so that no user experiences a compiling delay. The method of precompiling will depend on the servlet container you implement.

The Web container is smart enough to compile a JSP page on a need-only basis. Usually, a JSP page request is handled directly by executing the servlet class that was created from it. Only when a JSP page has changed since the last request for it does the system go through the process of creating a new servlet from that JSP page.

Examine Figure B.4, which demonstrates the detailed life cycle of a JSP page. The diagram illustrates that while a JSP page appears to be a single step to the user, in reality several important things are happening in the background. The most important of these is that a JSP page is compiled into a servlet, as shown at step 3a in the figure.

Figure B.4 demonstrates JSP pages' ability to do advanced processing. Clearly, running a JSP page is a several-step process. It's this layering of steps that permits a great degree of freedom in the creation of the various aspects of Web application projects. Another interesting fact that Figure B.4 points out is the ability to handle and process any user-defined file extension, as shown in section C of the figure. This is important, as it will permit us to create our own special extensions.

For example, say you have the extension .rpt to create and process XML-based reports. Any requested JSP page ending in .rpt can be mapped to a process to handle these reports. We use this capability on the JSP Insider Web site. Whenever a page with a .xml extension is requested, Tomcat automatically applies XSL templates to convert the XML document into a standard HTML page to be sent to the client. We show you how to expand JSP to do this in Chapter 10.

JSP XML Syntax

JSP has two forms of syntax: original blend (standard syntax) and XML syntax. Starting with JSP 1.2, a JSP page can be written entirely as an XML document. This is a great feature as it means we can apply many of the techniques we will use in this book directly to a JSP page. If you are new to JSP, be aware that the standard syntax is still the prevalent style of code for a JSP page. Over time, this will change and programmers will use the XML syntax more often. A programmer cannot mix the two versions of syntax within a single JSP file. Strangely enough, though, an included JSP page does not have to use the same syntax as the JSP page that is including it.

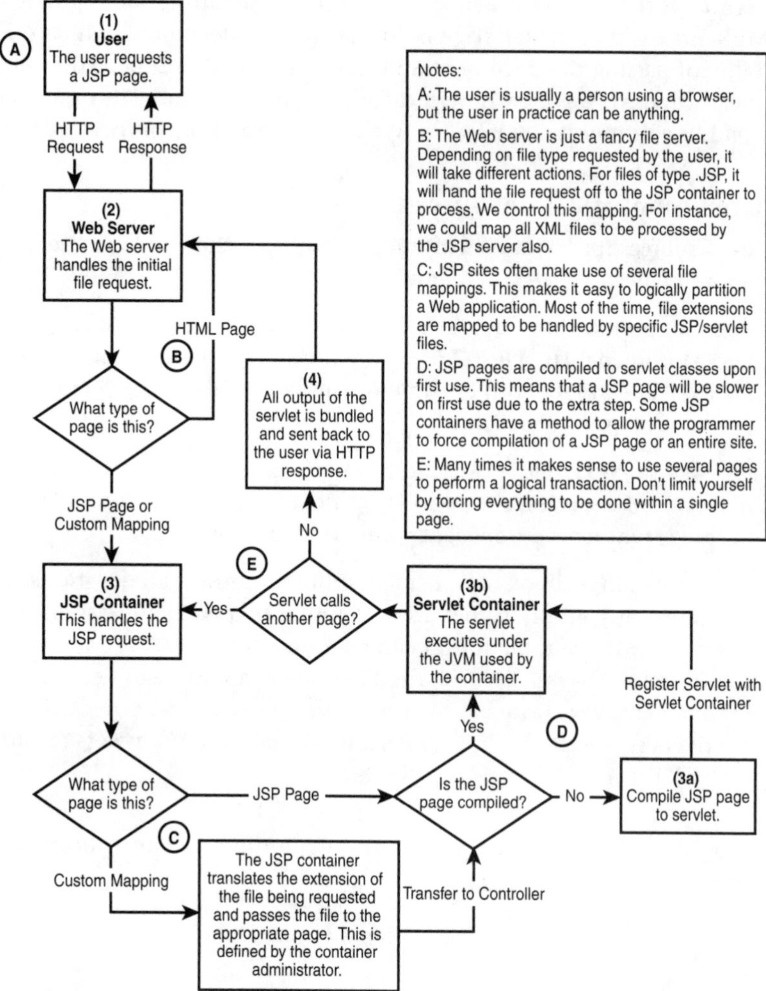

FIGURE B.4 The life cycle of a JSP page.

Does either style have an advantage over the other? Unless there is some special XML processing on a page, it really doesn't make a difference from a processing point of view which style is used within a page. The advantages and disadvantages pertain to the human factor. The advantage of standard syntax is that most JSP developers are used to it already, and most of the documentation is written relative to it. In addition, the standard syntax is easier to hand-code. The disadvantage of the XML syntax is that it is a little more awkward for humans to handle. The advantage of XML syntax is that the JSP page becomes an XML document, which opens up the possibility of parsing the document and modifying it according to the rules of XML. This means that XML syntax is perfect for tools that generate JSP, or for programmatically building or modifying JSP files. We cover an example of this in Chapter 15.

JSP Documentation Resources

The best resources for JSP documentation come from the Sun Web site. All JSP developers should have access to the following resources:

1. The JSP specification document explains how JSP works and is a great JSP reference document. The JSP 1.2 JavaDocs list all the methods and attributes that are available in JSP. Both documents can be found at `http://java.sun.com/products/jsp/download.html`.

2. Likewise, a JSP developer should have access to the servlet specification document and the servlet JavaDocs. These documents can be found at `http://java.sun.com/products/servlet/download.html`.

3. Finally, no single book or document will ever answer all questions. To aid in answering any question that arises, Sun has two excellent resources for developers. First, the Sun JSP forum can be found at `http://forum.java.sun.com/forum.jsp?forum=45`. Second, the JSP ListServ archive can be found at `http://archives.java.sun.com/archives/jsp-interest.html`. These forums are the best place to ask questions and look at others' answers regarding the use of JSP.

Added together, these resources will form the information foundation for any JSP developer.

Summary

In this appendix, we've reviewed some of the basics of JSP. While we haven't given you enough information to make you a full-fledged JSP programmer, we have covered enough basics to help start new programmers on the road to using JSP. Also at this point, you should have enough of an understanding of JSP to use the rest of the book.

C

Tag Library

IN THIS APPENDIX

- Tag Library Overview
- What Is a Tag Library?
- The Six Steps to Building Tag Libraries
- Tag Library Concepts
- Building a Tag Library
- General Notes

Tag libraries are a central feature of JSP. Concisely stated, tag libraries permit the JSP programmer to build reusable code that has a simple interface and is easy to package across many JSP projects. More than any other feature of JSP, tag libraries make JSP stand out from any other Web application solution. This appendix will give you a quick overview of what a tag library is and will walk you through the details of how to build them. However, only a brief taste of tag libraries can be given in an appendix of this size. After you get started here, we recommend that you review the JSP specification (`http://java.sun.com/products/jsp/download.html`), which has a complete and in-depth explanation of how tag libraries work.

In case you are wondering why there is a tag library reference in a JSP XML book, the answer is simple. Tag libraries give us a way to place code in our JSP pages using an XML-compliant interface. We made use of this feature in Chapter 15, "Advanced Application Design."

Tag Library Overview

Tag libraries exist for one reason: to enable the separation of business and presentation logic within a JSP page. All business logic should be placed in JavaBeans, and all presentation logic should be placed in tag libraries.

By using a tag library, the programmer can offer a simple XML-based interface through which anybody may access the tag library.

One way to maintain the separation of the business logic and presentation logic is by using tag libraries to access JavaBeans. Once a tag library is packaged in a JSP project, the XML tags are easy enough to use that non-programmers can use them to access more complicated programming logic.

What Is a Tag Library?

A tag library is a set of *custom actions* that can be invoked on a JSP page using a custom tag. A custom action is a reusable module of code used to perform repeating tasks.

Prior to the widespread use of tag libraries, JavaBean components were used in conjunction with scriptlets for performing what is now tag library processing. The disadvantage, which was stressed previously, is that the lack of separation of business logic and presentation logic made JSP pages difficult to maintain due to their complexity.

According to the JSP 1.2 specification, "A tag library abstracts functionality used by a JSP page by defining a specialized sub language that enables the more natural use of that functionality within JSP pages."[1]

Each tag library is a collection of custom actions. All custom actions compose that "specialized sub language" described in the preceding quotation. Each custom action uses an XML tag to invoke the processing code of the custom action and is composed of two parts:

- Tag handler—This Java class performs the processing required to implement the custom action.
- Tag library descriptor (TLD)—This descriptor primarily defines the XML interface to be used within the JSP pages and matches that XML interface to a tag handler.

In order to use these custom actions or tag libraries in a JSP page, you must declare the tag library directive. This is similar to the Java import statements.

Advantages

Advantages of tag libraries include the following:

1. Tag libraries facilitate faster development. They offer an easy way to modularize and reuse JSP code. All projects can use existing tag libraries, and thus existing code, directly in JSP pages. The XML interface is easy to use, and speeds up the process of building a JSP page by using "plug-and-play" programming.
2. Tag libraries make it easy to move code across projects. They are very portable between JSP applications. A tag library can be packaged as a JAR file and dropped into a project for use. The ability to reuse code from project to project is a major bonus to any JSP developer.

---

[1] *JavaServer Pages specification, p. 105. You can download this document from* `http://java.sun.com/products/jsp/download.html`.

3. Tag libraries permit the expansion of JSP. It's possible to replicate any action of the JSP specification through a tag library. This means that it's possible to expand JSP to do almost anything a project needs. If a better JSP include action is required, you can program your own.

4. Tag libraries help reduce maintenance. In a well-written JSP application, all logic resides in the centralized tag handler and JavaBeans. To update code, only the central files of the tag library need to be altered.

5. Expanding functionality is simple. The layering of logic makes it easy to add features to an existing tag library and have no impact on any of the existing pages using the tag. You can add attributes that introduce new behaviors to a tag while retaining old attributes and behaviors.

   For example, say you have a tag that colors all text blue:

   ```
   <BlueText> My Text </BlueText >
   ```

   Later in the project, you need to choose the shade of blue. Keeping the basic tag as is, we add an attribute called `shade`:

   ```
   <BlueText shade="teal"> My Text </BlueText>
   ```

   All of the old tags will still work as expected, but now we can use the new functionality to choose the shade.

Disadvantages

Tag libraries only have a single disadvantage worth mentioning: They create extra layers of processing. To completely separate presentation logic and business logic through the use of tags, extra layers are added to the process.

The Six Steps to Building Tag Libraries

The actual building of a tag library is a six-step process:

1. Place your business logic into a Java class file. Typically, this means using JavaBeans.

2. Create a tag handler. This Java class file contains the code that implements each tag's functionality.

3. Create a TLD (tag library descriptor) file. This file describes the tag library for the JSP system.

4. Create a distribution file. Tag libraries are portable and generally a programmer will package a tag library for distribution. This is optional.
5. Register the tag library. This step tells the JSP container where to find the TLD file. This can be as easy as dropping a JAR file into the JSP application.
6. Place the tag library on a JSP page.

Let's go through each of these steps, explaining them in greater detail.

Tag Library Concepts

The toughest part of building a tag library is understanding that it's a multiple-step process. Once you understand the overall process, it's easy to concentrate on each of the individual parts needed to build a tag library.

Isolating the Business Logic

To take advantage of the object-oriented nature of Java, reusable code should be placed outside the tag library in independent class containers. These classes are not part of the tag library. Rather, they are the code implemented by the tag library to perform part of the assigned task.

That is not to say that there isn't code within a tag library that executes. There is. It's called a tag handler, and it's a Java class file. But it's specifically written in such a way that only a JSP container can execute this class. For this reason, it is inaccessible to outside applications such as servlets, applets, and client-side Java applications.

Tag libraries are JSP specific. This means that any code within a tag library *cannot* be accessed by other Java applications. Moving the business logic out of the tag and into a JavaBean facilitates reuse of the code by other applications.

The Tag Handler

This is the core of a tag library. This class contains some of the logic needed to perform the tasks required when the tag library is used. This class will reference any outside material it needs, such as JavaBeans, and has access to all the information from your JSP page (through the `pageContext` object). It is this class (tag handler), which is only available through JSP pages, that will bring everything together to perform the tag library's assigned task.

One reason tag libraries are so powerful is that they have access to all the information needed to directly access the JSP page. The tag handler is the object within the tag library that gets access to the JSP page. This means that the tag handler has access to all the implicit objects tied to the JSP page. Any attributes declared within the tag on the JSP page are automatically passed down to the tag handler. Finally, the tag handler has direct access to any text data stored within the element that calls the tag handler.

Another powerful feature of the tag handler is the event framework that ties it back to the JSP page. This means that the tag handler and the JSP page communicate with each other during the processing of the tag element on the JSP page.

Because a tag handler is tied so strongly into JSP, any tag handler class must implement the `javax.servlet.jsp.tagext.Tag` interface. JSP takes the `Tag` interface and extends it to provide extra methods in the `IterationTag` and `BodyTag` interfaces. These three interfaces define the methods within a tag handler that a JSP page will call. In practice, most tag handlers are extended from two helper classes that JSP pages provide: the `TagSupport` class and the `BodyTagSupport` class.

Figure C.1 shows the event framework of a tag handler.

Here are the logical steps of a full-scale tag handler, based on the `BodyTag` interface:

1. The JSP container maintains a pool of existing tag handlers to reuse. If a tag handler doesn't exist yet, the JSP container instatiates a new tag handler object.

2. Any attribute defined in the tag on the JSP page is set. The tag handler is initialized with the JSP page's `pageContext` object.

3. The `doStartTag()` method is invoked when the start of the tag is encountered within the JSP page.

4. The JSP page creates the initial buffer to hold the `BodyContent` object. Note that the body of the tag is *not* evaluated in this step.

5. The `doInitBody()` method provides an opportunity to process the `BodyContent` buffer before the first evaluation of the tag body is placed into the buffer.

6. The JSP container evaluates the body of the tag and then places the data into the `BodyContent` object. If the tag doesn't implement the `BodyTag` interface, the `BodyContent` object is unavailable.

7. The `doAfterBody()` method is called after the JSP page evaluates the body of the tag element. This method permits the programmer to instruct the JSP container to reevaluate the body of the element. This allows tag libraries to perform looping logic. If `doAfterBody()` returns `EVAL_BODY_AGAIN`, the body will be reevaluated. If `doAfterBody()` returns `SKIP_BODY`, the body is skipped and `doEndTag()` will next be called by the system.

8. The method `doEndTag()` is invoked when the closing tag on the page is encountered.

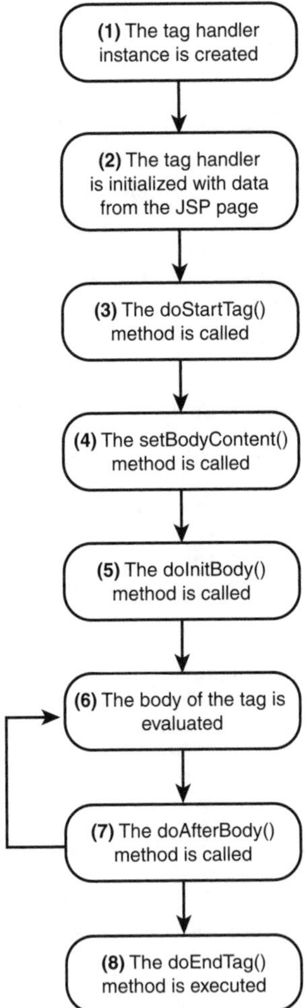

FIGURE C.1 The anatomy of a tag handler.

A couple of additional notes are important at this juncture:

- Most programmers will only place code within the `doStartTag()`, `doAfterBody()`, and `doEndTag()` methods. (Some programmers only put code in the `doStartTag()` method.)
- Typically, the `doStartTag()` method is used for initialization purposes or when dealing with empty tags. The `doAfterBody()` method is useful for building iterating tags. The `doEndTag()` method is where you should place clean-up code or final processes.

The example presented in Figure C.1 shows the processing steps of a fully functional tag handler based on the `BodyTag` interface or inherited from the `BodyTagSupport` class. Simpler tags built on the `TagSupport` class will have neither the `setBodyContent()` method nor the `doInitBody()` method.

It should be noted that the label "tag library" is misleading as it refers to a collection of tag handlers. A custom tag is a single tag handler, while a tag library is a collection of custom tags. However, the term "tag library" has come to mean either a custom tag or a collection of custom tags.

The Tag Library Descriptor (TLD)

A TLD is an XML file that describes a tag library. The data found in this file defines the following:

- The name of the tag library
- Each custom action within that tag library, including its attributes
- Which custom action matches each tag handler
- Documentation

It is through this information that the JSP container uses the TLD file to interpret how to handle each custom action declared on a JSP page.

A TLD file must end with a .tld extension. Usually the TLD file is stored within the `WEB-INF` directory of the JSP Web application.

In a strange sense, the TLD is what creates the "library" part of the tag library because it's here that the index pulls together separate tag handlers, resulting in a library. Later, when this appendix builds a TLD, the index nature of the TLD will become clearer. The TLD file is where all the custom tags are first referenced under a tag library collection name. This is the only place where the actual tag library is defined.

The DTD used to validate and define the TLD file can be found in the JSP specifications (`http://java.sun.com/products/jsp/download.html`).

Creating a Distribution File

Distribution files are not a requirement in building a tag library. However, it is easy to create such files, and it's recommended that you do so if the tag library is going to be packaged for any other Web applications to use.

The steps for creating a distribution files are as follows:

1. Create a JAR file. This is a zip file with a .jar extension.
2. Add the class files necessary for the tag library into the newly created JAR file.
3. Create and add a META-INF directory into the JAR file.
4. Within the META-INF directory, place the TLD file that describes this tag library.

Once the tag library is packaged, it is ready to be distributed into other Web applications. To distribute the packaged tag library, place the JAR file into the destination site's WEB-INF/lib directory. Tomcat requires a stop and restart in order to register the JAR file.

Registering the Tag Library

Once the tag library has been developed, the next step is to register it with the JSP container. This is automatically done when using a distribution JAR file, whose creation was described earlier. The registration instructions that follow will describe registering a tag library by hand, then through the use of a JAR distribution file.

The usual method of registering a tag library is to modify a JSP site's web.xml file found in the WEB-INF directory. Add a <taglib> element such as

```
<taglib>
  <taglib-uri>Your Unique Tag ID</taglib-uri>
  <taglib-location>The relative location of the TLD file</taglib-location>
</taglib>
```

At a minimum, a URI needs to be declared within a <taglib-uri> statement. The URI is a unique identifier that the JSP container will use to match with a tag library through its TLD file. Typically, the URI is a short unique identifier that makes sense for a tag. Sometimes programmers use URLs there, because they are unique.

The other piece of information is the physical location of the tag library TLD file. This information is stored in the <taglib-location> element, and is a relative path from the web.xml file.

After modifying the web.xml file, it's a good idea to restart your JSP container. This permits the JSP container to reinitialize itself with the new information.

The other common method of registering a tag library is through the use of a distribution JAR file. This file is placed in the destination Web site's WEB-INF/lib directory. Once it's installed, restart the JSP container and let the container automatically register the tag library.

While two other methods of registering a tag library exist, the methods mentioned here are the ones used throughout this book.

Using the Tag Library Declaration on a JSP Page

This is as simple as using a `taglib` directive to declare the existence of the tags. After the tag library has been declared on a JSP page, it can be used freely within that page. The `taglib` directive looks like the following:

```
<%@ taglib uri="registered URI" prefix="mytag" %>
```

The `URI` attribute is used to match with the registered URI name of the tag library. The `prefix` attribute is used to give a convenient tag handle to use within the page. For the previous `taglib` statement, any tag starting with the namespace `mytag` will call the "registered URI" tag library.

For instance, the following line of code calls the "hello" tag handler registered in the tag library referenced by the URI associated with the `mytag` prefix.

```
<mytag:hello>
```

In essence we are creating a variable that can be used throughout the JSP page in which it's declared. When this variable is declared, it's associated with a URI through which a tag library is referenced.

Building a Tag Library

Now, let's work through an example, building a tag library for database access. The tag library will take the results from a SQL statement and apply an XSL stylesheet to create formatted output.

Isolating the Business Logic

Chapter 7, "Successfully Using JSP and XML in an Application," produced several JavaBeans used to take a JDBC `ResultSet` and produce an XML output. The JavaBeans used are DatabaseParameter.java, XMLFromResult.java, and ProcessDom4J.java. This section will use these JavaBeans to illustrate how convenient it is to reuse code. Answers to any questions you might have regarding how to use or install these beans can be found in Chapter 7.

Building a Tag Handler

We need to build a new tag handler to access the previously created business logic components. Save the file shown in Listing C.1 as `webapps/xmlbook/WEB-INF/classes/xmlbook/tagappendix/DatabaseResultTag.java`.

LISTING C.1 A Tag Handler to Access and Return Results from a Database

```
package xmlbook.tagappendix;

import javax.servlet.jsp.tagext.*;
import javax.servlet.jsp.*;
import xmlbook.chapter7.*;
import org.dom4j.Document;

public class DatabaseResultTag extends TagSupport
{
    private DatabaseParameter database = null;

        public void setDatabase(DatabaseParameter data)  { database = data; }

        public DatabaseParameter getDatabase()       { return(database ); }

    private String SQL  = null;

        public void setSQL(String as_sql)            { SQL = as_sql; }

        public String getSQL()                       { return(SQL); }

    private String rootName = "Root";

        public void setRootName(String as_data)      { rootName = as_data; }

        public String getRootName()                  { return(rootName); }

    private String rowName = "Row";

        public void setRowName(String as_data)       { rowName = as_data; }

        public String getRowName()                   { return(rowName); }

    private String xsl = "";

        public void setXsl(String as_data)           { xsl = as_data; }

        public String getXsl()                       { return(xsl); }

    private boolean clearBuffer = false;
```

LISTING C.1 Continued

```
        public void setClearBuffer(boolean ab_data)   { clearBuffer = ab_data; }

        public boolean getClearBuffer()               { return(clearBuffer); }

    public int doStartTag() throws JspException
    {

        XMLFromResult result= new XMLFromResult(getRootName(),getRowName());
        JspWriter out = pageContext.getOut();


        try
        {  if (getClearBuffer()) out.clearBuffer();

           String ls_sql = getSQL();
           Document xmldata = result.createXML (getDatabase(), ls_sql);

           ProcessDom4J dealwithxml = new ProcessDom4J();

           if (xsl.length() == 0 || xsl == null)
           {dealwithxml.produceXML(out,xmldata);
           }
           else
           {String  ls_xsl  = pageContext.getServletContext().getRealPath(xsl) ;
            dealwithxml.applyXSL (out,xmldata,ls_xsl);
           }
        }
        catch (Exception e)
        {   try
            {out.print (" <p align=\"center\">" + e.toString() + "</p>");}
            catch (Exception tag_error)
            {throw new JspException(tag_error.toString());}
        }
        return SKIP_BODY;
    }
}
```

If upon compiling this file you run into errors about `org.xml.j4dom` being irresolvable, you need to install dom4j. To do so, download the dom4j files and place the dom4j.jar file into the `lib` directory found at the root of your Tomcat installation. (More specific instructions can be found in Chapter 7.)

Let's review the code in the tag handler. The first thing we see is the name DatabaseResultTag. It's a common practice to append the word Tag to the end of any tag handler class.

This particular tag doesn't need to handle data placed between the opening and closing tags that compose the custom action. The logic can get all the information it needs from the attributes of the custom action element.

The next block of code to review will be the properties. For example:

```
private DatabaseParameter database = null;

        public void setDatabase(DatabaseParameter data)   { database = data; }

        public DatabaseParameter getDatabase()            { return(database ); }
```

Properties are managed automatically by the JSP container. The JSP container manages these properties using the JavaBeans introspection tools to determine and set all properties. This means that all properties exposed for the tag handler must have getter and setter methods using the JavaBean standards. It should be noted that your own code should not use the setter methods, since it is the JSP container's job to maintain these properties. The properties can be of any type, including objects.

If a property is of a type other than String, two other steps will have to occur after the tag handler class is built. First, within the TLD file, any attribute that differs from type String needs an element of <type> in the web.xml file to fully define the expected type of that attribute. Second, when a property will be an object—as this first example is of type DatabaseParameter—the object needs to be passed in with a JSP expression statement (<%= %>). We will illustrate this as we move on in the example.

Remember, in this example we're not worried about the body text of the tag element. This leaves us with a choice to place the code within either the doStartTag() method or the doEndTag() method. In this case there isn't much difference.

If the doEndTag() is chosen, it is possible to halt execution of the JSP page, if necessary. We won't get into that here, but needed to mention that it's possible. However, it's generally bad practice to have the tag halt the processing of a page and is rarely done. Halting a JSP page should generally occur at the JSP page level, where all processes on the page can be stopped cleanly by the governing JSP page. If a tag halts a JSP page, it could cause conflicts with other processes occurring within the parent JSP, which the tag knows nothing about. As a component, a tag library shouldn't know about other processes and should only concentrate on its own process.

In this case, the `doStartTag()` is chosen because we can tell the tag handler to skip any body processing:

```
return SKIP_BODY;
```

In theory, this cuts down on unneeded processing within the tag handler. In a tag where processing of the body occurs, this choice becomes more critical relative to the timing of what's happening in your logic.

The next idea we will cover is the use of the `pageContext` object:

```
JspWriter out = pageContext.getOut();
```

The `pageContext` object can be used to give the tag handler access to all the implicit objects that the calling JSP page has access to at the time of the tag call. In the preceding line of code, we are getting a handle to the `out` implicit object.

Next, the tag handler checks to see whether the user wants the buffer cleared before sending out the XML output:

```
if (getClearBuffer()) out.clearBuffer();
```

Many times when dealing with XML output, whitespace from the JSP page will be introduced before the XML output. Since this tag is built to send XML/XSLT output, it makes sense to clear the output buffer of this whitespace.

The tag handler then takes the attributes sent in from the JSP page and calls the three classes discussed in Chapter 7 to create and output a processed XML document from a database SQL call. The only item of real interest is some work in the `catch` block:

```
catch (Exception e)
{   try
    {out.print (" <p align=\"center\">" + e.toString() + "</p>");}
    catch (Exception tag_error)
    {throw new JspException(tag_error.toString());}
}
```

The code has a `try-catch` block around the `print` statement. The `out.print` logic needs to catch the IO exception if it occurs. On the JSP page the servlet would do this for us. Also notice that the code repackages any exception as a `JspException` to send problems back to the JSP page. We repackage it as a `JspException` because the `doStartTag` already throws the `JspException` class. It's easier just to pass the `JspException` back up the exception food chain.

Overall, the logic here isn't much more difficult to deal with than that of a JavaBean. We have a little more work in the sense that the properties need to be created and the pageContext object queried for data. However, the code here is the intersection between the JSP page and other JavaBeans. As such, the slight amount of extra work is worth the increased functionality that the tag handler permits.

The Tag Library Descriptor

Now that we've created a tag handler, it is time to build a TLD file to define the tag handler for the tag library. The file in Listing C.2 should be saved as webapps/xmlbook/WEB-INF/xmldatabase.tld.

LISTING C.2 A TLD File to Define the XMLDatabase Tag Library

```
<?xml version="1.0" encoding="UTF-8"?>
<!DOCTYPE taglib PUBLIC "-//Sun Microsystems, Inc.//DTD JSP Tag Library 1.2//EN"
                        "http://java.sun.com/dtd/web-jsptaglibrary_1_2.dtd">

<taglib>
    <tlib-version>1.0</tlib-version>
    <jsp-version>1.2</jsp-version>
    <short-name>xmldatabase</short-name>
    <uri>xmlbook.xmldatabase</uri>
    <tag>
        <name>xmlresult</name>
        <tag-class>xmlbook.tagappendix.DatabaseResultTag</tag-class>
        <body-content>empty</body-content>
        <description>Database xml functionality</description>
        <attribute>
            <name>database</name>
            <required>true</required>
            <rtexprvalue>true</rtexprvalue>
            <type>xmlbook.chapter7.DatabaseParameter</type>
            <description>Pass in a Database property object </description>
         </attribute>
        <attribute>
            <name>SQL</name>
            <required>true</required>
            <rtexprvalue>true</rtexprvalue>
            <description>Pass in a Database SQL Statement </description>
        </attribute>
        <attribute>
            <name>rootName</name>
```

LISTING C.2 Continued

```
            <required>false</required>
            <rtexprvalue>true</rtexprvalue>
            <description>Define the root element name </description>
        </attribute>
        <attribute>
            <name>rowName</name>
            <required>false</required>
            <rtexprvalue>true</rtexprvalue>
            <description>Define element name for each row </description>
        </attribute>
        <attribute>
            <name>xsl</name>
            <required>false</required>
            <rtexprvalue>true</rtexprvalue>
            <description>The XSL style sheet to use </description>
        </attribute>
           <attribute>
            <name>clearBuffer</name>
            <required>false</required>
            <rtexprvalue>false</rtexprvalue>
            <type>boolean</type>
            <description>True to clear buffer before output</description>
        </attribute>
    </tag>

</taglib>
```

The first step is to create the actual tag library:

```
<taglib>
    <tlib-version>1.0</tlib-version>
    <jsp-version>1.2</jsp-version>
    <short-name>xmldatabase</short-name>
    <uri>xmlbook.xmldatabase</uri>
```

The tag library is assigned a unique URI and then we add each tag handler the system needs in this tag library:

```
<tag>
        <name>xmlresult</name>
        <tag-class>xmlbook.tagappendix.DatabaseResultTag</tag-class>
```

```
<body-content>empty</body-content>
<description>Database xml functionality</description>
```

The name element contains the name of the custom action. For a tag handler to work, we must define what class is driving the logic in the tag-class element. In this case, we also state that the element body must be empty. This helps the container run the tag more efficiently.

Next, the file defines the attributes that the tag handler needs:

```
<attribute>
    <name>database</name>
    <required>true</required>
    <rtexprvalue>true</rtexprvalue>
    <type>xmlbook.chapter7.DatabaseParameter</type>
    <description>Pass in a Database property object </description>
</attribute>
```

The name of the attribute is logically placed in a name element. The required tag indicates whether the attribute is required when used on the JSP page. In this case we must make sure that a JSP expression (<%= %>) is permitted to send the data into the attribute through the use of the rtexprvalue tag. Correctly defining this specification is very important as we are passing a non-String object through this attribute. The only way to pass in a Java object is to use a JSP expression.

By default, JSP will send attribute data as a String. However, at times it will be more useful to pass in an object. To do so, the attribute value must indicate the object it expects. For our example the attribute type is defined as follows:

```
<type>xmlbook.chapter7.DatabaseParameter</type>
```

We define the attribute as requiring a DatabaseParameter object. Once this attribute is defined, the tag handler will continue by listing the other attributes using the same XML structure.

Registering the Tag Library

Registering the tag library only requires a quick modification to the webapps/xmlbook/WEB-INF/web.xml file. Between the web.xml's root element <web-app> tags add the following:

```
<taglib>
  <taglib-uri>xmlbook.xmldatabase</taglib-uri>
  <taglib-location>/WEB-INF/xmldatabase.tld</taglib-location>
</taglib>
```

The taglib elements are placed after the final servlet-mapping tag within the web.xml file.

Stop and restart Tomcat and use the tag library we just built.

Using the Tag Library on a JSP Page

Listing C.3 shows a sample page using the tag library. Save this file as webapps/xmlbook/tagappendix/TestTag.jsp.

LISTING C.3 Creating a JSP Page to Use a Tag Library

```
<%@page contentType="text/html"
        import="xmlbook.chapter7.*,
                org.dom4j.Document"%>

<%@taglib uri="xmlbook.xmldatabase" prefix="xmldata" %>

<jsp:useBean class="xmlbook.chapter7.DatabaseParameter"
             id   ="DBconn"    scope="page" >
        <jsp:setProperty name="DBconn" property="databaseName"
                         value="xmlbook"/>
        <jsp:setProperty name="DBconn" property="driver"
                         value="org.gjt.mm.mysql.Driver"/>
        <jsp:setProperty name="DBconn" property="url"
                         value="jdbc:mysql://localhost/xmlbook"/>
</jsp:useBean>

<xmldata:xmlresult
 database    ="<%= DBconn %>"
 SQL ="select name as NAME,link as LINK,linktext as LINKTEXT from BannerAds"
 rootName    ="BANNERS"
 rowName     ="BANNERAD"
 xsl         ="chapter4/BannerAds.xsl"
 clearBuffer ="true"/>
```

This page requires that the MySQL database server be successfully installed and that the xmlbook database, with table BannerAds, be created.

The resulting data page, shown in Figure C.2, is similar to the one produced in Listing 4.2 in Chapter 4, "A Quick Start to JSP and XML Together," with the exception that here it has been created from a database query rather than from an XML file.

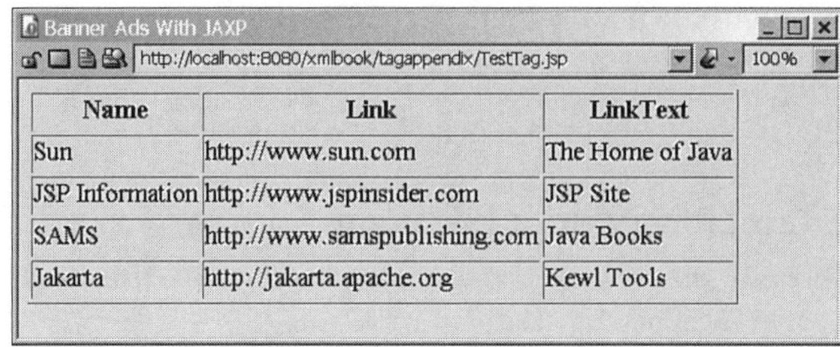

Name	Link	LinkText
Sun	http://www.sun.com	The Home of Java
JSP Information	http://www.jspinsider.com	JSP Site
SAMS	http://www.samspublishing.com	Java Books
Jakarta	http://jakarta.apache.org	Kewl Tools

FIGURE C.2 Results of the tag library call.

This output is basically the same as the earlier example, except that this one uses a tag that we created.

Let's look at the first line of the JSP page found in Listing C.4:

```
<%@taglib uri="xmlbook.xmldatabase" prefix="xmldata" %>
```

This line indicates that we have created a special namespace or tag prefix of `xmldata` to represent the tag library. In addition, the mapping `xmlbook.xmldatabase` is the URI the JSP container will use to find the tag library being used in this example.

To make our database connectivity object XML compliant, we created it as a JavaBean:

```
<jsp:useBean class="xmlbook.chapter7.DatabaseParameter"
             id   ="DBconn"    scope="page" >
        <jsp:setProperty name="DBconn" property="databaseName"
                         value="xmlbook"/>
        <jsp:setProperty name="DBconn" property="driver"
                         value="org.gjt.mm.mysql.Driver"/>
        <jsp:setProperty name="DBconn" property="url"
                         value="jdbc:mysql://localhost/xmlbook"/>
</jsp:useBean>
```

Referencing the object created by this `useBean` tag is a simple matter of using the ID "Dbconn." Many projects would store a database connectivity object within the application data space. It would then be simple to recall it and pass it directly to the tag.

The final step is to use the tag library itself:

```
<xmldata:xmlresult
 database    ="<%= DBconn %>"
 SQL ="select name as NAME,link as LINK,linktext as LINKTEXT from BannerAds"
```

```
rootName    ="BANNERS"
rowName     ="BANNERAD"
xsl         ="chapter4/BannerAds.xsl"
clearBuffer ="true"/>
```

Notice that a JSP expression (="<%= DBconn %>") was used to deliver the actual object to the tag handler. Also note that XML is case sensitive, so we had to make sure the SQL statement produced columns that matched the names of the XML elements (otherwise the XSL stylesheet wouldn't produce any results). Likewise, we had to tell the process the name of the row element and what names to expect for the root element. Again, we must match the XML file layout for our stylesheet to work.

General Notes

Before concluding this appendix, let's cover a few additional topics in greater detail.

Body Data

In order to access the body of the tag we need to implement the `BodyTag` interface. When the body is available, the JSP container will build the `BodyContent` object. This object will be created after the JSP container evaluates the body of the tag. This object will be passed to the tag handler when the `doInitBody()` method is invoked. Once created, `BodyContent` is available elsewhere in the tag handler until the `doEndBody()` method is finished processing.

The contents of `BodyContent` are the results after the JSP page has finished the evaluation. This means that the object will not contain any code or actions, just the results of the final invocation.

There is no limit to the amount of data a `BodyContent` object can contain other than the physical memory limitations of your server. Some care should be taken not to overload the object, since there is no way to automatically flush the buffer of the `BodyContent`.

Getting a handle of the `BodyContent` object requires a simple call to the `getBodyContent()` method.

In the typical tag library the `BodyContent` object and the data within it are converted to a `String` to be processed by the tag handler. The data is used either to perform an operation or as the base of some new output to be placed into the JSP output stream.

Design Notes

Tag libraries are flexible. A general rule is to avoid making a single tag handler do too much. It's a good idea to break logic into smaller reusable packages. As an example, we could have written several tags to perform the work of our single tag. It might be practical to take an approach similar to the DBTags database tags we examined in Chapter 1, "Integrating JSP and Data." The code is reproduced here:

```
<%@ taglib uri="http://jakarta.apache.org/taglibs/dbtags" prefix="sql" %>
<sql:connection id="connect">
  <sql:url>jdbc:mysql://localhost/xmlbook</sql:url>
  <sql:driver>org.gjt.mm.mysql.Driver</sql:driver>
</sql:connection>
```

Creating several custom tags could make our sample XML document tag library more flexible. In fact, it's also possible to make DBTags work alongside these tags. Because DBTags are an open source project, we could review their tag handlers' code and then merge the two to work together.

Empty Tags

Any tag library that is empty (such as `<action />`) will not invoke any methods that relate to tag body manipulation. This speeds up execution of the tags. As result, if a tag will always be empty, it's a good idea to build the tag from the TagSupport class. Also, indicate the fact that the tag will always be empty within the tag's description in the tag library descriptor file. The element would be set as follows:

```
<body-content>empty</body-content>
```

Threading

A tag handler instance will only permit one thread to execute at a time. The JSP container enforces this rule, and a programmer does not have to worry about thread safety of a tag handler. However, while a tag handler is thread safe, an instance of a tag handler can be reused many times. JSP containers will maintain a pool of tag handlers to speed execution of a tag library. The result is that while a tag library is thread safe, it is possible for threads to step on each other in dealing with shared data or objects at higher scopes. For example, we stated earlier that programmers shouldn't use the setter methods of any tag library property within the tag handler. The reason boils down to the fact that it's the JSP container's responsibility to do so. If the JSP container determines that a particular property is static across implementations, it may not reset the property after the initial setting of a pooled tag handler. This means that if one thread does modify the property, it may not be set to the proper value for the next thread. Note that this example depends on the way a JSP container is implemented and can vary from implementation to implementation.

Summary

This appendix has exposed you to the basics of tag libraries. If you choose to devote further study to tag libraries, you will discover how truly useful they are. As an example, it's possible to tie listener events within the TLD file for a tag library. Other features of tag libraries include the `doCatch` and `doFinally` methods, which permit a programmer to catch uncaught exceptions from the tag handler. Yet another feature is the `TagLibraryValidation` class that validates the use of tags on a JSP page. This appendix just scratches the surface of what is possible using a tag library. Throughout the book, you have encountered a few more advanced uses of tag libraries. As a JSP programmer, it's worth your time to learn how to use tag libraries to fill various everyday programming needs.

Summary

D XSL Reference

IN THIS APPENDIX

- XSLT and XPath
- Reference

The Extensible Stylesheet Language (XSL) was created for the presentation and formatting of XML documents for visual display. XSL is broken into three parts. The first, XSL Transformations (XSLT), is a set of XML elements used for transforming XML documents. The next part is XPath, which is an expression language used to access or refer to parts of an XML document; XPath is used in the XSL stylesheets to choose XML document parts to process or transform. The third part is XSL-FO (XSL Formatting Objects). This is an XML vocabulary for specifying formatting semantics, and is not covered here.

This appendix contains information related to XSLT and XPath. XSLT uses XPath for the selection of parts of an XML document. Once selected, these parts can be processed in various ways.

The appendix is broken into two sections. The first is a short discussion of XSLT and XPath, and the last is a quick reference of the commonly found tags and functions. An introductory discussion of how to use XPath expressions and XSLT can be found in Chapter 2, "Introduction to XML/XSL."

XSLT and XPath

XSL is based on recognition through matching. Each transformation is expressed as a set of rules that will match patterns found in the input. The transformation required is described, instead of providing sequential instructions to achieve it.

XSL works by matching nodes of XML documents through the matching capabilities of XPath. (If you don't know what a node is, read Chapter 2 first.) These nodes are selected through a combination of their location path in the tree structure, the text data contained therein, and the literal name of the element. After these nodes are selected, they can be processed through the rules of XSLT.

The set of rules transforms the tree structure, not the XML document itself. XSLT transforms the XML document through its content and structure, not the document itself. That means that the XML and XSL have to be parsed into a tree structure before they can be transformed. The transformation results in another tree that can be output or processed in some other way.

Context and Current Nodes

To use XSLT successfully, it is necessary to understand the difference between the context node and the current node. This knowledge will make XPath statements much easier to write.

The current node is always that node which is currently being processed, of the set of nodes causing the processing. The context node is the node that an XPath expression is currently matching through an XPath expression.

That is to say that each node being processed within an `xsl:template` element becomes the current node within the template body. This is also true of `xsl:for-each` elements. As each node of a node-set is being processed within an `xsl:for-each` structure, it becomes the current node.

Along the same lines, when that `xsl:for-each` element is closed, the current node will revert back to the node that it was before encountering the element.

The `.` always refers to the context node, whereas `current()` will always return the current node.

For example, let's suppose we had the following XML document. The first child element of the root contains descriptions for abbreviations, and the second element contains items that have abbreviated descriptions:

```
<?xml version="1.0" ?>
<ROOT>
    <KEYS>
        <LKUP abbv="AB">AB description</LKUP>
        <LKUP abbv="BC">BC description</LKUP>
        <LKUP abbv="CD">CD description</LKUP>
        <LKUP abbv="DE">DE description</LKUP>
        <LKUP abbv="EF">EF description</LKUP>
    </KEYS>
    <PRODUCTS>
        <ITEM desc="AB">MP3 player</ITEM>
        <ITEM desc="DE">Wrench</ITEM>
```

```
        <ITEM desc="EF">Car</ITEM>
    </PRODUCTS>
</ROOT>
```

Upon outputting the list of items, the descriptions have to be unabbreviated. This has been done in the following code. The `xsl:for-each` element selects the node-set consisting of all `ITEM` elements found descending from `PRODUCTS` elements that descend from the `ROOT` element. Each node of this set is processed one at a time in the body of the `xsl:for-each` element, and becomes the current node during that processing.

```
<xsl:for-each select="/ROOT/PRODUCTS/ITEM" >
    <xsl:value-of select="current()" />
    Description:
    <xsl:value-of select="/ROOT/KEYS/LKUP[./@abbv = current()/@desc]" />
    <hr />
</xsl:for-each>
```

In the following XPath expression, notice the use of `.` and `current()` together. This expression selects the text data of the `LKUP` element whose `abbv` attribute value is the same as the `desc` attribute value found in the `ITEM` element being processed.

```
/ROOT/KEYS/LKUP[./@abbv = current()/@desc]
```

The context node, namely the `LKUP` element that XPath selected, is referenced with `.`. In the same expression, the current node is referenced with the `current()` function. The current node is the `ITEM` element currently being processed within the `xsl:for-each` element.

Reference

This section is designed to serve as a quick reference for the more commonly used XSLT elements and XPath functions. It is by no means exhaustive.

In the following subsections, the word *`expression`* is used to denote the placement of an XPath statement.

XSLT Elements

The following XSLT elements are used together to create the declarative construct used to process an XML document representation. The definition of the unlisted XSLT elements can be found at `http://www.w3c.org/TR/xslt`.

The `<xsl:apply-templates select=expression />` **Element**
This instruction causes the set of nodes selected by *expression* to be processed using the appropriate template rules. The `xsl:sort` and `xsl:with-param` elements are permitted in this element's body.

The `<xsl:call-template name=string />` **Element**
This instruction invokes the template named *string*. This is analogous to a procedure call in other programming languages. The `xsl:sort` and `xsl:with-param` elements are permitted in this element's body.

The `<xsl:choose />` **Element**
This instruction causes one choice to be selected out of a number of alternatives. It is analogous to the `switch` keyword in Java. The `xsl:when` and `xsl:otherwise` elements are permitted in this element's body. At least one `xsl:when` element must be found within this element.

The following code demonstrates its structure:

```
<xsl:choose>
    <xsl:when test="$PageNum = 1">
          ...
    </xsl:when>
    <xsl:when test="$PageNum = $Total">
          ...
    </xsl:when>
    <xsl:otherwise>
          ...
    </xsl:otherwise>
</xsl:choose>
```

The `<xsl:for-each select=expression />` **Element**
This instruction selects a node-set using the XPath *expression*, and then processes each node of that node-set one by one using the instructions found in the body of this element. All elements are permitted in this element's body.

The `<xsl:if test=expression />` **Element**
This instruction encloses processing that will only occur if *expression* resolves to true. All elements are permitted in this element's body.

The `<xsl:otherwise />` **Element**
This instruction encloses the processing that will occur within an `xsl:choose` element when all `xsl:when` element expressions have resolved to `false`. This is analogous to the `default` keyword found in a `switch` structure in Java. This element can

only be found within an `xsl:choose` element and can contain any elements. See `xsl:choose` for an example.

The `<xsl:output method=string />` Element
This instruction controls the format of the serial output of the stylesheet. Some of the possible values for *`string`* are `xml`, `html`, and `text`. This element must be placed directly as a child of the root element, and other attributes exist for this element. No other elements are permitted in this element's body.

The `<xsl:param name=string select=expression />` Element
This element is used either directly beneath the root element to define a global parameter, or immediately within a template as a parameter local to the template. The name of the parameter is defined in *`string`*, and the default value is assigned using *`expression`*. No other elements are permitted in this element's body.

The `<xsl:sort select=expression />` Element
This instruction is used to sort a node-set prior to processing according to the node specified in *`expression`*. *`expression`* can select this node using its name or a number representing the child number to sort on. This element can only be placed within the `xsl:apply-templates` element, or as the first child of a `xsl:for-each` element. No other elements are permitted in this element's body.

The `<xsl:stylesheet version=string namespacedeclaration />` Element
This element will always be the root element of a stylesheet, and therefore will contain all elements of the stylesheet. The version *`string`* will contain the version of XSLT required by this stylesheet. Currently, this can only be 1.0. Also, at a minimum there will be one namespace declaration on this element. Typically, *`namespacedeclaration`* will be `xmlns:xsl = "http://www.w3.org/1999/XSL/Transform"`.

The `<xsl:template name=string match=expression />` Element
This element is used to contain a block of processing instructions for producing output. The combined contents of this element can be thought of and used like a function definition. It can either be a template named *`string`* and invoked with `xsl:call-template`, or it can match particular XML nodes through *`expression`* and `xsl:apply-templates`. All elements are permitted in this element. If a parameter is to be defined here, it must be the first child of this element. Also, this element must appear as a child of the `xsl:stylesheet` element. All elements are permitted in this element's body.

The `<xsl:value-of select=expression />` Element
This instruction results in the string value of *`expression`* being written to the output tree. No other elements are permitted in this element's body.

The `<xsl:variable name=*string* select=*expression* />` **Element**
This instruction creates a variable whose name is *string* and whose value is the result of *expression*. Unlike in most programming languages, XSLT variables cannot be updated once they are assigned an initial value. They retain their value until they go out of scope. No other elements are permitted in this element's body.

The `<xsl:when test=*expression* />` **Element**
This instruction defines actions to be performed if the condition in *expression* is `true`. This element can only be found within an `xsl:choose` element and can contain any elements. See `xsl:choose` for an example.

The `<xsl:with-param name=*string* select=*expression* />` **Element**
This instruction sets the value of the parameter named *string* to the value of *expression* when calling a template. This element can only be found in either `xsl:call-template` or `xsl:apply-templates` elements. No other elements are permitted in this element's body.

XPath Functions

The following XPath functions are available for use within any XPath expression. They are grouped according to return value, and some examples are provided.

The functions listed here by no means present an extensive list. Instead, these are the functions that have been most commonly used in stylesheet authoring. The complete listing of XPath functions can be found at `http://www.w3c.org/TR/xpath#corelib`.

Boolean Functions

The following functions return Boolean values. If the *argument* is not already a Boolean, it is first converted using the `boolean()` function, after which the function is evaluated.

`boolean(`*argument*`)`—returns the Boolean value of *argument*. The return values are as follows:

- `Number`—The number zero converts to `false`; all others convert to `true`.
- `String`—The empty string returns `false`; all else converts to `true`.
- `Node Set`—An empty node-set returns `false`; all else returns `true`.

`false()`—XPath doesn't have any Boolean constants available for XPath expressions. As a result, `false()` and `true()` can be used where a constant is required.

`not(`*argument*`)`—Results in the Boolean negation of the *argument* value: `false` if the *argument* is true, and `true` if the *argument* is false.

`true()`—See `false()`.

Number Functions

The following functions provide number-handling capabilities. If the `argument` is not already a number, it is first converted using the `number()` function, after which the function is evaluated.

`ceiling(`*`argument`*`)`—Results in the smallest integer that is greater than or equal to the numeric value of *`argument`*.

`floor(`*`argument`*`)`—Results in the largest integer that is less than or equal to the numeric value of *`argument`*.

`format-number(`*`argument`*`, `*`format`*`)`—Returns *`argument`* formatted according to the pattern and rules of the *`format`* string. The following characters can be used to define the *`format`* string:

- Pound (#)—Used to match one digit. If a digit is in the specified location of *`argument`*, it is output. Otherwise, it is rounded to fit the pattern.
- Zero (`0`)—Zero-digit, causes a `0` to be placed in this output position if there is no number present in *`argument`*. Otherwise, the number in this position is output.
- Period (`.`)—Decimal-point, always matches to decimal place of number. Results in the output of a decimal place if followed by `0`. Otherwise, decimal will only be output if number already contains one.
- Comma (`,`)—Grouping-separator, will be placed in the location specified by the pattern.
- Percent (`%`)—Multiply the number by 100 and show percentage.
- Semicolon (`;`)—Pattern separator. A pattern defined before this is for positive numbers, and a pattern found after this is for negative numbers.
- Literal—any character found inside the *`format`* string that is not one of the previously defined format characters can be output anywhere.

For example, the following expressions will return the noted results:

- `format-number(12.345, ##.##)` returns `12.35`
- `format-number(12345.1, ##.###)` returns `12345.1`
- `format-number(12.345, ##.0000)` returns `12.3450`
- `format-number(.1234, 00.00#)` returns `00.123`
- `format-number(1234.2, 00.###)` returns `1234.2`
- `format-number(1234.2, 0,0)` returns `1,2,3,4`

- `format-number(1234.2, 0,00.00)` returns `12,34.20`
- `format-number(.2345, 0.#%)` returns `23.5%`
- `format-number(2.345, $##.00;($##.00))` returns `$2.35`
- `format-number(-2.345, $##.00;($##.00))` returns `($2.35)`
- `format-number(2345, $##.00 dollars)` returns `$2345.00 dollars`

`number(`*`argument`*`)`—Returns the *`argument`* converted to a number.

- `Boolean`—`true` becomes one; `false` becomes zero.
- `String`—Leading and trailing whitespace is removed. The string is then converted to a number. If it fails, the resulting value will be `NaN` (not a number).
- `Node Set`—The node-set is converted to a string using `string()`. The resulting string is then converted to a number as in the preceding.

`round(`*`argument`*`)`—Returns *`argument`* rounded to the nearest integer.

`sum(`*`argument`*`)`—Returns the sum of all nodes in the node-set *`argument`*. It is an error if any node in the node-set cannot be successfully converted using `number()`. It is also an error if *`argument`* is not a node-set.

String Functions

The following functions provide XPath with string-handling capabilities. If the *`argument`* is not already a string, it is first converted using the `string()` function, after which the function is evaluated.

`concat(`*`arguments`*`)`—Returns a string consisting of the concatenation of all the *`arguments`*. There must be two or more values in *`arguments`*.

`contains(`*`string`*`, `*`substring`*`)`—Returns the Boolean value `true` if *`substring`* can be found in *`string`*; otherwise, it returns `false`.

`string(`*`argument`*`)`—Returns the string value of *`argument`*.

- `Boolean`—`true` becomes "true;" `false` becomes "false."
- `Number`—Integers are converted into a string representing their value.
- `Node Set`—The string value of the first node found is returned.

`substring(`*`string`*`, `*`start`*`, `*`length`*`)`—Returns a string created by taking *`length`* characters of *`string`*, starting from the *`start`* character position.

`translate(string, oldchars, newchars)`—Returns *`string`* with all the *`oldchars`* characters or strings found replaced with *`newchars`*.

Set Node Functions

The following functions either return node-sets or supply information in terms of node-sets.

`count(node-set)`—Returns the number of nodes found in *`node-set`*. There is an error if *`node-set`* is not a node-set.

`current()`—Returns the current node as a node-set. The current node is the node that is currently being processed when a set of nodes is being iterated. The current node does not change during the evaluation of expressions; the context node does.

`last()`—Returns a number that is the value of the context size. This function is useful when you are trying to create a comma-separated list from a node-set. Adding the commas within the following statement will prevent the addition of a comma after the last node has been processed:

```
xsl:if position()!=last()
```

`local-name()`—Returns a string whose value is the name of either the element or attribute without a namespace prefix whether or not there is one.

`name()`—Returns a string value of the node exactly as it appears in the source document. This will include any namespace prefixes.

`position(node)`—Returns a number that is the place number of *`node`* in the set of context nodes. For example, when iterating through a node-list using `xsl:for-each`, the position of each node processed will increment.

Index

Symbols

A

B

C

E

F

G

H

I

J

K-L

M

N

Q-R

S

T

U

V